Houghton Mifflin Science

DISCOVERYWORKS

HOUGHTON MIFFLIN

Boston • Atlanta • Dallas • Denver • Geneva, Illinois • Palo Alto • Princeton

Authors

William Badders
Elementary Science Teacher
Cleveland Public Schools
Cleveland, OH

Lowell J. Bethel
Professor of Science Education
The University of Texas at Austin
Austin, TX

Victoria Fu
Professor of Child Development
and Early Childhood Education
Virginia Polytechnic Institute and
State University
Blacksburg, VA

Donald Peck
Director (retired)
The Center for Elementary Science
Fairleigh Dickinson University
Madison, NJ

Carolyn Sumners
Director of Astronomy and Physical Sciences
Houston Museum of Natural Science
Houston, TX

Catherine Valentino
Author-in-Residence, Houghton Mifflin
West Kingston, RI

Acknowledgements appear on page H43, which
constitutes an extension of this copyright page.

Printed in the U. S. A.

ISBN 0-618-00830-6

8 9 10 RRD 08 07 06 05

CONTENTS

THINK LIKE A SCIENTIST

UNIT A — Systems in Living Things

THINK LIKE A SCIENTIST

CHAPTER 1 — Life Processes   A4

Digestion and Respiration   A32

Circulation and Excretion   A52

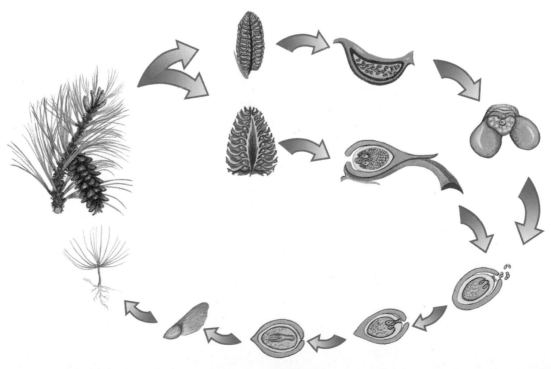

The Solar System and Beyond

The Solar System — B28

Stars and Galaxies — B52

Living in Space

How Matter Changes   C62

Water on Earth

UNIT E · Weather and Climate

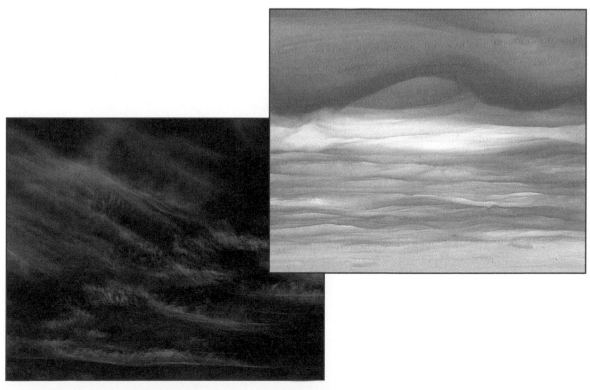

SCIENCE and MATH TOOLBOX

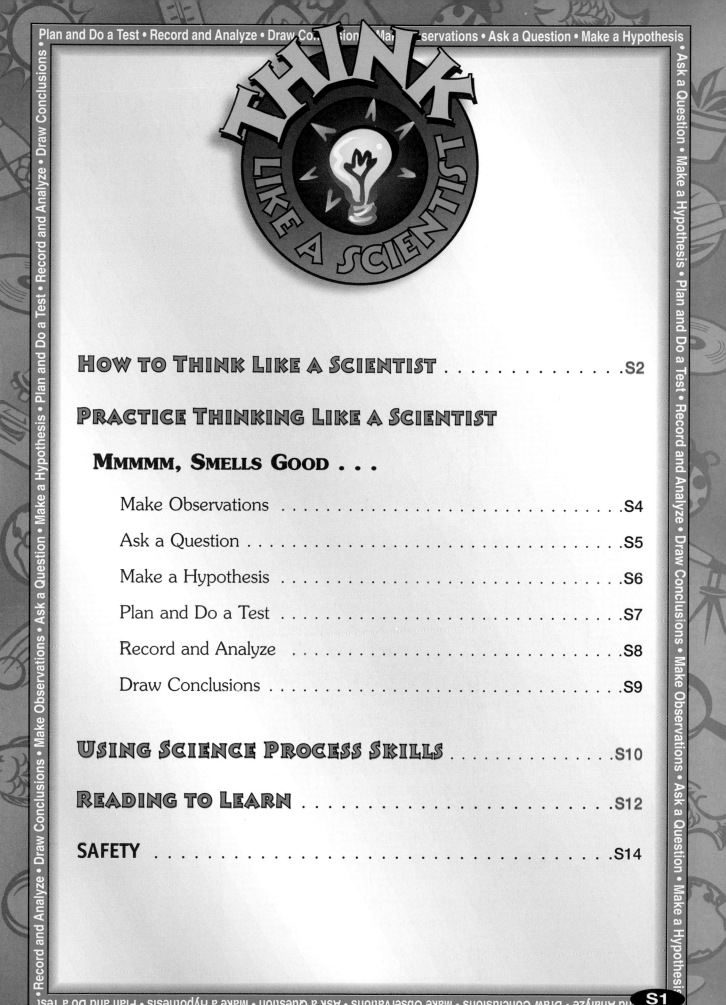

THINK LIKE A SCIENTIST

HOW TO THINK LIKE A SCIENTIST

THINK LIKE A SCIENTIST

Make Observations

To think like a scientist, learn as much as you can by observing things around you. Everything you hear, smell, taste, touch, and see is a clue about how the world works. As you test your ideas, you'll continue to make careful observations.

Make Observations

Ask a Question

Look for patterns. You'll get ideas. For example, you notice that you get static electric shocks on certain days but not on others. Ask questions such as this.

What conditions change from day to day that would affect static electric shock?

Make a Hypothesis

If you have an idea about why something happens, make an educated guess, or hypothesis, that you can test. For example, suppose your hypothesis is that static electric shock is more likely to occur on dry days than on humid ones.

Make Observations

S2

Plan and Do a Test

Plan how to test your hypothesis. Your plan would need to consider some of these problems.

How will you measure daily humidity?

How will you test for the presence of static electric shock?

Then test your hypothesis.

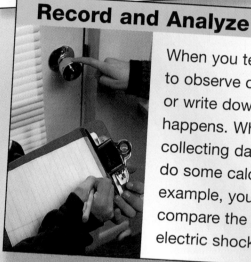

Record and Analyze

When you test your idea, you need to observe carefully and record, or write down, everything that happens. When you finish collecting data, you may need to do some calculations with it. For example, you may need to compare the frequency of static electric shock to daily humidity.

Make Observations

Draw Conclusions

Whatever happens in a test, think about all the reasons for your results. Sometimes this thinking leads to a new hypothesis. For example, besides humidity, might other weather conditions affect the frequency of static electric shock? If the frequency of static shocks increases as humidity decreases, what other weather conditions might affect static shocks?

Make Observations

Now read "Mmmmm, Smells Good . . ." to see scientific thinking in action.

Plan and Do a Test • Record and Analyze • Draw Conclusions • Make Observations • Ask a Question • Make a Hypothesis • Plan a

S3

THINK LIKE A SCIENTIST

PRACTICE THINKING LIKE A SCIENTIST

Mmmmm, Smells Good...

Make Observations

Carmen and Lou were on their way to lunch. As they walked into the school cafeteria, Carmen inhaled.

"Mmmmm, smells good, like freshly-made pizza. Just what I'm in the mood for," Carmen said. Lou sniffed and shook his head. "I can't smell anything. I have a cold."

The students sat and began eating their pizza. After a few bites, Lou told Carmen that he couldn't taste a thing—not the cheese, nor the onions and peppers, nor even the tomato sauce.

To learn about the world, you observe it. **Observations** can be made with any of the senses—sight, hearing, touch, taste, or smell.

Ask a Question

Carmen wondered why Lou couldn't taste the delicious pizza. Then she remembered what he said about having a cold and not being able to smell the pizza. Carmen thought to herself, "Does having a cold prevent you from tasting food, too?" She shared her question with Lou. Together they came up with another question that they wanted to investigate.

Are the sense of smell and the sense of taste related?

The students decided to try to find the answer to their question.

Scientific investigations usually begin with ideas that you're not sure about. Such ideas can help you ask a question that you really want to answer.

Make a Hypothesis

Carmen and Lou assumed that the nose detects odors, or smells. They also assumed that the tongue detects tastes, or flavors. They wondered if the ability to taste is reduced when the nose is blocked, as from a cold. They discussed the idea that the sense of taste might depend on the functioning of the sense of smell. Then Carmen and Lou chose this idea as their hypothesis.

When you use what you've observed to suggest a possible answer to your question, you're making a **hypothesis**. Make sure that your hypothesis is an idea that you can test. If you can't test your hypothesis, try changing it.

Plan and Do a Test

Carmen and Lou designed an experiment to test their hypothesis. They cut up four different fruits—banana, strawberry, orange, and peach—into small, equal-sized samples. They set up two groups of three students each.

Students in Group 1 were blindfolded and asked to taste and identify a sample of each fruit. As each group member tasted the samples, only Carmen and Lou were present. This kept the other group members from hearing the responses.

Students in Group 2 were also blindfolded. In addition these students wore a nose clip, the kind used by swimmers. The nose clip blocked their sense of smell as they tasted and tried to identify the fruit samples. Again, only Carmen and Lou were present for this part of the test.

One way to try out your hypothesis is to use a test called a controlled experiment. The setups in this kind of experiment are identical in all ways except one. The one difference is the variable. In Carmen and Lou's experiment the variable is the use of the nose clip.

Plan and Do a Test • Record and Analyze • Draw Conclusions • Make Observations • Ask a Question • Make a Hypothesis • Plan

S7

Record and Analyze

As each blindfolded student tried to identify a fruit, Carmen and Lou recorded their responses. They used a chart like the one shown to keep track of the data from the experiment.

Next, Carmen and Lou carried out their experiment two more times with different groups. When they analyzed all the data they noticed that the results each time were similar.

When you do an experiment, you make observations so that you can obtain information called data. You need to write down, or record, this data and then organize it. Graphs and tables are ways to organize data. Analyze the information that you collect by looking for patterns. To see if your results are reliable, repeat the experiment several times.

Taste Test

✔ = correct
X = incorrect

Group	Students tested	banana	strawberry	orange	peach
Group 1 (blindfold only)	Jill	✔	✔	✔	✔
	Rick	✔	✔	X	X
	Marna	✔	X	✔	✔
Group 2 (blindfold and nose clip)	Sal	X	X	✔	X
	Erin	✔	X	X	✔
	Toni	X	X	X	X

Draw Conclusions

From the information that they collected, Carmen and Lou concluded that the results of their experiment supported their hypothesis. When a person's nose is blocked, as from a cold, the sense of taste and the sense of smell are affected.

After you have analyzed your data, you should use what you learned to draw a conclusion. A **conclusion** is a statement that sums up what you learned. The conclusion should be about the hypothesis you made. A hypothesis supported by a lot of evidence may be called a **theory**.

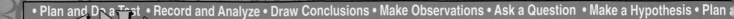

USING SCIENCE PROCESS SKILLS

Observing involves gathering information about the environment through your five senses—seeing, hearing, smelling, touching, and tasting.

Classifying is grouping objects or events according to common properties or characteristics. Often you can classify in more than one way.

Measuring and Using Numbers involves the ability to make measurements (including time measurements), to make estimates, and to record data.

Communicating involves using words, both speaking and writing, and using actions, graphs, tables, diagrams, and other ways of presenting information.

Inferring means coming to a conclusion based on facts and observations you've made.

Predicting involves stating in advance what you think will happen based on observations and experiences.

Collecting, recording, and interpreting data

all involve gathering and understanding information. This skill includes organizing data in tables, graphs, and in other ways. Interpretation includes finding patterns and relationships that lead to new questions and new ideas.

Identifying and controlling variables

involves determining the effect of a changing factor, called the variable, in an experiment. To do this, you keep all other factors constant, or unchanging.

Defining operationally

means to describe an object, an event, or an idea based on personal observations. An operational definition of a plant might be that it is a green living thing that is attached to soil and that does not move around.

Making a hypothesis

is suggesting a possible answer to a question or making an educated guess about why something happens. Your hypothesis should be based on observations and experiences.

Experimenting

is testing your hypothesis to collect evidence that supports the hypothesis or shows that it is false.

Making and using models

includes designing and making physical models of processes and objects, or making mental models to represent objects and ideas.

THINK LIKE A SCIENTIST
READING TO LEARN

Wanderers in the Night Sky

Reading Focus What is the difference between a star and a planet?

Other than the Sun and the Moon, most of the objects in the night sky look about the same to the unaided eye. They all seem to be just tiny points of light. Are all of those shiny objects stars? If not, what are they? And how can you tell which ones are which?

You can begin to answer these questions yourself by simply looking a little bit longer and a little more closely at those points of light in the sky. If you do, you'll soon realize that they are *not* all exactly alike.

A Different Sort of "Star"

Have you ever seen the "morning star"? This is an object that seems to be a very bright star. It can be seen at certain times on the eastern horizon (hə-rī'zən), just before the Sun rises. The

horizon is the line formed where the Earth and sky seem to meet. If you lo closely at this bright object, it seems shine with a steady light. Almost all t other "stars" seem to twinkle.

If you observe the morning star through a telescope, it will no longer look like a tiny point of light. Instead you'll see a small round disk. This object, in fact, has phases like the Moon does, so you might see either fairly full disk or a thin crescent.

If you use a more powerful telesc to observe the morning star, you'll s larger disk. But no matter how pow your telescope is, most of the other stars in the sky will still appear to b just tiny points of light.

If you look for the morning star eral days in a row, you'll notice son thing else. It's moving! And it's mo not just *along with* all the other sta but *in relation to* the other stars, including the Sun.

Over a period of weeks, you'll s the morning star move closer and closer to the Sun until it disappear the Sun's glare. Then something e more interesting happens. The sa object reappears in the west just a sundown as the evening star!

▲ The "morning star"

B16

Before You Read

1. **Scan** each page.
   - titles
   - subheads
   - highlighted words
   - photos and illustrations
   - captions

2. **Identify** the main topic.

3. **Ask** yourself what you know about the topic.

4. **Predict** what you will learn by turning subheads into questions.

Scientists use scientific methods when they do experiments. They also use special methods when they read to learn. You can read like a scientist, too. Just follow the steps below.

▲ The Sun, Moon, and planets appear to move in the same narrow band across the sky.

Of all the starlike objects easily seen by the unaided eye, only five are like the morning star. That is, they shine steadily rather than twinkle, appear in a telescope as disks rather than points of light, and move against the backdrop of the other stars.

These five objects share one other trait with the morning star. They can only be seen in a certain part of the sky. Although they all move, these "stars" appear only in a narrow band. That band is roughly the same as the path of the Sun and the Moon across the sky.

The Wandering Planets

The ancient Greeks called these five special objects "wandering stars." In English, we call them *planets*—a name that comes from the Greek word for "wanderer." These five objects—and a few others like them that are not easily seen by the unaided eye—are really in a different class from stars. They are planets.

A **star** is a huge globe of hot gases that shines by its own light. The Sun is a star. It just appears bigger because it's much closer to Earth than are other stars. A **planet** is a large object that circles a star and does *not* produce light of its own. We can see planets only because they reflect sunlight.

The morning and evening star is really Venus, one of nine known planets that revolve around our Sun. Until very recently, scientists thought there were only nine planets in the universe. By 1998, however, astronomers had discovered 13 planets circling other nearby stars. ■

INVESTIGATION 1 WRAP-UP

REVIEW

1. How do a star and a planet differ?

2. What motion of the Earth causes the Sun to seem to rise and set each day?

CRITICAL THINKING

3. The constellation Leo is visible in the east on a January evening but in the west on a July evening. Explain why.

4. Explain why the Earth has seasons.

B17

While You Read

1. **Look** for words that signal cause and effect and sequence.

2. **Make** inferences and draw conclusions.

3. **Ask** questions when you don't understand and then reread.

After You Read

1. **Say** or **write** what you've learned.

2. **Draw**, **chart**, or **map** what you've learned.

3. **Share** what you've learned.

SAFETY

The best way to be safe in the classroom and outdoors is to use common sense. Prepare for each activity before you start it. Get help from your teacher when there is a problem. Always pay attention.

Stay Safe From Stains

- Wear protective clothing or an old shirt when you work with messy materials.
- If anything spills, wipe it up or ask your teacher to help you clean it up.

Stay Safe From Flames

- Keep your clothes away from open flames. If you have long or baggy sleeves, roll them up.
- Don't let your hair get close to a flame. If you have long hair, tie it back.

Make Wise Choices About Materials

- Use only the amount of material you need.
- Recycle materials so they can be reused.
- Take care when using valuable tools so they can be used again.

Stay Safe From Injuries

- Protect your eyes by wearing safety goggles when you are told that you need them.
- Keep your hands dry around electricity. Water is a good conductor of electricity, so you can get a shock more easily if your hands are wet.
- Be careful with sharp objects. If you have to press on them, keep the sharp side away from you.
- Cover any cuts you have that are exposed. If you spill something on a cut, be sure to wash it off immediately.
- Don't eat or drink anything unless your teacher tells you that it's okay.

Stay Safe During Cleanup

- Wash up after you finish working.
- Dispose of things in the way that your teacher tells you to.

HAIR Keep it out of the way of a flame.

EYES Wear safety goggles when you are told to.

MOUTH Don't eat or drink ANYTHING unless your teacher tells you it's okay.

HANDS Keep your hands dry around electricity. Cover any cuts. Wear gloves when told to. Wash up after you finish.

DON'T MAKE A MESS If you spill something, clean it up right away. When finished with an activity, clean up your work area. Dispose of things in the way your teacher tells you to.

CLOTHES Keep long sleeves rolled up. Protect yourself from stains. Stay away from open flames.

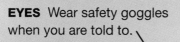

MOST IMPORTANTLY

If you ever hurt yourself, or one of your group members gets hurt, tell your teacher right away.

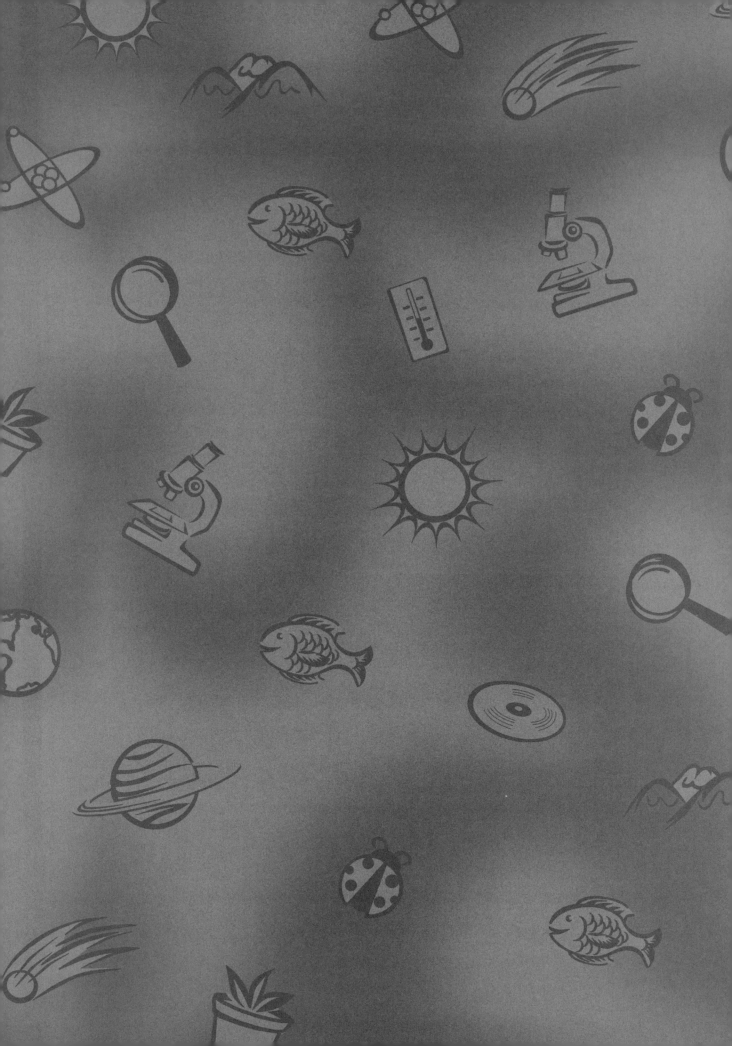

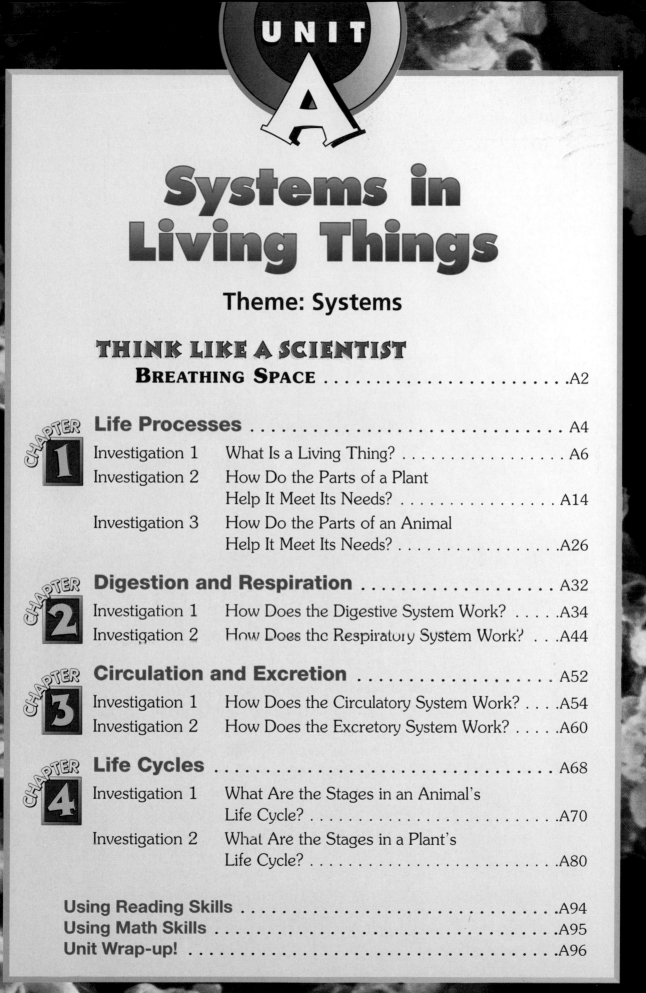

UNIT A

Systems in Living Things

Theme: Systems

THINK
LIKE A SCIENTIST

BREATHING SPACE

You are looking inside the gas-exchange organ of the human body—the lung. In this magnified image, you can see some of the many tiny sacs (the dark spaces) that fill with air each time you breathe. The orange-colored spheres are red blood cells, which pick up oxygen from the lungs. The lungs are just one of the many kinds of organs that work together in the body to keep you alive and healthy.

THINK LIKE A SCIENTIST

Questioning In this unit you'll study the life processes and systems of plants and animals. You'll investigate questions such as these.

- What Is a Living Thing?
- How Does the Respiratory System Work?

Observing, Testing, Hypothesizing In the Activity "Lung Power," you'll observe a working model of a lung. You'll also hypothesize what happens in your body when you breathe.

Researching In the Resource "Breathing Basics," you'll gather more information about the parts of the respiratory system and how the parts work together.

Drawing Conclusions After you've completed your investigations, you'll draw conclusions about what you've learned— and get new ideas.

CHAPTER 1

LIFE PROCESSES

How can you tell the difference between a living thing and a nonliving thing? What are the parts of a plant? of an animal? Which systems of living things allow them to eat, grow, and repair injured parts? In this chapter you'll explore the answers to these questions.

Connecting to Science
ARTS

Topiary Artist Linda Rodriguez has an unusual job. She creates animals from plants! The animals that Linda Rodriguez creates are sculptures called topiaries (tō′pē er ez). She is a topiary artist for the San Diego Zoo. Her job is to make sculptures of lions, tigers, bears, and other zoo animals. She makes her sculptures in two different ways. Sometimes she allows bushes to grow. Then she snips the bushes into different animal shapes. Other times she begins with a hollow mesh frame. She packs the frame tightly with moss and then roots ivy in the moss. As the ivy grows, Linda Rodriguez cuts and trains the growing plants to the shape of the frame. Her knowledge of living things— both plants and animals—helps make her creations realistic as well as fun!

Coming Up

◀ Linda Rodriguez sculpts an
ivy-covered animal.

A5

INVESTIGATION 1

WHAT IS A LIVING THING?

Can you tell whether something is alive just by looking at it? Seeds appear lifeless, but they can grow into giant trees. Some silk flowers look very much alive. Yet, when you touch them, you know they are fakes. In this investigation you'll explore the main features that make living things different from nonliving things.

Activity

Alive or Not?

What information do you need to determine if something is alive or not? In this activity you'll become a detective. Your job will be to ask the right questions to learn if something is a genuine living thing or if it is a clever fake.

MATERIALS
• *Science Notebook*

Procedure

1. Look at the pairs of photos on this page and on A7. You'll need to decide which photo in each pair shows something that is alive.

A1

A2

B1

B2

2. **Observe** each pair of photos carefully. In your *Science Notebook,* **record** a general description of the objects in each pair. Be sure to identify both the letter and number of the object you are describing.

3. For each pair of objects, look for clues that suggest which of the pair is alive. **Talk with your group** and together **brainstorm** a list of questions about each pair of objects. The questions should help you decide whether each object is alive or not.

4. Make a list of tests you could carry out to find out whether the objects are alive or not. **Describe** the tests you would carry out for each pair of objects.

C2

C1

Analyze and Conclude

1. In your *Science Notebook,* make a chart that lists the tests your group came up with for step 4. In the chart, explain how each test would help you know which object in each pair was alive and which was not.

 See **SCIENCE** *and* **MATH TOOLBOX** page H11 if you need to review *Making a Chart to Organize Data.*

2. Have one member of your group list six things, some of which are living and some of which are nonliving. Decide whether your tests could help identify each thing as living or nonliving.

3. Based on the results of this activity, **make a generalization** about what characteristics, or traits, distinguish living things from nonliving things.

D2

E1

E2

D1

Activity

Observing Plant Cells

The part of the onion you eat is actually a ball of leaves called a bulb. Onions, like all plants, are made up of basic units called cells. Look at an onion through a microscope to see what plant cells look like.

MATERIALS

- goggles
- onion
- tweezers
- microscope slide
- iodine solution
- toothpick
- cover slip
- microscope
- *Science Notebook*

SAFETY //////

Wear goggles during this activity. Be careful when handling glass slides. Iodine will stain clothing and is poisonous if swallowed.

Procedure

1. Take a section of an onion and snap it in half. A thin piece of skin should separate from the section. Peel this piece off with tweezers, as shown below.

2. Place the onion skin on a microscope slide. Add one drop of iodine solution. Use a toothpick to smooth out the wrinkles. Cover the onion skin with a cover slip.

 See **SCIENCE** and **MATH TOOLBOX** page H2 if you need to review *Using a Microscope.*

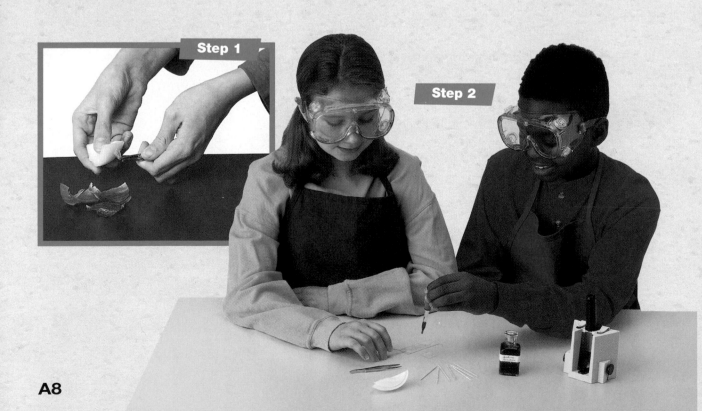

Step 1

Step 2

3. **Observe** the onion skin under a microscope at low power and **draw** what you see in your *Science Notebook*. Then **observe** the skin under high power and draw what you see.

4. The small circular structure that turned deep red inside the onion cell is called a nucleus (nōō'klē əs). **Label** the nucleus in your drawings.

5. The boundary of the cell is called the cell wall. **Label** the cell wall in your drawing.

Step 3

Analyze and Conclude

1. Like all living things, plants are made of cells. **Describe** the appearance of the cells that you observed.

2. A cell wall is found only in plant cells, not in animal cells. **Hypothesize** what job the cell wall has.

3. Suppose you looked through a microscope at cells from an unknown living thing. How could you tell whether you were looking at plant cells or animal cells?

INVESTIGATE FURTHER!

EXPERIMENT

Use a dropper to add two drops of water to a microscope slide. Place a single *Elodea* leaf in the water and cover it with a cover slip. Observe the leaf under a microscope's low power. Then study the leaf under high power and make a sketch of what you see. Describe any structures that you see in the leaf cell that you did not see in the onion cell in the activity. Infer what the functions of such structures are, based on the leaf's role in a plant.

It's Alive!

RESOURCE

Reading Focus How do plants and animals differ in the way they carry out their life processes?

Living things are all around you. Every tree, every blade of grass, and every insect is alive. Scientists have found life on the highest mountains and in the deepest oceans. They have discovered life on bare rocks and in snowbanks.

Alive—Or Not?

As the activity on pages A6 and A7 shows, it can be difficult to tell whether an object is living or nonliving. Montana moss agate (ag'it), for example, has fooled many people. This rock contains green streaks that "grow" and are often mistaken for moss or roots. The streaks are actually mineral crystals. The crystals grow, but not the way that living things grow.

▲ Moss agate, a kind of rock. Moss agate as seen through a microscope (*inset*).

Look closely at the objects in the ocean beach scene below. Which ones do you think are alive?

Many of the seemingly lifeless objects in this scene are really alive. ▼

Corals are sea animals that form colonies of limestone homes. When the corals die, the hard limestone remains, forming a coral reef.

The hard shell of a mollusk was once the home of a soft-bodied animal.

Sand dollars are small flat sea animals that are often mistaken for smooth stones.

Seaweed can look like thick strips of rubber when it dries.

A10

Life Processes

A **cell** is the basic unit of living things. Some simple organisms consist of only one cell. Most living things are composed of many cells. These cells work together to carry out the life processes of that organism. **Life processes** are the functions that a living thing must carry out in order to stay alive and produce more of its own kind.

Living things, as you have seen, can sometimes look like they are nonliving. What trait separates living from non-living things? A living thing carries out basic life processes. For example, all living things must take in **nutrients** (noo′trē ənts), which are substances that are needed for an organism to live and grow. Living things also increase in size and change in other ways during their life cycle.

The basic life processes are listed in the table that follows. Examples are given of how plants and animals carry out these processes. Look for ways that the life processes are alike and different in plants and animals.

Comparing Life Processes

Life Process	Plants	Animals
Taking in materials, such as nutrients and gases	Take in carbon dioxide from air and take in water and minerals from soil	Take in oxygen from the air and nutrients from the food they eat
Releasing energy in food to carry out life processes	Release energy from the food they make	Release energy from the food they eat
Giving off wastes	Give off oxygen as a waste product of food making; also give off carbon dioxide and water as waste products	Give off carbon dioxide and other waste products
Reacting to surroundings	Stems grow toward a source of light; roots grow toward a source of water.	Move to find food, water, and suitable temperatures
Growing and developing	Increase in size and undergo change during their life cycle	Increase in size and undergo change during their life cycle
Reproducing	Most form seeds that result from the union of male and female reproductive cells	Produce offspring that result from the union of male and female reproductive cells

Cells—The Building Blocks of Life

Reading Focus How do plant and animal cells differ from each other?

Recall that the cell is the basic unit that makes up living things. It is the building block of both plants and animals. Each cell contains various parts, each with its own unique role in keeping the cell alive.

Comparing Plant and Animal Cells

The activity on pages A8 and A9 shows plant cells. Plant and animal cells have certain parts in common. There are also some cell parts that are unique to, or occur only in, plant cells. Other cell parts are unique to animal cells.

The drawings on page A13 show a typical plant cell and a typical animal cell. Notice the colored numbers pointing to the cell parts. You'll see that some parts are found in both kinds of cells. Some parts are found only in plant cells; others are found only in animal cells.

Cells Work Together

How do cells work together to form a living thing? Different cells working together form a **tissue** (tish'o͞o). Muscle cells, for example, work with many other muscle cells to form muscle tissue. Different types of tissues work together to form an **organ**, such as the liver, heart, stomach, and small intestine.

In plants, as in animals, there are tissues and organs. For example, cells containing green pigment work together to form leaf tissue. Groups of tissues together form plant organs, such as the leaf, stem, and root. Each organ performs a certain function that helps the plant, or animal, maintain life.

Groups of organs work together to form an **organ system**, such as the circulatory system. The circulatory system brings oxygen to each cell of the body and removes waste products in animals. Together, groups of organ systems form a living thing, such as a pine tree, a cat, or a person.

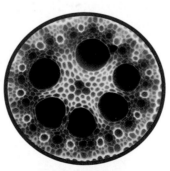

◀ Plant cells— a cross section of a root

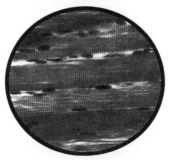

◀ Animal cells— skeletal muscle

Comparing Plant and Animal Cells

❶ CELL MEMBRANE A thin layer that surrounds all cells, the **cell membrane** allows water and dissolved materials to pass into and out of the cell.

❷ NUCLEUS (nōō′klē əs) The **nucleus** controls all the cell's activities and is very important in cell reproduction.

❸ VACUOLE (vak′yōō ōl) A **vacuole** is a large storage area filled with a liquid that contains various substances.

❹ CYTOPLASM (sīt′ō plaz əm) The jellylike substance that fills much of the cell; other cell structures are found in the **cytoplasm**.

❺ CHLOROPLAST (klôr′ə plast) The structure in which food making occurs, the **chloroplast** contains the green-colored pigment chlorophyll.

❻ CELL WALL The **cell wall** is the tough outer covering of a plant cell that gives it a rigid shape; it is made of cellulose.

❼ MITOCHONDRION (mī tə kŏn′drē ən) The **mitochondrion** is the structure in which energy from food is released.

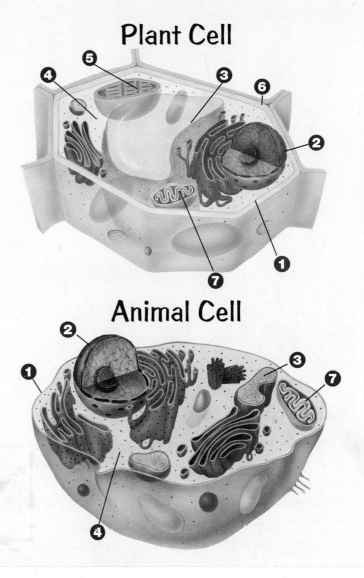

Plant Cell

Animal Cell

INVESTIGATION 1 WRAP-UP

REVIEW

1. List at least three basic life processes. Give examples of how plants and animals carry out these processes.

2. Draw and label a picture of a typical plant cell.

CRITICAL THINKING

3. How can a nonliving thing be mistaken for a living thing? How can a living thing be mistaken for a nonliving thing? Give examples of each.

4. Make a table that compares a typical plant cell with a typical animal cell.

INVESTIGATION 2

HOW DO THE PARTS OF A PLANT HELP IT MEET ITS NEEDS?

How do you obtain nutrients? Your body needs food to function. You have breakfast, lunch, and dinner. Sometimes you munch a snack in between. How does a plant, such as a geranium, get nutrients? You will investigate the parts of a plant and find out which ones help a plant get what it needs.

Activity

Take It Apart

Seed plants, such as a geranium and a maple tree, have the same basic parts—roots, stems, and leaves. As they mature, these plants develop flowers, fruits, and seeds. Examine a seed plant and get to know its parts.

MATERIALS
- goggles
- potted plant
- hand lens
- metric ruler
- newspaper
- plastic knife
- cut flower
- *Science Notebook*

SAFETY /////
Wear goggles during this activity.

Procedure

1. With other members of your group, **observe** a potted plant. In your *Science Notebook*, **list** all the plant parts you can see. **Infer** what parts might be hidden from view.

2. **Examine** the leaves. **Describe** and **record** their shape. Compare the width of a leaf to its length. Describe the thickness, texture, and color of a leaf. Describe how the leaves are attached. **Record** your observations. **Draw** a leaf.

3. **Observe** the stem. **Record** whether the stem has branches. Note whether the main stem is stiff or flexible. **Record** your observations.

Step 2

4. Carefully hold the pot upside down over a newspaper. Tap the bottom of the pot gently until the plant and soil come out. If the soil is stuck to the pot, use a plastic knife to loosen it. You may remove some of the soil so that you can observe plant parts that were hidden. **Record** your observations.

5. Note whether your plant has a flower. If your plant doesn't have a flower, **examine** a cut flower. Use a hand lens to **observe** the structures in the center of the flower. **Record** your observations. **Draw** the flower, showing all of its structures.

Analyze and Conclude

1. What are the main parts of a flowering plant?

2. On your drawings of a leaf and a flower, **label** any parts that you can identify.

3. In what ways is your plant similar to a tree? On what do you base your conclusions?

4. If you have ever examined other plants, **compare** ways in which these plants were different from the plant you observed in this activity. How were they the same?

Technology Link CD-ROM

INVESTIGATE FURTHER!

Use the **Science Processor CD-ROM**, *Plants* (Investigation 1, Inside Plants) to find out more about the parts of plants. View a magnified stem and leaf and learn about the inner workings of these plant parts.

Step 4

RESOURCE

Roots and Stems

Reading Focus How are roots and stems alike and different?

Roots

Did you know that when you sit under a shady tree on a hot summer day, you are seeing half the tree or less? For all of the tree that you see above ground, there is an equal or even greater part below ground—the roots.

The **roots** are the underground foundation of a plant. Roots anchor the plant and absorb water and minerals. Roots also help transport these materials to other parts of the plant. Some roots, such as those of a carrot and a beet, also store food.

Types of Roots

FIBROUS ROOTS Plants such as grasses have a system of branching roots called fibrous roots.

TAPROOT Some plants, such as a carrot or a dandelion, have one main root, or taproot, that stores food.

Some plants have one main root, called a taproot. Other plants have many, branching roots, called fibrous roots. Compare these two types of roots in the drawing on page A16.

Study the drawing that shows the inside of a root. What type of tissue carries water toward the stem? What type of tissue carries nutrients from the leaves and stem into the root? What other kinds of tissue are found in a root? The root hairs near the tip of a root are very important. Water and minerals enter the root through these tiny structures. The drawing at the right shows how water and minerals move from the root hairs into the root's main transport system. Roots are observed in the activity on pages A14 and A15.

TRANSPORT IN A ROOT   The arrows show the paths of water and minerals into a root. ▼

xylem   phloem   cortex   epidermis

root hair

water
minerals

Inside a Root

CORTEX This layer connects the epidermis with the inner core.

XYLEM TISSUE This tissue is made of tubes that carry water and minerals from the soil upward.

EPIDERMIS This layer of cells covers the root.

PHLOEM TISSUE This tissue is made of tubes that carry sugars and other nutrients from the leaves through the stem and down to the root.

ROOT HAIRS These are tiny extensions that take in water and minerals.

ROOT CAP The tip of the root, called the root cap, pushes the root through the soil.

Stems

The root is connected to the next main part of the plant—the stem. The **stem** is the part of a plant that connects the roots and the leaves. The stem supports the other above-ground parts of the plant, the leaves and flowers. The transport tissues that you saw in the roots on page A17 continue through the stem and into the leaves and flowers. Water and minerals move through the xylem tissue toward the leaves.

Sugar, the food made by the plant, moves through the phloem tissue toward the roots.

Stems vary in structure. Small flowering plants, such as buttercups and daisies, have short, thin, some-what soft stems. The trunks of large trees, such as oaks and maples, are hard, sturdy, and may be more than 30 m (100 ft) in height! Compare the nonwoody and woody stems in the drawings on this page. ■

CUTAWAY VIEW OF NONWOODY PLANT STEM This stem has thick walls and fibers running through it. The fibers give the stem its strength. This view shows the xylem and phloem cells that make up the transport system of the stem. Daisies and dandelions have nonwoody stems.

CUTAWAY VIEW OF WOODY PLANT STEM This trunk, which is actually a woody stem, is formed of many layers of cells. These layers have an outside protective covering called bark. This view shows the transport system of xylem and phloem. Each year the xylem cells form new layers of growth called annual rings.

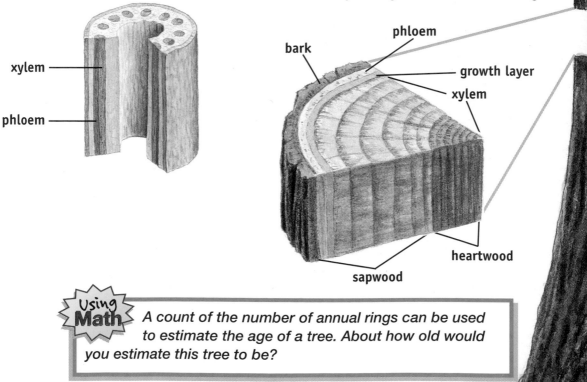

xylem

phloem

bark

phloem

growth layer

xylem

heartwood

sapwood

Using **Math** *A count of the number of annual rings can be used to estimate the age of a tree. About how old would you estimate this tree to be?*

Leaves

Reading Focus What are the parts of a leaf, and what is the function of each?

In autumn in some parts of the country, you will find great numbers of fallen red, yellow, and brown leaves. Why do plants have so many leaves? What do leaves do?

Look at the picture below of two kinds of leaves. A **leaf** is a plant part that grows out of the stem and is the food-making factory of a plant. The thin flat part of a leaf is called the blade. The blades of broad-leaved plants are often shaped so that the greatest amount of leaf is exposed to the Sun. Sunlight is an essential part of **photosynthesis** (fōt ō sin'thə sis), the food-making process in plants. The leaves of

Types of Leaves

NEEDLE LEAVES Plants such as a pine, a spruce, and a fir have needle leaves. The shape of these leaves helps reduce water loss.

BROAD LEAF Plants such as a maple and an oak are called broad-leaved trees and have broad flat leaves.

VEINS Along with the petiole, the veins form the transport system of the leaf. Water enters the leaf through the veins.

BLADE The blade is the broad flat part of a leaf.

PETIOLE The petiole is an extension of the xylem and phloem tubes of the stem.

Structure of a Leaf

UPPER EPIDERMIS Cell layer that protects the leaf from drying out

PALISADE LAYER Columnlike cells where food making occurs

SPONGY LAYER Loosely-packed cells where food making occurs and where veins are located

VEIN Structure that contains xylem tissue, which transports water, and phloem tissue, which transports sugar and other nutrients

LOWER EPIDERMIS Cell layer that protects the leaf and allows for the exchange of gases

both broad-leaved plants and needle-leaved plants, such as a pine and a spruce, carry on this process.

Inside a Leaf

A typical leaf may be very thin, but it contains many cells, as shown above. If you cut across a leaf, producing a cross section, you'll find several layers of cells. The leaf's main function is to pro-duce food for the plant. The structure of a leaf is well suited to that purpose.

Photosynthesis takes place in the two middle layers of cells. The top and bottom layers protect the leaf and keep it from drying out. Openings in the bottom layer allow for the exchange of gases with the environment. A leaf also contains many veins, which help transport water and manufactured food. ■

▲ The pointy spines of a cactus do not make food. They protect the stem from animal intruders. Cactus spines are modified leaves.

▲ In pea plants some leaves function as tendrils. They twist around objects and support the plant.

Energy Traps

Reading Focus What is needed for photosynthesis to occur, and what does this process produce?

Imagine that you're walking home from school and you begin to feel hungry. It would be great if you could manufacture a tasty snack on the spot. But you can't, of course. Your body can't produce its own food. But plants can.

Making Food

Plants produce their own food by using light energy, carbon dioxide, and water. Plants can't move around to find these things. But they can trap light energy and collect the substances they need to make their own food.

Plants trap energy in their leaves. Some leaf cells contain hundreds of disklike parts called chloroplasts. Recall that chloroplasts are tiny cell structures that contain a green pigment called chlorophyll. This pigment collects light energy from the Sun. Chlorophyll works much like a solar panel, absorbing light energy, which is then stored as food energy.

Chlorophyll uses the Sun's light energy to change two substances, carbon dioxide and water, into food. Carbon dioxide is a gas found in air. It enters the plant through tiny holes

usually found on the underside of the leaves. Water enters the plant through the roots. Recall that transport tissue carries water from the roots to the stems to the leaves.

The food produced by a plant is called glucose (glо̄о̄′kо̄s), a form of sugar. The process of using light energy to combine carbon dioxide and water to produce glucose is called photosynthesis. *Photo-* means "light," and *synthesis* means "joining together."

Chloroplasts are tiny green disklike cell parts that trap energy during photosynthesis. (*A*) Groups of chloroplasts (*B*) one enlarged chloroplast

Photosynthesis

light energy
carbon dioxide + water ➜ glucose + oxygen

Plants trap light energy from the Sun during photosynthesis.

sunlight

■ Carbon dioxide (CO_2) enters the leaf through holes in its surface.

■ Oxygen (O_2), a waste product of photosynthesis, is released.

Glucose ($C_6H_{12}O_6$) is produced in the leaf cells.

Water (H_2O) enters roots through root hairs at the tips of roots.

Comparing Photosynthesis and Cell Respiration

Photosynthesis	Cell Respiration
Occurs in plants	Occurs in plants and animals
Food-making process	Food-using process
Occurs in the cell part called the chloroplast	Occurs in the cell part called the mitochondrion
Traps light energy and produces glucose	Releases energy in glucose
carbon dioxide + water $\xrightarrow{\text{light energy}}$ glucose + oxygen	glucose + oxygen → carbon dioxide + water + energy

The drawing on page A22 shows the process by which plant cells produce glucose. In addition to glucose, photosynthesis produces a "waste" product. This waste product, oxygen, is one that humans and other animals need to survive. Oxygen and any leftover water leave the plant by way of the same tiny openings in the leaves through which carbon dioxide enters.

Storing and Using Energy

Plants store the glucose they produce. Most plants store extra glucose in the form of starch, a chemical made up of chains of simple sugars. Starch can be stored in different parts of plants. For example, starch is stored in leaves of lettuce. It is stored in roots of radishes and in leafstalks of celery. Starch is also stored in grains of wheat and used to make bread.

How is energy from glucose released so that it can be used by cells? It is released during a process called **cell respiration** (res pə rā'shən). Cell respiration occurs inside each cell in tiny cell parts called mitochondria. In the mitochondria, glucose joins with oxygen, and the energy stored in the glucose is released.

During cell respiration, water and carbon dioxide are released as waste products. The energy released is used by plants and animals for cell growth and repair and for carrying out their life processes. The table above compares photosynthesis and cell respiration. How do these processes compare? ■

Starch is stored in celery leafstalks, radish roots, and lettuce leaves. ▼

Internet Field Trip

Visit **www.eduplace.com** to find out more about the life processes of plants.

Plant Responses

> **Reading Focus** What are some ways a plant responds to its environment?

Have you ever seen someone grow a sweet potato plant in a glass of water? If so, you probably noticed that the roots grow down into the glass. The stems grow up, usually toward a light source. The sweet potato plant is reacting, or responding, to its environment. A plant response to conditions in the environment is called a **tropism** (trō′piz əm).

Growth Toward Gravity

Roots respond to Earth's gravity by growing toward the center of Earth. Growing toward the center of Earth is a geotropic response. The word *tropism* comes from a Greek word that means "a turning." The word part *geo-* means "Earth." So *geotropism* is a turning (of the roots) toward Earth. This growth response ensures that the roots will grow down into the soil, the plant's source of water and nutrients. Leaves and stems have the opposite response to gravity. They grow away from Earth's center. This response helps ensure that leaves and stems will be exposed to sunlight, which the plant needs to make its food.

Growth Toward Light

Leaves and stems grow toward a source of light. Growing toward light is a phototropic response. *Photo-* means "light." You have probably seen the leaves of houseplants turned toward a bright light source. Stems may also bend toward that light source. The bending of stems occurs because they are actually growing toward light. Such growth allows the leaves to capture the greatest amount of light, which is needed for the process of photosynthesis. What can you do with a houseplant to keep the stems and leaves from bending in one direction?

Growth Toward Water

When plant roots are in soil that has lots of water in one area, they grow toward the wet area. This kind of growth is a hydrotropic response. (*Hydro-* means "water.") However, roots do not "know" where the moisture is. They do not "try" to find the water. Instead, when roots come into contact with moist soil, they continue to grow toward the moisture. Roots touching only very dry soil may grow very slowly or not at all.

Hanging On

Some plants have threadlike parts called tendrils that wrap around objects to support the plant. This response is another kind of tropism called thigmotropism, or response to touch. (*Thigmo-* means "touch.") Picture 4 on page A25 shows the thigmotropic response of a pea plant.

① Roots showing a geotropic response. ② Leaves showing a phototropic response.
③ Two plants showing a hydrotropic response. ④ Tendrils curling around garden stakes,
showing a thigmotropic response.

INVESTIGATION 2 WRAP-UP

REVIEW

1. Draw a leaf, such as a maple leaf, and label the veins, blade, and petiole.

2. Describe the roles of xylem tissue and phloem tissue in stems.

CRITICAL THINKING

3. Explain why the parts of the word *photosynthesis (photo-* and *synthesis)* help explain the process of photosynthesis.

4. What do you think would happen to the roots of a plant if you turned the plant upside down for two weeks? Explain.

HOW DO THE PARTS OF AN ANIMAL HELP IT MEET ITS NEEDS?

Roots, stems, and leaves help a plant meet its needs. Animals have body parts, too. These parts appear very different from those found in plants. But surprisingly, an animal's body parts have the same basic job as a plant's parts—to help the organism meet its needs.

Activity

Come and Get It

You know that a plant's roots absorb water. And you've learned that carbon dioxide is taken in through its leaves. A plant uses these materials to make food. Unlike plants, animals must obtain food from their environment. Find out what body parts help a snail do this.

Procedure

1. Obtain a garden snail from your teacher. Place the snail on the inside wall of a plastic container.

2. Use a hand lens to observe the snail. In your *Science Notebook*, **make a sketch** of the snail. **Label** any body parts that you can identify.

Step 2

3. **List** each body part that you labeled. **Infer** the job done by each part listed. **Record** your inferences.

4. Add food to the plastic container and place the snail near the food. **Observe** the snail's behavior. **Record** your observations.

5. **Identify** any body parts that you think help the snail obtain food. **Describe** these body parts.

6. **Compare** your observations with those of another group of students in your class.

Analyze and Conclude

1. **Make a chart** that compares the basic needs of a snail with those of a plant. List any similarities.

2. **Compare** the way that a snail obtains food with the way a plant obtains food.

3. Both a snail and a plant use food. **Hypothesize** whether the food is used for the same purpose in both organisms. Explain your reasoning.

UNIT PROJECT LINK

For this Unit Project you will create a museum display comparing systems in a plant, an invertebrate, and a vertebrate. Research where each organism lives and what it eats. Write a brief report as part of your display.

Technology Link

For more help with your Unit Project, go to **www.eduplace.com**.

Science in Literature

STOP THE DISAPPEARING ACT

"Follow the trunks of the trees as they rise straight up from the forest floor. You'll see them open like umbrellas, branching out to form the rooflike canopy of the rain forest. In this dense layer of green, leaves bathed in full sunlight absorb energy and use it to make food."

Why Save the Rain Forest?
by Donald Silver
Illustrated by Patricia J. Wynne
Julian Messner, 1993

Read about the role of rain forest trees in keeping carbon dioxide from building up in the air. In *Why Save the Rain Forest?* Donald Silver describes the importance of photosynthesis in balancing the life-support systems of Earth.

Staying Alive!

Reading Focus What life processes do all living things carry out?

A Look Back

You've compared the structure of plant cells and animal cells. You learned that plants obtain and use materials from their environment. You also learned that through the process of photosynthesis, plants are able to produce their own food.

You've seen how plant organs—roots, stems, and leaves—help plants meet their needs. Animals must also meet their needs. Like plants, they have organs and systems that help meet those needs. Let's take a look at the organ systems of two animals—the frog and the human.

Frogs and Plants—Alike or Not?

Like a plant, a frog carries out basic life processes. The frog obtains and digests food. Digestion is the process of breaking down food into nutrients that cells can absorb. The digested food provides the frog with the energy needed to carry out its life processes. The nutrients in food are also used to build new cells and to repair damaged cells. A plant uses food in these same ways.

As it carries out its life processes, a frog produces waste products, which are removed from the body. Plants also produce and release waste products as they carry out their life processes.

Organ Systems of a Frog

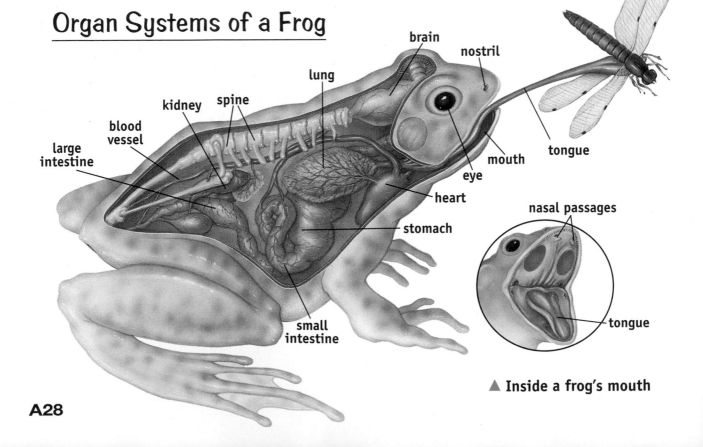

▲ Inside a frog's mouth

Food Getting and Digesting

A major difference between a frog and a plant involves the way each obtains food. In the presence of light, plants take in water and carbon dioxide and make sugar, which is their food. They give off oxygen as a waste product of the food-making process. All animals, including frogs, must obtain their food from their surroundings. They must then digest, or break down, the food to release the energy it contains.

A frog has a group of organs, the digestive system, that work together to digest food. As you read, find parts of the frog's digestive system in the drawing on page A28.

A frog's digestive system begins at its mouth. A frog uses its tongue to obtain food. Notice from the drawing that a frog's tongue is attached to the front of its mouth. By flicking out its sticky tongue, a frog can catch passing insects.

Next, the frog swallows the insect whole, without chewing. Frogs have very tiny teeth that are good for gripping, not biting or chewing! The food is pushed down the frog's throat in an interesting way. As the frog blinks, its large eyeballs push the insect down its throat!

The mouth connects to a short tube, the esophagus (i säf′ə gəs), that connects to the stomach. Partly digested food remains a short time in the stomach and then moves on to the coiled small intestine. Digestion continues in this organ.

Digested food containing nutrients is absorbed from the small intestine into the bloodstream. The bloodstream carries the nutrients to all the frog's cells. The small intestine joins to a large intestine, which narrows to a rectum. Undigested food leaves the body through an opening at the end of the rectum.

Gas Exchange

The cells of a frog's body use oxygen to break down sugar obtained from food. Oxygen is brought into a frog's body by its respiratory system. Air, which contains oxygen, passes through a frog's mouth and down a tube to the lungs. Here, oxygen is picked up by the frog's transport system. At the same time, the transport system picks up carbon dioxide, a waste gas. The carbon dioxide is carried from the blood to the lungs and is then exhaled, or breathed out.

Transporting and Excreting

The circulatory system is the frog's transport system. A frog's circulatory system includes a heart that pumps the blood through blood vessels to all parts of the frog's body. Blood carries oxygen and digested food to the body's cells.

As the frog carries on its life processes, its cells produce waste products. If allowed to build up, these wastes become harmful. Wastes are removed, or excreted, from the frog's body by the excretory (eks′krə tôr ē) and digestive systems.

Blood traveling through the body carries carbon dioxide and other wastes from cells. Blood passes through the kidneys, which are organs of the excretory system that filter the blood. The kidneys remove wastes, minerals, and excess water from the frog's blood. The liquid wastes are stored in a bladder and then passed out of the body.

Human Body Systems

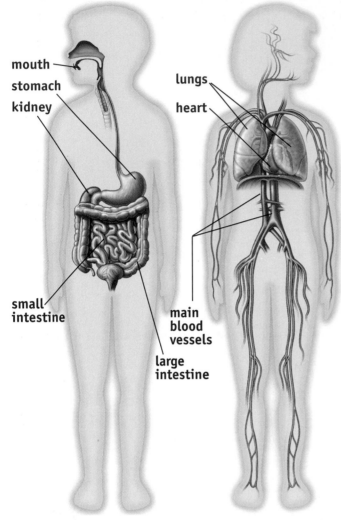

You've just learned about what's inside a frog. What would you find inside a human body? The same life processes that keep a frog alive also keep a human being alive. People must digest food and get rid of the waste products of digestion. They must breathe in air and release the waste products of respiration. They must also circulate the nutrients that are made available during digestion.

The drawings on this page show four human body systems. On the left is a drawing of the digestive and excretory systems. On the right is a drawing of the circulatory and respiratory systems. You can probably recognize some of the organs in these four systems. For example, find the stomach, kidneys, lungs, and heart.

In the next two chapters, you'll learn in more detail how human body systems work to keep the body alive and well.

mouth
stomach
kidney

small
intestine

lungs

heart

main
blood
vessels

large
intestine

▲ **The digestive and excretory systems**

▲ **The circulatory and respiratory systems**

INVESTIGATION 3 WRAP-UP

REVIEW

1. Describe the major difference in food-getting between plants and animals.

2. Why is it vital for living things such as frogs to digest food?

CRITICAL THINKING

3. How is the transport system of a plant similar to the transport system of a frog? How do the systems differ?

4. Explain how the digestive and circulatory systems work together to supply nutrients and energy to the body's cells. Use information about the frog to support your answer.

REFLECT & EVALUATE

Word Power

Write the letter of the term that best matches the definition. *Not all terms will be used.*

1. Cell structure that controls all the cell's activities
2. Plant responses to conditions in the environment
3. Functions that a living thing must carry out to stay alive
4. Jellylike substance that fills most of a cell
5. Food-making process in plants
6. Chlorophyll-containing structure in a plant cell

a. chloroplast
b. cytoplasm
c. life processes
d. nucleus
e. organ
f. photosynthesis
g. tropisms
h. vacuole

Check What You Know

Write the word in each pair that correctly completes each sentence.

1. Tubes that carry nutrients from the leaves through the stem and down to the roots are (xylem, phloem) tissue.
2. The process by which animal cells and plant cells use oxygen to release energy in foods is (photosynthesis, cell respiration).
3. The outermost layer of an animal cell is the (cell membrane, cell wall).

Problem Solving

1. A potted plant is growing on a windowsill in bright light. The plant is rotated one-half turn each morning. How would this turning affect the way the plant's stems grow?
2. In your own words, explain why a leaf can be called an "energy trap."
3. Explain the function of digestion; use digestion in a frog to support your explanation.

PORTFOLIO Make a sketch of this plant cell. Label the parts. In a short paragraph describe how the parts in a drawing of an animal cell would be different from the parts in a drawing of a plant cell.

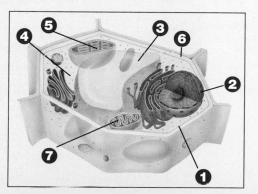

CHAPTER 2

DIGESTION AND RESPIRATION

Human body systems consist of many organs working together. What happens to the food that we eat? What is the purpose of breathing? In this chapter you'll explore the workings of two important body systems—the digestive system and the respiratory system.

Connecting to Science
CULTURE

Ancient Remedies Treatment for problems of the digestive system dates back to ancient times. As long ago as 2500 B.C. the Chinese treated various digestive disorders with acupuncture. Acupuncture is a treatment in which very thin needles are placed into the body at key points. This treatment has been proven to control appetite and to reduce stomach upset.

The ancient Chinese also used plants to treat digestive disorders. Plants used in this way are called herbs. The yellow underground stem of Chinese rhubarb has been used for more than 2,000 years to regulate digestion. Another herb used as medicine since ancient times is garlic. The Chinese, Babylonians, Greeks, Romans, Hindus, and Egyptians all used garlic to treat various intestinal disorders. Read on to learn more about the human digestive system.

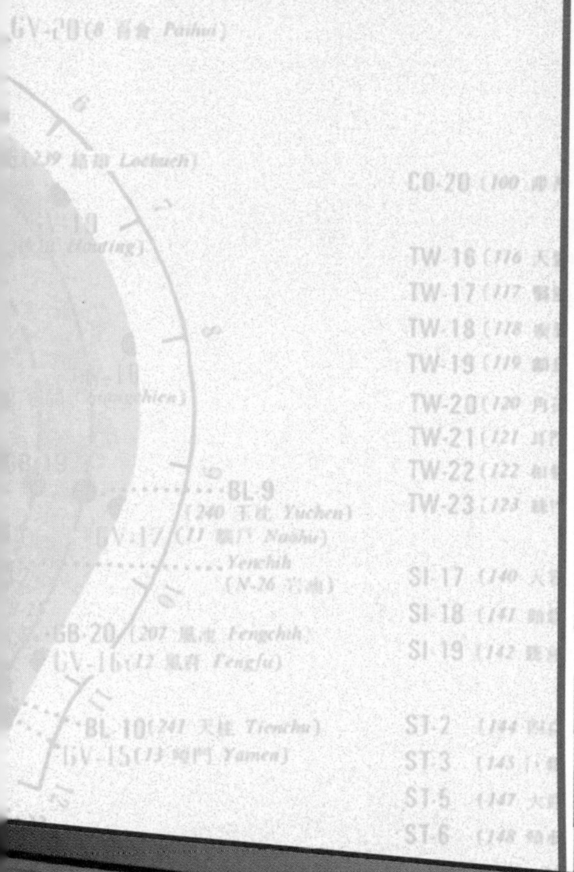

Coming Up

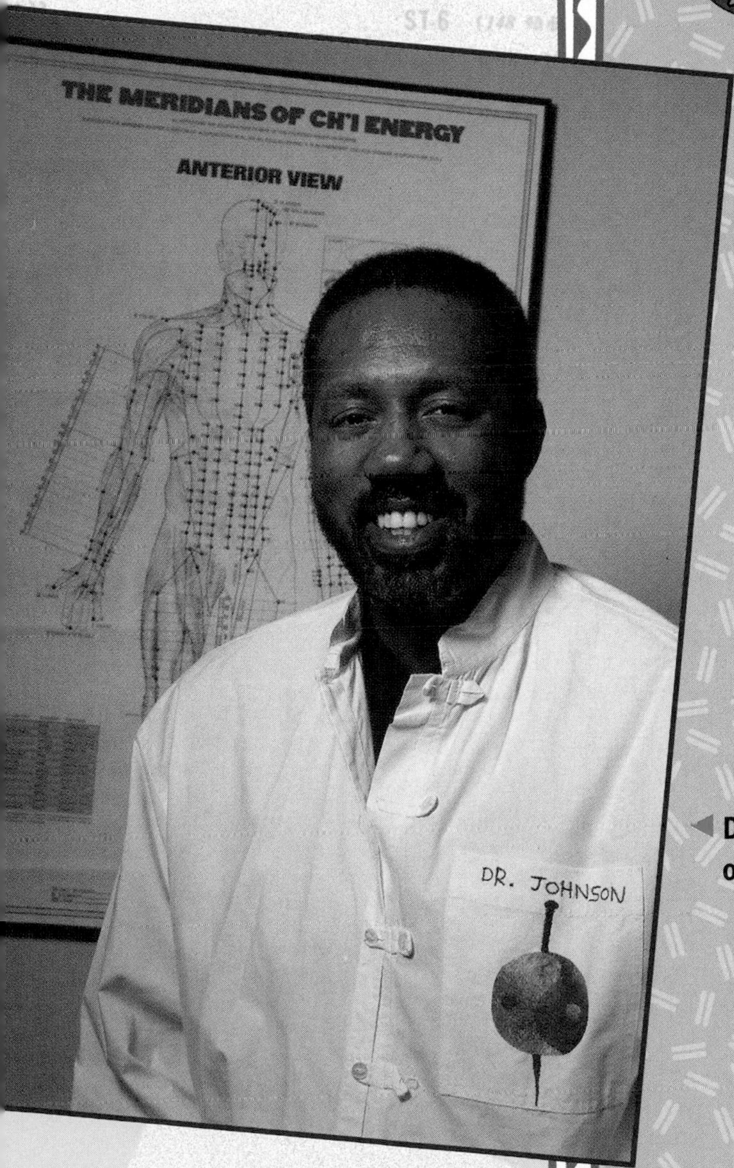

THE MERIDIANS OF CH'I ENERGY
ANTERIOR VIEW
DR. JOHNSON

Dr. Malcolm Johnson in front of a chart of acupuncture points

INVESTIGATION 1

HOW DOES THE DIGESTIVE SYSTEM WORK?

Did you ever swallow a large piece of food without properly chewing it? How did that feel? For food to be used by your body, it must be broken down by the digestive system. The breakdown begins in the mouth.

Activity

Sink Your Teeth Into This

Have you ever looked very carefully at your teeth? Are they all the same size and shape? Are the edges of your teeth smooth or ragged? Find out in this activity.

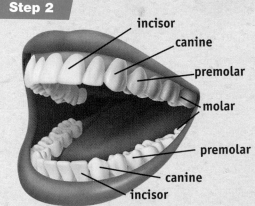

Step 2

incisor
canine
premolar
molar
premolar
canine
incisor

MATERIALS

- mirror
- celery stick
- *Science Notebook*

SAFETY

During this activity, eat foods only with your teacher's permission.

Procedure

1. Use a mirror to **observe** your teeth. Count the number of teeth in your lower jaw. Then count the number of teeth in your upper jaw. **Record** these numbers in your *Science Notebook*. **Compare** the numbers with those of other students in your class.

2. Look for four main kinds of teeth in your mouth. Look at the drawing to the right, which shows the teeth in a person's mouth. In your *Science Notebook*, **list** the four kinds and describe how they are alike and how they are different.

3. **Talk with group members** about how the four kinds of teeth differ. **Infer** why these teeth are different.

4. Close your teeth and **observe** how the upper teeth and lower teeth meet. In your *Science Notebook,* **describe** how your teeth meet. Note whether the way the teeth meet affects how you chew your food.

5. Eat a celery stick. Note which teeth you use to bite the celery. Note which teeth you use to chew the celery. **Record** this information in your *Science Notebook.*

Analyze and Conclude

1. How many teeth do most students have in their lower jaw? in their upper jaw? Is there a difference between the kinds of teeth in the upper jaw and the lower jaw?

2. In what ways do you use your front teeth? In what ways do you use your back teeth? How do the shapes of the front teeth and the back teeth differ? **Describe** how the shape of your teeth is related to how you use them.

INVESTIGATE FURTHER!

RESEARCH

Find pictures of the teeth of different animals such as a squirrel, a deer, a bear, an alligator, and a wolf. Compare the shapes and sizes of the teeth. Find out the diet of each animal. Hypothesize whether diet and tooth shape are related.

Science in Literature

WHEN FOOD GOES DOWN THE "WRONG WAY"

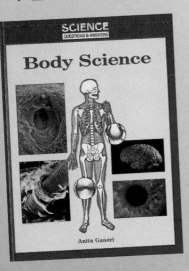

Body Science
by Anita Ganeri
Dillon Press, 1992

"When you swallow a piece of food, a flap called the epiglottis covers the top of your windpipe, and the food goes down your esophagus and into your digestive system. But this process can go wrong. If you accidentally breathe in as you swallow the food, the epiglottis opens up. Then the food gets into your windpipe. You may choke on it. . . ."

Does your food ever go down the "wrong way"? Does your stomach ever rumble? Find out about your digestive system and many other parts of the human body as you read *Body Science* by Anita Ganeri.

Activity

How Sweet It Is

Some foods contain sugar. You'll use a glucose test strip to find out if glucose, a kind of sugar, is present in certain foods. You'll also find out how a chemical called an enzyme (en'zīm) can change a sugar from one form to another.

Procedure

1. Use a marker to label four paper cups *apple juice*, *orange juice*, *cranberry juice*, and *milk*.

2. Use a dropper to add ten drops of apple juice to the first paper cup. Wash the dropper thoroughly. Then add ten drops of orange juice to the second paper cup.

3. Wash the dropper. Add ten drops of cranberry juice to the third cup. Wash the dropper again. Add ten drops of milk to the fourth cup.

4. You will use a glucose test strip to find out if the liquid in each cup contains the sugar glucose. A glucose test strip changes from light green to dark green or brown when it contacts glucose. In your *Science Notebook*, **make a chart** like the one shown below. **Predict** what will happen to the test strip when each liquid is tested. **Record** your predictions in your chart.

Glucose Present?		
Food	**Prediction**	**Result**
apple juice		

See **SCIENCE** and **MATH TOOLBOX** page H11 if you need to review **Making a Chart to Organize Data.**

5. **Test** each liquid by dipping a dry glucose test strip into each cup. **Record** your results in your chart.

6. Lactose is a kind of sugar found in milk. Lactase is a chemical, called an enzyme, made by the body. Lactase breaks down lactose to simple sugars, such as glucose. Put one drop of lactase into the cup of milk. Now dip a dry glucose test strip into the milk. **Record** your observations.

Analyze and Conclude

1. What happened to the glucose test strip in the apple juice, orange juice, cranberry juice, and milk? Which liquid contained glucose? How do you know?

2. Compare the two glucose test strips you used in the milk both before and after you added the lactase. How were they alike or different? **Infer** what could have caused a difference in the results.

3. Recall that lactase breaks down lactose, the sugar in milk. Some people do not make enough lactase. If such people drink milk or milk products, they can become ill. **Hypothesize** how these people might be able to drink milk without becoming ill.

Step 5

UNIT PROJECT LINK

For the plant that you selected for your museum display, research the plant system that allows for gas exchange. For the two animals you chose, research the respiratory system of each. Create a display that compares all three systems. Your display might include posters, models, or another medium of your choice.

TechnologyLink

For more help with your Unit Project, go to **www.eduplace.com**.

How Digestion Starts

Reading Focus How is food digested as it moves from the mouth to the stomach?

Your Stomach "Speaks"

Your body sends you signals when it is time to eat. Many people feel tired, weak, or even grouchy when they're hungry. Yet it isn't really food the body needs. The body's cells need chemicals called nutrients (noo′trē ənts) for energy, to build new cells, to repair damaged cells, and to control body processes.

Foods provide tasty packaging for nutrients. After you take a bite, food travels through about 9 m (30 ft) of digestive organs. These organs make up the human **digestive system**, in which food is broken down into a form that body cells can use.

From Your Plate to a Cell

The digestive organs grind, mash, and churn food into smaller and smaller particles. They also release chemicals that soften food and change it from one form to another. Once food has been changed to a form that cells can use, it passes out of the digestive system. The nutrients from food pass into the bloodstream and then to the body's cells.

Digestion in the Mouth

Think about your last meal. The digestive process probably began before you took your first bite. At just the sight and smell of the food, your salivary (sal′ə ver ē) glands went to work.

The drawing at the bottom of page A39 shows your salivary glands, which are located under your tongue and near your ears. The glands produce **saliva** (sə lī′və), the watery liquid that moistens the mouth and food. Each day as much as $1\frac{1}{2}$ L (about 6 c) of saliva flow into your mouth. Saliva begins the chemical breakdown of the food.

The Role of the Teeth

When you eat solid food, you bite off pieces with your front teeth, the incisors (in sī′zərz). The incisors are cutting teeth as the activity on pages A34 and A35 shows. The teeth on either side of them are canines, which tear food. To help the digestive process, you chew your food well with your back grinding teeth, the premolars and molars.

From about 6 months to 26 months of age, your baby teeth grow in. Then those teeth fall out and are replaced by permanent teeth. All your permanent teeth will appear by age 20. Look at the drawing of teeth on page A39 and find the four main kinds of teeth. The cutting, tearing, and grinding action of the teeth physically breaks food into smaller pieces, helping digestion.

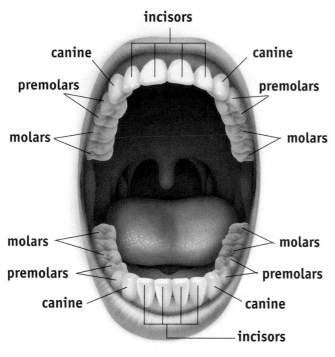

incisors

canine • canine

premolars • premolars

molars • molars

molars • molars

premolars • premolars

canine • canine

incisors

▲ **Teeth in an adult's mouth**

Your teeth would not work very well without your tongue. The tongue is the muscular organ that helps you swallow and pushes food against your teeth. After you bite, slice, and tear food, your tongue pushes it to the grinding surfaces of the back teeth.

As you chew, your salivary glands produce chemicals called **enzymes** (en′zīmz), which help break down food. Ptyalin (tī′ə lin) is an enzyme in saliva that breaks starch into simple sugars. After food is ground and mixed with saliva, it becomes a soft, wet mass. This mass of food is ready to be swallowed.

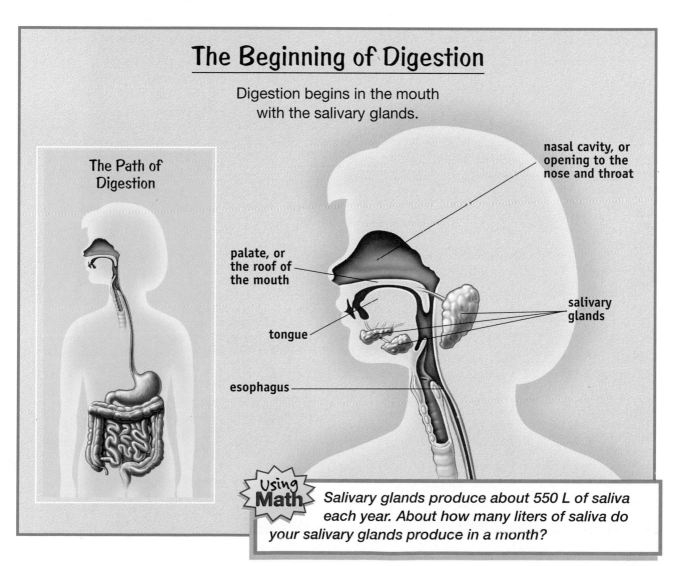

The Beginning of Digestion

Digestion begins in the mouth with the salivary glands.

The Path of Digestion

nasal cavity, or opening to the nose and throat

palate, or the roof of the mouth

salivary glands

tongue

esophagus

Using Math

Salivary glands produce about 550 L of saliva each year. About how many liters of saliva do your salivary glands produce in a month?

A39

Swallowing

You control the start of a swallow. When the food is moist and soft, your tongue pushes it to the back of the throat. Once food reaches the back of the throat, automatic processes take over. Then the food cannot go down the "wrong pipe"—the trachea, or windpipe.

Look at the numbers in the drawings below to see what happens during the automatic part of swallowing.

Choking

Sometimes the automatic processes of digestion fail. Suppose you talk and laugh while eating. The food in your mouth can enter the nose or the windpipe. You can even choke. A person trained in giving the Heimlich maneuver (hīm′lik mə nōō′vər) can help to dislodge the stuck food. First, the trained person wraps his arms around the choking person under that person's ribs.

Stages of Swallowing

❶ The tongue pushes food to the back of the throat.

❷ The back part of the palate (pal′ət) rises up to close the opening to the nose. (This keeps food from backing up into the nose.)

❸ A flap of tissue closes the trachea, keeping food from entering it.

❹ Throat muscles squeeze food to the top of the esophagus (i säf′ə gəs). The **esophagus** is the muscular tube that connects the mouth to the stomach.

❺ The palate lowers, opening the passage to the nose.

❻ The flap of tissue to the windpipe rises.

❼ Food is now safely in the esophagus.

❽ Food will continue moving toward the stomach.

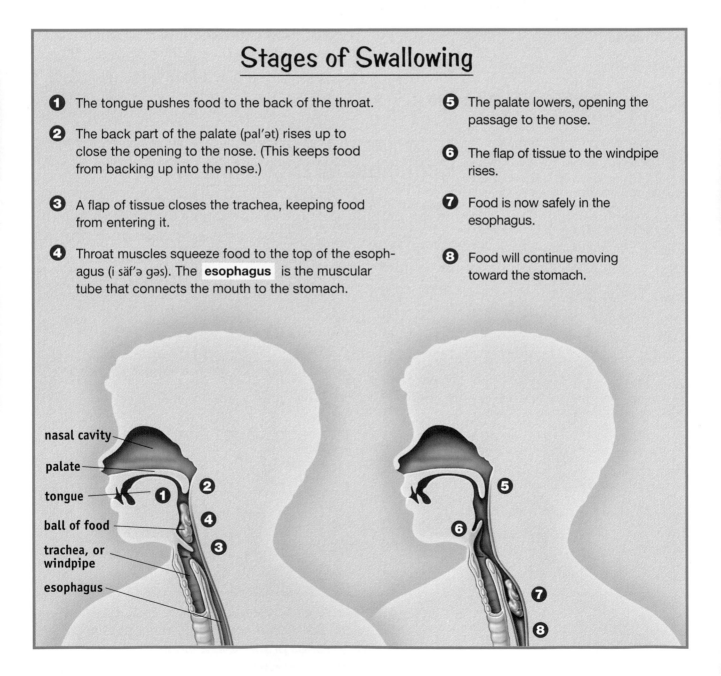

nasal cavity
palate
tongue
ball of food
trachea, or windpipe
esophagus

Then he presses strongly in and up under the breastbone. This action can help to force the stuck food up and out of the windpipe.

Down to the Stomach

The esophagus moves food along, using a wavelike motion known as **peristalsis** (per ə stal'sis). Rings of muscles contract, or tighten, above the mass of food. At the same time, rings of muscles below the food relax. This contracting and relaxing of muscles pushes the food down to the stomach.

The esophagus ends at the **stomach**, a muscular organ that stores food and helps digest it. Between the esophagus and the stomach is a round muscle that acts as a gatekeeper. This muscle opens, allowing the swallowed food into the stomach. Once the food is in the stomach, the muscle closes, preventing the food from moving back into the esophagus.

In the Stomach

An adult's stomach can hold about 1 L (1 qt) of food. The food stays in the stomach two to six hours, where it is further broken down.

Even before food reaches the stomach, glands in the stomach lining begin to produce digestive juices. One juice, hydrochloric acid, is strong enough to make a hole in a carpet or dissolve metal. Why, then, isn't the stomach digested by its own acid? The walls of the stomach and other digestive organs are protected. They produce mucus (myoo'kəs), a slippery material that forms a thick, protective coating inside digestive organs.

The stomach also makes digestive enzymes. Some stomach enzymes begin to break down the proteins found in meat, eggs, dairy products, and beans. Like the esophagus, the stomach undergoes peristalsis. Waves of muscle action mash and churn the food and digestive juices. The food soon becomes a thick, soupy liquid called chyme (kīm). Then it is ready to leave the stomach.

Two to six hours after food is swallowed, chyme begins to leave the stomach. Sugars and starches leave first, then proteins. Fats remain in the stomach longest. A few simple chemicals, such as sugar, alcohol, and some medicines, pass directly from the stomach to the bloodstream. But most nutrients are passed along for further digestion. ■

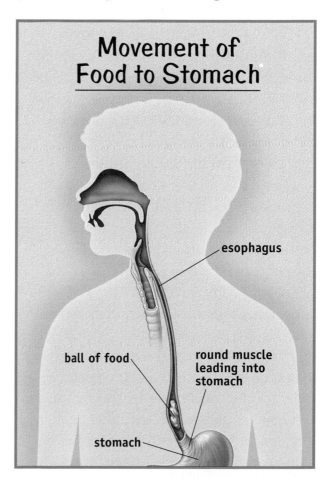

Movement of Food to Stomach

esophagus

ball of food

round muscle leading into stomach

stomach

How Digestion Ends

Reading Focus What happens to food after it leaves the stomach?

Digestion in the Small Intestine

Did you know that a person can live without a stomach? How can this be? Look at the drawing. Recall that the main role of the stomach is to store food, not digest it. Most nutrients are absorbed into the bloodstream in the next part of the digestive system—the small intestine. The **small intestine** is the long, coiled organ where most digestion takes place.

The "small" intestine is not really small. About 6 m (20 ft) long, it can be three times as long as the body it occupies. You can see that it is coiled, allowing it to fit inside the body. It is called the *small* intestine because it is narrower than the *large* intestine.

Recall that in the stomach, food becomes a soupy liquid called chyme. Chyme from the stomach enters the first part of the small intestine. Then, over the next five hours, the digestive process is completed. The small intestine produces digestive juices and enzymes, such as the enzyme lactase. As the activity on pages A36 and A37 shows, lactase changes lactose, a sugar found in milk, to glucose, a simpler form of sugar.

Other organs work with the small intestine. Find the liver in the drawing. The liver is an organ that performs

more than 500 functions in several body systems. One function in digestion is to produce bile, which breaks fats into smaller pieces.

Made in the liver, bile is stored in the gallbladder, a small pear-shaped organ. The gallbladder supplies bile to the small intestine as it is needed. Another organ, the pancreas, lies behind the stomach and is connected to the small intestine.

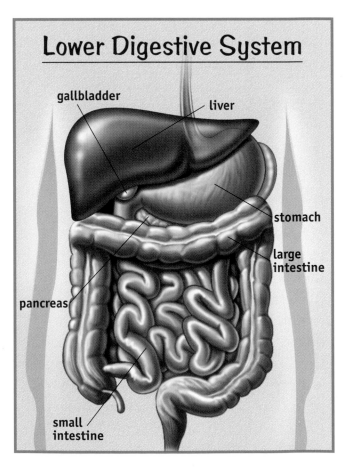

Lower Digestive System

The pancreas produces pancreatic juices. These juices are a mixture of digestive enzymes and other substances that aid in digestion.

Absorption in the Small Intestine

Most carbohydrates, proteins, and water are absorbed in the second part of the small intestine. Vitamins and minerals that dissolve in water are also absorbed there.

In the wall of the small intestine are **villi** (vil′ī), shown below. Villi are like the loops on a terry-cloth towel. In the villi is a network of blood vessels. Dissolved nutrients pass from the small intestine through these vessels into the blood. The blood then carries the nutrients to every cell in the body.

Waste Removal

After food passes through the small intestine, some material, such as fiber, still remains undigested. Fiber helps move food through the digestive system. But humans cannot digest fiber. It must be passed out of the body.

Peristalsis moves undigested matter into the large intestine. The **large intestine**, also called the colon, is the organ that absorbs water and salts from undigested material. It returns much of the water through its walls to the bloodstream. The large intestine also moves undigested material out of the body. About 24 to 48 hours after a meal is eaten, the undigested materials pass out of the body through an opening called the anus (ā′nəs). ■

Using Math At left is a cross section of the small intestine, with a closeup of three villi. The small intestine is about 7 m (23 ft) long and contains about 700,000 villi per meter. About how many villi can be found in the small intestine?

INVESTIGATION 1 WRAP-UP

THINK IT WRITE IT

REVIEW

1. What is the function of the digestive system? Describe digestion in the mouth and the stomach.

2. Explain why a person can live without a stomach.

CRITICAL THINKING

3. As food moves through the digestive system, it is changed in two main ways. Identify these two changes. Explain the role of the mouth, stomach, small intestine, and large intestine in these changes.

4. Describe the structure of the small intestine. How does this structure aid in the absorption of nutrients?

HOW DOES THE RESPIRATORY SYSTEM WORK?

Breathe in. Hold that air. Then breathe out. What is going on inside your body when you inhale and exhale? In this investigation you'll learn what is happening to air as it moves through your respiratory system.

Activity
Breathing Rates

Your breathing rate is how often you inhale in one minute. Find out what things affect this rate.

Procedure

Sit in a chair in a relaxed position. Have a group member **count** the number of times you breathe in during one minute. Have another member use a timer to keep track of the time. **Record** the number in your *Science Notebook*.

Predict how exercise will affect your breathing rate. **Record** your prediction. Run in place for one minute. Then **count** and **record** how many times you breathe in during one minute.

Analyze and Conclude

1. How did exercise affect your breathing rate? **Infer** why exercise had this effect.

2. **Hypothesize** about other things that could affect your breathing rate. Explain your ideas.

Activity
Lung Power

Without special devices you can't look inside your chest to observe how your lungs work. But you can make a working model of a lung in this activity.

MATERIALS
- 2 balloons (1 small, 1 large)
- drinking straw
- tape
- scissors
- small clear plastic bottle with bottom cut off
- modeling clay
- *Science Notebook*

Procedure

1. Work with your group to **build a model** of a lung. Pull the opening of a small balloon over one end of a drinking straw. Use tape to attach the balloon to the straw.

2. Cut the neck off a large balloon. Have a group member hold a plastic bottle from which the bottom has been cut off. Stretch the balloon over the cut end of the bottle. Secure the balloon with tape.

3. Push the end of the straw with the small balloon into the mouth of the bottle. Then use modeling clay to seal the mouth of the bottle and to hold the straw in place.

4. **Predict** what will happen to the small balloon when you pull down and push up on the large balloon. **Record** your prediction in your *Science Notebook*.

5. **Observe** what happens when you pull down and then push up on the large balloon. **Make drawings** of your observations.

Step 3

Analyze and Conclude

1. What happened to the small balloon when you pulled down on the large balloon? What happened when you pushed up?

2. Based on observations of your model, **hypothesize** what happens in your body when you breathe.

3. You have just made a model of the way the lungs work. **Describe** at least one way in which this model differs from a real lung.

Breathing Basics

Reading Focus What happens when you breathe in and breathe out?

Breathing is the process by which the body takes in "fresh" air containing oxygen and pushes out "used" air containing waste gases. The parts of the body that work together to take air into the body and push it back out form the **respiratory system**. The drawing below illustrates the parts of this system.

Air Enters

What happens when you take in a breath of air, or inhale? Air can enter through either the mouth or nose.

Your nose both warms and moistens the air you breathe. Small hairs inside the nose trap dust and other particles in the air. If tiny particles slip past the hairs, they are trapped by mucus. On page A41 you read about mucus in the digestive system. The respiratory system is also lined with a sticky layer of mucus.

From your mouth or nose, the inhaled air moves to the back of your throat. There it enters the trachea (trā′kē ə), or windpipe. The **trachea** is the air tube that connects the throat to the lungs. Find the trachea below.

To feel your trachea, gently move your hand up and down the front of your neck. You will feel bumpy rings of cartilage (kärt′′l ij), a tough but bendable material. Cartilage helps the trachea keep its shape. Without cartilage, the trachea would collapse when you inhale.

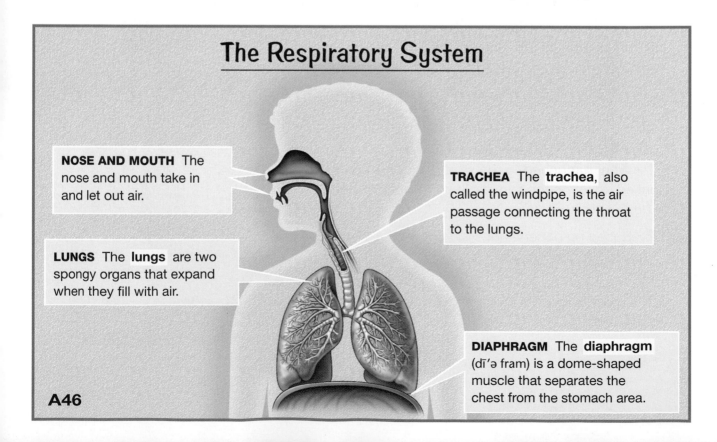

The Respiratory System

NOSE AND MOUTH The nose and mouth take in and let out air.

LUNGS The **lungs** are two spongy organs that expand when they fill with air.

TRACHEA The **trachea**, also called the windpipe, is the air passage connecting the throat to the lungs.

DIAPHRAGM The **diaphragm** (dī′ə fram) is a dome-shaped muscle that separates the chest from the stomach area.

Muscles Do the Work

The activity on page A45 shows that the breathing process starts in your chest. The process depends on the diaphragm and the muscles between your ribs. Follow the numbered steps in the drawing to see what happens during breathing.

Inhaling

1. When you begin to inhale, the rib muscles tighten and get shorter, pulling the chest out and up.

2. The diaphragm tightens and moves down, further increasing the space inside the chest.

3. When the space inside the chest increases, the lungs expand and air rushes in.

Air flows in.

Diaphragm moves down.

Exhaling

1. When you begin to exhale, the rib muscles relax and get longer and the chest gets smaller.

2. The diaphragm relaxes and moves up, making less space inside the chest.

3. Air is forced out of the lungs as the space in the chest gets smaller.

Air flows out.

Diaphragm moves up.

Breathless!

Your breathing rate is the number of times you inhale each minute. When you're sleeping or sitting quietly, your rate is slow. If you're walking, the rate increases, since your body needs a greater amount of oxygen supplied to the lungs. If you're exercising heavily, your breathing rate increases still more. The only way to get more oxygen into the body is to breathe more quickly and deeply. The activity on page A44 shows how a person's breathing rate increases during exercise. ■

Exchanging Gases

Reading Focus Which gases are exchanged inside the lungs?

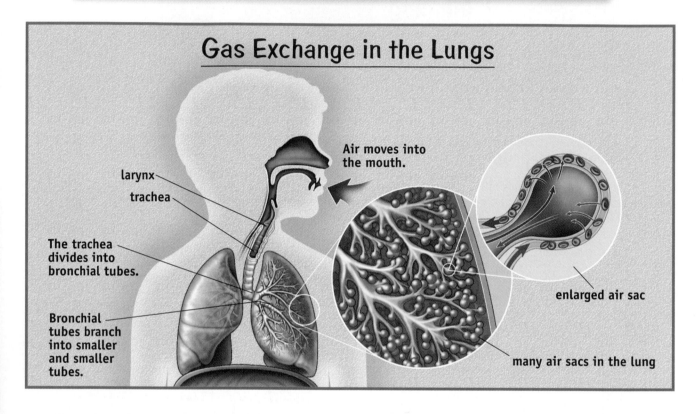

Gas Exchange in the Lungs

Air moves into the mouth.

larynx

trachea

The trachea divides into bronchial tubes.

Bronchial tubes branch into smaller and smaller tubes.

enlarged air sac

many air sacs in the lung

Imagine that you're going to dive into a deep pool. Inhale and hold your breath for as long as you can. At some point, probably within a minute, you have no choice—the muscles in your chest force you to breathe. This is your body's response to the fact that cells could soon be in danger of injury. They need oxygen for energy. And they must get rid of waste gases that are building up. Breathing meets both these needs.

The Bronchial Network

How does the oxygen you inhale get to the cells that need it? After passing through the nose or mouth, air enters the larynx (lar'iŋks), or voice box. The **larynx** is the part of the throat that is used in speaking.

Look at the drawing and find the parts described here. Below the larynx is the trachea. In the middle of the chest, the trachea splits to form two **bronchial tubes**. The bronchial tubes carry air from the trachea to the lungs. One tube enters each lung. Inside the lungs the bronchial tubes branch out into smaller and smaller tubes, much as tree branches do. The branches get smaller until they are like the tiniest twigs. Each twig ends in a tiny air sac.

A48

Through the Wall

The spongy tissue of the lungs has millions of tiny air sacs. These **air sacs** are thin-walled chambers through which oxygen moves into the blood. Around the thin wall of each air sac is a network of tiny blood vessels. Oxygen from inhaled air passes into the air sacs, through the thin walls, and into blood vessels. Here the oxygen is picked up by the blood. Once oxygen passes into the blood, it is carried to the cells where it is needed.

For the air sacs to do their jobs, their walls must be kept clean. For example, when the walls become coated with tobacco smoke, they cannot take in enough oxygen. These delicate air sacs can also be injured by particles in air, called air pollutants, that are breathed in.

An Even Exchange

To release the energy in digested nutrients, cells need oxygen. In releasing this energy, the cells produce a waste product, the gas carbon dioxide. This gas can be dangerous to the cells. In fact, too much of it can poison them. When the blood delivers oxygen to the cells, it takes back the carbon dioxide that is given off. The carbon dioxide is carried by the blood back to the air sacs in the lung.

An exchange of gases takes place in the air sacs. The inhaled air brings oxygen to the air sacs in the lung. As oxygen passes from the air sacs to the blood, carbon dioxide passes from the blood to the air that fills the air sacs.

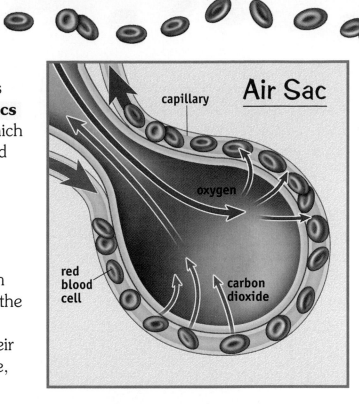

capillary

Air Sac

oxygen

red blood cell

carbon dioxide

▲ **Gas exchange in an air sac**

Out With the Old

Next, the carbon dioxide in the air sacs must be pushed out of the body. When you hold your breath, the buildup of carbon dioxide signals your body to breathe. From the air sacs, the air passes through the bronchial tubes. After passing through the trachea, it travels through the larynx and out through the mouth or nose.

Exhaled air contains less oxygen than inhaled air and more carbon dioxide than inhaled air. If you breathe on a mirror, you'll notice that the exhaled air also picks up water vapor inside the body. Breathe on a mirror and see for yourself!

Internet Field Trip

Visit **www.eduplace.com** to learn more about the human body.

How You Say It

Moving air allows you to speak. Air flowing through the larynx helps you produce speech sounds. Notice your breathing as you speak. Are you inhaling or exhaling? You need exhaled air to speak.

In the larynx are bands of tissue called vocal cords, shown below. If they are stretched tightly, air flowing between them makes them vibrate. When they vibrate, they produce sounds. Find the larynx in the drawing. Then find your own larynx and place your hand over it. Make a sound. When the sound begins, you'll feel a vibration in the larynx.

When you speak, the muscles in your larynx stretch the vocal cords. Stretched tightly, they are close together. Exhaled air passing through the larynx makes the vocal cords vibrate, producing sound.

Both the respiratory and digestive systems need a way to transport substances to the cells. In the next chapter you'll learn about this transport system.

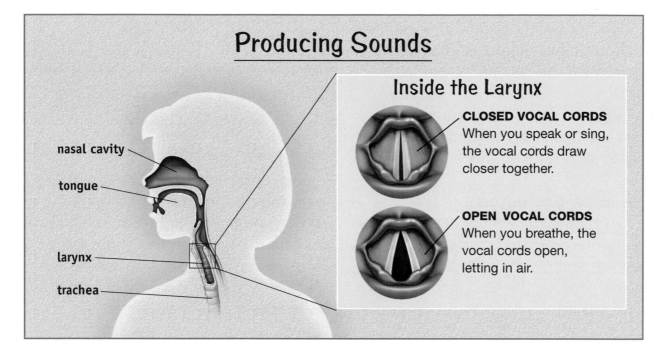

Producing Sounds

nasal cavity

tongue

larynx

trachea

Inside the Larynx

CLOSED VOCAL CORDS
When you speak or sing, the vocal cords draw closer together.

OPEN VOCAL CORDS
When you breathe, the vocal cords open, letting in air.

INVESTIGATION 2 WRAP-UP

REVIEW

1. Starting with the nose, list the main parts of the respiratory system.

2. Describe gas exchange in the air sacs.

CRITICAL THINKING

3. Describe the movement of the lungs and diaphragm when you exhale and when you inhale. Relate this to air flow into and out of the body.

4. During exercise, breathing rate increases. How would you expect an increase in the breathing rate to affect the heart rate? Give reasons for your answer.

REFLECT & EVALUATE

Word Power

Write the letter of the term that best matches the definition. *Not all terms will be used.*

1. The long, coiled organ where most digestion takes place
2. A watery liquid that moistens the mouth and food
3. The air passage connecting the throat to the lungs
4. The muscular tube that connects the mouth to the stomach
5. Looplike structures through which dissolved nutrients pass into the blood

a. bronchial tubes
b. esophagus
c. large intestine
d. peristalsis
e. saliva
f. small intestine
g. trachea
h. villi

Check What You Know

Write the term in each pair that best completes each sentence.

1. When you exhale, you release (oxygen, carbon dioxide).
2. The teeth used mainly for grinding are the (incisors, molars).
3. A tough, but bendable, body material is (mucus, cartilage).
4. When you inhale, the diaphragm moves (up, down).

Problem Solving

1. Imagine that you've just taken a bite out of an apple. Describe what happens to this apple as it moves from your mouth through your digestive system.

2. Pneumonia causes liquids to build up in the air sacs. Based on what you've learned, describe how pneumonia can affect gas exchange. Explain how this might affect the entire body.

BUILD YOUR PORTFOLIO

Copy this drawing of an air sac in the lungs. Explain what the disklike objects are and why they are in different colors. Then explain what the arrows show about gas exchange in the air sac.

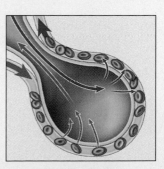

CHAPTER 3

CIRCULATION AND EXCRETION

Your body has a network of connecting tubes that are part of a transport system. These tubes carry materials vital to your body's cells. In this chapter you will explore the transport system's role in supplying needed materials to cells and in removing waste products from those cells.

PEOPLE USING SCIENCE

Medical Illustrator You can see the work of Richard LaRocco on many pages in Chapters 2 and 3 of this unit. He is a medical illustrator, an artist who specializes in drawings of the human body systems. By the age of 16, Richard LaRocco had decided to pursue art as a career. His art teacher, Mrs. Brosch, encouraged him to take art seriously and to develop his skills. His college studies at the Rochester Institute of Technology included human anatomy, medical illustration, and graphic design.

In his work, Richard LaRocco often begins with a paper-and-pencil sketch. Then he goes "high-tech." He scans the art into a computer and completes the work with an "electronic pen." Thinking about art as a career? Richard LaRocco's advice: Learn to draw very well and draw all the time!

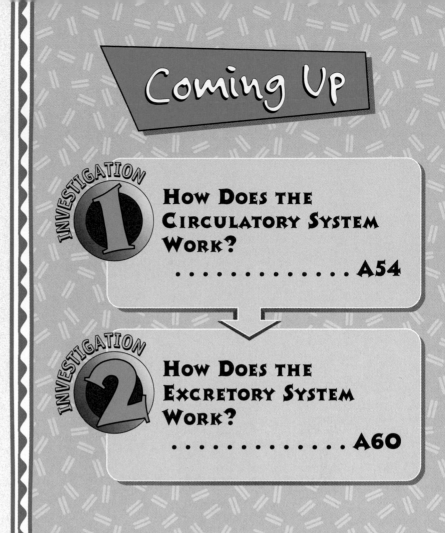

◄ Richard LaRocco at work on a drawing of the upper digestive system

HOW DOES THE CIRCULATORY SYSTEM WORK?

The circulatory system, the body's transport system, has three main parts—the heart, the blood vessels, and the blood. In this investigation you'll explore how these three parts work together to transport nutrients and remove wastes.

Activity

Squeeze Play!

How hard does a human heart work to pump blood? Try this activity and find out!

MATERIALS
- rubber ball
- timer
- *Science Notebook*

Procedure

Squeeze a rubber ball hard and then release it. **Predict** how many times you can squeeze the ball in one minute. **Record** your prediction in your *Science Notebook*. While a group member times you, count how many times you can squeeze the ball in one minute. **Record** the number. Repeat this two more times. Next, try to squeeze the ball 70 times in one minute. See how long you can continue at that rate. **Record** your results. **Compare** your results with those of other groups.

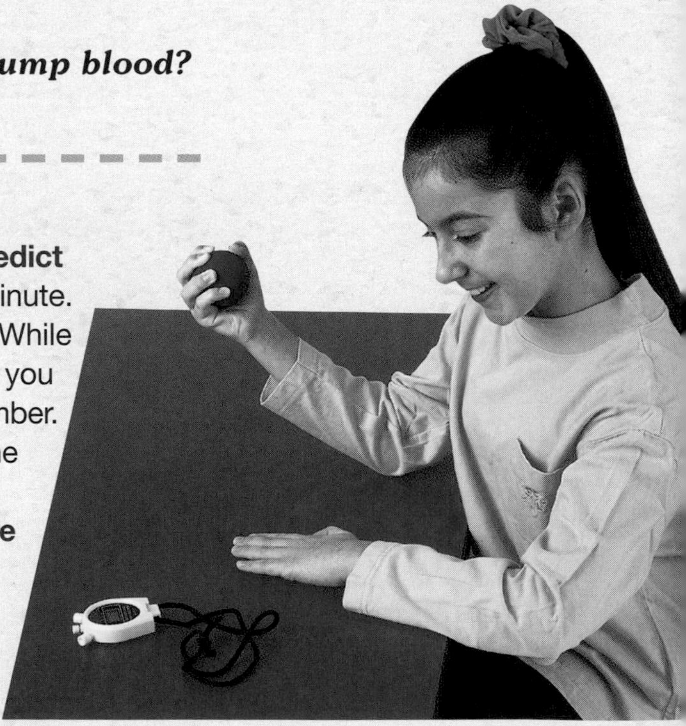

Analyze and Conclude

1. On average, the heart beats about 70 times per minute. How long could you squeeze the ball at the rate of 70 squeezes per minute without stopping?

2. What does this activity tell you about the heart?

Activity

In a Heartbeat

You've learned that the average person's heart beats about 70 times each minute. Find out how hard your own heart is working and what factors affect it.

Step 1

Procedure

1. Find your pulse in your wrist, as shown. The **pulse** is the throbbing you can feel in a blood vessel caused by the beating of your heart.

2. Count how many times your heart beats in one minute. This is your heartbeat rate. **Record** this number in your *Science Notebook*.

3. Repeat step 2 two more times. Find the average of the three rates. **Record** the average heartbeat rate.

 See **SCIENCE** *and* **MATH TOOLBOX** page H5 if you need to review *Finding an Average.*

4. Predict whether your heartbeat rate will change if you exercise. **Record** what you think the rate for one minute will be after exercising.

5. Run in place for one minute. Immediately afterward, find your heartbeat rate as you did in step 2. Then rest for five minutes.

6. Repeat step 5 two more times. Find and **record** the average of the three heartbeat rates.

Analyze and Conclude

1. Compare your average heartbeat rate before and after exercising.

2. Infer why exercise would cause changes in your heartbeat rate.

UNIT PROJECT LINK

For your chosen plant, research the system that allows for transport of water, minerals, and sugars. Then research the circulatory system in the two animals chosen. Compare these three systems. How are they alike? How are they different? Add materials, such as models or posters, to your display that show how these systems compare.

 **Technology** *Link*

For more help with your Unit Project, go to **www.eduplace.com**.

The Circulatory System

Reading Focus What is the job of the circulatory system?

The **circulatory system** is the transport system of the human body. It carries oxygen and nutrients to all cells and then removes carbon dioxide and other wastes. There are three main parts to this system—the heart, the blood vessels, and the blood. The **heart** is the pump that pushes the blood throughout the entire system. A vast network of tubes, called **blood vessels**, carries the blood. **Blood** is a tissue made up of a liquid called plasma and several types of cells. Blood carries materials to and from the body's cells.

Look at the drawing below to find the main organs of the circulatory system. Then follow the steps to see how blood circulates throughout the body.

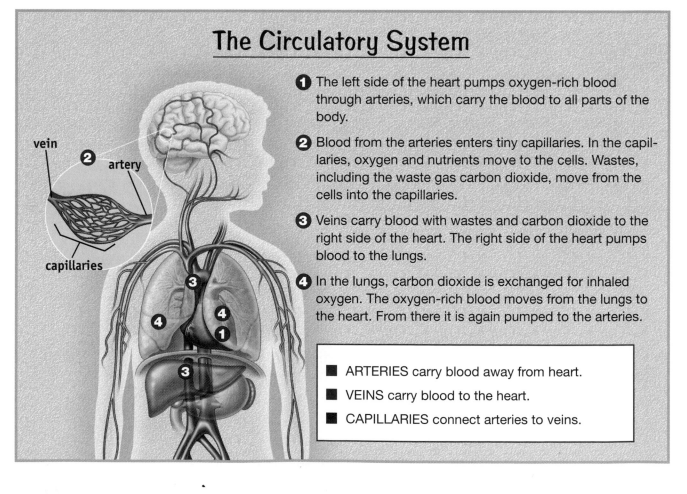

The Circulatory System

vein

artery

capillaries

1 The left side of the heart pumps oxygen-rich blood through arteries, which carry the blood to all parts of the body.

2 Blood from the arteries enters tiny capillaries. In the capillaries, oxygen and nutrients move to the cells. Wastes, including the waste gas carbon dioxide, move from the cells into the capillaries.

3 Veins carry blood with wastes and carbon dioxide to the right side of the heart. The right side of the heart pumps blood to the lungs.

4 In the lungs, carbon dioxide is exchanged for inhaled oxygen. The oxygen-rich blood moves from the lungs to the heart. From there it is again pumped to the arteries.

- ■ ARTERIES carry blood away from heart.
- ■ VEINS carry blood to the heart.
- ■ CAPILLARIES connect arteries to veins.

Circulation in the Heart

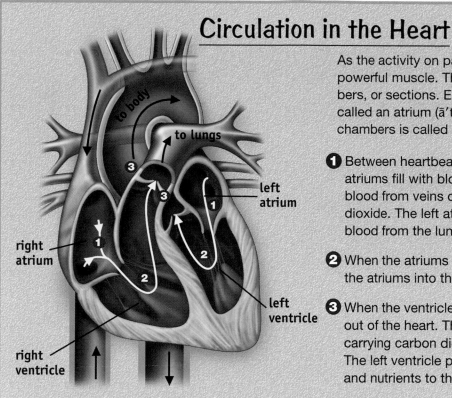

to body

to lungs

3

3

1

left atrium

right atrium

1

2

2

left ventricle

right ventricle

As the activity on page A54 shows, the heart is a powerful muscle. The heart consists of four chambers, or sections. Each of the two top chambers is called an atrium (ā′trē əm). Each of the two lower chambers is called a ventricle (ven′tri kəl).

1 Between heartbeats, the heart relaxes and both atriums fill with blood. The right atrium fills with blood from veins carrying wastes and carbon dioxide. The left atrium fills with oxygen-rich blood from the lungs.

2 When the atriums contract, blood is forced from the atriums into the ventricles.

3 When the ventricles contract, they pump blood out of the heart. The right ventricle pumps blood carrying carbon dioxide and wastes to the lungs. The left ventricle pumps blood carrying oxygen and nutrients to the rest of the body.

The Blood-Vessel Network

The blood vessels form a network through which the heart pumps blood. There are three kinds of blood vessels—arteries, capillaries, and veins.

Arteries are blood vessels that carry blood away from the heart. Most arteries carry oxygen-rich blood, which is bright red. The thick, muscular walls of the arteries stretch when the heart pumps blood into them. Large arteries branch many times into smaller arteries.

The smallest arteries lead into tiny blood vessels called **capillaries**. The capillaries connect the smallest arteries with the smallest veins. Look at the capillaries in the inset drawing on page A56. What happens inside the capillaries?

Veins carry blood from the capillaries to the heart. As blood travels to the heart, the many small veins join to form large veins, much like streams join to form rivers.

Blood and Its Parts

Blood is a fluid made up of blood cells and platelets in a pale yellow liquid called plasma. Plasma contains water, nutrients, wastes, and salts. Red blood cells give blood its color. They carry oxygen from the lungs to the body's cells. They carry carbon dioxide back to the lungs. White blood cells fight germs and break down dead cells. The number of white cells increases when the body is fighting infection. Platelets are tiny discs in plasma that help the blood clot, or thicken.

The Pulse

Your arteries expand and contract as blood pushes through them. You can feel a throbbing where arteries are close to the skin. The throbbing caused by blood rushing into the arteries when the lower chambers of the heart contract is called a **pulse**. Pulse rate is measured in the activity on page A55. ■

Ancient Blood Transfusions

Reading Focus Why could the Incas safely receive blood more than 500 years ago?

Why would a medical treatment work well in one part of the world and have mixed results in another? This medical mystery stumped scientists until they learned more about blood.

Early Transfusions

The mystery begins more than 500 years ago with the Incas. The Incas were a group of people who lived along the western coast of South America. Inca doctors learned how to give blood transfusions to injured people who had lost a lot of blood. A blood transfusion is the transfer of blood from one person to another person. Inca doctors let the blood pass from a blood vessel of a healthy person, through a tube, to a blood vessel of an injured person. This was often a lifesaving measure.

When blood transfusions were tried in Europe in the 1600s, many patients died. In 1818 an English doctor, James Blundell, saved 11 of 15 patients by giving them blood. He noticed that when transfusions failed, the blood cells in the patient were stuck together.

Blood Types

In 1901 the mystery began to unfold. Karl Landsteiner, an Austrian-born doctor working in the United States, found that there are several types of human blood. He named these blood types A, B, AB, and O. He also learned that a **recipient** (ri sip'ē ənt), a person who receives blood, can only safely be given blood of a certain type. Blood from the **donor**, the person who gives blood, must be matched to the recipient's blood. If the blood types don't match, the blood cells clump, or stick together. This clumping of cells causes illness or death.

Look at the table on page A59 to see which recipients can receive blood from which donors. What clues does the table give for solving the mystery?

▲ Machu Picchu, the site of ancient Inca ruins

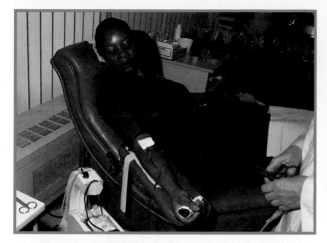

▲ When blood is donated, it is also typed.

▲ Blood cells clumped in mismatched blood

Scientists now think the reason the Incas were successful in blood transfusions was that most of them had type O blood. In western Europe the most common blood types were A and O. It's likely that many early blood transfusions in western Europe failed because of mismatched blood, which caused the blood cells to stick together.

Today, blood is typed when it's drawn. That means it's tested to find out what type it is. Then each unit of blood is labeled by type. As a safety

Blood Types	
Recipient (receives blood)	**Donor** (gives blood)
A	A or O
B	B or O
AB	A, B, AB, or O
O	O

measure, some donor red blood cells are mixed in a tube with some of the patient's plasma. If these mixed cells clump, the blood isn't used. ■

INVESTIGATION 1 WRAP-UP

THINK IT
WRITE IT

REVIEW

1. What are the main parts of blood? Briefly describe each part.

2. Name and describe the three types of blood vessels.

CRITICAL THINKING

3. How does the blood entering the right atrium differ from the blood entering the left atrium? Account for the difference.

4. One blood type is called the "universal donor." From the table above, tell which blood type is the universal donor and explain what is meant by that term.

HOW DOES THE EXCRETORY SYSTEM WORK?

Your body gets energy when it "burns" nutrients. Just as burning wood produces ash, "burning" nutrients produces wastes in your body. In this investigation you'll find out about a body system that gets rid of body wastes, such as water and salts.

Activity

Peering at Pores

Skin is the largest body part. How does it help you get rid of wastes? Find out.

- -

Procedure

Observe the skin on your arms and hands with a hand lens. In your *Science Notebook*, **record** all the features you observe. **Make a sketch** of what you see through the hand lens. Then **compare** observations with your group members. As a group, **list** the things the skin does for the body. **Record** your group's list. Give reasons for each item you put on the list. **Compare** your list with those of other groups.

Analyze and Conclude

1. What are some of the features you saw on your skin? What do you think these features do for the body?

2. How do you think the skin helps the body get rid of wastes?

A60

Activity

Your Watery Body

Your body needs water to help it get rid of wastes. You take in much of this water in the liquids that you drink. In this activity you'll measure how much liquid you drink in one day.

MATERIALS
- metric measuring cup
- plastic cup
- marker
- *Science Notebook*

Procedure

1. **Predict** how much liquid you'll drink in one day. Include all liquids. **Record** your prediction in your *Science Notebook*.

2. **Make a chart** like the one shown below.

Drinks in a Day		
Time	Type of Liquid	mL of Liquid

3. Make a plastic cup into a liquids measurer. Use a measuring cup to add 50 mL of water to the plastic cup. Use a marker to mark the water line. Label this mark *50 mL*. Add another 50 mL and mark the new water line. Label this mark *100 mL*. Continue marking the cup in this way to its top. Use your liquids measurer as your drinking glass for one day.

See **SCIENCE** and **MATH TOOLBOX** *page H7 if you need to review* **Measuring Volume.**

4. In your chart, **record** all the liquids you drink during one day. **Record** the time you drink the liquid, the type of liquid, and the amount. Rinse out the measurer each time you use it.

5. **Compare** your results with those of other students.

Analyze and Conclude

1. How much liquid did you drink during the day?

2. Was your intake of liquid about the same as, more than, or less than that of other students?

INVESTIGATE FURTHER!

RESEARCH

Find out how much liquid doctors think a person should drink each day. Research what effect a person's age, weight, health, and activity have on the amount of liquid suggested. Find out the percentage of water in common foods and research the percentage of water in a human body.

The Excretory System

Reading Focus How does the body get rid of wastes?

Your body is constantly busy—even while you are asleep. It is building and replacing cells, releasing energy from food, and maintaining parts that keep the body running smoothly.

All this activity creates body wastes. The human body has a system for ridding itself of harmful wastes produced by the cells. This system is called the **excretory** (eks'krə tôr ē) **system**. The picture below shows the main parts of the excretory system.

Notice that the excretory system includes organs that are part of other body systems. The lungs are part of the respiratory system. But they also

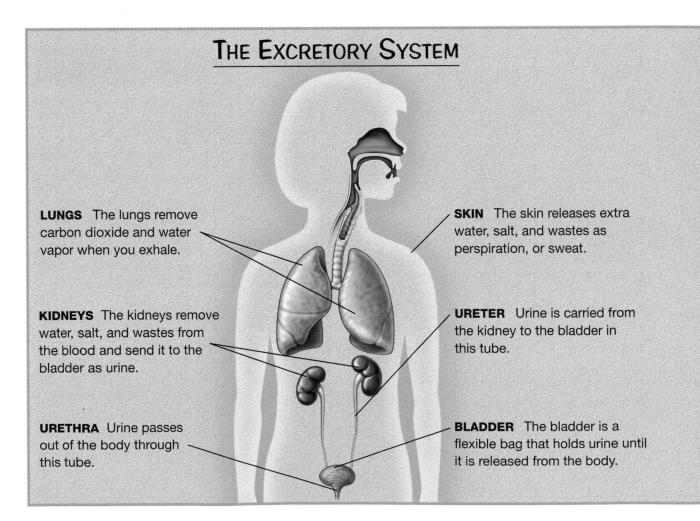

THE EXCRETORY SYSTEM

LUNGS The lungs remove carbon dioxide and water vapor when you exhale.

KIDNEYS The kidneys remove water, salt, and wastes from the blood and send it to the bladder as urine.

URETHRA Urine passes out of the body through this tube.

SKIN The skin releases extra water, salt, and wastes as perspiration, or sweat.

URETER Urine is carried from the kidney to the bladder in this tube.

BLADDER The bladder is a flexible bag that holds urine until it is released from the body.

remove many wastes in exhaled air. For example, the lungs remove excess water. It leaves the body as water vapor, or water in the form of a gas.

But the major waste-removal job of the lungs is to release the wastes formed when carbohydrates and fats are broken down in the cells of the body. Carbohydrates and fats are broken down by oxygen, releasing energy. The carbon in these materials combines with the oxygen to produce carbon dioxide, a waste gas. The carbon dioxide passes into the blood. Then the blood carries this waste gas to the lungs. From the lungs the carbon dioxide is exhaled.

How the Kidneys Work

The **kidneys** are two organs that clean and filter the blood. The filtering of the blood results in the yellowish liquid called **urine** (yoor'in). Kidneys remove excess water and salts. They also remove the wastes that are produced when proteins are broken down into smaller molecules.

From the drawing on page A62 you can see the location of the kidneys. They lie on either side of the spine. Each kidney weighs less than 0.225 kg (about 0.5 lb) and is about the size of a fist.

The drawing on this page shows a closeup of one of millions of tiny filtering units in the kidney. These units, or nephrons (nef'ränz), are found in the outer layer of the kidney. Each unit has a cup-shaped end packed with a tightly coiled ball of capillaries.

Blood passes through the nephron and is filtered under pressure, removing wastes and water. The filtering of blood by the nephron produces urine. The urine drains out of the filtering units into tubes in the middle part of the kidney. From there the urine drains through larger tubes into the bladder, where it collects. Small round muscles keep the urine in the bladder until it is ready to be emptied. When about 250 mL (1 c) of urine has collected, a person has an urge to empty the bladder.

On average, an adult passes about 1.5 L (1.6 qt) of urine per day. Only a small fraction of the water filtered by the kidneys passes into the urine. To help keep a healthy balance of fluids, the kidneys send most of the water and some salt and nutrients back to the blood.

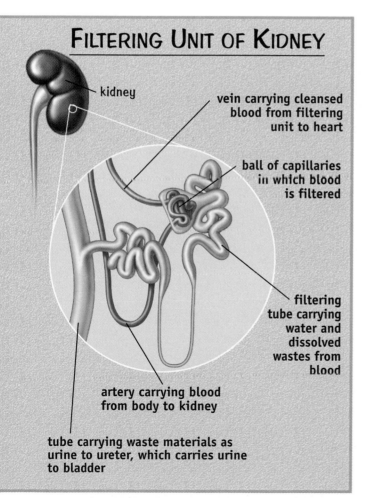

FILTERING UNIT OF KIDNEY

kidney

vein carrying cleansed blood from filtering unit to heart

ball of capillaries in which blood is filtered

filtering tube carrying water and dissolved wastes from blood

artery carrying blood from body to kidney

tube carrying waste materials as urine to ureter, which carries urine to bladder

The Skin

A person also loses water and wastes through the skin. Weighing about 4 kg to 7 kg (9 lb to 15 lb) in an adult, the skin is the largest organ in the body.

The skin removes wastes and water by perspiring, or sweating. Sweating is the release of water, salts, and wastes through pores in the skin. Look at the drawing below. Notice the **sweat glands**, which are small coiled tubes that end at pores on the skin's surface. These pores can be observed in the activity on page A60.

The main function of sweating is to cool the body. When the body produces extra heat, such as during exercise, the circulatory system delivers more blood to the capillaries near the skin. Water, carrying heat, passes into the skin tissues and moves to the sweat glands. This water then reaches the skin surface as perspiration, or sweat. As water evaporates from the skin, it removes some of the heat from the body.

Sometimes a person can lose too much water, salt, and minerals through sweating. Working hard in hot weather, a person can lose as much as 3 L (3 qt) of water! The kidneys can adjust the level of water in the body. But a person needs to drink extra water on a hot day or after exercise to replace the lost water. ■

Internet Field Trip

Visit **www.eduplace.com** to learn more about human body systems.

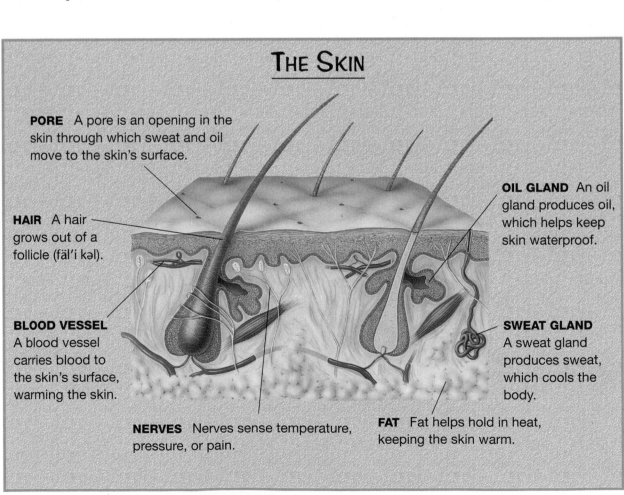

THE SKIN

PORE A pore is an opening in the skin through which sweat and oil move to the skin's surface.

HAIR A hair grows out of a follicle (fäl'i kəl).

BLOOD VESSEL A blood vessel carries blood to the skin's surface, warming the skin.

OIL GLAND An oil gland produces oil, which helps keep skin waterproof.

SWEAT GLAND A sweat gland produces sweat, which cools the body.

NERVES Nerves sense temperature, pressure, or pain.

FAT Fat helps hold in heat, keeping the skin warm.

Goose Bumps

RESOURCE

Reading Focus What causes goose bumps, and how are they helpful?

Does your skin get covered with little bumps when you are cold or frightened? You probably call these bumps "goose bumps" or "goose pimples." Are goose bumps helpful? Look at the pictures on page A66 to see what causes them. These pictures show two sections of skin. On the left is warm skin. On the right is cold skin.

When you are cold, several things occur. Nerves in the skin signal the brain that it's cold. Small muscles at the bottom of each hair contract, pulling each hair straight up. At the same time, blood vessels near the skin's surface become narrower. Blood flows through blood vessels that are deep within the skin. This process helps to keep the skin warm.

When all the hairs on the skin stand on end, they trap air close to the skin's surface. This layer of trapped air helps to keep the skin warm. As the hair stands straight up, it pulls on the skin

Science in Literature

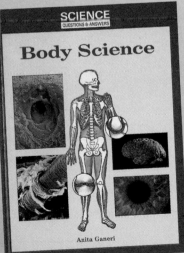

Body Science
by Anita Ganeri
Dillon Press, 1992

WHY IS BLOOD RED?

"Your red blood cells contain a special substance called hemoglobin, which carries oxygen around your body and also gives blood its red color. As your blood flows through your lungs, the hemoglobin takes in oxygen and carries it throughout your body. When the hemoglobin is filled with fresh oxygen, it looks red."

Do you have more questions about your blood and your heart? Many of your questions will be answered by this colorful and informative book. Check out *Body Science* by Anita Ganeri.

around it, forming a bump. This bump is the goose bump!

Do other animals besides humans get goose bumps? Yes! Animals with fur or hair also get cold. When this happens, the hair or fur stands straight up, trapping air that helps to keep the animal warm. Now think about a frightened animal, such as a cat. The fur on a frightened cat fluffs out. This makes the cat look bigger to its enemies. The cat's enemies may stay away if the cat looks scary.

Since humans don't have a thick coat of fur or hair, goose bumps don't do a lot to keep them warm. But goose bumps can let you know when it's time to put on a sweater or to stop watching a scary movie! ■

Using Math *What Celsius temperatures might cause the reactions shown? What Fahrenheit temperatures might do the same?*

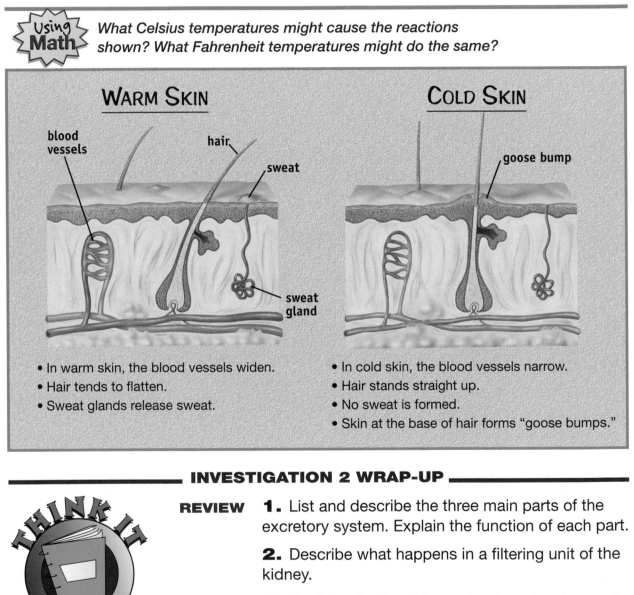

WARM SKIN

blood vessels
hair
sweat
sweat gland

- In warm skin, the blood vessels widen.
- Hair tends to flatten.
- Sweat glands release sweat.

COLD SKIN

goose bump

- In cold skin, the blood vessels narrow.
- Hair stands straight up.
- No sweat is formed.
- Skin at the base of hair forms "goose bumps."

INVESTIGATION 2 WRAP-UP

THINK IT WRITE IT

REVIEW

1. List and describe the three main parts of the excretory system. Explain the function of each part.

2. Describe what happens in a filtering unit of the kidney.

CRITICAL THINKING

3. Explain why the skin can be thought of as part of the excretory system.

4. How is a bird with fluffed-up feathers like a person with goose bumps?

REFLECT & EVALUATE

Word Power

Write the letter of the term that best matches the definition. *Not all terms will be used.*

1. A tissue that carries materials to and from the body's cells
2. Blood vessels that carry blood from the capillaries to the heart
3. Blood vessels that carry blood away from the heart
4. A pair of organs that clean and filter the blood
5. A person who gives blood for transfusions
6. Blood vessels that connect the smallest arteries with the smallest veins

a. arteries
b. blood
c. capillaries
d. donor
e. heart
f. kidneys
g. recipient
h. veins

Check What You Know

Write the term in each pair that best completes each statement.

1. Urine passes out of the body through the (ureter, urethra).
2. Tiny discs that help blood to clot are called (platelets, pores).
3. The two lower chambers of the heart are the (atriums, ventricles).

Problem Solving

1. Explain how the filtering units of the kidneys are somewhat like the air sacs in the lungs.

2. While fixing his bicycle, a boy cut a large blood vessel in his hand. Every few seconds, the blood would spurt out. What would this tell you about the kind of blood vessel that was cut? Explain your answer.

Copy this drawing of the excretory system. Identify parts *a–e*. Briefly describe the function of each part. Which of these parts also belongs to another body system? Name that system.

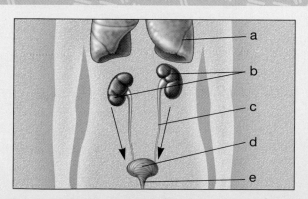

CHAPTER 4

LIFE CYCLES

All living things pass through a life cycle. They might crack out of an eggshell or sprout from a seed. Some live only a few days; others live more than one hundred years. In this chapter you'll explore the life cycle of several different animals and plants.

PEOPLE USING SCIENCE

Animal Nutritionist Dr. Diane A. Hirakawa is a specialist in the field of animal nutrition. She develops tasty, nutritious pet food suited to the age, activity, and health of pets. "Animals always greet you with a wag of a tail or a lick on the face," writes Dr. Hirakawa, who chose her career because she loves animals.

Dr. Hirakawa is Senior Vice President of Research and Development at The Iams Company, producers of pet foods. To prepare for her career, Dr. Hirakawa studied companion animal biology in college. Then she earned a Ph.D. in nutritional biochemistry. In 1995 she coauthored a book on animal nutrition. Her book deals with dietary needs of animals at different stages in their life cycle.

Coming Up

▲ These dogs are eating food suited to the life cycle stage they are in.

A69

INVESTIGATION 1

WHAT ARE THE STAGES IN AN ANIMAL'S LIFE CYCLE?

Are there any babies in your family? Are there any people older than 80? All living things pass through stages. In this investigation you'll explore the life cycle of several different animals.

Activity

Life Cycle of a Brine Shrimp

Do animals change as they age? What is the importance of change in the life of an animal? By observing changes in the life of a tiny animal, the brine shrimp, you'll discover answers to some of these questions.

Procedure

1. Obtain some brine shrimp eggs from your teacher. Use a hand lens and microscope to examine the eggs. Note their size, color, and texture. **Record** your observations in your *Science Notebook*.

See **SCIENCE** and **MATH TOOLBOX** *page H2 if you need to review* ***Using a Microscope.***

2. With your group, **brainstorm** questions about how the brine shrimp grow and develop. **Record** your questions.

A70

3. Prepare an egg hatchery. Obtain room-temperature salt water from your teacher. Add 250 mL of this water to a plastic cup. With a red marker, mark the level of water on the outside of the cup.

4. Sprinkle one fourth of a teaspoon of brine shrimp eggs into the cup. Check with your teacher. You may need to add a pinch of yeast to the water as food for the brine shrimp. Stir the mixture. Place the hatchery in a warm place, where it will not be disturbed.

Step 7

5. Make a chart like the one shown below. Leave enough space to record three weeks of observations.

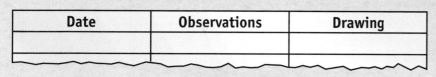

Date	Observations	Drawing

6. Observe the egg hatchery the next day. **Record** your observations.

7. Each day for three weeks, use a dropper to carefully remove a few eggs. **Observe** them with a hand lens and through a microscope. **Record** any changes you notice. **Draw** what you see when you observe the brine shrimp with the hand lens and the microscope. Return the brine shrimp you observe to the plastic cup. As water evaporates from the cup, add salt water up to the red line.

8. Compare your observations with those of other members of your class.

Analyze and Conclude

1. What stages of development did you observe in the brine shrimp?

2. Were your questions about the brine shrimp's growth answered by the activity? Explain.

3. What changes occurred in the brine shrimp at each stage?

4. What stage was reached by about the twentieth day? **Infer** why this stage is important.

INVESTIGATE FURTHER!

EXPERIMENT

Can you speed up the life cycle of a brine shrimp? Write a step-by-step procedure for an experiment that would reduce the number of days needed for eggs to hatch and grow into adults. You may wish to use a computer, including CD-ROM programs, to record and analyze the results of your experiment.

A71

The Human Life Cycle

Reading Focus What are the main stages in the human life cycle?

Where are you in your life cycle? You've changed a lot since you were a tiny baby. Now you're just a couple of years from being a teenager. Find out about the stages that humans pass through from infancy to old age.

Infancy

Infancy is a stage that lasts from birth to about age 1. At birth an infant is almost completely dependent on its parents for survival. Through the first year, the baby gains control of its muscles and other systems. As a baby develops, it can sit up, creep, then crawl, stand, and walk. During this period the infant is growing at a tremendous rate.

An infant shows traits that are inherited, or passed down, from its parents. For example, the infant might have inherited straight black hair from its father and dimples from its mother.

Childhood

Childhood is a stage that lasts from about age 1 to about age 12. This stage begins with the ability to walk. Most children learn to walk from 9 months to about 15 months. Through the first year of childhood, the growth spurt of infancy continues. The growth rate is fairly steady from age 4 until age 11 or 12.

▲ The human life cycle

During childhood a person learns many skills that will be used for the rest of life. A child learns how to speak his or her parents' language by imitating what the parents say. A lot is learned from the child's environment. A child may learn about the pain of touching a hot stove. Through such a painful experience, the child learns to stay away from a hot stove.

Adolescence

Adolescence lasts from about age 11 to about age 18 to 20. It is during this stage that a person grows into adulthood. A second growth spurt occurs, and the adult body takes shape. During this stage a person becomes able to reproduce.

Adulthood

Adulthood is the stage that begins at the end of the teenage years and lasts the rest of a person's life. Early in this stage, the body is at the peak of its physical abilities. This is usually when the person has the greatest strength and greatest physical endurance. Responsibilities during this stage may include raising a family and earning a living. Physical ability declines in later adulthood.

In the United States, a male born in 1993 can expect to live an average of 72.2 years. A female born in 1993 can expect to live an average of 78.8 years. As medical science advances, people are able to live longer and more healthfully. ■

The Life Cycle of an Insect

> **Reading Focus** What are the stages in the life cycle of a beetle?

You've learned about the stages in the life cycle of a human. You know that a baby looks somewhat like an adult human being—just much smaller! With some kinds of animals, each stage in the life cycle is very different. The animal looks very different at each stage. It also lives in different places and eats different kinds of food. The beetle, which is an insect, is such an animal.

How a Beetle Changes

A beetle goes through four distinct stages in its life cycle. Animals that go through these four stages are said to pass through **complete metamorphosis** (kəm plēt′ met ə môr′fə sis). Refer to the table on page A75 to see what happens at each stage.

The **egg** is the first stage in the beetle's life cycle. An adult beetle lays her eggs in the openings of wet decaying wood or in soil. The **larva**, also called a grub, is the wormlike stage that follows the egg stage. A beetle larva eats wet decaying wood or other rotting material in soil. As the grub eats and develops, it gets larger. Once it reaches a certain size, it molts, or sheds its outer skin. After it molts, the larva comes out, a bit larger than before.

The **pupa** (pyoo′pə) is the stage between the larva and the adult. During this stage, the beetle might look like it's at rest. Actually the insect is going through many changes. It changes color and develops a hard outer case. Adult organs form, and the beetle develops wings. The insect may stay in this stage for a few days or several weeks, depending on the kind of beetle it is. The photograph on this page shows the inside of the pupa case.

The **adult** is the final stage in the beetle's life cycle. The adult beetle comes out of the pupa fully grown. It now has six legs, two pairs of wings, complex mouth parts, and adult organs.

▲ **Lengthwise section of a beetle pupa, showing the developing insect**

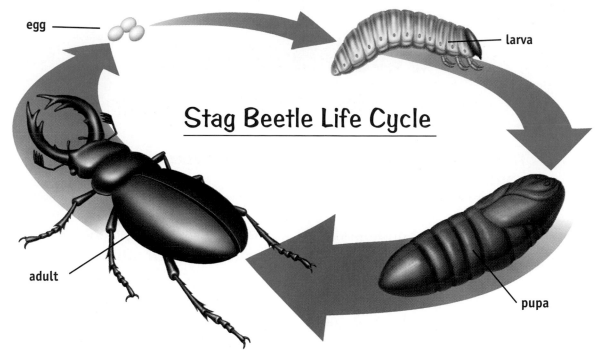

Stag Beetle Life Cycle

egg — larva

adult

pupa

The adult male and adult female beetle mate. Then the female lays her eggs in wet decaying wood. The entire cycle begins again.

The Moth and the Butterfly

Like beetles, moths and butterflies go through complete metamorphosis. They pass through the same four stages—egg, larva, pupa, and adult.

There are a few differences between the life cycles of beetles, moths, and butterflies. The table below shows you these differences and the names given to each of the stages. You are probably most familiar with the terms *cocoon* and *caterpillar*. Notice that the pupa stage of a moth is called a cocoon. The pupa stage of a butterfly is called a chrysalis (kris′ə lis). ■

Life Cycles of Three Insects

Beetle	Moth	Butterfly
egg	egg	egg
larva (grub)	larva (caterpillar)	larva (caterpillar)
pupa	pupa (cocoon)	pupa (chrysalis)
adult (beetle)	adult (moth)	adult (butterfly)

Vertebrate Life Cycles

Fish and humans share an important characteristic. A fish, like a human, is a **vertebrate** (vur'tə brit), an animal with a backbone. Vertebrates have a series of bones that make up their backbone.

A Fishy Story

Some kinds of fish live in fresh water and some live in salt water. Some kinds live in both fresh water and salt water at different times in their life cycle. The drawings on page A77 show the life cycle of a fish that you might eat for dinner—the salmon.

Adult salmon live in the ocean. When it's time to reproduce, these fish return to the same freshwater stream where they hatched. Salmon may swim as far as 3,220 km (2,000 mi) to where they hatched.

This behavior—returning to the fresh-water stream—is instinctive (in stiŋk'tiv)

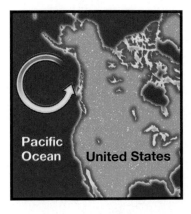

◄ **The yellow arrow on this map shows the great distance the salmon swims from its hatching place to the ocean and back again.**

Pacific Ocean   United States

behavior. It is behavior that the salmon inherits, or is born with. A salmon does not have to learn to do this.

As she prepares to lay her eggs, the adult female salmon forms several nests in the gravel at the bottom of the stream. She lays 2,000 to 17,000 sticky eggs. The adult male salmon releases male sex cells over the eggs.

When a male sex cell joins with an egg, or female sex cell, the result is called a fertilized egg. A young salmon develops from a fertilized egg. Each fertilized egg forms a yolk sac, which is food for the tiny fish.

At the next stage, the salmon looks like a tiny spotted fish. By the time a young salmon is two years old, it takes on the silvery color of the adult fish. It begins the long journey from its fresh-water home to the ocean.

After swimming great distances to the ocean, the adult male and female salmon remain in the ocean until they are ready to reproduce. When the females are ready to lay eggs, all adults swim upstream, against the flow of water, to the same freshwater river where they hatched. After the female lays her eggs and the male releases male sex cells over the eggs, the adult salmon die. Then the cycle continues.

Salmon Life Cycle

1 The adult female lays thousands of eggs in a gravel nest in a freshwater river or stream.

egg

2 Each fertilized egg forms a yolk sac on which the tiny young fish feed.

yolk sac

6 The adult female lays eggs in a nest. The adult male fertilizes them, and the cycle begins again.

3 The young fish at this stage is called a fry and looks like a tiny spotted salmon.

5 The adult salmon swim upstream to where they began life.

4 After spending 1–2 years in freshwater rivers, the salmon, now called smolt, swim to the ocean. Smolt look like small adult fish.

Internet Field Trip

Visit **www.eduplace.com** to learn more about life cycles.

A77

It's for the Birds

Woodpeckers use their pointed beaks to hunt for insects in bark. They sleep in larger holes that they drill in the sides of trees. Hunting for insects and drilling holes is instinctive. That is, a woodpecker is born with the ability to drill holes. This bird inherits from its parents the ability to drill holes in wood.

Woodpeckers mate for life. After a courtship dance in the spring, a pair of birds mate. Then the female lays up to fourteen eggs in a hole drilled in a tree. Male and female birds take turns sitting on the eggs to warm them. Inside each egg, a tiny woodpecker is developing.

In about 12 days, the young bird pecks open the shell. It comes out with wrinkly pink skin and no feathers. Its eyes don't open for 8 days. The young birds remain in the hole in the tree, and the parent birds bring caterpillars for their young to eat. The parents defend the young birds from enemies. This behavior by the adults is also instinctive. In a couple of weeks, the baby birds have grown feathers. By four weeks of age they are ready to learn to fly and hunt for themselves.

The family remains together throughout the summer. By November the birds are ready to live on their own. Each young woodpecker drills a hole in a tree for shelter and seeks a mate. Next spring the young woodpeckers will reproduce, and the cycle will continue.

Science in Literature

SECRETS OF SURVIVAL

"When it is time for the butterflies to lay their yellow eggs, the passionflower leaves provide the perfect spot. Once the eggs hatch, the emerging caterpillars chomp into the vine's leaves without being harmed by the poison. Why? The caterpillars are able to store the poison inside their bodies. They use it as a weapon against birds that eat caterpillars. . . ."

Why Save the Rain Forest?
by Donald Silver
Illustrated by Patricia J. Wynne
Julian Messner, 1993

Find out about the amazing ways that butterflies survive in the rain forest. Read these stories of survival in *Why Save the Rain Forest?* by Donald Silver.

These eggs will hatch in about twelve days.

Newly hatched birds are blind and helpless.

Very young birds are fed by their parents.

Woodpecker
Life Cycle

An adult woodpecker drills a hole for a nest.

These birds search for insects in a tree trunk.

INVESTIGATION 1 WRAP-UP

THINK IT
WRITE IT

REVIEW

1. Describe the four main stages in the life cycle of an insect that goes through complete metamorphosis.

2. Name and describe four stages in the human life cycle. Name a learned and an inherited trait.

CRITICAL THINKING

3. Compare the human life cycle with the bird life cycle. Consider such things as how an infant and a young bird obtain food.

4. Compare the life cycle of a butterfly with that of a beetle. How are they alike? How are they different?

A79

INVESTIGATION 2

WHAT ARE THE STAGES IN A PLANT'S LIFE CYCLE?

Which came first—the acorn or the oak tree? The answer may always be a matter of opinion. In this investigation you'll explore how plants change during their life cycle.

Activity

The Secret of a Seed

You put a seed in soil and keep it moist. In a few days a tiny new plant with roots, a stem, and leaves appears. How can a new living plant come from a seed that seems lifeless? Find out what secrets a seed holds!

Procedure

1. **Examine** and **compare** a lima bean seed and a corn kernel, which is actually a corn seed. **Record** your observations in your *Science Notebook*. **Make drawings** of the seeds.

2. Carefully peel off the thin outer coverings of a lima bean and a corn kernel. **Observe** each covering with a hand lens. **Record** the differences and similarities you see.

Step 3

3. Gently split open the bean seed with either your fingernail or a plastic knife. Spread open the two halves of the bean seed and **examine** each half with a hand lens. **Draw** what you observe. **Record** your observations.

Math Hint

As you examine each half of the seed, note any symmetric shapes or structures.

4. Predict what you will find inside the corn kernel. Then use the knife to carefully cut the corn kernel in half lengthwise through the side. Lay the halves flat.

5. Examine each half with the hand lens. **Compare** the inside of the corn kernel with the inside of the bean seed. **Draw** the inside of the corn kernel. **Discuss** what you have observed with other members of your group.

6. Use a toothpick to scrape off a bit of the material that fills up each seed. **Examine** the material with the hand lens. **Compare** the material from the bean seed with that from the corn seed.

Analyze and Conclude

1. How was the covering of the lima bean seed different from the covering of the corn kernel? How was it similar? **Infer** the purpose that each covering serves.

2. What structures did you find inside each seed?

3. Hypothesize the function of the material that fills up each seed.

4. What can you **infer** about seeds from this activity?

UNIT PROJECT LINK

Research the life cycles of the same three organisms you have been using in your museum display. Use posters or models to show how their life cycles compare. Point out how their life cycles are alike and how they are different. Add these materials to your display. Invite other classes to view the completed display.

Technology Link

For more help with your Unit Project, go to **www.eduplace.com**.

Activity

It's Just a Stage

Infant, child, adolescent, adult are the stages of the human life cycle. In this activity you'll use fast-growing radish seeds to find out if plants have similar life-cycle stages.

MATERIALS

- small flowerpot
- fast-growing radish seeds
- soil
- water
- liquid houseplant fertilizer
- dropper
- good source of artificial light
- metric ruler
- red marker
- cotton swab
- *Science Notebook*

SAFETY

Do not eat any seeds or soil!

Procedure

1. Fill a small flowerpot with soil. Place 4 fast-growing radish seeds in the pot, spaced evenly apart near the rim. Cover them lightly with soil. Water the seeds. Using a dropper, add liquid houseplant fertilizer to the soil according to the package directions.

2. Place the flowerpot under a good source of artificial light. Keep the light on 24 hours a day. Check the soil each day, making sure to keep it moist, not wet, at all times. When the seeds sprout, assign each tiny plant a different number to help you keep track of its growth. Write the number on the pot, near each plant.

3. In your *Science Notebook*, **make a chart** for recording height as the plants grow. **Measure** and **record** each plant's height each day. Then **make a line graph** that shows the growth of each plant. As the plants grow, **record** your observations and **draw** the plants.

Plant #	Height (cm)				
	Day 1	Day 2	Day 3	Day 4	Day 5
1					

See **SCIENCE** *and* **MATH TOOLBOX** page H13 if you need to review *Making a Line Graph.*

A82

Step 4

4. When the stems are 5 cm tall, use a red marker to make a dot on the stem just below the leaves. Each day **measure** and **record** the distance between the soil and the dot.

Math Hint *Measure and record the distance at the same time each day.*

5. If your plants form flowers, follow your teacher's instructions for using cotton swabs to transfer pollen from the flower of one plant to the flower of another plant. **Record** your method of pollination.

6. Continue to **observe** your plants. If fruits are produced, open several when they are ripe and **examine** the contents.

Analyze and Conclude

1. Seedlings are the tiny plants that first appear above the soil. How many days after planting seeds did most seedlings appear? If you saw flower buds, how many days after planting did they appear? If your plants formed fruits, how many days did it take for them to form fruits with seeds?

2. What can you **infer** about stem growth from the measurements you made each day?

3. What stages in the life cycle of a plant did you observe?

4. What stage in the plant's life cycle is similar to the life-cycle stage you are in? Explain your answer.

From Flower to Fruit

Reading Focus How do fruits and seeds form from a flower?

How would you encourage someone to visit you? You might prepare some food, put on your best clothes, and make sure you smell good. That's just what many flowers do to attract insects. When an insect visits a flower, however, the visit begins the process that ends with seed production.

The flower is the reproductive organ of a flowering plant. Some kinds of plants have flowers that produce both male and female sex cells. Other kinds have flowers that produce either male or female sex cells. When an insect visits a flower, it transfers the male sex cells from one flower to another. This transfer is part of the process of sexual reproduction in the flower. During **sexual reproduction** a male sex cell joins with a female sex cell to produce a fertilized (fʉrt″l īzd) egg. In flowering plants, this fertilized egg develops into a tiny plant enclosed in a seed. Through sexual reproduction, the tiny plant inherits traits, such as petal color and leaf shape, from each parent plant.

How a Fruit Forms

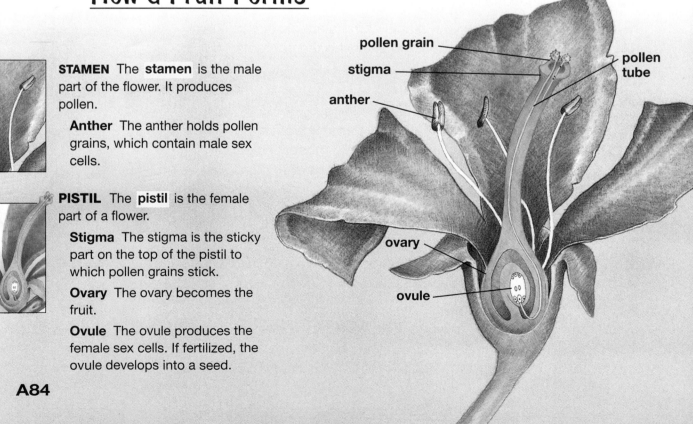

STAMEN The **stamen** is the male part of the flower. It produces pollen.

Anther The anther holds pollen grains, which contain male sex cells.

PISTIL The **pistil** is the female part of a flower.

Stigma The stigma is the sticky part on the top of the pistil to which pollen grains stick.

Ovary The ovary becomes the fruit.

Ovule The ovule produces the female sex cells. If fertilized, the ovule develops into a seed.

pollen grain

pollen tube

stigma

anther

ovary

ovule

A84

Producing Seeds and Fruits

Look at the pictures on pages A84 and A85 to see how seeds and fruits are formed. The first step in producing seeds is the transfer of pollen grains from the male part of a flower (the stamen) to the female part of another flower (the pistil). The **pollen grain** contains the male sex cell. When an insect, a bird, or a bat brushes against an anther, which contains the pollen grains, some of the pollen sticks to the animal's body. As the animal moves to the next flower, some pollen brushes off its body onto the stigma, which is at the tip of the pistil. This transfer of pollen grains is called **pollination** (päl ə nā'shən).

Some flowers are pollinated when wind or rain carries pollen to them from another flower. These flowers usually are not scented or brightly colored. They do not attract animals for pollination.

Pollination can take place only between plants of the same kind. For example, if pollen from an apple blossom lands on a tulip, no pollination occurs. A tulip must be pollinated by pollen grains from another tulip.

Inside the ovule, the fertilized egg forms an **embryo** (em'brē ō), a tiny new plant. Other cells in the ovule produce a food supply for the embryo. The ovule then forms a protective seed coat around the embryo and its food supply, forming a seed. In the activity on pages A80–A81, bean seeds and corn seeds are opened to reveal a tiny embryo and its food supply. Every seed contains these basic parts. The activity on pages A82 and A83 shows the germination of a seed and its growth into a flowering plant. As growth continues, the flower forms a fruit and seeds.

The ovary surrounding the seed or seeds enlarges and develops into a **fruit**. The fruit protects the seeds as they grow. Some fruits, such as cherries, have only one seed; others, such as oranges, have many seeds. ■

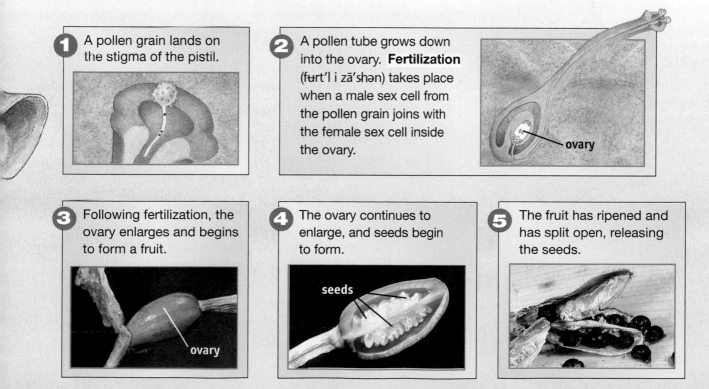

1 A pollen grain lands on the stigma of the pistil.

2 A pollen tube grows down into the ovary. **Fertilization** (fʉrt'l i zā'shən) takes place when a male sex cell from the pollen grain joins with the female sex cell inside the ovary.

ovary

3 Following fertilization, the ovary enlarges and begins to form a fruit.

ovary

4 The ovary continues to enlarge, and seeds begin to form.

seeds

5 The fruit has ripened and has split open, releasing the seeds.

The Story of a Flowering Tree

Reading Focus What are the main stages in the life cycle of a flowering tree?

The Story of a Flowering Tree

In late spring, red maple seeds ripen and fall off the tree. The seeds are inside the fruit, connected in pairs. A thin "wing" allows the wind to carry the seeds away from the parent tree.

As they fall to the ground, many seeds are eaten or hidden, to be eaten at a later time by insects and small animals, such as squirrels. Some fruits lie on the ground long enough to open and release the seeds.

1 **GERMINATION** Water in the soil softens the seed coat of a maple seed. **Germination**, or sprouting, occurs. Inside the seed, the embryo grows. This tiny embryo has inherited traits, such as leaf shape, from two parent plants. As the root grows into the soil, it absorbs nutrients and water, and the rest of the embryo sprouts. The tiny plant uses food stored in the seed leaves that surround it.

2 **SEEDLING** As its stem appears above the ground, the plant becomes a seedling. True leaves develop in the familiar shape of the red maple. Then, with the cooler days of fall, the seedling stops growing. Chlorophyll in its leaves disappears, leaving behind the bright colors that were there all along.

3 **SAPLING** In spring, buds appear on the stem and new leaves develop. As the stem becomes taller and thicker, bark forms. The roots grow deep and wide. They support the growing plant and provide it with water and nutrients. Last year's seedling has become a sapling, or young tree.

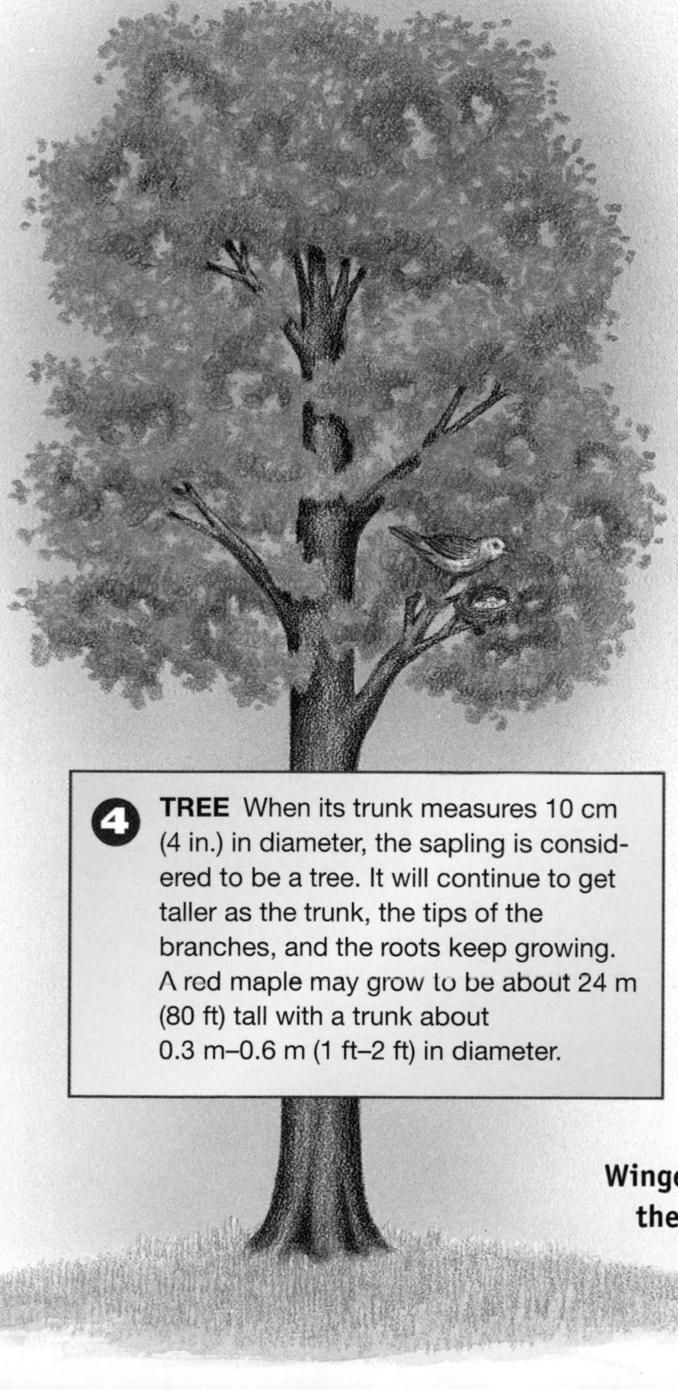

The first spring that a young maple grows flowers, it is considered to be a mature tree. A maple tree produces some flowers with female sex cells, other flowers with male sex cells, and a third kind of flower with both female and male sex cells. These flowers are pollinated when the wind carries pollen grains from the anther of one flower to the stigma of another flower. After fertilization occurs, the flowers produce the winged seeds that once more begin the red maple's life cycle. ■

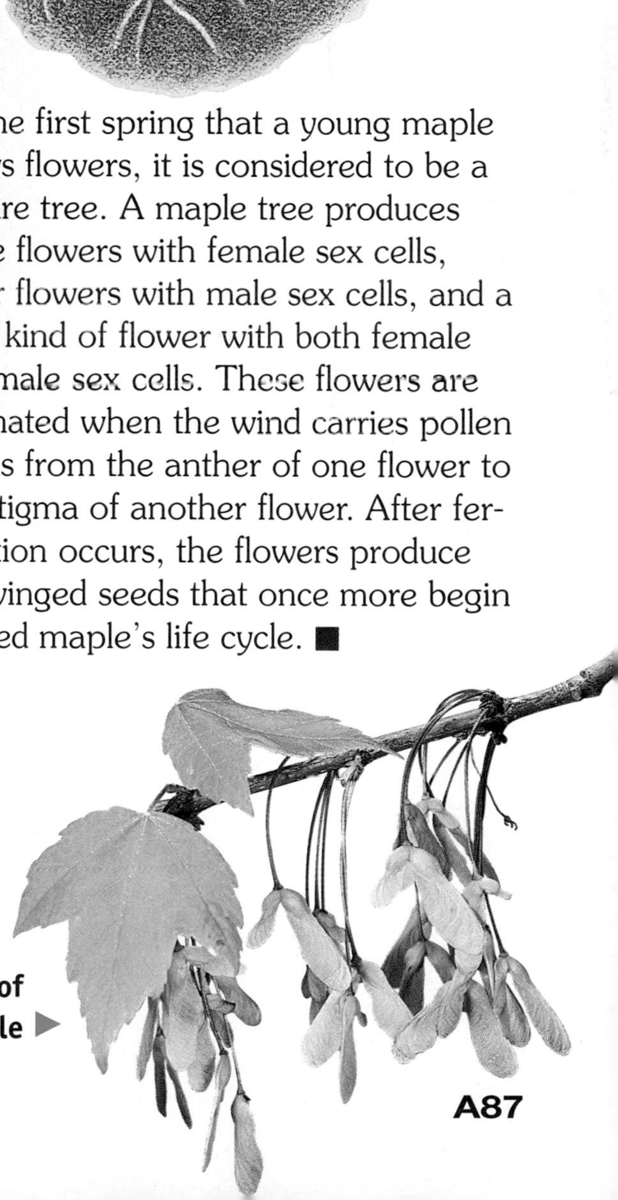

4 **TREE** When its trunk measures 10 cm (4 in.) in diameter, the sapling is considered to be a tree. It will continue to get taller as the trunk, the tips of the branches, and the roots keep growing. A red maple may grow to be about 24 m (80 ft) tall with a trunk about 0.3 m–0.6 m (1 ft–2 ft) in diameter.

Winged seeds of the red maple ▶

The Life of a Bristlecone Pine

Reading Focus How long has this bristlecone pine been growing?

One of the oldest living things on Earth is a bristlecone pine named Methuselah. Methuselah has been growing in Great Basin National Park in California's White Mountains for about 4,600 years!

Today only a small portion of Methuselah is still alive. We know how old Methuselah is because scientists used a tiny hollow drill to bore into the tree. They removed a thin core of wood. From this core, they counted the annual rings, which tell the tree's age.

If the twisted, wind-battered tree called Methuselah could talk, what might it tell us about the important events that have occurred during its lifetime? The time line shows some of the events during Methuselah's long life.

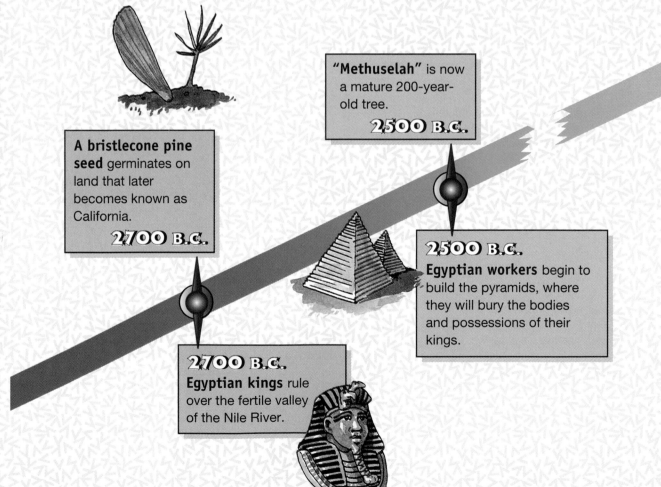

A bristlecone pine seed germinates on land that later becomes known as California.

2700 B.C.

"Methuselah" is now a mature 200-year-old tree.

2500 B.C.

2700 B.C.
Egyptian kings rule over the fertile valley of the Nile River.

2500 B.C.
Egyptian workers begin to build the pyramids, where they will bury the bodies and possessions of their kings.

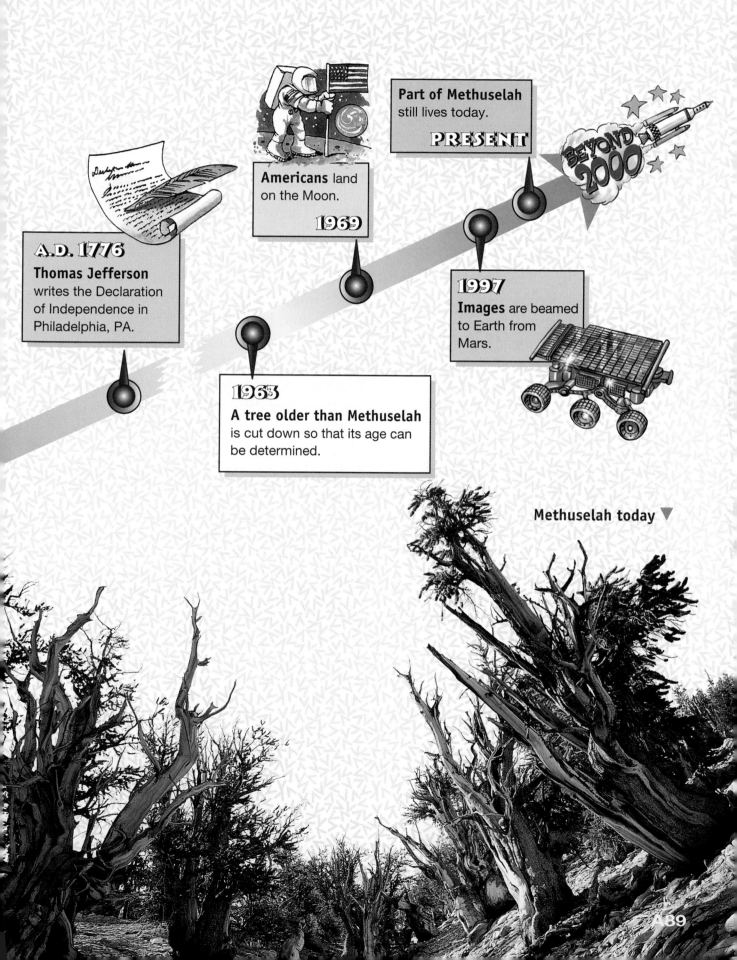

A.D. 1776
Thomas Jefferson writes the Declaration of Independence in Philadelphia, PA.

Americans land on the Moon.
1969

Part of Methuselah still lives today.
PRESENT

BEYOND 2000

1963
A tree older than Methuselah is cut down so that its age can be determined.

1997
Images are beamed to Earth from Mars.

Methuselah today ▼

Growing Plants Without Seeds

Reading Focus What are two ways that new plants can grow without seeds?

SCIENCE TECHNOLOGY & SOCIETY

When you plant seeds, you are planting the result of sexual reproduction—the joining of male and female sex cells from the parent plants. However, you can also grow new plants without using seeds. Such plants are produced by asexual reproduction. In asexual reproduction, offspring are produced from one or more cells of a single parent.

Cuttings

One way to produce new plants without planting seeds is by using cuttings. For example, with some kinds of plants you can cut a length of stem that has one or more leaves. The stem will grow roots when placed in water for a few days or weeks. The rooted stem can then be planted in soil and will grow into an entire new plant. This is a type of asexual reproduction. The new plants grown this way are clones, or exact copies of the parent plants.

Tissue Culture

Another type of asexual reproduction is tissue culture. A group of cells that works together is called a *tissue.* *Culture* is another word for "growing." Tissue culture is growing new plants in the laboratory from the cells of other

plants. The growth is done in test tubes or in culture plates.

When might a plant be grown through tissue culture instead of from a seed? Suppose most plants in a crop are affected by a disease. Then one of the plants is found to have a trait making it resistant to disease. Tissue from this healthy plant is grown by means of tissue culture. Since the new plant tissue is exactly like that of the parent plant, the new plants grown are also resistant to disease. Tissue culture can lead to a disease-resistant crop.

A leaf cutting (*left*) and plants grown from tissue culture in test tubes (*right*). ▼

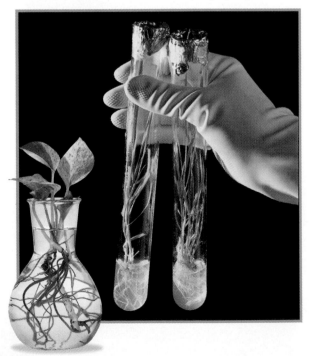

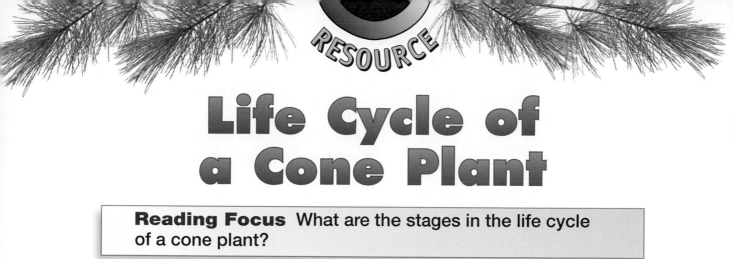

Life Cycle of a Cone Plant

Reading Focus What are the stages in the life cycle of a cone plant?

You've probably seen pine cones lying on the ground beneath a tall pine tree. Have you ever wondered what pine cones are?

Trees that produce cones are called **conifers**. The word *conifer* means "cone-bearing." Conifers have a life cycle that is similar to that of flowering plants. But instead of producing flowers and fruits, they produce cones. Seeds form inside the cones.

A pine is a type of conifer, or cone-producing tree. Both male and female cones grow on a pine tree. Compare the male and female cones in the photograph on this page.

What's in a Cone?

During winter the male cone produces pollen grains. Recall that the pollen grains contain the male sex cells. As the male cones grow in the spring, they open, releasing the pollen grains. Wind carries the pollen grains to the female cone.

In the spring, female cones are soft and green. Like flowers, the female cones contain ovules from which the seeds grow. The female cone produces a sticky material that traps the pollen grains. The process by which pollen grains from the male cone are transferred to the female cone is pollination.

After the pollen becomes trapped in the female cone, a pollen tube grows from the pollen into the ovule. Male sex cells from the pollen travel to the egg inside the ovule. Fertilization occurs when the male sex cell and the female sex cell, or egg, unite. From these two parts, the seed will grow. After fertilization, the female cone grows

Female cone of white pine (*left*); **male cones** (*right*)

seed ▶

▲ **pollen grains**

A91

larger, becomes woody, and the spaces between the scales close.

What's in a Seed?

Like a seed in a flowering plant, the seed in a cone plant contains three main parts. It contains an embryo, a layer of food used by the very young plant, and a seed coat that protects the seed.

In the fall the female cone opens and the seeds are released and carried by the wind. Many will be eaten by animals. Those that remain will not germinate until spring. A young tree grows for several years before it is mature and produces cones. When it produces male and female cones, the life cycle begins again. ■

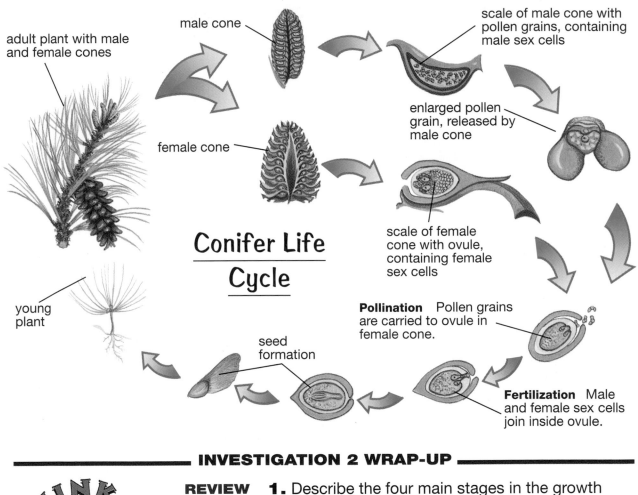

male cone

scale of male cone with pollen grains, containing male sex cells

adult plant with male and female cones

enlarged pollen grain, released by male cone

female cone

scale of female cone with ovule, containing female sex cells

Conifer Life Cycle

Pollination Pollen grains are carried to ovule in female cone.

young plant

seed formation

Fertilization Male and female sex cells join inside ovule.

INVESTIGATION 2 WRAP-UP

THINK IT WRITE IT

REVIEW

1. Describe the four main stages in the growth of a maple seed into an adult tree.

2. Describe how seeds and fruit form in a flower. Identify some inherited traits in plants.

CRITICAL THINKING

3. List two ways in which a female cone is like a flower. List two ways in which it is different.

4. Compare the life cycle of a flowering plant to that of a cone plant.

REFLECT & EVALUATE

Word Power

Write the letter of the term that best completes each sentence. *Not all terms will be used.*

a. cone
b. conifer
c. fertilization
d. fruit
e. invertebrate
f. larva
g. pollination
h. pupa
i. vertebrate

1. The ovary surrounding the seed or seeds develops into a _____.

2. The wormlike stage in the life cycle of an insect is called a _____.

3. A tree that bears cones is a _____.

4. The process that takes place when a male sex cell from a pollen grain joins with a female sex cell inside an ovary is _____.

Check What You Know

Write the term in each pair that best completes each sentence.

1. The stage of metamorphosis at which an insect appears to be at rest but is actually changing is the (larva, pupa) stage.

2. In a human life cycle a person is most likely to have a growth spurt during (adulthood, adolescence).

3. The reproductive organ of a maple tree is the (leaf, flower).

Problem Solving

1. Drawings showing an insect's life cycle are often in the shape of a circle. Explain why.

2. Seeds of flowering plants usually have a hard seed coat and a supply of food. How does this structure help a plant?

3. Make a table that shows how the life cycles of a salmon and a woodpecker are alike and different.

BUILD YOUR PORTFOLIO

Make a sketch of this flower. On your sketch, label all the numbered parts. Show which part of the flower will grow into the fruit.

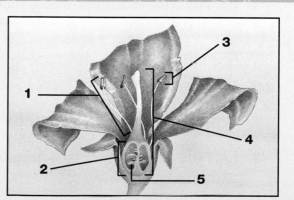

Main Idea and Details

When you read science, it's important to recognize which facts and details support or explain the main idea. First identify the main idea by looking for clues such as a title, or a topic sentence that states the main idea. Then look for statements that support that idea.

> Look for clues to find the main idea.
>
> Look for statements, facts, and details that support the main idea.

Read the paragraph below. Then complete the exercises.

From Flower to Fruit

The flower is the reproductive organ of a flowering plant. Some kinds of plants have flowers that produce both male and female sex cells. Other kinds have flowers that produce either male or female sex cells. When an insect visits a flower, it transfers the male sex cell from one flower to another. This transfer is part of the process of **sexual reproduction** in the flower. During sexual reproduction a male sex cell joins with a female sex cell to produce a fertilized egg. In flowering plants, this fertilized egg develops into a tiny plant enclosed in a seed. Through sexual reproduction, the tiny plant inherits traits, such as petal color and fruit shape, from each parent plant.

1. Write the letter of the sentence that states the main idea of the paragraph.

   a. The flower is the reproductive organ of a flowering plant.

   b. Tiny plants inherit traits, such as petal color and fruit shape, from each parent plant.

   c. Some plants produce both male and female sex cells.

   d. The fertilized egg develops into a tiny plant.

2. What clue helped you find the main idea?

3. List the most important facts and details that support the main idea.

 **Line Graph**

Bamboo is a fast-growing giant grass. The 24-hour growth of a shoot of one species of bamboo is shown on the line graph below.

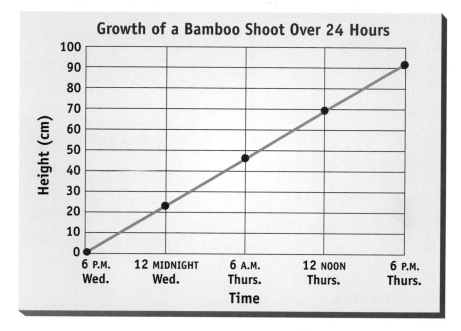

Use the information in the graph to complete the exercises that follow.

1. What does the line on the graph represent? Estimate how much the bamboo shoot grows in one hour. Explain.

2. In the line graph above, the line is a straight line. Is the line of every line graph a straight line? Explain.

You may want to use a calculator for Exercises 3 and 4.

3. Some bamboo species can grow to a height of 37 m. If the bamboo shoot shown continued growing at the rate shown, how long would it take to reach a height of 37 m? Round your answer to the nearest whole number.

4. Suppose another species of bamboo grows at one half the rate of the bamboo species shown on the graph. How long would it take a shoot of that species to grow to a height of 10 m? Round your answer to the nearest whole number.

WRAP-UP!

On your own, use scientific methods to investigate a question about systems in living things.

THINK LIKE A SCIENTIST

Ask a Question

Pose a question about plants or animals that you would like to investigate. For example, ask, "How does turning a seedling upside down affect the direction in which its roots grow?"

Make a Hypothesis

Suggest a hypothesis that is a possible answer to the question. One hypothesis is that the roots of a seedling that is turned upside down will curve downward and grow toward the ground.

Plan and Do a Test

Plan a controlled experiment to find the effect that turning a seedling upside down has on the direction in which roots grow. You could start a number of seedlings growing on wet paper towels placed inside sealed clear plastic bags. Develop a procedure that uses these materials to test the hypothesis. With permission, carry out your experiment. Follow the safety guidelines on pages S14–S15.

Record and Analyze

Observe carefully and record your data accurately. Make repeated observations.

Draw Conclusions

Look for evidence to support the hypothesis or to show that it is false. Draw conclusions about the hypothesis. Repeat the experiment to verify the results.

WRITING IN SCIENCE
Letter of Request

Write a letter to request information about lung diseases and their prevention. Use these guidelines to write your letter of request.

• Find the Internet addresses of helpful Web sites that have reliable information.

• Use the parts of a formal letter: heading, inside address, greeting, and closing.

• Clearly state your request.

• Include a self-addressed, stamped envelope.

UNIT B

The Solar System and Beyond

Theme: Scale

THINK LIKE A SCIENTIST

A COMET'S TALE

Comet Hale-Bopp was discovered on June 23, 1995. Astronomers, scientists who study the sky, anxiously waited to see clear views of this new visitor to the sky. On March 30, 1997, this photo of the comet was taken in Finland. Hale-Bopp is seen here above the greenish glow of the aurora borealis. Through their study of comets, astronomers have learned such things as what a comet is made of and how to predict when a comet will make a return visit. Astronomers look forward to uncovering many more secrets of the sky.

THINK LIKE A SCIENTIST

Questioning In this unit you'll learn about the solar system, stars, and living in space. You'll investigate questions such as these.

- What Is the Life Cycle of a Star?
- What Is It Like to Travel in Space?

Observing, Testing, Hypothesizing In the Activity "Making a Telescopic Camera," you'll compare the image you see through the camera you make with the real image. You'll hypothesize what astronomers might do to make their images of stars brighter.

Researching In the Resource "Telescopes," you'll gather more information about the tools that astronomers use.

Drawing Conclusions After you've completed your investigations, you'll draw conclusions about what you've learned—and get new ideas.

EXPLORING THE NIGHT SKY

In the daytime sky the Moon, when visible, is a pale ghost. Seen on a clear night, it's round and full at times. At other times it's a curved sliver that looks like a comma. And what about the stars? On a dark, clear night you'll see hundreds and hundreds of them twinkling. Many, many objects are visible in the night sky. What could you see with a telescope?

PEOPLE USING SCIENCE

Astronomer From a hilltop Carolyn and Eugene Shoemaker scan the sky with a telescope. Carolyn Shoemaker is an astronomer, a scientist who studies bodies in space through a telescope. Eugene is a geologist and amateur astronomer, who worked until 1993 for the U.S. Geological Survey. Carolyn and Eugene are among the leading comet discoverers in the world.

In March 1993, the Shoemakers and David Levy, another comet hunter, discovered a comet on a collision course with Jupiter. Sixteen months later, this comet slammed into Jupiter, producing one of the greatest collisions ever observed. This comet was named Shoemaker-Levy 9, in honor of its discoverers.

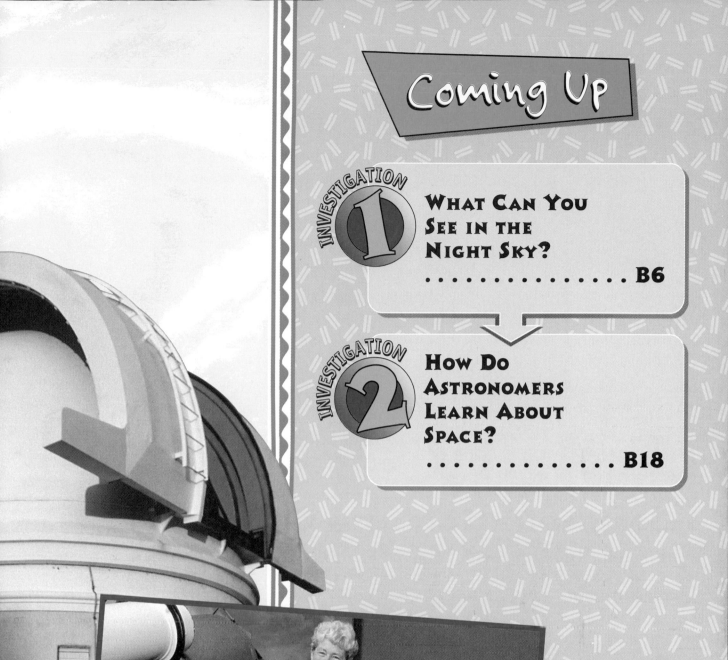

Coming Up

From left to right, David Levy, Carolyn Shoemaker, and Eugene Shoemaker (*inset*).

B5

WHAT CAN YOU SEE IN THE NIGHT SKY?

Star light, star bright,
First star I see tonight,
I wish I may, I wish I might
Have the wish I wish tonight.

Have you ever looked for the "first star" in this nursery rhyme? What do astronomers see when they look at the night sky?

Activity

Constellation in a Can

Individual stars are much easier to identify once you've learned to recognize star patterns called constellations. Learn a few of them now!

Procedure

1. Place the bottom of a 35-mm film canister on a piece of tracing paper. Trace a circle around the canister.

2. Select one of the constellation patterns your teacher will provide. Use a black marker to trace that pattern inside the circle you drew on the tracing paper.

MATERIALS

- goggles
- black plastic 35-mm film canister
- tracing paper
- constellation patterns
- black marker
- scissors
- tape
- pushpin
- *Science Notebook*

SAFETY /////

Wear goggles when punching holes.

3. Cut out the circle, leaving about 3 cm of paper all the way around it.

4. Place the circle of tracing paper over the outside bottom of the film canister, with the drawing to the inside. Tape the paper to the canister.

5. With a pushpin, punch a small hole through the paper and the canister bottom for each star in the pattern. Remove the paper and tape from the canister.

6. Hold the film canister up to the light and look through it. Turn the canister counterclockwise and **observe** the constellation pattern inside.

7. Trade canisters with your classmates. Try to **identify** the other students' constellations. **Compare** what you see inside their canisters to the star pattern your teacher gave you.

Analyze and Conclude

1. In your *Science Notebook,* **make a list** of the patterns that you could identify and another list of the ones you could not.

2. **Analyze** how turning the canisters affects the way the constellations appear. **Draw** four pictures that show four different views of your own constellation as you turn your canister around.

3. **Hypothesize** why constellations might look different at different times of the night.

Technology Link CD-ROM

INVESTIGATE FURTHER!

Use the **Science Processor CD-ROM**, *The Solar System & Beyond* (Investigation 1, Starry Night) to find out more about constellations. You can see the movement of constellations at different times of the night and different seasons of the year.

Activity

Making a Planisphere

Do the constellations always appear in the same positions in the sky? How can you predict when and where a particular constellation will be visible? Here's one way.

Procedure

1. Cut along the dashed lines on the horizon mask provided by your teacher. Be sure to cut out the large oval and the small slits.

2. Cut along the outer edge of the star wheel provided by your teacher.

3. With a paper fastener, punch a small hole in the center of the star wheel where the star Polaris is. Then use the fastener to attach the star wheel to the middle of a piece of cardboard, as shown.

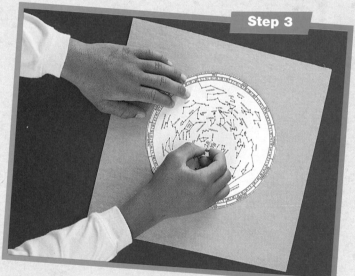

Step 3

4. Attach the corners of the horizon mask to the cardboard with glue, as shown, so that the outer portion of the star wheel is visible around the outer circular edge of the horizon mask. The wheel should turn freely behind the mask.

5. You have now made a planisphere, a map of the sky that can show the positions of the stars at different times. To use it, find the time of year you're interested in on the star wheel. Then turn the wheel until that date lines up with the hour you're interested in on the horizon mask. The stars in the sky at that time will have the same pattern as they do in the oval window of your planisphere.

Step 4

6. Use your planisphere to see how the Big Dipper and the Little Dipper will look at 8:00 P.M. tonight. **Draw** these star patterns in your *Science Notebook* and mark the compass directions to match those on the horizon mask. **Label** your drawing with today's date and the time 8:00 P.M.

7. **Predict** how the Big Dipper and Little Dipper will look at 11:00 P.M. tonight. Use the planisphere to check your prediction. **Draw** these star groups again with their compass directions, the date, and the new time. How will these two star groups change during the three hours from 8:00 P.M. to 11:00 P.M.?

8. **Predict** how the Big Dipper and Little Dipper will look at 11:00 P.M. three months from now. Check your prediction. Then **draw** these star groups with their compass directions, the date, and the time. How will these two star groups change during the next three months?

Analyze and Conclude

1. Based on what you learned in steps 6 and 7, **infer** how the appearance of the Big Dipper and the Little Dipper will change throughout the entire night tonight.

2. Based on what you learned in steps 7 and 8, **infer** how the appearance of these two star groups would change throughout an entire year if you looked at them at the same time every night.

3. **Hypothesize** what might cause these changes. Do you think the stars are really moving in the way they appear to move in the sky? If not, what else might explain their apparent motion? Do you think the changes you see occurring nightly and the changes you see throughout the year are caused by the same thing? Explain your reasoning.

Internet Field Trip

Visit **www.eduplace.com** to learn more about the constellations.

INVESTIGATE FURTHER!

EXPERIMENT

Go outside on the next clear night. Set your planisphere for the correct date and time. Hold it overhead, with the compass directions oriented correctly. Then identify the brighter constellations in the sky.

EAST
MARCH

HORIZON

FEBRUARY

JANUARY

SOUTH

DECEMBER

HORIZON

CAPRICORNUS

AQUILA

SAGITTARIUS

SERPENS
CAUDA

PEGASUS
Great Square

CYGNUS
Northern
Cross

ANDROMEDA

CEPHEUS

CASSIOPEIA

LYRA
Vega

Deneb

HERCULES

URSA
MINOR
Little
Dipper
Polaris

DRACO

OPHIUCHUS

CORONA
BOREALIS

Antares

SCORPIUS

SERPENS
CAPUT

BOÖTES

Big Dipper
URSA MAJOR

Arcturus

Star Patterns in the Sky

Reading Focus What are constellations, and what are some well-known examples?

Have you ever been out on a clear night and just looked up to see what you could see in the sky? Even if you live in a city with lots of bright lights, you can still spot dozens of stars. If you live in or visit the country, you can see thousands of beautiful, sparkling objects in the night sky.

How do you find your way around the sky? It's easy to learn! The activities on pages B6 to B9 help with recognizing star patterns and in knowing what might be seen on a certain night.

Identifying Groups of Stars

The activities show pictures of constellations (kän stə lā′shəns). A **constellation** is a group of stars that forms a pattern in the night sky.

Throughout history, different cultures have identified and named such star patterns. Today's astronomers recognize a total of 88 constellations.

The constellations that can be seen from Earth's Northern Hemisphere received their names from Greek and Roman mythology. Leo, Pisces (pī′sēz), and Taurus, for example, were named for a lion, two fish, and a bull. Orion (ō rī′ən) and Cassiopeia (kas ē ō pē′ə) are the names of a hunter and a queen in Greek and Roman myths.

The Southern Hemisphere's constellations probably aren't very familiar to you. These star patterns were named between the 1400s and the 1700s, when explorers from Europe first sailed south of the equator. The constellations they sighted were named for tools they used and for objects and animals they saw. Telescopium, for instance, was named for the telescope, and Tucana was named for the South American bird called a toucan.

Using **Math** *The constellation Taurus is shown at the left. If line segments are used to show Taurus, what geometric shapes can you find?*

When you think of constellations, which ones come to mind first? The most widely recognized star patterns are probably the Big Dipper and the Little Dipper. These two are not really constellations by themselves, however, but are portions of two larger constellations. The Big Dipper is part of the constellation called Ursa Major, the Great Bear. The Little Dipper belongs to Ursa Minor, the Little Bear.

▲ **The constellation Orion**

The Big Dipper and the Little Dipper are so well known not just because of their recognizable shapes, but also for where they are in the sky. What's most important is that these two patterns can always be found in the same area of the northern sky. Polaris, the star at the tip of the Little Dipper's "handle," is known as the North Star because it always appears almost exactly above the North Pole. You'll learn why Polaris does this—and why other stars don't—as you go through this investigation.

A Map of the Sky

Today's constellations no doubt started out as pictures in the minds of our ancestors, much as you might see castles or dragons in clouds during the daytime. But constellations also serve an important practical purpose. They provide us with a map of the sky.

Since the sky is so huge, it can be difficult to tell someone where to find a certain object in it. But constellations divide the sky into 88 imaginary sections, just as a map of the United States divides the country into 50 states. Astronomers use constellations to identify the "address" of a certain sky object, just as you use your state to identify where you live. We say that the bright reddish star Betelgeuse (bet″l jōōz), for example, is located within the constellation called Orion. Rigel (rī′jəl), a bright bluish star, is also part of Orion. It marks Orion's heel.

Now that you have a map, won't it be easier to find your way around the sky? One clear night, look up and see how many of the constellations you find! ∎

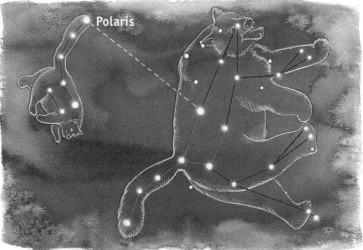

▲ **The constellations Ursa Minor and Ursa Major**

Polaris

Why the Stars Appear to Move

Reading Focus How do Earth's movements affect what you see in the sky?

Look at the picture at the right. What are all those rings? They're the tracks of stars as they move throughout the night!

The tiny circle in the center is the track of Polaris, the North Star. This object hardly seems to move at all, while most of the other objects in the sky appear to revolve around it. If you point a camera at Polaris and leave the shutter open, you will take a picture like this one.

While you can watch the northern constellations circle Polaris every night, other changes in the sky take place over many months. Both types of changes are modeled in the planisphere activity on pages B8 and B9.

Orion is a good example of a constellation whose position shifts slowly with the seasons. On a late autumn evening, it can be seen low in the eastern sky. If you look for Orion on future autumn evenings, you'll find that it appears to move higher and higher in the sky. It reaches its highest position in the sky in

▲ A time exposure photograph of the northern night sky

mid-December. Then, on winter evenings the constellation is found in the western sky. By early spring, it can only be seen on the western horizon. By late spring, Orion has completely disappeared from the sky for the summer.

Two Kinds of Movement at Once

How can you explain the apparent daily and yearly movements of the constellations? To better understand what you're seeing, try this exercise.

Imagine you're a pitcher on the mound in a baseball game. You wind up and throw a curveball—a ball that spins as it flies through the air. Suppose that a housefly lands on your baseball and hangs onto its stitches as it races toward home plate. What will that insect see as the ball flies through the air?

Let's suppose you released the ball so that it spins from side to side, instead of from top to bottom. As the baseball rotates, the fly will see the player at third base appear to race by several times. But the girl playing third base hasn't really moved. She has only appeared to move, from the fly's point of view, because the ball on which the fly sits is spinning.

But the ball isn't just spinning. It's also traveling from the pitcher's mound toward home plate. As it does, the fly's view of the girl at third base changes. At first, the fly sees her from the side. But as the ball nears the plate, the fly is able to see the girl from the front.

The third-base player hasn't really moved. Instead, it's the fly who has moved. And yet, to that insect on the baseball, the girl has appeared to turn toward the fly and move backward. The girl appears to move farther and farther away as the fly's viewing angle and the distance between the ball and third base have changed.

Earth Rotates and Revolves

If you can imagine a fly on a baseball, you can imagine yourself standing on a planet. The planet is Earth, and just like the baseball, it moves in two ways at once.

First, Earth spins. To be more precise, it rotates on its **axis**, an imaginary rod stretching through the planet between the North and South Poles. Earth takes 24 hours, or one day, to turn completely around on its axis and finish one **rotation**, even though it is spinning at a great speed.

Second, as Earth rotates, it also moves from one part of space to another. Rather than following a straight line, Earth follows a roughly circular orbit

A curveball spinning and moving toward home plate in a baseball game (*above*) may be compared to Earth rotating and revolving in space (*below*).

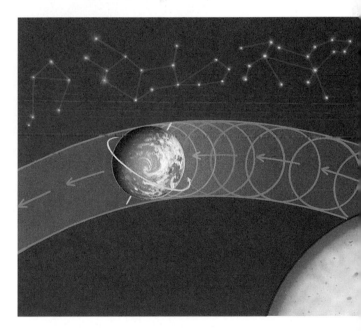

around the Sun. The distance Earth travels in its orbit around the Sun is so great that each round trip—one **revolution**—takes about 365 days, or one year.

Earth is so huge and its gravity is so strong that you cannot feel the planet rotate or move through space in its orbit. But evidence for both kinds of motion is all around you.

Earth's rotation, for example, makes the Sun appear to rise in the east and set in the west. When a spot on Earth rotates away from the Sun, it's night for that location.

Earth's revolution around the Sun and the tilt of Earth's axis cause seasons. The tilt of the axis causes the angle at which the Sun's rays strike Earth and the number of hours of daylight at any location to change in a regular pattern. Summer and winter in the Northern and Southern Hemispheres are opposite. When one hemisphere is tilted toward the Sun, the other is tilted away from the Sun. For example, when it is summer in the United States, it is winter in Argentina.

The Stars' Apparent Motion

Can you now see why the stars appear to move? Think back to the fly on the baseball. Do you remember the third-base player who seemed to be moving but was actually standing still?

▲ Earth's rotation makes the stars appear to circle Polaris.

The stars are like the player, and Earth is like the baseball. It's our planet's rotation that makes the stars appear to move each night from east to west.

It's worth noting here that the stars are *not* in fact standing still. They're just so far away that they'd *seem* to be motionless if Earth itself weren't moving. But that's a story for Chapter 3!

To people viewing the sky from Earth, only the North Star appears almost motionless. That's because the North Star lies directly above the North Pole—the northern tip of Earth's axis. This makes Polaris seem like the center of the sky, with all the other stars revolving around it.

Earth's revolution around the Sun means that different stars appear in the sky at different times of the year. The viewing "window" that we look through—the direction in space that the night side of Earth faces—keeps changing as Earth moves in its orbit. Each month we see about 30° of new star groups in the east and lose sight of 30° of old star groups in the west. Different constellations wait to greet us as we sail along through space. ■

Moving Bears of the Native Americans

Reading Focus What does the Micmacs' story about the Celestial Bear help to explain?

Scientists call it Ursa Major. Most people know it as the Big Dipper. To the Micmac Native Americans of eastern Canada, this pattern of stars is known as the Celestial Bear.

When the Micmacs look at the night sky, they see a bear in the four stars that we think of as the "dipper." Earth's daily rotation and yearly revolution make it appear that the bear is moving. The Micmacs have created a story about why the position of the bear keeps changing.

They say that in early May the bear climbs out of her "den"—a circle of stars higher up in the sky—and is pursued by seven hunters. The three stars behind her that form the "handle" of the dipper are hunters named Robin, Chickadee, and Moose Bird. Following close by are hunter stars called Pigeon, Blue Jay, Hoot Owl, and Saw-whet.

In midsummer the bear runs across the northern sky trying to get away from her pursuers. In mid-autumn she "stands up" to defend herself. At this time of year, the four stars near the Big Dipper set below the horizon. So only three hunters remain to pursue the bear. In late autumn the bear falls on her back and the three hunters catch her. The bear's blood falls to Earth and turns the autumn leaves bright red.

This story is the Micmacs' way of describing what they observed about the movement of the stars and the changing of the seasons. The story is based on activities in their everyday lives. The Micmac story can help you remember how the stars appear to change position. ■

The Big Dipper as seen by the Micmacs ▼

Wanderers in the Night Sky

Reading Focus What is the difference between a star and a planet?

Other than the Sun and the Moon, most of the objects in the night sky look about the same to the unaided eye. They all seem to be just tiny points of light. Are all of those shiny objects stars? If not, what are they? And how can you tell which ones are which?

You can begin to answer these questions yourself by simply looking a little bit longer and a little more closely at those points of light in the sky. If you do, you'll soon realize that they are *not* all exactly alike.

A Different Sort of "Star"

Have you ever seen the "morning star"? This is an object that seems to be a very bright star. It can be seen at certain times on the eastern horizon (hə-rī′zən), just before the Sun rises. The

▲ The "morning star"

horizon is the line formed where the Earth and sky seem to meet. If you look closely at this bright object, it seems to shine with a steady light. Almost all the other "stars" seem to twinkle.

If you observe the morning star through a telescope, it will no longer look like a tiny point of light. Instead you'll see a small round disk. This object, in fact, has phases like the Moon does, so you might see either a fairly full disk or a thin crescent.

If you use a more powerful telescope to observe the morning star, you'll see a larger disk. But no matter how powerful your telescope is, most of the other stars in the sky will still appear to be just tiny points of light.

If you look for the morning star several days in a row, you'll notice something else. It's moving! And it's moving not just *along with* all the other stars, but *in relation to* the other stars, including the Sun.

Over a period of weeks, you'll see the morning star move closer and closer to the Sun until it disappears in the Sun's glare. Then something even more interesting happens. The same object reappears in the west just after sundown as the evening star!

▲ The Sun, Moon, and planets appear to move in the same narrow band across the sky.

Of all the starlike objects easily seen by the unaided eye, only five are like the morning star. That is, they shine steadily rather than twinkle, appear in a telescope as disks rather than points of light, and move against the backdrop of the other stars.

These five objects share one other trait with the morning star. They can only be seen in a certain part of the sky. Although they all move, these "stars" appear only in a narrow band. That band is roughly the same as the path of the Sun and the Moon across the sky.

The Wandering Planets

The ancient Greeks called these five special objects "wandering stars." In English, we call them *planets*—a name that comes from the Greek word for "wanderer." These five objects—and a few others like them that are not easily seen by the unaided eye—are really in a different class from stars. They are planets.

A **star** is a huge globe of hot gases that shines by its own light. The Sun is a star. It just appears bigger because it's much closer to Earth than are other stars. A **planet** is a large object that circles a star and does *not* produce light of its own. We can see planets only because they reflect sunlight.

The morning and evening star is really Venus, one of nine known planets that revolve around our Sun. Until very recently, scientists thought there were only nine planets in the universe. By 1998, however, astronomers had discovered 13 planets circling other nearby stars. ■

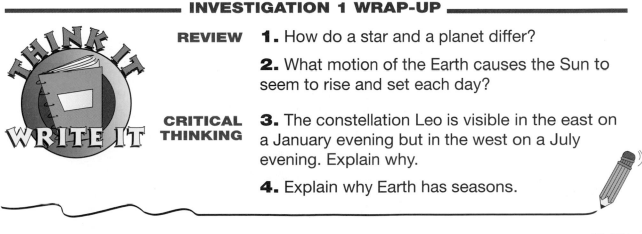

INVESTIGATION 1 WRAP-UP

REVIEW

1. How do a star and a planet differ?

2. What motion of the Earth causes the Sun to seem to rise and set each day?

CRITICAL THINKING

3. The constellation Leo is visible in the east on a January evening but in the west on a July evening. Explain why.

4. Explain why Earth has seasons.

HOW DO ASTRONOMERS LEARN ABOUT SPACE?

How can you learn about objects that are as far away as stars and planets? This is a problem that has puzzled scientists for centuries. Two solutions to this problem are to use telescopes and to collect material that has fallen to Earth from space. You can do these things, too!

Activity

Making a Telescopic Camera

Astronomers use many tools to help them study the sky. In this activity you'll build a simple version of one of those tools.

Procedure

1. Hold a convex lens above a table and directly below a ceiling light. Adjust the height of the lens above the table until an image of the ceiling light appears on the table.

2. Measure the distance between the lens and the table. Then cut a cardboard tube so that it's about three fourths of this length.

MATERIALS

- convex lens
- metric ruler
- 2 cardboard tubes
- scissors
- tape
- wax paper
- *Science Notebook*

SAFETY //////

Never look at the Sun through a lens. Your eyes could be injured. Do not use the lens to focus sunlight.

Step 1

See **SCIENCE** *and* **MATH TOOLBOX** page H6 if you need to review *Using a Tape Measure or Ruler.*

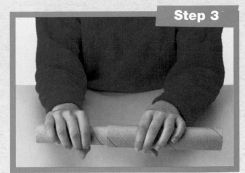

Step 3

3. Cut a second cardboard tube of the same length. Then cut this second tube lengthwise. Overlap the edges and tape them so that this tube is slightly narrower in diameter than the first tube. This narrower tube should slide smoothly inside the first tube.

4. Using tape, attach the lens to the open end of the wider tube.

5. Cut a square of wax paper to cover the open end of the smaller tube. Tape the wax paper in place. You have now made a simple type of telescopic camera—a device that projects a magnified image of distant objects onto film (or, in this case, wax paper).

Step 6

6. Aim the lens of your camera toward a bright area—perhaps out a window. Look at the wax paper at the other end of the camera. Slide the tubes until you get a clearly focused image on the wax paper.

Analyze and Conclude

1. Compare the image on the wax paper with the real scene. In your *Science Notebook,* **make a list** of the ways in which the image is different from the real thing.

2. In a real camera on a telescope, film is used instead of wax paper. **Make a list** of other ways in which your cardboard-tube camera differs from a real camera on a telescope.

3. Is your image on the wax paper brighter than the real object? **Hypothesize** what astronomers might do to make their images of faint stars brighter.

UNIT PROJECT LINK

For this Unit Project you will turn your classroom into a simulated space station. On large sheets of paper, draw windows for your space station. Within the windows, draw the stars of several constellations that are near each other in the sky. Then use your telescopic camera to take sightings on certain stars.

 TechnologyLink

For more help with your Unit Project, go to **www.eduplace.com**.

Activity

Mining for Meteorites

Have you ever seen a "falling star"? Do you know what one looks like up close? Find out!

MATERIALS
- magnet
- clear plastic bag
- rainwater in a large pan
- hand lens
- craft stick
- microscope slide
- microscope
- *Science Notebook*

SAFETY
Clean up spills immediately.

Procedure

1. Place a magnet inside a clear plastic bag. Then run the bag-covered magnet through the rainwater your teacher has collected.

Step 1

2. Use a hand lens to look carefully at the outside of the bag. If you find any small spheres, or round objects, use a craft stick to scrape them onto a microscope slide.

3. **Observe** the objects through a microscope. If they still look like round objects, what you probably have are meteorites—pieces of space dust that came to Earth as falling stars!

 See **SCIENCE** and **MATH TOOLBOX** page H2 if you need to review *Using a Microscope.*

Analyze and Conclude

1. **Infer** what material your meteorites contain. What part of the activity provided you with this information?

2. **Hypothesize** what might cause most meteorites to be rounded in shape.

Step 2

3. **Hypothesize** how small meteorites could end up in rainwater. In your *Science Notebook*, **draw** a picture of Earth that shows where you think your meteorites were before they fell to the ground during a rain shower.

Telescopes

Imagine that you're living hundreds of years ago. All that you know about the stars and planets is based on what you can see with your unaided eyes. Then you learn of a new device called a telescope—a viewing instrument that can magnify distant objects.

You aim your telescope at the speck of light called Jupiter. Until now, Jupiter looked to you like a very bright star. But today, instead of appearing as a tiny point of light, Jupiter can be clearly seen as a round disk. Not only that, but four smaller points of light—previously invisible to you—can now be seen close to Jupiter. As you watch through the telescope each night, it becomes obvious that the four smaller objects are moons. They circle Jupiter, just as our own Moon orbits Earth. What an amazing discovery this is!

The person who actually made this discovery in the seventeenth century was the great Italian scientist Galileo Galilei. What he found changed people's views of the universe. He made his observations by using one of the most useful devices ever developed by human beings—the telescope.

The two main types of telescopes are pictured on the next page. A **refracting** (ri frakt'iŋ) **telescope** is an instrument for viewing distant objects that uses two lenses to gather light and produce an image. The telescope looks like a long, narrow tube, such as a sea captain might use. You look directly through the tube. Light from a distant object is focused by a large lens and then magnified by a smaller lens before it reaches your eye. The camera in the activity on pages B18 and B19 uses a simple single-lens refracting system.

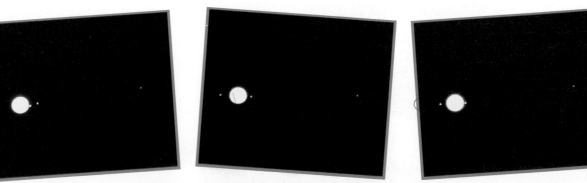

▲ Galileo discovered four moons of Jupiter by viewing scenes like these through his telescope.

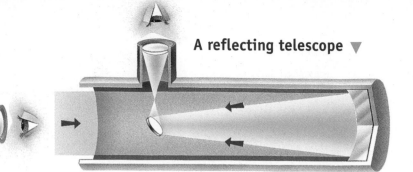

A refracting telescope ▼

A reflecting telescope ▼

A **reflecting telescope** gathers light in a curved mirror at the back of its tube. It then reflects and focuses the light on a smaller mirror near the front. The small mirror is often angled to send the image out through an eyepiece on the side of the tube. The eyepiece contains lenses that can be changed to give you different magnifications.

Because it's easier to build large mirrors than large lenses, the largest telescopes in the world are reflectors. A mirror has only one surface that must be precisely made. A lens must be shaped perfectly from top to bottom! Since a mirror reflects light, a mirror's bottom surface can rest on a supporting structure. Light must pass through a lens, so a lens has to be supported around the edge. The world's largest reflecting telescope, at McDonald Observatory, in Texas, has mirrors with a combined diameter of 11 m (436 in.). The lens of the world's largest refracting telescope, at Yerkes Observatory, in Wisconsin, is only about 1 m (40 in.) in diameter.

Wonders in the Heavens

No one is sure who made the first telescope, although many historians believe it was a Dutch spectacle-maker named Hans Lippershey. It is known, however, that by the early 1600s the Dutch had learned how to line up two curved lenses

◄ **The observatory at Palomar Mountain, California, contains a 5-m (200-in.) reflecting telescope.**

▲ The Hubble Space Telescope (HST) is shown here about to be released from an orbiting space shuttle. HST is about 13 m (43 ft) long and 4 m (13 ft) wide.

in a tube and look through them to make faraway objects appear closer.

As soon as Galileo heard about the Dutch invention, he set out to make his own telescope. Soon he had built several, each one more refined and more powerful than the last. Then he did something no one else had ever done. He took his most powerful telescope outside and looked up.

Galileo's telescope could bring the heavens only 30 times closer, yet what he saw astounded him! The Moon became an alien wonderland covered by deep craters and towering mountains. And there were many more stars than he had ever imagined, some gleaming with newly visible colors.

An important advance over Galileo's telescope came from the English scientist Sir Isaac Newton. The simple lenses of his day distorted color, but a mirror did not. So Newton designed a reflecting telescope that would collect light in a mirror before passing it through a lens.

Since Newton's time, astronomers have learned new ways to use telescopes to see things the human eye cannot see. For example, astronomers can capture pictures of very faint objects. They used to do this by attaching a camera to a telescope's eyepiece and exposing the film for long periods of time. Today, most astronomers use equipment to send telescope images directly to computers.

Putting Telescopes in Space

Today there is a large telescope in orbit around Earth. The Hubble Space Telescope (HST) is positioned beyond our planet's atmosphere, so it avoids distortions caused by looking through the air. Even though the mirror in the HST is smaller than that of many telescopes on Earth, it can see more clearly and see objects that are fainter and farther away than telescopes on the ground can see. Space telescopes can even see wavelengths of light that aren't visible from Earth's surface. ■

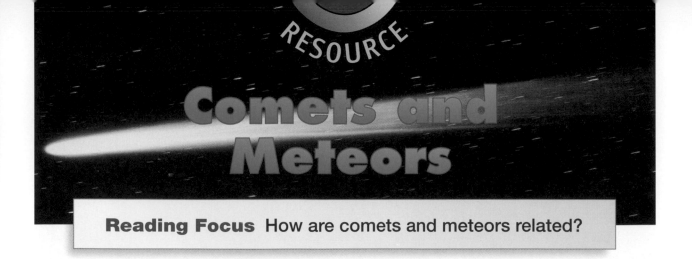

Comets and Meteors

Reading Focus How are comets and meteors related?

Pretend that you're a giant. Build yourself a huge snowball, about 5 km (3 mi) wide. Stuff some dirt and rocks in with the snow. Let the whole thing freeze rock-hard. Then send it hurtling through space at about 250,000 km/h (150,000 mph).

Aim your snowball so that it will swing in toward the Sun, go completely around it, and then head out into the most distant regions of the solar system before it returns. The snowball's path should look like a long thin oval. Congratulations! You have now made and launched your own **comet**, an icy ball that contains dust and rock and travels in an elliptical (ē lip'ti kəl) orbit around the Sun.

Snowballs That Melt in the Sun

From Earth a comet can look like a ball of fire. Yet real comets begin just as your imaginary one did, as giant chunks of ice. At the core, comets are mostly frozen water, ammonia, and methane,

mixed with enough dust and debris to create what you might call a "dirty snowball."

A comet spends most of its life drifting through the cold outer reaches of the solar system. But when its orbit brings it closer to the Sun, that's when the show begins!

Because the main body of a comet is made of frozen material, it is doomed to slow destruction by the Sun's heat. But the fiery look of a comet is not because the comet is burning up in the heat of the Sun. Instead, as the comet approaches the Sun, its body begins to melt, releasing its frozen gases into space. These gases spread out to form a huge misty head around the comet's front end.

A comet's tail is made of gases and grains of dust—the "dirt" streaming off the dirty snowball. A stream of charged particles given off by the Sun, called the solar wind, causes a comet's tail to point

Using Math *Halley's comet—shown at the top of this page as a telescope on Earth would see it—follows a 76-year orbit. It was last seen from Earth in 1986. How old will you be when it can be seen again?*

away from the Sun. No matter in which direction the comet is moving, its tail always points away from the Sun.

Some comets with very long orbits have only appeared once during recorded history. Others have reappeared regularly many times. The most famous one, Halley's comet, revolves around the Sun once every 76 years.

Comets: The Meteor Makers

The dirt particles left behind by the comet can drift toward Earth as Earth orbits the Sun. These particles then speed up into Earth's atmosphere and burn up there as "shooting stars," or **meteors** (mē'tē ərz).

Not all meteors come from comets, but comets do appear to cause many

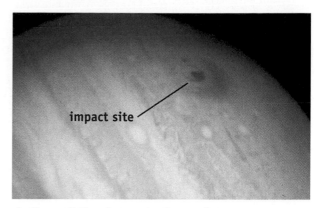

▲ One of the impact sites of comet Shoemaker-Levy 9 on the planet Jupiter

large meteor showers. The meteors that do not come from comets come from rocky material called asteroids. Most meteors burn up before they reach the ground. Sometimes meteors from asteroids can fall to Earth. The material that lands is called a **meteorite** (mē'tē ər īt).

Science in Literature

OBSERVING THE NIGHT SKIES

"Amateur astronomers . . . discover most of the new comets that pass through the inner Solar System. Comets, which are mountain-sized chunks of frozen gases, ice, and rock, are of great scientific interest because they can tell us more about how the Solar System formed. Each year, one or two new ones are found."

Stars, Clusters and Galaxies
by John Gustafson
Julian Messner, 1992

This information about the discovery of new comets comes from *Stars, Clusters and Galaxies* by John Gustafson. In this book you will find a wealth of information and tips for observing the galaxies in the night sky, as well as directions for making your own telescope.

Using Math *The Barringer meteor crater in Arizona has a diameter of about 1,200 m (4,000 ft). Estimate the distance around the crater.*

Collisions between comets and planets are rare, but when they do occur, the results can be spectacular! In July 1994, a comet called Shoemaker-Levy 9 struck the planet Jupiter. The photograph at the top of page B25 shows where the comet struck the planet. After the collision, the scars on Jupiter were two to three times the size of Earth!

Most scientists believe that Earth's dinosaurs became extinct because a comet or an asteroid struck our planet 65 million years ago. But the chances of something like that happening today are very, very small. When material from space does reach Earth—in the form of a meteorite—scientists can then examine and study it.

Meteorites are made of either metal or rock. The tiniest ones—like those in the activity on page B20—are so light that they often remain suspended in the atmosphere until a rain shower brings them to Earth.

Astronomers think that material from comets may date back more than 4 billion years, to the time of Earth's beginnings. By studying meteorites, scientists can learn about comets and the origins of the solar system. ■

INVESTIGATION 2 WRAP-UP

THINK IT WRITE IT

REVIEW

1. What are the two main kinds of telescopes?

2. What is the name of the telescope that orbits Earth?

CRITICAL THINKING

3. Suppose you could build a telescope anywhere on Earth. Where would you build it, and what kind of telescope would it be? Explain the reasons for your choices.

4. How does studying meteorites help scientists learn about comets?

REFLECT & EVALUATE

Word Power

Write the letter of the term that best matches the definition. *Not all terms will be used.*

1. Device that has two lenses and is used for seeing distant objects
2. Huge globe of hot gases that shines by its own light
3. Group of stars that forms a pattern in the night sky
4. Yearly movement of Earth around the Sun
5. Imaginary rod stretching between Earth's North and South Poles.

a. axis
b. constellation
c. planet
d. reflecting telescope
e. refracting telescope
f. revolution
g. rotation
h. star

Check What You Know

Write the term in each pair that best completes each sentence.

1. The seasons of the year are caused by Earth's (rotation, revolution).
2. The "morning star" is actually (Venus, Polaris).
3. The powerful telescope that orbits Earth is named after (Galileo, Hubble).

Problem Solving

1. Use what you have learned about the apparent motion of the stars to explain how stars might be used as a navigational tool.
2. With your unaided eye you see an object in the night sky. It looks like a bright point of light. How would you go about identifying this object?

BUILD YOUR PORTFOLIO

Copy this drawing of the Little Dipper as it appears at 7:00 P.M. in the February sky. Then redraw the picture to show how it will appear at 1:00 A.M. the same night. Label Polaris in each drawing. Add an arrow to show the direction in which the constellation appears to be moving. Then explain why the constellation appears to move.

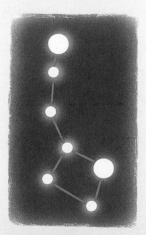

CHAPTER 2

THE SOLAR SYSTEM

When you look out into the vast reaches of the sky, do you wonder about the planets? To those who live upon it, Earth seems enormous. Actually, Earth is a medium-sized planet among the nine planets that orbit the Sun. How Earth compares to the other planets has fascinated people for ages.

PEOPLE USING SCIENCE

Aerospace Engineer Dr. Aprille Ericsson-Jackson is an aerospace engineer at the NASA Goddard Space Flight Center. As part of her work, she conducts simulations for spacecraft designs. A simulation is an attempt to duplicate on Earth a situation found in space. From the simulation, Dr. Ericsson-Jackson suggests changes in the spacecraft's design.

In junior high school, she realized she had an aptitude for mathematics and science. Dr. Ericsson-Jackson is the first African American woman with a Ph.D. in Engineering to work at the NASA Goddard Space Flight Center. By serving as a career advisor, mentor, and friend, Dr. Ericsson-Jackson encourages students to enter careers in science, math, and engineering.

Coming Up

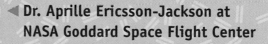

◀ Dr. Aprille Ericsson-Jackson at NASA Goddard Space Flight Center

INVESTIGATION 1

WHAT IS THE SOLAR SYSTEM MADE OF?

Our solar system's diameter is about 11.8 billion km. Can you picture that? Start walking at a rate of 5 kilometers per hour. Don't stop! You will walk a distance equal to the solar system's diameter in about 275,000 years. Now learn about the objects that make up our solar system and how they came to be.

Activity

When to Go Planet Watching

You've learned that the planets in our solar system seem to move across a narrow band in the sky. In this activity you'll discover how the planet Mars really moves in space. And you'll see how that motion affects the way Mars looks in Earth's night sky.

- -

Procedure

1. Use a colored pencil to **make a drawing** in your *Science Notebook* like the one on this page, but larger. Your drawing should show the Sun, Earth's orbit around the Sun, and the larger orbit of the planet Mars around the Sun.

2. Choose two small round objects to represent Earth and Mars. Place each object on your drawing at any location along each planet's orbit.

3. Use another colored pencil to trace around each object and show its position in your drawing. **Label** the two traced objects *Earth* and *Mars*.

Step 1

Earth

Mars

4. With a ruler, **measure** how far apart the two planets are in your drawing. **Record** that measurement.

See **SCIENCE** and **MATH TOOLBOX** page H6 if you need to review *Using a Tape Measure or Ruler.*

5. Move both planet models along their orbits until you have them as close together as they can be. **Draw** these positions, using a third color. Then **measure** and **record** the new distance between the two objects.

6. Move both planet models along their orbits until you have them as far apart as they can be. **Draw** these positions, using a fourth color. **Measure** and **record** the distance between the objects.

Analyze and Conclude

1. Look at the locations of the Sun, Earth, and Mars when Mars is as close to Earth as it can be. **Predict** what time of day you'd see Mars in Earth's sky when the real planets are positioned this way. **Infer** whether Mars would be visible from the daytime or nighttime side of Earth.

2. **Observe** the locations of the Sun, Earth, and Mars when Mars is as far from Earth as it can be. **Predict** what time of day you would see Mars when the real planets are positioned this way. **Infer** whether the daytime or night-time side of Earth would be facing Mars. Where would Mars appear to be in Earth's sky in relation to the Sun? Would you be able to see Mars from Earth at this time?

3. Look at the first positions you chose for the Earth and Mars objects. **Predict** whether you'd be able to see Mars from Earth if the planets were positioned in this way.

INVESTIGATE FURTHER!

Use the **Science Processor CD-ROM**, *The Solar System & Beyond* (Investigation 2, Planet Explorer) to find out more about the solar system and to take an imaginary trip to a planet.

Step 4

Activity

Comparing Planetary Distances

MATERIALS
- 10 index cards
- 400-sheet roll of toilet paper
- calculator
- *Science Notebook*

How far from Earth and from the Sun are the other eight planets? How can you better understand such large distances in the solar system? Here's one way to do it.

- -

Procedure

1. To **create a model** of planetary distances, go with nine other students to a large open area. One student represents the Sun while the others represent the nine planets.

2. Each student should label an index card with the name of the body he or she represents.

3. The Sun student should sit on the floor with one hand holding down the end of a roll of toilet paper. The planet students should unroll the toilet paper and count the sheets. As each student comes to the sheet number that's listed on the table for his or her planet, that student should sit. The student should then place the index card on the sheet representing his or her planet's average distance from the Sun.

Step 3

Planet	Sheet Number
Mercury	3
Venus	between 5 and 6
Earth	between 7 and 8
Mars	between 11 and 12
Jupiter	40
Saturn	74
Uranus	149
Neptune	233
Pluto	305

4. Back in the classroom, use a calculator to find the distance between each two neighboring planets in terms of toilet paper sheets. Make calculations for the distances between Mercury and Venus, Venus and Earth, Earth and Mars, and so on. Record the results in your *Science Notebook.*

See **SCIENCE** *and* **MATH TOOLBOX** page H4 if you need to review *Using a Calculator.*

Step 4

5. **Calculate** and **record** the distance in sheets between each planet and Earth.

Analyze and Conclude

1. **Compare** the distances between neighboring planets. Which two are closest together? Which two are farthest apart? As a group, which set of planets is closest together—those nearest the Sun or those farther out?

2. With other students, **hypothesize** about the effects of a planet's distance from the Sun. Which planets would be hottest? Which would be coldest? What would the Sun look like from each one? How long would a year be on each planet? **Compare** your ideas with those of your classmates.

3. Suppose you want to send a radio signal from Earth to each of the other planets at the time when each planet is closest to Earth. Which planet would receive a signal most quickly? Which would take the longest to get a signal? Use the results of step 5 to make a list of the planets according to their distance from Earth.

UNIT PROJECT LINK

Future trips to other planets may begin from an Earth-orbiting space station. Create a docking port for your simulated space station. Begin to collect information so that you can decorate the docking port area with travel posters of different planets and moons. Which ones would you and your classmates like to visit most?

Technology Link

For more help with your Unit Project, go to **www.eduplace.com**.

Earth's Neighborhood— The Solar System

Reading Focus Starting with the Sun, what is the order of planets in the solar system?

On pages B10 and B11, the way the sky is divided up into 88 constellations is compared to the way the United States is divided up into 50 states. In the same way, you can consider a solar system to be a "neighborhood" in the sky.

A **solar system** consists of a star and the objects that revolve around it. A model of our own solar system is shown here. In addition to the Sun, our solar system includes nine known planets and the moons that orbit those planets. It also includes many smaller objects, such as comets and the small rocky bodies known as asteroids. The force of gravity keeps planets in orbit around the Sun.

The activity on pages B32 and B33 shows the relative distances between planets. The planets are tiny compared to those distances. To show the planets clearly, on pages B34 and B35 they are drawn much larger than they should be, compared to the size of their orbits.

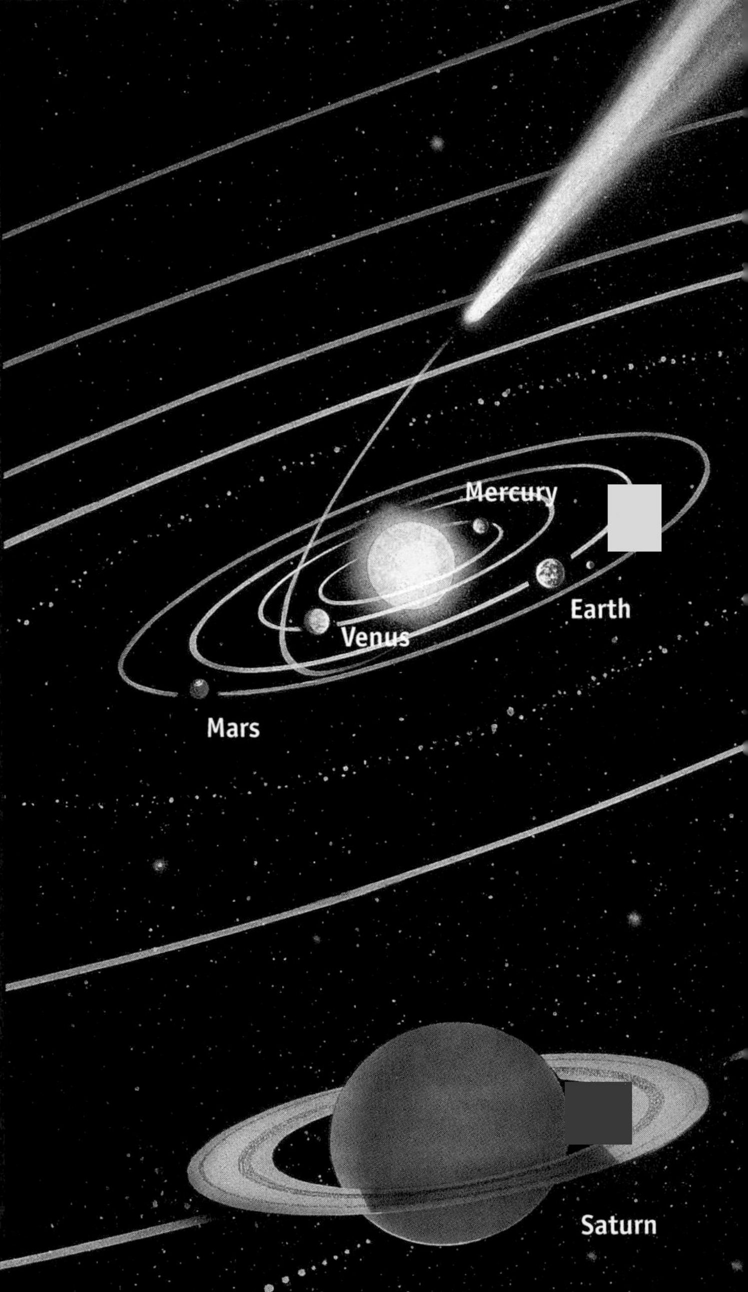

Mercury

Earth

Venus

Mars

Saturn

Pluto

Neptune

Uranus

asteroid belt

Jupiter

Planet	Average Distance From the Sun (in millions of km)	Period of Revolution (in Earth years)	Number of Known Moons
Mercury	58	0.24	0
Venus	108	0.62	0
Earth	150	1.00	1
Mars	228	1.88	2
Jupiter	778	11.86	16
Saturn	1,429	29.46	18
Uranus	2,875	84.01	15
Neptune	4,504	164.79	8
Pluto	5,900	248.60	1

Using Math *In Earth days, how long is one year on Mercury? Round your answer to the nearest whole day.*

Ptolemy Was Right—and Wrong

Reading Focus What is the heliocentric model of the solar system, and what other model came before it?

"Pygmies placed on the shoulders of giants see more than the giants themselves." It may seem to you that this saying has little to do with science. But it applies to two giants in the world of astronomy. One of these men was totally wrong about a major principle. Yet his work prepared the way for later astronomers to arrive at a better understanding of the universe. That man's name was Ptolemy (täl'ə mē).

Ptolemy lived in Egypt in the second century A.D. He tried to understand why the planets seem to wander across the sky. After charting their movements, he worked out a model that seemed to explain what he was seeing.

The Maya in Central America use astronomical observations to create the most accurate calendar in the world. **300**

Greek philosopher Aristarchus proposes that Earth and the other planets are spheres that revolve around the Sun.

260 B.C.

A.D. **145**
Ptolemy, an astronomer studying in Egypt, popularizes the theory that the Sun, Moon, and planets all revolve around a motionless Earth.

Sun

Earth

▲ **Ptolemy's model of the solar system**

3000 B.C.
The Chinese begin recording and predicting the apparent movements of the Sun, Moon, and planets.

B36

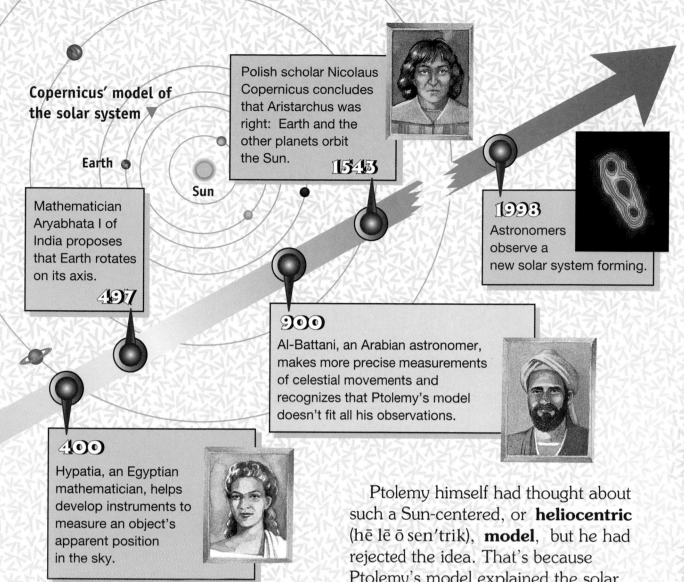

Copernicus' model of the solar system ▼

Earth

Sun

Mathematician Aryabhata I of India proposes that Earth rotates on its axis.
497

Polish scholar Nicolaus Copernicus concludes that Aristarchus was right: Earth and the other planets orbit the Sun.
1543

1998
Astronomers observe a new solar system forming.

900
Al-Battani, an Arabian astronomer, makes more precise measurements of celestial movements and recognizes that Ptolemy's model doesn't fit all his observations.

400
Hypatia, an Egyptian mathematician, helps develop instruments to measure an object's apparent position in the sky.

Ptolemy's model was an Earth-centered, or **geocentric** (jē ō sen'trik), **model**. To him that seemed perfectly logical, since Earth appeared to Ptolemy to be steady and unmoving. To explain the motions of the Sun, Moon, and planets, he reasoned that they all must revolve around Earth.

Ptolemy's model was used for more than 1,000 years. But in 1543 a Polish clergyman, Nicolaus Copernicus, put forth a different idea. He placed the Sun at the center of the universe and suggested that all the planets, including Earth, revolve around it.

Ptolemy himself had thought about such a Sun-centered, or **heliocentric** (hē lē ō sen'trik), **model**, but he had rejected the idea. That's because Ptolemy's model explained the solar system based on the best data available to him at the time. It's a basic principle in science that you can't get the right answer if you don't have all the necessary information. But you can't wait for everything to be discovered before you try to use what you know, either.

That's where "standing on the shoulders of giants" comes in. When Copernicus came along, he had a head start because he was able to build on Ptolemy's work. By adding his own observations to Ptolemy's, Copernicus could create a more accurate theory. That theory formed the basis for all of modern astronomy. ■

Birth of the Universe

Reading Focus How do scientists think that the universe was formed?

▲ **Formation of the universe according to the big-bang theory**

Where did the universe and our solar system come from? This is one of the biggest questions that human beings have ever asked. The answer may never be completely discovered or proved to everyone's satisfaction. But based on all the evidence people have uncovered over the centuries, this is what most scientists consider the best explanation they have so far.

The Big Bang

All the matter and energy that exist make up the **universe**. At one time, all of this matter and energy was concentrated in an incredibly tiny, extremely hot, unbelievably dense ball. (The word *dense* in this case means "very closely packed.")

Then all at once, at least 14 billion years ago, this ball of matter and energy exploded. The explosion sent a vast cloud of matter swirling out in all directions into space.

Time passed—*lots* of time. As it did, little by little, concentrations of matter began to form within the massive, expanding cloud. Each separate concentration was huge beyond anything we can imagine. Together these concentrations must have been millions of times bigger than Earth and all the planets combined in order to have contained enough material to condense into all the objects that now exist.

But condense they did, due to gravity. Gravity is the force that causes bodies to be attracted to each other. Very slowly, each clump of matter began to contract. Different clumps joined together, forming bigger clumps. And as these bigger clumps contracted, they began to spin. At the same time, each clump continued to move outward, away from all the other clumps.

These huge spinning collections of matter would eventually become galaxies, which are giant clusters of stars.

The story you've just read is commonly known as the **big-bang theory** of the origin of the universe.

The Sun and Planets Form

More time went by—billions of years. Then, within one of the galaxies, one particular collection of gas and dust began to condense. This was an event of special importance to us, for this material would eventually form our solar system! Refer to the drawings as you read about this event.

As the cloud of gas and dust rotated and flattened, most of the material collected in the center, where it would become our Sun. At the same time, in the swirling clouds around this future Sun, separate spinning clouds of matter began condensing to form the planets, including Earth. By about 4.6 billion years ago, the major objects in our solar system were in place.

What was happening in our own neighborhood was just one tiny chapter in a much larger story. For throughout the billions of kilometers of outer space, other collections of matter were also condensing. These collections formed other galaxies, other stars, and even— scientists think—other planets around those stars.

How Do We Know It's All True?

How do scientists know that the big bang happened this way? Well, they don't, not for certain. But the evidence continues to mount as we gather more and more data about the universe. Piecing together the cosmic puzzle of our origins is a tremendous job. ■

Formation of the Solar System

1 Gas and dust cloud spins in space.

2 Material condenses and the Sun and planets begin to form.

3 The solar system forms.

INVESTIGATE FURTHER!

RESEARCH

Research other scientific theories on the birth of the universe. Compare these theories as to their strengths and weaknesses.

Mission to Mars!

Reading Focus What can rocks on Mars tell about the planet?

▲ The Mars landscape, as seen during the Mars Pathfinder mission at the Jet Propulsion Center in Pasadena, California

STS
SCIENCE TECHNOLOGY & SOCIETY

In July 1997 the eyes of everyone in the mission control room in Houston, Texas, were glued to the TV screen. What were they watching? Their attention was on Shark, Half Dome, and Moe —three of the rocks named by mission scientists on the surface of Mars. The scientists were awed by the sight of the detailed images beamed back by Mars Pathfinder from the surface of Mars!

The Mission

Pathfinder was the first successful United States Mars mission since 1976. Its lander was equipped with a camera to take detailed pictures of the planet's rocks. It carried devices to measure and record daily Mars weather. To cushion the landing, the Pathfinder carried airbags. These airbags, looking like a huge white skirt, are shown on page B41.

Mars and the Internet

The Mars Pathfinder mission got world-wide interest. Images were shown on a NASA Web site for the whole world to see. Anyone on the Internet— from school students to senior citizens—could view what the scientists were seeing. On one single day, July 8, 1997, the Web site was visited about 47 million times!

What's the cost of sending an unpiloted spacecraft to Mars? It's about the same as making a major motion picture. Unpiloted flights cost much less than flights with people onboard. Even without a crew, a mission can gather a lot of information. Robots such as Pathfinder's Mars rover, Sojourner, collect data from the surface of the planet. Sojourner gathered information about the Martian rocks and sent the information back to Earth.

What Rocks Tell

Why study rocks? Every rock has a story to tell about where it came from and what it's made of. Here's what Martian rocks suggest to scientists about Mars. Billions of years ago, Mars

▲ This photograph, taken with the aid of a microscope, shows possible traces of microorganisms in a Mars meteorite.

▲ Sojourner, the Mars rover (*left*) and Mars Pathfinder, the lander (*right*). Airbags are under the lander.

was more Earthlike. Rounded pebbles on the surface have led scientists to believe that a long time ago there was water on Mars. That time was about 1.8 to 3.5 billion years ago. Since then, Mars has been dry and very cold.

Could the presence of water mean that life once existed on Mars? Scientists aren't sure about what other conditions were needed to spark life. Some doubt that Mars ever had an environment that could support life

forms. Others think it is possible that life existed on the red planet.

Scientists have found 13 meteorites on Earth thought to be from Mars. At least one of these meteorites has features that are thought by some to be once-living microbes. Scientists do not have other strong evidence that there has been life on Mars. Future missions, however, will build on the evidence gathered by Mars Pathfinder. ■

INVESTIGATION 1 WRAP-UP

REVIEW

1. Name the nine planets in our solar system in order. Start with the planet closest to the Sun.

2. Describe the big-bang theory of the origin of the universe.

CRITICAL THINKING

3. You have read about and probably made models of the solar system. Explain how a model can help you understand the solar system. How does a model differ from the real thing?

4. Compare the heliocentric model of the Sun and planets with the geocentric model.

INVESTIGATION 2

HOW DO THE PLANETS DIFFER?

My Very Elegant Mother Just Served Us Nine Pickles. This sentence is a tool that will help you remember the names of the planets in order of their distance from the Sun. The first letter of each word is the same as the first letter of a planet. Now learn what distance from the Sun has to do with the characteristics of each planet.

Activity

Measuring Planet Sizes

Which planets are the biggest? Which are the smallest? How large is the difference between them? Find out!

Step 2

Procedure

1. Make an Earth ruler like the one pictured on the facing page. Place the edge of a sheet of paper just below the picture. **Draw** lines on the paper's edge at exactly the same places as the lines in the picture. Number the spaces on your ruler as shown.

Pluto Neptune Uranus Saturn

2. Place your Earth ruler over the picture of each planet on these two pages. Use the ruler to **measure** the distance across the middle of each planet in terms of Earth diameters. **Record** each measurement.

3. **Rank** the planets from smallest to largest.

4. Using graph paper, **make a bar graph** showing the diameters of the nine planets. **List** the planets' names on one side of the graph and the number of Earth diameters on the other.

See **SCIENCE** and **MATH TOOLBOX** page H3 if you need to review *Making a Bar Graph.*

Analyze and Conclude

1. With classmates, **hypothesize** about the differences between the larger planets and the smaller ones. For example, how strong might each planet's gravity be compared to Earth's gravity? **Hypothesize** how gravity might affect whether or not a planet has an atmosphere. **Discuss** and **compare** your ideas.

2. Imagine that you live on a moon of each planet. Assume that each moon is about the same distance from its planet as Earth's Moon is from Earth. **Predict** how much of the sky each of the planets would fill.

3. **Compare** the pictures of large planets with those of small planets. **Make a list** of the differences you observe.

INVESTIGATE FURTHER!

RESEARCH

Look at the order of the planets. Are the biggest planets close to the Sun or far away? Hypothesize why those giant planets are located where they are. Look in an astronomy book that tells about the origins of the solar system to find out scientists' theories about this.

EARTH RULER (*Earth diameters*)

| 1 | 2 | 3 | 4 | 5 | 6 | 7 | 8 | 9 | 10 | 11 | 12 | 13 | 14 | 15 | 16 | 17 | 18 | 19 | 20 |

Jupiter

Mars

Earth

Venus

Mercury

Sun

The Inner Planets

Reading Focus What are some characteristics of the four planets closest to the Sun?

The inner planets of our solar system are Mercury, Venus, Earth, and Mars. All four planets are close to the Sun and are like Earth in size, in density, and in their mostly rocky makeup. Because of these likenesses they are known as **terrestrial** (tə res'trē əl) **planets**, meaning those that are Earthlike.

Two of the inner planets and all of the outer ones have satellites. Astronomers use the terms **moon** and **satellite** when they refer to natural objects that revolve around a planet. (The word *satellite* can also mean an orbiting object built by people.) Now find out about each of the inner planets.

☿ MERCURY

MERCURY is the closest planet to the Sun and the second smallest of the nine planets. It looks a lot like Earth's Moon, with a rocky surface covered by craters. Mercury has almost no atmosphere, just faint traces of helium and one or two other gases that it probably "captured" from the Sun. Surface temperatures on Mercury get hot enough to melt lead. This speedy planet takes about three months (measured in Earth time) to revolve around the Sun.

♀ VENUS

VENUS is the second planet from the Sun. Although it's named after the Roman goddess of beauty, it's not a very pleasant place. The Venusian (vi n$\overline{oo}$'-shən) atmosphere consists mainly of carbon dioxide with sulfuric acid clouds. It's so dense that the atmospheric pressure on the planet's surface is tremendous. Temperatures there reach about 500°C (900°F).

Venus' clouds appear featureless in normal light, but certain cameras reveal swirling patterns (*above right*). Radar provided this computer-generated view of the surface (*right*). ▶

⊕ EARTH

EARTH is the only planet in the solar system on which life is known to exist. It's the third planet from the Sun and the largest of the four inner planets. Earth has a vast core of molten metal and rock, with a thin crust of solid rock. Our planet's atmosphere is about 78 percent nitrogen and 21 percent oxygen, plus traces of other gases. As seen from space, Earth is one of the most beautiful planets, with bright blues indicating the abundant water and swirling whites, its scattered clouds.

☾ MOON

The Moon is Earth's only natural satellite. It has no atmosphere and is one of the largest satellites in the solar system. The force of gravity keeps the Moon in orbit around Earth. The Moon is the brightest object in Earth's night sky. This brightness is caused by the reflection of the Sun's light off the Moon's surface. The Moon rotates on its axis and moves around Earth once each month. During this cycle, the Moon passes through phases, so from night to night the lighted part of the Moon appears to change shape when seen from Earth.

♂ MARS

▲ **The features on Venus** range from smooth plains to volcanic mountain ranges. A computer created this false-color ground view from radar data.

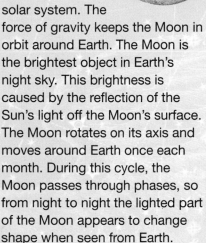

MARS, the fourth planet from the Sun, resembles Earth more than any other planet. Mars is smaller and less dense than Earth, which gives it less gravity and a thinner atmosphere. But the Martian day is only 41 minutes longer than the Earth day, and the planet has four seasons similar to those on Earth. Surface temperatures on Mars dip down to −90°C (−130°F) and seldom rise above 0°C (32°F). Iron oxide gives Martian soil the reddish color of rust. There are also white polar caps that grow and shrink with the seasons, and dark patches that were once mistaken for canals or vegetation. We now know that these dark areas come and go as dust storms cover and uncover darker rock.

▲ **Venus' surface** was photographed by a probe that landed on the planet.

MARS continued

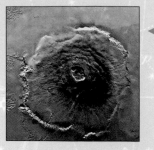

◄ **Olympus Mons**
(ō lim'pəs mänz) is a huge extinct volcano on Mars, nearly three times the height of the tallest mountain on Earth.

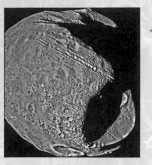

◄ **Phobos** (fō'bəs) is a Martian satellite just 27 km (16 mi) long. Its companion moon Deimos (dī'məs) is even smaller. Many scientists think these rough-shaped objects are asteroids that were captured by Mars' gravity.

◄ Sojourner, the Mars rover, scooped up soil and rock samples.

Science in Literature

THE FACES OF VENUS

"Venus is very nearly as large as the Earth but is a very hostile place. Its surface is hidden beneath deadly clouds of sulphuric acid droplets. The atmosphere consists mainly of carbon dioxide and is so heavy that any astronaut on the planet's surface would be crushed. The atmosphere retains so much heat that the surface temperature is about 880°F, hot enough to melt lead."

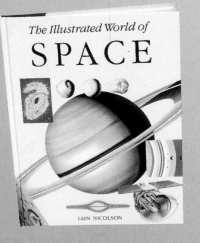

The Illustrated World of Space
by Iain Nicolson
Simon & Schuster
Books for Young Readers, 1991

There are lots of beautiful pictures and interesting facts in *The Illustrated World of Space* by Iain Nicolson. Read it to find out what might happen to the Earth and the Sun in 5 or 6 billion years.

The Outer Planets

Reading Focus What are some characteristics of the five planets farthest from the Sun?

Four of the five planets farthest from the Sun are very much alike. They're quite large in comparison to the inner planets, and they have ring systems. They're also made up mostly of substances that would be gases on Earth. For this reason, Jupiter, Saturn, Uranus, and Neptune are often referred to as the **gas giants**. The outermost known planet, Pluto, seems to be more like the inner terrestrial planets in size and composition. Take a closer look at this planet and its neighbors.

♃ JUPITER

JUPITER is the fifth planet from the Sun and the largest planet in our solar system. When the solar system was forming, Jupiter almost became a star. But the nuclear reactions that keep the Sun burning could not occur, and so Jupiter cooled and became a planet instead. It's composed mainly of gaseous and liquid hydrogen and helium. The gases probably surround a small rocky core. The planet's upper atmosphere features swirling cloud bands and the Great Red Spot, a huge circular storm that's lasted for centuries. Jupiter has a set of rings, but they're so thin and dark that they're practically invisible.

Io (ī′ō), a satellite of Jupiter, is the most volcanically active object we know of in the solar system. This rocky moon's volcanoes regularly coat the satellite's surface with lava. ▶

Io's volcanoes send up towering plumes of gas, visible in this false-color view. ▶

♄ SATURN

SATURN is the sixth planet from the Sun and the last planet you can easily see with your unaided eye from Earth. It's almost as big as Jupiter, with a very similar composition and banded atmosphere. Strong winds sweep across Saturn almost constantly, reaching speeds of 1,800 km/h (1,100 mph). The planet's spectacular rings are its most distinctive feature.

▲ **Saturn and some of its moons** are shown in this composite photo. Saturn has the most known satellites of any planet. Some have rocky surfaces and others are ice-covered.

▲ **Saturn's rings** are shown in a false-color view that brings out their details. The planet's ring system is made up of countless ice and rock fragments. These fragments orbit so closely together that the rings look solid from a distance.

▲ **Titan**, the largest of Saturn's satellites, is the only moon in the solar system with a dense atmosphere. Its haze is shown clearly in this false-color photo. Titan's atmosphere may resemble that of early Earth.

♅ URANUS

♆ NEPTUNE

URANUS (yŏŏr'ə nəs), blue-green in color, is the seventh planet from the Sun. Like Jupiter, it has thin, dark rings that are too faint to be easily photographed. Since this planet can't readily be seen from Earth without a telescope, its existence wasn't recognized until the 1700s. Because of its distance from the Sun, Uranus is very cold, with temperatures near -215°C (-355°F) in the cloud tops.

NEPTUNE was discovered in the 1800s. It's a planet very similar to Uranus, but it doesn't have a severely tilted axis. Neptune's rings, like those of Jupiter and Uranus, are too faint to be seen from a distance. While Uranus' cloud tops present a pretty bland face, Neptune's atmosphere has swirling blue and white features.

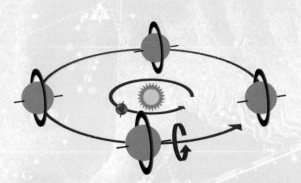

▲ **The tilt of Uranus' axis** is the most unique feature of this planet. In contrast to Earth's axis, Uranus' axis is tilted way over on its side. As Uranus revolves around the Sun, its poles take turns pointing toward the Sun.

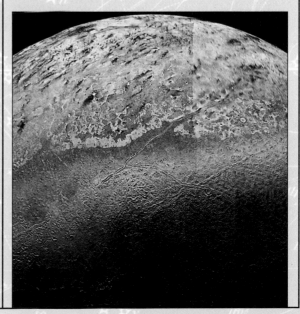

Triton is a rocky, ice-covered moon of Neptune that seems to be active despite being very cold. It has geyserlike features that send up plumes of material into Triton's thin atmosphere. ▼

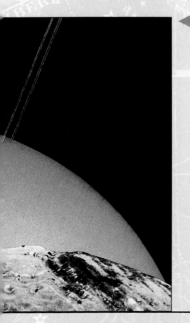

◀ **Uranus and its moon Miranda** (mə ran'də) are seen in this computer-generated photo. The picture shows what Uranus' faint rings might look like from nearby. Miranda has been called the most bizarre object in the solar system. Scientists think the patchwork appearance of its surface resulted when the moon was torn apart by collisions and then was reassembled by its own gravity.

♇ PLUTO

PLUTO is the most remote planet in the solar system— at least, it usually is! It's also the smallest planet, about the same size as Earth's Moon. Not much is known for sure about Pluto, since no space probe has ever visited it. Indeed, Pluto is so small and so far away that only Earth's most powerful telescopes can see it at all. The Hubble Space Telescope took this photo (*above*), which shows the planet and its one known moon, Charon (ker′ən). It's cold beyond imagination on Pluto, probably never warmer than −223°C (−370°F).

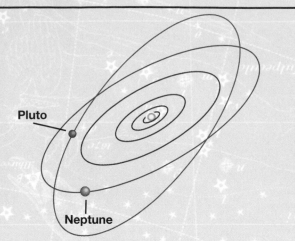

Pluto

Neptune

▲ **Pluto's unusual orbit** makes it the ninth planet most of the time but sometimes brings it inside the orbit of Neptune. When that happens, Pluto becomes the eighth planet and Neptune is the ninth! Pluto was closer to the Sun from 1979 to 1999.

◄ **Pluto's surface** may look something like this artist's view. Scientists think that Pluto's rocky ground is covered with a frost of frozen gases, under a very light atmosphere of methane and nitrogen. The artist has pictured the moon Charon and the tiny-looking Sun in Pluto's sky.

Internet Field Trip
Visit **www.eduplace.com** to learn more about the solar system.

INVESTIGATION 2 WRAP-UP

THINK IT WRITE IT

REVIEW

1. Compare Earth and the Moon.

2. Name and describe the sixth planet from the Sun.

CRITICAL THINKING

3. Describe some ways that the inner planets and the outer planets are alike and different.

4. Suppose you could set up a scientific outpost on any planet. Where would you build it? Explain your choice.

REFLECT & EVALUATE

Word Power

Write the letter of the term that best completes each sentence. *Not all terms will be used.*

1. Other than Pluto, the outer planets are called ——.
2. The idea that the Sun, Moon, and planets revolve around a motionless Earth is the ——.
3. How the universe began is described by the ——.
4. A star with objects revolving around it is a ——.
5. Earthlike planets are also called ——.

a. big-bang theory
b. gas giants
c. geocentric model
d. heliocentric model
e. satellite
f. solar system
g. terrestrial planets

Check What You Know

Write the term in each pair that best completes each sentence.

1. Scientists have a theory that our solar system formed about (10,000 years, 4.6 billion years) ago.
2. Mercury, Venus, Earth, and Mars are all (outer planets, inner planets).
3. The planet with the Great Red Spot is (Uranus, Jupiter).

Problem Solving

1. A friend tells you that Mars is the planet most like Earth. Explain why you agree or disagree.
2. Use sketches to illustrate some scientists' theories on how the solar system formed.

Use the information given here to help you arrange the planets in order of increasing distance from the Sun. Use the information from the chapter to make a labeled drawing of the solar system showing the relative sizes of the planets.

Planet	Period of Revolution (in Earth years)	Planet	Period of Revolution (in Earth years)
Saturn	29.46	Jupiter	11.86
Mars	1.88	Earth	1.00
Pluto	248.60	Mercury	0.24
Venus	0.62	Neptune	164.79
Uranus	84.01		

CHAPTER 3

STARS AND GALAXIES

The main entrance to an ancient ceremonial hall in New Mexico was built to face the North Star. The ceilings of some caves in Arizona are covered with ancient drawings of stars. Native Americans identified and located stars and planets thousands of years ago. Why did they do it? How accurate were they?

Connecting to Science
CULTURE

Ancient Astronomer Two thousand years ago in Mexico, a large city was laid out according to knowledge of the Sun, Moon, planets, and stars. Pyramids dedicated to the Sun and Moon were constructed in the city. A hall was built so that on the first day of spring it would align a distant point on Earth with the Sun.

Carved rocks found throughout the Americas were used to mark the rising and setting of stars. Early Native Americans designed a 365-day calendar and determined the four compass directions from their knowledge of the night sky.

Coming Up

◄ An ancient Native American rock carving of stars in New Mexico

WHAT ARE STARS, AND HOW DO THEY DIFFER?

When you look at the stars at night, do they all look the same? The next chance you get, look carefully at the night sky. You might be surprised at some of the differences you can observe among the stars.

Activity

Capturing Colors

Stars come in many colors. Find out how astronomers observe the colors in starlight.

MATERIALS

- lamp with a clear-glass bulb
- red and green filters
- spectroscope
- colored pencils
- *Science Notebook*

SAFETY

Do not touch the bulb.

Procedure

In a dark room, view a glowing light bulb. **Describe** what you see in your *Science Notebook*. **Observe** the bulb through a red filter, then through a green filter. **Describe** what you see through each. **Observe** the bulb through a spectroscope. **Draw** a color picture of the band of light, or spectrum, that you see. Place the red filter over the opening of the spectroscope, view the bulb, and **draw** a color picture of what you see. Do the same with the green filter.

Analyze and Conclude

1. How did the filters and the spectroscope affect the appearance of the bulb? Based on your observations, what can you **infer** about white light?

2. **Hypothesize** how astronomers might use spectroscopes and filters to help them obtain information about the stars.

Activity

How Big Is Betelgeuse?

Stars come in many sizes. Betelgeuse is a giant red star. Our Sun is a medium-sized yellow star. What would our solar system be like if Betelgeuse were our star? Find out!

Step 2

Procedure

1. On a large sheet of paper, **draw a model** of the solar system from the Sun to Jupiter. First, place a dot in the center of the paper. This dot represents the Sun in your model.

2. Using the data from the table below and a compass, **draw** the orbits of Mercury, Venus, Earth, and Mars. Use a string and pencil, as shown, to draw the orbit of Jupiter. Label each orbit.

3. Finally, **draw** a circle 12 cm in diameter (a radius of 6 cm) around the Sun in your model. Shade everything inside this circle red. This circle represents the giant red star Betelgeuse.

Math Hint *Remember, a diameter is a line segment that connects two points on a circle and passes through the center of the circle.*

Analyze and Conclude

1. Based on your model, **compare** the relative sizes of the Sun and Betelgeuse.

2. In your *Science Notebook*, **hypothesize** what would happen to Earth if our Sun were to grow to the size of Betelgeuse. Use your model to support your hypothesis.

Planet	Distance From the Sun
Mercury	1.2 cm
Venus	2.2 cm
Earth	3.0 cm
Mars	4.6 cm
Jupiter	15.6 cm

How Stars Differ

Reading Focus How are stars classified?

When Galileo first looked through his telescope at the night sky, he noticed differences among the stars. Some were extremely bright, but others seemed dim and plain. Scientists now know that stars differ from one another in many ways. Four of the obvious differences involve brightness, size, temperature, and color.

The Characteristics of Stars

You don't need a telescope to know that some stars are brighter than others. Stars also range in size from dwarfs to supergiants. The largest body in our solar system, the Sun, is an average-sized star with a diameter of about 1.4 million km (865,000 mi). A supergiant can have a diameter 1,000 times that of the Sun. Some dwarf stars have diameters less than half that of Earth.

The temperature and color of a star are closely linked. In fact, temperature determines a star's color, as it sometimes determines the color of heated materials on Earth. For example, melted iron that glows with a white light is hotter than heated iron that glows with an orange light.

Stars show a wide range of colors, indicating different temperatures. Astronomers use spectroscopes to study the light given off by stars, in much the same way as one is used to study light in the activity on page B54.

The surface temperatures of the hottest stars may be as high as 50,000°C (90,000°F). These stars shine with a bluish light, while the coolest stars shine with a red light. The table below shows the relationship between star color and temperature.

Star Color and Temperature		
Star Color	**Surface Temperature**	**Examples**
Blue	11,000°–50,000°C	Regulus, Rigel
Blue-white	7,500°–11,000°C	Deneb, Sirius
White	6,000°–7,500°C	Canopus, Procyon
Yellow	5,000°–6,000°C	The Sun, Alpha Centauri
Orange-red	3,500°–5,000°C	Aldebaran, Arcturus
Red	2,000°–3,500°C	Betelgeuse, Proxima Centauri

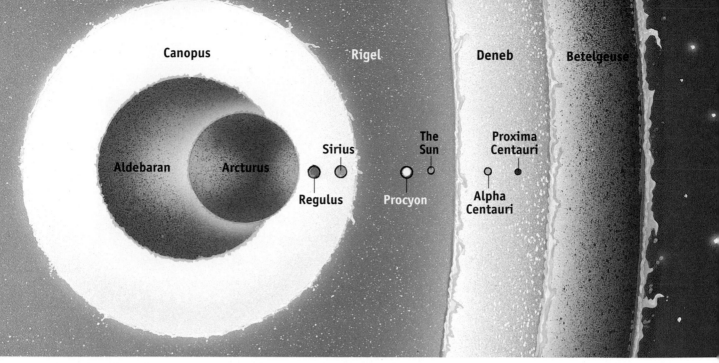

▲ **Stars of various sizes and colors**

The picture above shows the relative sizes of the stars in the table. Find the red star Betelgeuse, which is modeled in the activity on page B55. Now find the red star called Proxima Centauri. These two stars are the same color and so have similar surface temperatures. But, as you can see, stars of the same color can vary greatly in size.

How a Star Gets Its Energy

Although stars have different visible features, they all have one thing in common: the way they produce energy. A star is a huge ball of hot glowing gases. In the center of the star, energy comes from nuclear reactions that change hydrogen into helium. It's as if millions of hydrogen bombs were going off every second inside the star.

Unlike a hydrogen bomb, a star doesn't explode and fly apart. Its mass is so great that it is held together by its own gravity. So the energy released by the nuclear reactions moves throughout the star, generating heat and light. ■

INVESTIGATION 1 WRAP-UP

REVIEW

1. What are four ways in which stars differ from one another?

2. What is the temperature range of a "cool" star? of a "hot" star?

CRITICAL THINKING

3. How does our Sun differ in size and temperature from the star Rigel?

4. When viewed from Earth, a red star and a blue star appear to be equally bright. What could you infer about these two stars?

INVESTIGATION 2

HOW FAR AWAY ARE THE STARS?

If you traveled beyond our solar system at the speed of light, you could reach the closest one of these objects in about four years. What are these objects? They are stars.

Activity

Star Light, Star Bright

As you look up at the twinkling stars, some seem very bright. Others seem dim and almost disappear into the blackness of night. In this activity, find out why all stars don't shine with the same brightness.

MATERIALS
- grease pencil
- 2 flashlights of the same size
- transparent tape
- large sheet of white paper (poster size)
- metric ruler
- metric tape measure
- *Science Notebook*

Procedure

1. Use a grease pencil to **label** one flashlight *A* and another flashlight *B*. In your *Science Notebook*, **make a chart** like the one shown below.

Flashlight	Distance From Wall	Diameter of Circle of Light	Brightness
A			
B			

2. Attach a large sheet of white paper to a wall at about shoulder height. Darken the room.

3. Have one student stand at least 1 meter from the white paper. Ask this student to shine flashlight *A* on the paper.

4. Have a second student stand at least twice the distance from the paper as the first student is standing. Ask this student to shine flashlight *B* on the same paper, to the right of the light from flashlight *A*.

5. Have a third student use a metric ruler to **measure** the diameters of the central spots of light from flashlight *A* and flashlight *B*.

See **SCIENCE** and **MATH TOOLBOX** page H6 if you need to review *Using a Tape Measure or Ruler.*

6. With a measuring tape, **measure** the distance from the wall to flashlight *A*. Then **measure** the distance from the wall to flashlight *B*. **Record** this information in your *Science Notebook.*

7. **Compare** the brightness of the circles of light from each flashlight. **Record** which circle is brighter and which is dimmer.

8. **Compare** your results with those of other groups in your class.

Analyze and Conclude

1. What is the relationship between the distance of the flashlight from the paper and the diameter of the circle of light formed? **Hypothesize** why this relationship exists.

2. What is the relationship between the distance of the flashlight from the wall and the brightness of the circle of light?

3. From this activity, what can you **infer** about the apparent brightness of two identical stars at different distances from the Earth?

Step 4

INVESTIGATE FURTHER!

EXPERIMENT

Write a hypothesis on the appearance from Earth of a large star and a small star that are the same distance from Earth. Plan an experiment that would model how two stars of different sizes but the same distance from Earth would look from Earth. Tell what equipment you would use. Write the steps of the experiment. After you discuss the experiment with your teacher, actually do it.

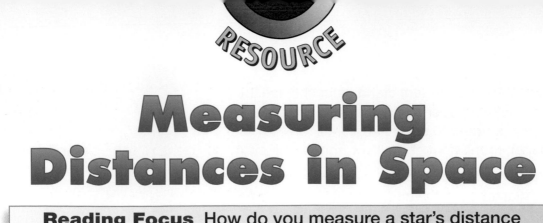
Measuring Distances in Space

Reading Focus How do you measure a star's distance from Earth?

Incredibly large distances separate stars from Earth. Scientists can't run a tape measure across space to measure these distances. Instead, they measure something called parallax (par'ə laks).

To understand parallax, try this exercise. Close one eye. Hold up one finger at arm's length. Line up your finger with a reference point, such as a mark on a chalkboard. Keeping your finger and head still, open your closed eye, and close the eye that was open. Observe how your finger *appears* to move in relation to your reference point.

In this exercise, nothing actually moved. But your finger appeared to shift position because you were viewing it from a slightly different location with your other eye. Such an apparent shift in position is called parallax.

Astronomers use parallax to figure out distances to nearby stars. As shown below, they view a star from two different places in Earth's orbit. Then they measure how far the star appeared to move in relation to other, more distant stars. They use this information to calculate the distance to the star.

Distance and Brightness

The measure of a star's brightness is called magnitude (mag'nə tood). Astronomers use a device called a photometer to measure how bright a star *appears* to be. That is the star's **apparent magnitude**, and it depends

▲ A student's finger appears to shift due to parallax, just as a star's position against more distant stars appears to shift.

on two things: (1) how far away the star is, and (2) the star's absolute magnitude. **Absolute magnitude** is a measure of how bright the star really is.

Imagine looking at a bonfire and a match. If these two sources of light are the same distance from you, the bonfire will seem brighter. However, if the bonfire is a kilometer away and the match is at arm's length, the match will appear brighter. The "absolute magnitudes" of the two light sources won't have changed—but their apparent magnitudes will vary with distance.

Astronomers can find the absolute magnitude of a star if they know the

star's apparent magnitude (which can be measured) and its distance from Earth (using the parallax method). They can also use apparent magnitude to estimate the distance to faraway stars, where parallax cannot be used.

Because distances between stars are so great, astronomers measure these distances using units called light-years. A **light-year** is the distance that light travels in one year. The speed of light is about 300,000 km (186,000 mi) per second. So a light-year is about 9.5 trillion km (5.9 trillion mi). Imagine having to write out numbers this great. ■

Using Math

The stars in the Big Dipper lie at different distances from Earth. About how much farther from Earth is the farthest star than the nearest?

200 180 160 140 120 100 80 60 40 20

light-years from Earth

INVESTIGATION 2 WRAP-UP

REVIEW

1. What is a star's absolute magnitude?

2. On what two things does a star's apparent magnitude depend?

CRITICAL THINKING

3. The star Sirius (sir'ē əs) appears to be about ten times brighter than the star Deneb. Yet scientists have found that Deneb gives off much more light than Sirius does. How can you explain this puzzling situation?

4. Why is the light-year a useful unit for measuring distances to stars?

INVESTIGATION 3

WHAT IS THE LIFE CYCLE OF A STAR?

The stars that you see today are the same ones that ancient astronomers viewed thousands of years ago. But stars do change over very long periods of time. In this investigation you'll discover the different stages a star can go through.

Activity

MATERIALS
• Science Notebook

Studying Nebulas

A nebula (neb'yə lə) *is a cloud of gases and dust in space. In this activity you'll learn about the role nebulas play in the life cycle of stars.*

▲ A nebula in Vela   ▲ The Orion Nebula   ▲ The Horsehead Nebula

B62

Procedure

1. Each of the six photographs on these two pages shows a nebula. Study the photos carefully and **describe** each one in your *Science Notebook*.

2. Astronomers think that stars form from the gases and dust that make up nebulas. **Identify** the photo or photos that show evidence that stars may have recently formed or may be forming now. **Describe your reasons** for choosing these photos.

3. It is thought that the gases and dust in nebulas come from old stars that have exploded. **Identify** the photo or photos that support this hypothesis. **Describe the evidence** you see in those photographs.

4. Under certain conditions, stars may form in groups or clusters. **Identify** the photo or photos that provide such evidence. **Explain the evidence** you see.

Analyze and Conclude

1. Compare the nebulas in the photographs. What characteristics do they have in common? How are they different?

2. Explain why you think astronomers study nebulas to learn about the life cycle of stars.

Technology Link CD-ROM

INVESTIGATE FURTHER!

Use the **Science Processor CD-ROM**, *The Solar System & Beyond* (Investigation 3, A Star Is Born!) to view the life cycle of a star.

▲ **The Helix Nebula**   ▲ **The Lagoon Nebula**   ▲ **The Pleiades**

The Life Cycle of a Star

Reading Focus What are the stages in the life cycle of a star?

Although a star is not a living thing, it has a "life cycle." Like a living thing, a star passes through several stages as it ages. These stages include birth, growth and development, middle age, old age, and death.

The life cycle of a star covers a huge span of time. For example, our Sun is a middle-aged yellow star of average size and temperature. It has been shining for about 4.6 billion years. It should continue to shine for another 4.6 billion years before it begins to change very much.

The Birth of a Star

Huge clouds of gases and dust, called **nebulas**, are scattered through many regions of space. Nebulas provide the raw materials from which stars form. Under certain conditions, portions of a nebula begin to contract, forming clumps of spinning gases. Over millions of years, gravity causes these clumps to shrink, or condense, into dense pockets of matter within the nebula. These pockets of matter form the beginnings of stars and are called **protostars** (prō'tō stärz).

Stages in the life cycle of stars. Each star's fate depends on its mass. ▼

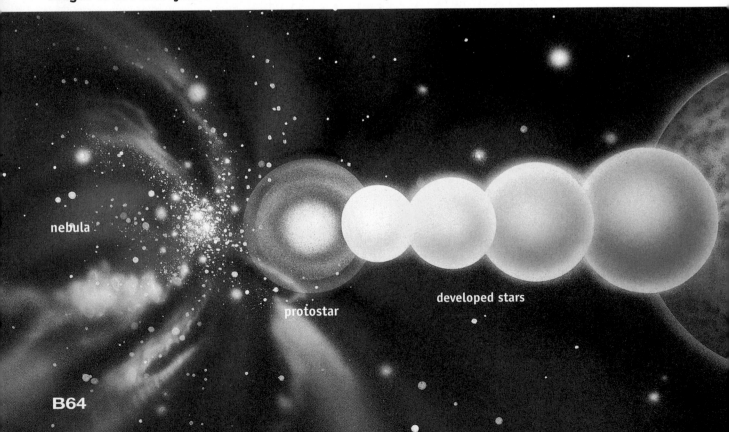

nebula

protostar

developed stars

As a protostar condenses, its particles are squeezed closer together, creating great pressure at the center. This pressure causes the core of the protostar to become very hot. When the core's temperature reaches about 10,000,000°C, nuclear reactions begin, releasing tremendous amounts of energy. At this point the protostar stops shrinking and begins to shine. It is now a star.

The Life of an Average Star

How long does a star "live"? The main factor that determines a star's life span—and the kind of death it will have—is the star's mass. A star of medium mass, like our Sun, shines for billions of years by changing its hydrogen into helium.

Eventually, though, the star's hydrogen fuel begins to run out. The star's core, now made up mostly of helium, shrinks and releases energy as it

collapses. This energy, when added to the energy of the remaining nuclear reactions, causes the outer layers of the star to expand far out into space. The star swells to many times its original size.

As the outer layers expand, they move farther from the star's hot core. The outer layers cool, the light reddens, and the star becomes a **red giant**. This is what will happen to our Sun, though not for billions of years.

After a long period as a red giant, the last traces of fuel will run out. Then the Sun will collapse again. It will become a **white dwarf**, not much larger than Earth is now. At this stage, the Sun will still be shining, but only dimly. The particles of matter in the Sun will be packed tightly together at a density a million times greater than that of water. Finally the Sun will die completely and become a cool, darkened **black dwarf**.

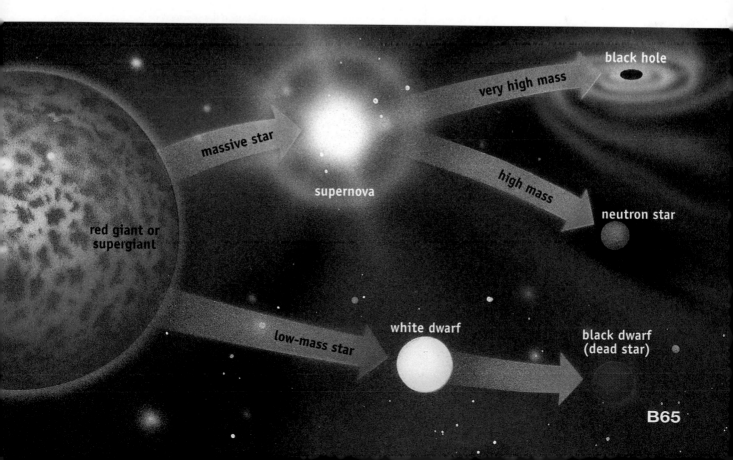

red giant or supergiant
massive star
supernova
very high mass
black hole
high mass
neutron star
low-mass star
white dwarf
black dwarf (dead star)

How Massive Stars Die

Stars that begin with much greater mass than our Sun live shorter lives. They also end their life in a much more spectacular fashion.

When a massive star forms, enormous pressure is created as it condenses. Although the early part of the life of a massive star is much like that of an average star, the larger star reaches the red-giant stage much sooner.

After that, the star's life is a constant battle between two opposing forces. The outward pressure caused by ever-increasing core temperatures opposes the inward push of gravity. As this battle is waged, the massive star may expand and contract several times before its "death."

When the star's fuel is finally used up, the outer layers of the star fall into the core at tremendous speeds. The great pressure created by the star's rapid contraction can result in a gigantic explosion known as a **supernova**. This is one of the most dazzling events in the universe. A supernova can appear as a bright "new" star in Earth's sky. It can produce as much light as an entire galaxy. The material released by a supernova includes elements from which future stars may be created. The Crab Nebula, shown on page B67, is the remains of a supernova.

Science in Literature

The Illustrated World of Space
by Iain Nicolson
Simon & Schuster Books
for Young Readers, 1991

BLACK HOLES— FACT OR FICTION?

"The pull of a black hole's gravity increases dramatically near its edge. The nose of an approaching spacecraft would be dragged toward the black hole, causing it to stretch. This stretching force (called a 'tidal force') would become so strong that the spacecraft would quickly be torn to shreds."

Black holes are one of the amazing features of space that you can read about in *The Illustrated World of Space* by Iain Nicolson. The book has some beautiful pictures that help you appreciate the incredible size of the universe.

▲ The Crab Nebula is what remains of a supernova observed by Chinese astronomers nearly 1,000 years ago.

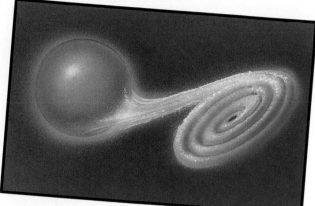

▲ A black hole—normally invisible—might be detected if material from a nearby star is pulled into it.

Neutron Stars and Black Holes

The life of a massive star doesn't end with a supernova. Some matter remains after the explosion. This material may become one of two space features. The surviving shrunken core of the star can become either a neutron star or a black hole.

In a **neutron star**, the collapse of the core is so powerful that it crushes the star's remaining matter. A typical neutron star is less than 20 km (12 mi) in diameter. Its material is so tightly packed that only a spoonful would weigh as much as a billion tons on Earth!

The collapse of the core of a massive star may be so powerful that it does not stop at the stage of a neutron star. The star may keep shrinking until it has collapsed to a tiny region, or point, with a very strong gravitational field. This region or point is called a **black hole**. The gravitational attraction of a black hole is so strong that absolutely nothing can escape it—not even light! ■

Internet Field Trip

Visit **www.eduplace.com** to learn more about the life cycle of a star.

━━━ INVESTIGATION 3 WRAP-UP ━━━

REVIEW **1.** What is meant by the phrase "a star's life cycle"?

2. How long does a medium-sized star, such as our Sun, "live"? What fuel does it use?

CRITICAL THINKING **3.** Compare the life cycle of an average-sized star with the life cycle of a very massive star.

4. The matter that makes up a star today may have been part of another star that died billions of years ago. How can this be?

INVESTIGATION 4

WHAT ARE GALAXIES, AND HOW DO THEY DIFFER?

Sometimes a point of light in the night sky looks like a single star. Actually it is a huge group of stars so far away that their light seems to come from a single source. Learn about these star collections, or galaxies.

Activity

Classifying Galaxies

Each night, astronomers study distant galaxies. In this activity you can observe and compare some, too.

Procedure

1. The photographs on these pages show several different galaxies. Study each galaxy carefully and **describe** it in your *Science Notebook*.

▲ The Large Magellanic Cloud   ▲ Galaxy NGC 7217   ▲ The Whirlpool Galaxy

▲ Galaxy NGC 1365

▲ The Centaurus A Galaxy

▲ The Small Magellanic Cloud

2. Different galaxies may have characteristics in common. These characteristics can be used to classify galaxies into groups. Study the photos on these pages again. Then **classify** the galaxies into two or more groups.

Analyze and Conclude

1. Based on your observations, **identify** one or more characteristics that all the galaxies have in common.

2. Identify the characteristics you used to classify the galaxies. How many different groups did you have?

3. Astronomers recognize three general classes of galaxies: spiral, elliptical, and irregular. Use these terms to **classify** each of the galaxies on these pages.

4. Before galaxies were properly identified, astronomers thought that such objects were nebulas. Recall that nebulas are huge clouds of gases and dust. **Compare** the characteristics of galaxies with those of nebulas. Why might astronomers have confused nebulas with galaxies?

The Milky Way and Other Galaxies

Reading Focus What is the Milky Way Galaxy like?

If a visitor from outer space asked you your address, what would you say? You'd probably mention a house or an apartment number, a street, a city or a town, and a state. You could then add a country and even a planet—Earth. But how could you tell the visitor the location of your planet?

Earth and eight other planets are members of a solar system, all revolving around a star we call the Sun. The solar system belongs to a gigantic cluster of stars known as the **Milky Way Galaxy**.

Our Sun is just one of more than 100 billion stars that make up the Milky Way.

Is there anything bigger than a galaxy? Yes, there is! You, your planet, your solar system, and your galaxy are all part of the universe. Recall that the universe includes absolutely everything that exists.

Building Blocks of the Universe

A **galaxy** is a huge collection of stars. A typical galaxy may contain hundreds of billions of stars, all revolving

The drawing shows the Milky Way Galaxy as it might look from another galaxy. Using a fraction, estimate the distance our solar system is from the center of the galaxy and its outer edges.

location of our solar system

▲ An elliptical galaxy　　　　▲ A spiral galaxy　　　　▲ An irregular galaxy

around a central core. Galaxies can be thought of as building blocks of the universe. The reason is that they're the largest single structures that astronomers have identified so far. There may be as many as 100 billion galaxies in the universe.

Edwin Hubble (1889–1953) is the man for whom the Hubble Space Telescope is named. Hubble was a well-known American astronomer who spent many years studying galaxies. He found that they can be classified into three basic groups, based on their shapes. Galaxies are classified in the activity on pages B68 and B69.

The most common type of galaxy is an elliptical galaxy that is shaped like a slightly flattened sphere, with no clear features. The second most common type is a spiral galaxy, with arms that make it resemble a pinwheel spinning in space. The third type of galaxy is irregular, having no definite shape.

The Milky Way Galaxy

The Milky Way is not a "special" galaxy in any way—except, of course, that you and everyone you know live inside it! The Milky Way is a spiral galaxy with at least two arms that extend out from a central bulge. This bulge is some 3,000 light-years in diameter. The solar system is in one of the spiral arms, about 26,000 light-years from the center. A trip from one side of our galaxy to the other, traveling at the speed of light, would take about 100,000 years.

From our location in one of the galaxy's arms, the Milky Way appears as a broad band of light stretching across Earth's night sky. You can see this band for yourself if you're out in

INVESTIGATE FURTHER!

RESEARCH

Learn more about how Edwin Hubble discovered that all galaxies are moving away from each other. Look up the term *Doppler effect* in a dictionary. Find out how the Doppler effect operates in everyday life—for example, when you hear a sound produced by a moving object, such as the whistle of a passing train. Then learn how Hubble applied this principle when he studied the colors of light produced by distant galaxies.

the country, away from bright city lights, on a clear, moonless night. The stars and dust clouds of our galaxy seem to form a milky-white path across the sky, giving the galaxy its name.

How Do Galaxies Move?

Every galaxy, in addition to rotating around its own imaginary axis, is also moving in another way. It was Edwin Hubble, in 1929, who discovered the second way that galaxies move.

While studying the light given off by distant galaxies, Hubble came to an amazing conclusion. He found that most galaxies seemed to be moving away from planet Earth. What would explain such an observation?

Hubble was smart enough to realize that his findings didn't mean that Earth lay at the center of the universe. He wasn't about to become another Ptolemy! Instead, Hubble realized that *all* galaxies, including our own Milky Way, are moving rapidly *away* from one another.

For help in visualizing this expanding universe, imagine a deflated balloon with many dots on its surface. What happens to the dots as you inflate the balloon? They all move away from one another. This is similar to what's going on in the universe. Pretend you're looking out from a dot that represents the Milky Way Galaxy. All the other dots on the balloon will appear to be moving away from you—even though you too are moving!

▲ **The expanding universe can be compared to a balloon that's being inflated.**

Hubble's discovery of the expanding universe later became an important part of the big-bang theory, which you learned about in Chapter 2. Hubble helped astronomers realize that the universe, a big place right now, is getting bigger and bigger all the time! ■

INVESTIGATION 4 WRAP-UP

REVIEW

1. What is the difference between a galaxy and the universe? Which is larger?

2. Name and describe three types of galaxies.

CRITICAL THINKING

3. In the past, many astronomers thought that the universe was steady and unchanging. How did Edwin Hubble's discovery and conclusions contradict that view of the universe?

4. Describe a simple model that explains Edwin Hubble's theory of the universe.

CHAPTER 3 REVIEW

REFLECT & EVALUATE

Word Power

Write the letter of the term that best matches the definition. *Not all terms will be used.*

1. Unit used to measure distances between stars
2. Huge cloud of gases and dust that can be found in many regions of space
3. Pockets of matter that form stars
4. Gigantic collection of stars
5. How bright a star appears to be

a. absolute magnitude
b. apparent magnitude
c. galaxy
d. light-year
e. nebula
f. protostars
g. supernova
h. white dwarf

Check What You Know

Write the term in each pair that best completes each sentence.

1. Edwin Hubble discovered that galaxies are moving (toward, away from) each other.
2. When a star collapses into a tiny region, it is called a (protostar, black hole).
3. The final stage in the life cycle of a star like our Sun is a (nebula, black dwarf).
4. The general shape of the Milky Way Galaxy is (spiral, elliptical).

Problem Solving

1. Two stars have the same absolute magnitude, yet one seems very bright and the other very dim. Explain how this could happen.
2. Make a list showing the relative size of each of the following, from the smallest to the largest: planet, galaxy, universe, solar system, black dwarf.
3. Describe the movement of the Milky Way Galaxy as seen from another galaxy.

Identify each type of galaxy. Explain which is most like the Milky Way Galaxy. Make a drawing of the Milky Way Galaxy and indicate the position of our solar system.

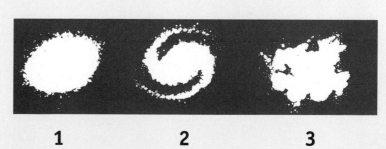

1   2   3

B73

CHAPTER 4

LIVING IN SPACE

"Houston? We have just received a signal that may have been sent by alien beings! Request advice." Will the International Space Station send this kind of message some day? What should we be doing to prepare for such an event?

PEOPLE USING SCIENCE

Astronaut Dr. Ellen Ochoa once said, "Only you put limitations on yourself about what you can achieve, so don't be afraid to reach for the stars." She took her own advice quite literally, becoming the first Latina astronaut to fly in space. She flew in space shuttle missions in 1993 and 1994 and has logged almost 500 hours in space.

She grew up in California and earned her doctorate in electrical engineering at Stanford University. She has won several honors, including the Women in Aerospace Outstanding Achievement Award. In addition to her accomplishments in the space program she holds patents for optical technologies and is both a classical flutist and a private pilot.

Coming Up

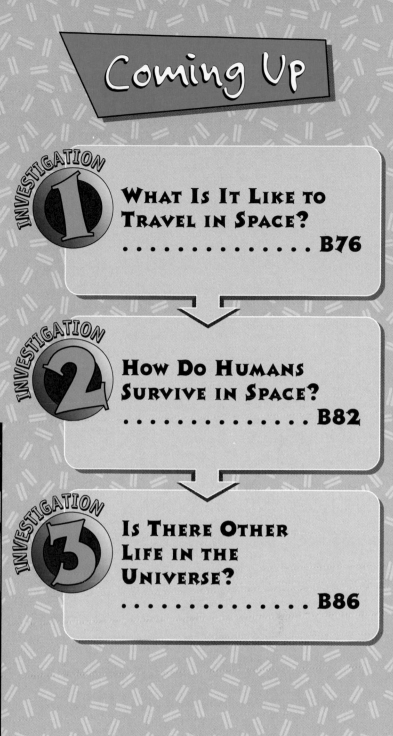
◀ Dr. Ellen Ochoa in orbit aboard the space shuttle

INVESTIGATION 1

WHAT IS IT LIKE TO TRAVEL IN SPACE?

Imagine floating as if you had no weight at all. This is what you would experience if you were in orbit on a space shuttle. In this investigation you'll learn what causes the experience of "weightlessness" and how it can make many everyday activities unique.

Activity

Free Falling

What does the term free fall *mean? How does it affect astronauts? Find out!*

MATERIALS

- goggles
- paper cup
- string
- scissors
- metal washer
- *Science Notebook*

SAFETY /////

Wear goggles during this activity.

Procedure

1. Punch small holes on opposite sides of a paper cup, below the rim. Make a handle by pushing each end of a string through one of the holes. Then tie a knot in each end.

2. Next put a shorter length of string through a washer. Tie both ends of this string to the handle. The washer should hang about even with the top of the cup, as shown.

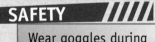
Step 2

3. Hold the cup with one hand. Hold the handle of the cup with the other hand. Release only the handle as you continue to hold the cup. **Observe** what happens. **Record** the results in your *Science Notebook*.

Step 3

4. Hold the cup by the handle at waist height. Then release both the cup and handle. With members of your group, watch the objects fall. Listen for the sound of the cup hitting the floor and the sound of the washer hitting the bottom of the cup. **Record** when you hear each sound.

5. Repeat step 4 at least three times. Make sure the objects fall straight to the floor without hitting each other on the way. Make sure you can tell when the two sounds occur. **Observe** whether each sound always occurs at about the same time.

6. Draw four pictures showing step 4. Show what the cup setup looks like (a) just before you let it drop, as you hold it up by the strings; (b) when it's falling in midair; (c) at the moment the cup touches the floor; and (d) at the moment the washer touches the bottom of the cup.

Analyze and Conclude

1. Compare how the washer fell in step 3 with the way the washer and cup fell in step 4. **Suggest a hypothesis** to explain the differences you observed.

2. Pretend you are a tiny bug sitting on the washer. How would you feel when the washer is released? How would the cup below you look as both objects fall toward the ground in step 4? Would the cup appear to stay the same distance away from you or not? At what point would you start to move closer to the cup?

3. An astronaut in a spaceship orbiting Earth is said to be in "free fall," with both the astronaut and the space-ship "falling" around Earth. **Infer** how this activity might relate to astronauts feeling weightless in orbit. If the imaginary bug on the washer represents an astronaut, what does the cup represent?

4. Infer some ways that free fall would affect an astro-naut. **Discuss** your inferences with your group.

INVESTIGATE FURTHER!

EXPERIMENT

Punch a small hole in the side of a plastic-foam cup, near the cup's bottom. Fill the cup with water and hold it over a sink. What happens? Refill the cup with your finger over the hole. With your teacher's supervision, observe the hole as you drop the cup into the sink from as great a height as possi-ble. What happens? Suggest a hypothesis that would explain your observations.

Activity

Eating and Drinking in Space

Can you swallow in space if you are in free fall? Try this activity and see.

Procedure

1. Pour water into a sealable plastic bag until the bag is about half full. Insert a plastic straw into the top of the bag.

2. Seal the bag around the straw. Wrap tape around the straw where it enters the bag to keep water from escaping.

3. Prop up one end of a bench by placing books under the legs, so that this end is 7 or 8 cm higher than the other. Lie on your stomach on the bench, with your feet at the high end and your head extending out over the low end.

4. Have a group member hold the plastic bag so that it is several centimeters below your head. Try to suck water into your mouth through the straw.

Step 2

Analyze and Conclude

1. In your *Science Notebook*, **describe** the path of the water from the bag to your stomach. Is it going uphill or downhill?

2. **Hypothesize** whether gravity is necessary when you eat. Does gravity move food from your mouth to your stomach? How do you know?

3. Based on your experiment, **infer** whether astronauts can drink from a squeeze bottle in space.

Step 4

Living in Free Fall

Reading Focus What is it like to be inside a spacecraft orbiting Earth?

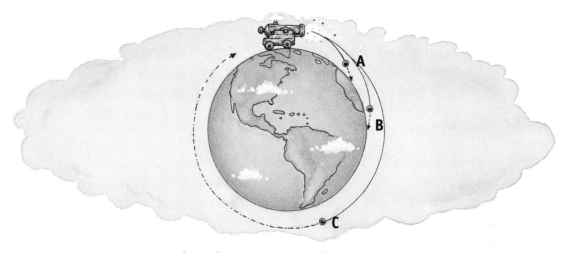

▲ An imaginary cannonball goes into orbit.

Imagine that you had a huge cannon, like the one in the picture above. If you shot a cannonball, like ball *A*, as shown, it would arc down toward the ground because of Earth's gravity. If you shot a second ball, ball *B*, with more speed, it would go farther before it fell. If you could shoot a third cannonball, ball *C*, with so much speed that the arc of its fall matched the curve of Earth, the ball would go into orbit.

The third cannonball would still be falling because of Earth's gravity, but Earth's gravitational pull would also keep the cannonball from flying off into space. All other things being equal, the imaginary ball would keep falling forever around and around Earth. That's what it's like to be in orbit and experience **free fall**, the motion of a freely falling object.

Coasting "Weightless" in Space

People often refer to free fall as "weightlessness" or "zero gravity." Although these terms describe the way objects appear to behave in free fall, they are not completely accurate.

Astronauts are not really totally weightless in space. They just feel that way because they and their spacecraft are falling. Have you ever gone high up on a swing and felt weightless for a split second at the top? You weren't *really* weightless—but you *were* in free fall for an instant!

There's still plenty of gravity present in an orbiting spacecraft. You'd have to be millions of kilometers farther away

Internet Field Trip

Visit **www.eduplace.com** to find out more about living in space.

to escape the effects of Earth's gravity. It's just that you don't feel the effects of gravity in free fall, because there's nothing resisting your fall.

Most of the time, an orbiting spacecraft coasts with its engines off, literally just falling around planet Earth. Astronauts inside the craft are falling along with it, just as the washer falls along with the cup in the activity on pages B76 and B77. Like an imaginary bug on a washer, the astronauts feel weightless as they fall.

On Board the Space Shuttle

For a space shuttle crew, weightlessness is both enjoyable and challenging. Imagine being able to float all over the shuttle's cabin, with hardly any effort! All you need to get around is a little push.

Most astronauts experience a little motion sickness at the beginning of a space flight, but then they adjust to weightlessness. Soon they can eat, drink, sleep, and do just about anything else they might do on Earth.

Food and drink must be kept in sealed packages and consumed carefully so that pieces and droplets don't float around the cabin. Each crew member has a sleeping bag that can be tied to the wall, floor, or ceiling. If the bag weren't tied down, the dozing astronaut would float around the space shuttle.

Taking showers or baths in space is difficult, so shuttle astronauts wash by wetting a cloth with a water gun. Instead of plumbing that relies on gravity, the shuttle toilet uses suction to draw the waste away like a vacuum cleaner.

The human body is suited to function where the pull of gravity is resisted by Earth's surface. In free fall the body undergoes many changes, which are described on page B81.

When astronauts return to Earth, it takes just a short time for their muscles to adjust to gravity again. But weightlessness for long periods could have permanent effects on the human body. Many questions must be answered before humans can take extended trips in space.

An orbiting space shuttle and the astronauts inside it are in free fall. ▼

Technology Link
CD-ROM

INVESTIGATE FURTHER!

Use the **Science Processor CD-ROM**, *The Solar System and Beyond* (Investigation 4, Shuttle Ride) to take a journey on a space shuttle and learn how it feels to be in space.

When free fall begins, blood moves from your legs toward your head. Your face swells, and you feel like you have a stuffed-up nose. You must drink extra liquids to replace lost fluids until your body reaches a new fluid balance.

Your heart has less work to do to pump blood in free fall. It may become a little smaller—and a lot lazier—until it resumes its normal workload on Earth.

Your waistline gets thinner as your body's fluids are redistributed. Because gravity no longer compresses your spine, you'll be about 2.5 cm (1 in.) taller in space.

Your bones lose calcium in space. Doctors aren't sure if the body can fully recover from the calcium loss caused by a very long space flight.

All the muscles of your body have much less work to do in space. You should exercise as much as possible to keep your muscles in shape.

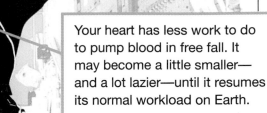

▲ **How the human body adjusts to free fall**

INVESTIGATION 1 WRAP-UP

REVIEW

1. Describe some of the challenges faced by astronauts living in a space shuttle.

2. Describe three changes that take place in the body during free fall.

CRITICAL THINKING

3. Explain why the term *zero gravity* is not completely accurate in describing conditions in an orbiting spacecraft.

4. Astronauts train for weightlessness by riding in a plane that goes into a steep dive. How is the dive like being in orbit?

HOW DO HUMANS SURVIVE IN SPACE?

What would you pack for a trip to another planet? You'd need more than just a change of clothing! What would you eat and drink? What would you breathe? What would you use for shelter? In this investigation you'll think about what humans need to survive and then explore some answers to these questions.

Activity

Survival on the Moon

What are the most important supplies you'd need to survive on the Moon? Pretend you're a stranded astronaut and figure out the answer.

Procedure

1. Imagine that your spacecraft has just crash-landed in daylight on the Moon. You were scheduled to meet the command ship 320 km (about 200 mi) away on the lighted surface of the Moon, but the rough landing has destroyed all the equipment on board. All that is left are the 15 items listed at the right. Your crew's survival depends on reaching the mother ship. Some supplies will be critical for the long trip to meet the command ship. But you don't want to carry the extra weight of items you cannot use.

MATERIALS
• **Science Notebook**

first-aid kit containing bandages, medicines, injection needles, and related items

packages of food concentrate

solar-powered portable heating unit

self-inflating life raft

magnetic compass

map of the stars

box of matches

2 large tanks of oxygen

parachute silk

2 pistols

packages of powdered milk

solar-powered radio receiver and transmitter

nylon rope

signal flares

5 containers of water

2. In your *Science Notebook*, make a list of the 15 items. Number the items in order of importance, with the number 1 indicating the most important item for survival. **Discuss** your choices with your group before assigning each number. Keep in mind that you might wish to use some items for purposes other than those originally intended.

Analyze and Conclude

1. Identify the objects that are most critical to your survival. Why are they so important?

2. Identify the objects that are useless. Why?

3. Identify any objects you could use in ways for which they were not originally intended. How would you use them?

4. Compare your group's rankings with the rankings provided by your teacher, which come from NASA—the U.S. space agency. Subtract to find the difference between each item's NASA ranking and your own group's ranking for it. Add up all the differences to find your total score.

5. Compare your score to the figures below to see how well your group did.

UNIT PROJECT LINK

For your space-station simulator, create a life-support storage area and a kitchen. In the life-support storage area, use large sheets of paper as the fronts of storage lockers for water and oxygen tanks. Decide what foods you would store in the kitchen and how much water and oxygen you'd need for one month. Plan a space meal, using only foods that astronauts can store and eat easily in free fall.

Technology Link

For more help with your Unit Project, go to **www.eduplace.com**.

0–25	Excellent
26–32	Good
33–45	Average
46–55	Fair
56–70	Poor
71–112	Stay home!

International Space Station

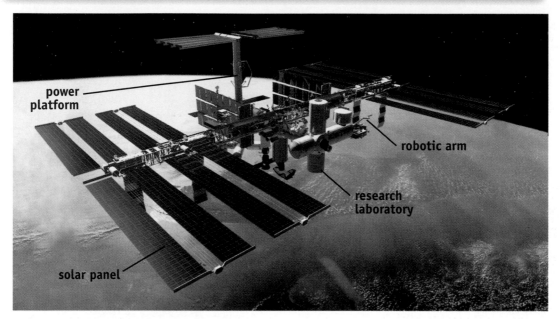

power platform

robotic arm

research laboratory

solar panel

▲ **The completed ISS will be longer than a football field. With its solar panels it will be 108.6 m (358.4 ft) long and 79.9 m (263.7 ft) wide.**

An international space project is underway. Scientists and engineers from 16 countries are designing and building the International Space Station (ISS). The first four crews to live and work on the ISS come from the United States and Russia. These crews are constructing the ISS in space.

Spacewalks

From 1998 to 2004, more than 90 spacewalks have been scheduled. Astronauts will spend hundreds of hours building the ISS. When finished, it will be home for up to seven astronauts.

Why build a space station? First, it's a great adventure to be able to live and work in space. Second, the ISS is a permanent space laboratory with people working in it for as long as a year.

The ISS provides a unique environment that is nearly free of the effects of gravity. This condition of very low gravity is called **microgravity**. Many experiments in medical science are planned for the ISS under microgravity. The results of these experiments may help fight diseases such as the flu, diabetes, cancer, and AIDS.

Living in Space

All the living and nonliving things on Earth together form a self-contained system. The food, water, carbon dioxide, oxygen, and nitrogen that are needed for life are here on Earth.

When astronauts go out into space on short trips, they don't need to worry about recycling resources. They just carry enough food, water, and oxygen to last the length of the trip. But for longer voyages, such as on the International Space Station, they need to recycle water, carbon dioxide, and other materials.

On the ISS the astronauts will grow wheat, rice, soybeans, and peanuts in space gardens. By growing their own food, ISS crews will be less dependent on shipments from Earth. They'll also be investigating how well plants grow in microgravity.

The food the astronauts eat on the ISS is "out of this world." Cooks in the best kitchens on Earth are working hard to give the ISS crews tasty and nutritious foods. The astronauts have a microwave oven, rice cooker, bread machine, and machine for making tofu and soy milk.

Space Tools

New tools assist the astronauts in their work. One is a 16.5 m (55 ft) long robotic "arm" that can move along the outside of the ISS and pick up large, heavy objects. This robotic arm, called the "Canadian Hand," helps astronauts assemble and maintain the space station. Another tool is a robotic "eye" that can fly around and inspect the outer surface of the ISS for trouble spots. ■

The robotic arm, known as the "Canadian Hand" ▼

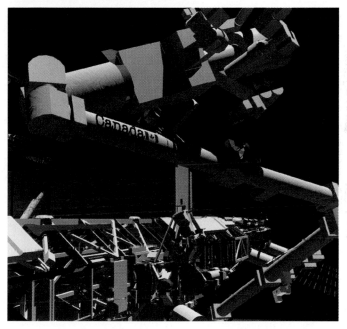

INVESTIGATION 2 WRAP-UP

REVIEW

1. What is microgravity?

2. Give an example of how the ISS could help people on Earth.

CRITICAL THINKING

3. Why do you think it's a good idea to make the space station an *international* project?

4. Suppose you could live for a year on the ISS. Give reasons why you would or would not want to go on this mission.

IS THERE OTHER LIFE IN THE UNIVERSE?

Have you ever watched a science fiction movie about aliens from outer space? How did the movie director imagine they looked? In this investigation you'll learn what astronomers think the possibilities are for finding life beyond planet Earth.

Activity

A Postcard From Earth

If intelligent life exists beyond Earth, that life could be very different from intelligent life as we know it. How would you communicate with a being from another planet? Give it a try!

Procedure

1. On the front side of a blank postcard, **draw** a scene of Earth. Use your scene to tell about Earth and about yourself. Be careful not to draw things that might confuse an alien being who is unfamiliar with Earth.

2. On the back side of the card, **draw** a diagram or map that might tell an alien being where your planet is located. Remember that residents of another planet may not be able to read English or any other Earth language. Use symbols that might mean something to an alien being.

Step 2

Analyze and Conclude

1. Exchange postcards with a classmate.

2. In your *Science Notebook*, make a list of all the things you are able to learn about Earth from your classmate's post-card. Look for as many things as possible.

3. Make a second list of all the things in the postcard that could be misinterpreted. Look at the card as if you were a being from another planet. You wouldn't even know when a picture was right side up!

4. **Share** your lists with your classmate. See if the two of you can think of ways to improve both postcards. Make a third postcard with ideas that you've thought up together.

5. **Infer** how easy or hard it might be for humans to communicate someday with beings from another planet. What might some of the problems be? What ways of communicating might work best? What things might alien beings and humans have in common that could help us understand one another?

▲ **How would you try to communicate with another species here on Earth?**

INVESTIGATE FURTHER!

EXPERIMENT

Plan an experiment that would test how humans communicate with another species, such as a chimpanzee or a dolphin. Begin by writing a hypothesis that you could test. Decide what steps you would take. Then list any special equipment you would need. How might your experiment be applied to communicating with beings from another planet?

Messages to the Stars

Reading Focus What are some ways scientists are trying to communicate with alien beings?

How would you talk to an extraterrestrial (eks trə tə-res'trē əl)? What would you say, and how would you say it? And just what *is* an extraterrestrial, anyway?

The word **extraterrestrial** can be used to describe anything that comes from beyond Earth. Meteorites, for example, are said to be of extraterrestrial origin. But when most people say *extraterrestrial*, they mean a living being from outer space.

Humans tend to think a lot about the possibility of life on other planets. Some people even believe that Earth has already been visited by aliens traveling in unidentified flying objects, or UFOs. But no proof exists that anything like this has ever happened.

Even though scientists are doubtful about the idea that aliens have visited Earth, many scientists do think it's possible for life to *exist* beyond our own planet. Some scientists have even gone so far as to try to send a message to any extraterrestrial civilization that might be out there, waiting.

One method of communicating with an alien civilization would be by using pictures, as is done in the activity on pages B86 and B87. That's what the

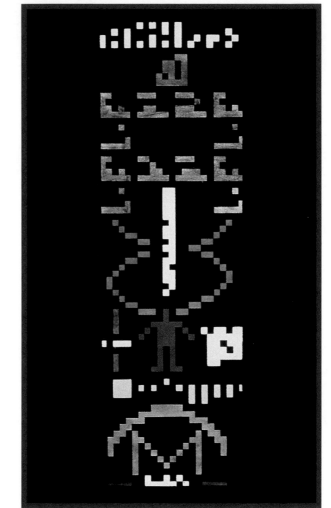

▲ **Frank Drake's radio message**

scientists did who launched the *Pioneer 10* and *11* space probes back in 1972.

Each Pioneer spacecraft was equipped with a gold plaque that was designed to tell any extraterrestrials it might encounter what the beings were like who made it and where it came from. On each plaque is a drawing of a man and a woman and a map of our solar system. A line shows the probe's course away from Earth.

Another way to communicate is to use radio or television signals. Without meaning to, humans have been broadcasting messages for decades! Ordinary radio and TV signals travel at the speed of light out into space. If there are any aliens out there, the first sign they get of intelligent life on Earth could be a broadcast of music!

Scientists have used a radio telescope to send messages out into space intended for any extraterrestrials they might reach. In 1974, astronomer Frank Drake sent out a pattern of on-and-off signals that could be decoded into pictures of a human, a DNA molecule, and our solar system.

The most elaborate message yet is one that relies heavily on sound. In 1977 this message was placed on board the *Voyager 1* and *2* probes which explored the outer solar system.

Each Voyager probe carries a disk made of gold-plated copper, designed to operate like an old-fashioned phonograph record. Called *The Sounds of Earth,* each 30-cm (12-in.) disk includes greetings spoken in 54 different Earth languages. There is also music that ranges from Beethoven to African and Mexican folk songs to jazz and rock. There are natural sounds such as a barking dog, the song of a whale, and the cry of a newborn baby.

Each Voyager record has instructions on how to play it. However, before the aliens can receive their message, they will have to figure out how to build their own record player! ■

▼ **The Voyager message disk**

▲ **A Voyager space probe receives its message disk.**

The Search for Intelligent Life

Reading Focus Do you think there is life on other planets?

Men and women from every era have spent time dreaming about the possibility of life existing on other planets. Despite possible evidence that tiny organisms may have once lived on Mars, scientists haven't found a single living cell from another planet. But every time we get a clearer peek into the universe, we come closer to answering questions about extraterrestrial life.

How We Search for Life

Radio telescopes are one of the major ways we get that clearer peek. A radio telescope is not a telescope in the visual sense at all. You can't look through one and see anything. Instead, a **radio telescope** is a gigantic antenna that receives radio signals.

The first radio telescope was built in 1931 as an aerial for studying static

Science in Literature

SPACE SHIPS WANTED

"Wanted: A small space ship about eight feet long, built by a boy, or by two boys, between the ages of eight and eleven. . . . No adult should be consulted as to its plan or method of construction. An adventure and a chance to do a good deed await the boys who build the best space ship. Please bring your ship *as soon as possible* to Mr. Tyco M. Bass, 5 Thallo Street."

So begins the adventure of *The Wonderful Flight to the Mushroom Planet* by Eleanor Cameron. You can still enjoy this space adventure even though it was written a half century ago.

The Wonderful Flight to the Mushroom Planet
by Eleanor Cameron
Little, Brown and Company, 1954

Book 1 in the Mushroom Planet Series

THE WONDERFUL FLIGHT TO THE MUSHROOM PLANET
Eleanor Cameron

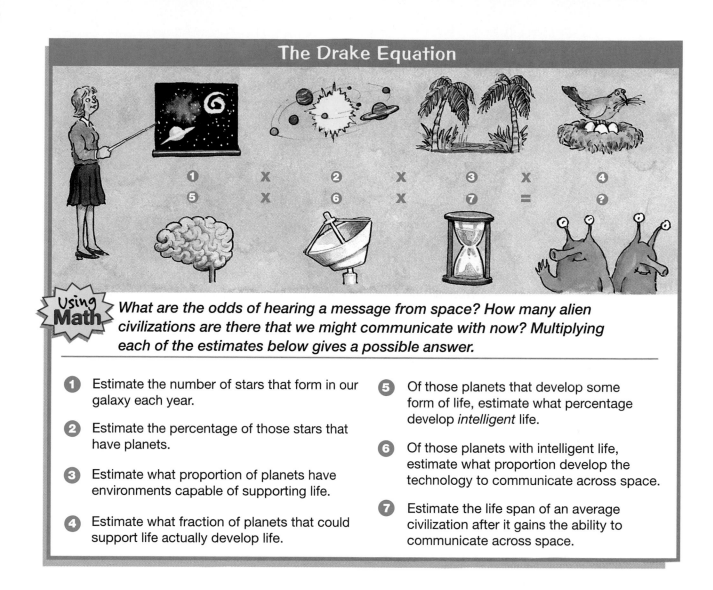

The Drake Equation

Using Math

What are the odds of hearing a message from space? How many alien civilizations are there that we might communicate with now? Multiplying each of the estimates below gives a possible answer.

1. Estimate the number of stars that form in our galaxy each year.

2. Estimate the percentage of those stars that have planets.

3. Estimate what proportion of planets have environments capable of supporting life.

4. Estimate what fraction of planets that could support life actually develop life.

5. Of those planets that develop some form of life, estimate what percentage develop *intelligent* life.

6. Of those planets with intelligent life, estimate what proportion develop the technology to communicate across space.

7. Estimate the life span of an average civilization after it gains the ability to communicate across space.

that was interfering with radio transmissions. Scientists found that this "static" was coming from the Milky Way. They soon discovered that radio waves are generated naturally by stars, planets, and other objects in space.

Astronomers interested in the possibility of extraterrestrial life realized that radio might be a good way to detect a distant civilization. If humans have been unintentionally sending radio signals out into space since the 1920s, perhaps alien beings have also been broadcasting news of their existence.

In the 1960s, astronomer Frank Drake began listening for radio signals from nearby stars that are like the Sun. This was the beginning of what we now call the search for extraterrestrial intelligence, or SETI. Today, SETI involves radio telescopes as large as 304 m (about 1,000 ft) in diameter that can pick up faint signals from as far away as 15,000 light-years.

Frank Drake has considered the odds that SETI might someday be successful. The equation he developed to estimate those odds is shown in the box above. Look especially at the last factor in the equation. Factor 7 may seem out of place with the rest, but it's one of the most important pieces of the puzzle.

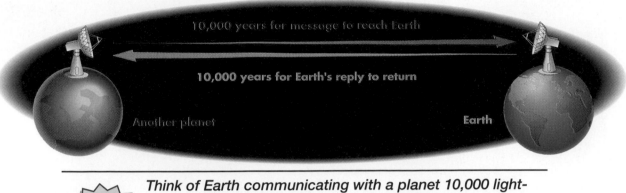

10,000 years for message to reach Earth

10,000 years for Earth's reply to return

Another planet

Earth

> **Using Math** *Think of Earth communicating with a planet 10,000 light-years away. Suppose a message from Earth was sent today and a return message was sent on the day it was received. In what year would it reach Earth?*

Remember how large the distances between stars are? What if a civilization 10,000 light-years from Earth were to send a radio message in our direction? Traveling at the speed of light, that message would take 10,000 years to reach us. If aliens sent the message today, would humans still be here to receive it in 10,000 years? If they were, and if they immediately sent a reply, would the civilization that sent the first message still be around to receive the answer after another 10,000 years? That would be 20,000 years after they sent their first signal.

What if aliens had sent a message out 20,000 years ago? After a 10,000-year

trip, the message would have reached Earth around 8000 B.C. Would anyone have had a radio back then to pick up the signal?

When you look at the Drake equation on the previous page, it should be clear to you that there are no firm numbers for any of its steps. Nobody knows how often planets develop or how often intelligent life evolves. Many scientists think it's probable that life exists elsewhere in the universe, but the chance that we'll have a two-way conversation with that life appears slim. If we keep on trying, however, someday we may just get lucky! ∎

INVESTIGATION 3 WRAP-UP

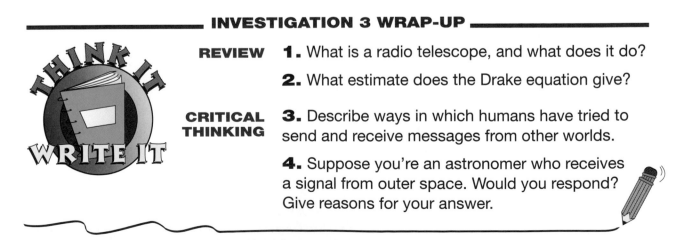

REVIEW

1. What is a radio telescope, and what does it do?

2. What estimate does the Drake equation give?

CRITICAL THINKING

3. Describe ways in which humans have tried to send and receive messages from other worlds.

4. Suppose you're an astronomer who receives a signal from outer space. Would you respond? Give reasons for your answer.

REFLECT & EVALUATE

Word Power

Write the letter of the term that best completes each sentence. *Not all terms will be used.*

1. A huge antenna that receives radio signals is a/an ___.
2. The condition of very low gravity is ___.
3. The near-weightlessness that an astronaut experiences when in orbit is called ___.
4. A living being from outer space is known as a/an ___.

a. extraterrestrial
b. free fall
c. International Space Station
d. microgravity
e. refracting telescope
f. reflecting telescope
g. radio telescope

Check What You Know

Write the term in each pair that best completes each sentence.

1. An object in orbit stays in orbit because of (weightlessness, gravitational pull).
2. Astronauts in free fall become (shorter, taller).
3. The Drake equation estimates the odds of communicating with (beings from another planet, humans traveling to Mars).

Problem Solving

1. Suppose that scientists received a radio signal and determined that it came from alien beings on another planet. Do you think humans would be able to communicate with those who sent the signal? Why or why not?
2. What are some advantages and disadvantages of sending robots to do research in space?

BUILD YOUR PORTFOLIO

Copy this drawing of the cannonballs and Earth. Explain why cannonball C orbits Earth but cannonballs A and B do not.

Drawing Conclusions

Writers often imply, or hint at, more information than they actually state. They give you clues and expect you to figure out the rest, using what you already know. Suppose an author writes "The car slid across the road, spun around, hit a fence, and came to rest in a snowbank." You can conclude that the road was slippery from snow or ice and that condition is what probably caused the accident.

Consider these questions as you draw conclusions.

- What did the author write?
- What do I know?
- What is my conclusion?

Read the paragraph. Then complete the exercises that follow.

Putting Telescopes in Space

Today there is a large telescope in orbit around Earth. The Hubble Space Telescope (HST) is positioned beyond our planet's atmosphere, so it avoids distortions caused by looking through the air. Even though the mirror in the HST is smaller than that of many telescopes on Earth, it can see more clearly and see objects that are fainter and farther away than telescopes on the ground can see. Space telescopes can even see wavelengths of light that aren't visible from Earth's surface.

1. **Which statement is a conclusion you can draw from the paragraph? Write the letter of that statement.**

   a. It was easy to place the HST in space.

   b. Earth's atmosphere limits what we can learn about space.

   c. The mirror in the HST is too small to see beyond Earth's atmosphere.

   d. The HST has changed our understanding of the Sun.

2. **What was the most important clue in helping you draw that conclusion?**

Analyze Data

The table compares gravity on other planets to gravity on Earth.

Surface Gravity on the Planets								
Planet	Mercury	Venus	Earth	Mars	Jupiter	Saturn	Neptune	Uranus	Pluto
Gravity	0.38	0.90	1.00	0.38	2.64	1.14	0.91	1.20	0.04

 Notice that gravity on Earth
is equal to 1.

Use the information in the table to complete the exercises that follow.

1. On which planet is gravity closest to Earth's gravity?

2. On which planet would an object weigh about the same as it would on Mars?

3. On which planets would your science textbook weigh less than it does on Earth? On which planets would it weigh more?

4. What is the difference in gravity between the planet with the greatest gravity and the planet with the least gravity?

5. Suppose a newly-discovered planet has gravity equal to three times that of Venus. In terms of its gravity, which of the known planets would the new planet be most like?

You may wish to use a calculator for Exercises 6 through 8.

6. Gravity on Saturn is about three times the gravity of which planets?

7. Gravity on Earth is about six times greater than gravity on the Moon. What decimal number might be used to represent the moon's gravity?

8. If a book weighed 1 pound on Pluto, how many pounds would it weigh on Earth?

WRAP-UP!

On your own, use scientific methods to investigate a question about the solar system.

THINK LIKE A SCIENTIST

Ask a Question

Pose a question about a planet, a star, or another object in the night sky that you would like to investigate. For example, ask, "If I am standing at the South Pole, can I see the star Polaris?"

Make a Hypothesis

Suggest a hypothesis that is a possible answer to the question. One hypothesis is that Polaris, also called the North Star, cannot be seen by someone standing at the South Pole.

Plan and Do a Test

Plan an experiment that uses models to determine whether Polaris can be seen from the South Pole. You could begin by using a globe of Earth and a paper circle to represent Polaris. Develop a procedure that uses these materials to test the hypothesis. With permission, carry out your experiment. Follow the safety guidelines on pages S14–S15.

Record and Analyze

Observe carefully and record your data accurately. Make repeated observations by moving the objects in your model.

Draw Conclusions

Look for evidence to support the hypothesis or to show that it is false. Draw conclusions about the hypothesis. Repeat the experiment to verify the results.

WRITING IN SCIENCE
Research Report

Research information about comets and what scientists hope to learn from them. Present your findings in a research report. Use these guidelines to prepare your report.

- Gather information from several sources.
- Organize the information in order of importance.
- Draw a conclusion from your research.

B96

UNIT C

The Nature of Matter

Theme: Scale

THINK
LIKE A SCIENTIST

BERRY, BERRY COLD

Have you ever seen a tree or a bush after an ice storm? If so, it may have looked something like the tree in the photo. The day before the photo was taken, the branches and berries were dry. During the night, rain covered the tree with water. Then a drop in the air temperature caused the water to lose heat. The result is ice-encrusted berries. Scientists study such changes in water and in other kinds of matter. They also study how energy is related to these changes.

THINK LIKE A SCIENTIST

Questioning In this unit you'll study how changes in energy are related to changes in state, such as freezing and melting. You'll investigate questions such as these.

- How Does Energy Affect Matter?
- How Can Matter Change?

Observing, Testing, Hypothesizing
In the Activity "Cooling Race," you'll compare the cooling rates of water mixed with ice cubes and water mixed with crushed ice. You'll hypothesize what happens to heat energy in the water as it cools.

Researching In the Resource "Particle Energy," you'll learn about the relationship between temperature, heat, and the energy of particles that make up matter. You'll also find out how this energy is involved in changes in state.

Drawing Conclusions After you've completed your investigations, you'll draw conclusions about what you've learned—and get new ideas.

CHAPTER 1

CHARACTERISTICS OF MATTER

When you take ice cubes from the freezer of your refrigerator, you are removing solid chunks of water. Yesterday, you put liquid water in the ice-cube trays. Besides becoming cold and solid, how else has the water changed? Have the mass, density, and volume of the water been affected?

PEOPLE USING SCIENCE

Glaciologist Erik Blake surveys the bleak, white landscape around him. As a glaciologist (glā shē äl'ə-jist), or scientist who studies glaciers, he is exploring Hubbard Glacier in Canada's Yukon Territory.

A glacier is a giant mass of ice that moves slowly over land. The Hubbard Glacier is among the largest in North America. The glacier is a natural laboratory for Blake. He seeks to understand how it moves and the kinds of wildlife found in this harsh environment. By studying ice cores taken from deep in the glacier, he can learn what conditions were like thousands of years ago, when the ice formed.

Where a glacier meets the ocean, great mountains of ice break off and fall into the sea. Yet these massive ice mountains float! What questions would you like to ask about how glacial ice differs from liquid water?

Coming Up

◀ Erik Blake, glaciologist

HOW CAN YOU DESCRIBE MATTER?

Suppose you were asked to compare a brick and a basketball. List the characteristics you would use to describe each object. Could another person identify both objects based on your lists?

Activity

A Matter of Mass

A golf ball and a table-tennis ball are about the same size. Which contains more matter? How can you measure the amount of matter in an object?

MATERIALS

- 3 sealed containers, labeled *A, B,* and *C*
- balance and masses
- *Science Notebook*

Procedure

1. Look at the three containers your teacher will provide. Without picking them up, **compare** their sizes and shapes. **Record** your observations in your *Science Notebook*.

2. Now pick up each container, but don't shake it. Based on the way the containers feel, arrange them in order from heaviest to lightest.

3. **Make a chart** like the one shown.

4. Using a balance, **measure** in grams the **mass**—the amount of matter—of each container. **Record** the results in your chart.

Container	Mass (g)	Contents
A		
B		
C		

Step 2

See **SCIENCE** and **MATH TOOLBOX** page H9 if you need to review *Using a Balance.*

Step 4

5. One container is filled with sand, one with water, and one with cotton. Based on your observations, **infer** which material is in each container. In the *Contents* column of your chart, **record** your inferences. Then open each container and check your inferences.

Analyze and Conclude

1. By studying and handling the containers, what can you **infer** about the amount of space taken up by each of the materials?

2. What did you learn about the amount of matter in each container? How did you learn this?

3. **Describe** what you learned about mass and matter by doing this activity.

Science in Literature

CAN ICE SINK?

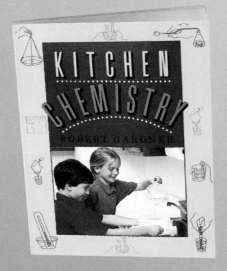

Kitchen Chemistry
by Robert Gardner
Julian Messner, 1988

"Place an ice cube in a glass of water. Why do you think it floats? . . . Now add an ice cube to half a glass of alcohol. Why do you think the ice sinks?

An ice cube will float in cooking oil, but just barely. It's beautiful to see because the melting ice forms giant drops of water that flow ever so slowly through the clear, thick oil. It's like watching rain drops falling in slow motion."

Read *Kitchen Chemistry* by Robert Gardner to find out how to complete this experiment and for other fun ways to explore matter.

Activity

A Matter of Space

Does a softball take up more space than a shoe? Try to describe the amount of space each of these objects takes up. Does the amount of matter an object contains affect how much space it takes up?

Procedure

1. If you place some cotton in one container and an equal mass of sand in another container, **predict** which material will take up more space.

2. Fill a plastic bag with cotton balls. Put as much cotton as you can in the bag without squashing it down.

3. Use a balance to **measure** the mass of the cotton. **Record** this measurement in your *Science Notebook*.

4. Remove the bag of cotton from the balance. Place another plastic bag on the empty balance pan. Add sand to the bag until it has the same mass as the bag of cotton.

5. Pour the sand from the plastic bag into a measuring cup. **Measure** and **record** how many milliliters of sand were in the bag. Then pour the sand back into its original container.

 See **SCIENCE** *and* **MATH TOOLBOX** page H7 if you need to review *Measuring Volume.*

Step 5

6. Take the cotton balls from the bag and push them down into the measuring cup. **Record** how many milliliters of cotton you have. You may have to fill the cup more than once.

Analyze and Conclude

1. Which bag contained more mass, the bag of cotton or the bag of sand?

2. Which material took up more space, cotton or sand?

3. Can an object's volume be determined just from its mass? Explain your answer.

Activity
Checking for Purity

The sphere and cube are about the same size. One is made of clay; the other is a mixture of clay and some lighter material. How can you tell which is which?

Procedure

1. Study a clay ball and a clay cube carefully. You may handle them, but do not change either object's shape or size. **Make inferences** about the mass and volume of each object and **record** your inferences in your *Science Notebook*.

Step 1

 Math Hint *Record your inferences using the >, <, or = symbols.*

2. **Measure** and **record** the mass of each object.

3. Half fill a measuring cup with water. **Record** the water volume in milliliters.

4. Carefully place the ball in the measuring cup. **Observe** what happens to the water level. **Record** the new volume reading. **Calculate** the volume of the ball. Then remove the ball, shaking any excess water into the measuring cup.

5. Repeat step 4 with the cube.

Analyze and Conclude

1. What did you **infer** about the mass and volume of the two objects in step 1?

2. How did the masses of the ball and cube compare?

3. What did the changing water level in the measuring cup tell you about each object?

4. **Hypothesize** which object is made of pure clay and which is made of clay and some lighter material. Give evidence to support your hypothesis.

Measuring Mass and Volume

Reading Focus How can you find the mass and volume of an object?

▲ **Which package would you rather be holding?**

It's a cold day, and you and a friend are standing at a bus stop. You've been shopping, and you each have a package to hold. One package is quite heavy; the other is lighter but is larger and more bulky. Which package would you choose to hold?

Like everything around you, the packages are made up of matter. **Matter** is anything that has mass and volume. In fact, the problem of which package is easier to hold involves these two physical properties—mass and volume. As seen in the activities on pages C6 to C8, these properties can be measured. To review and practice your skills for measuring these and other

properties, read pages H6 to H9 in the Science and Math Toolbox.

Mass

The heaviness of each package is directly related to its mass. **Mass** is a measure of how much matter something contains. Weight is a measure of the force of gravity acting on a mass. So the more matter an object contains—the greater its mass—the more it will weigh.

A spring scale, which is used to weigh objects, measures the effect of gravity on an object. To find an object's mass, you have to use a balance, like the one shown on page C11.

Finding the Mass of an Object
The mass of an object is found by placing the object in one pan of a balance and objects of known masses in the other.

The most common metric units used to measure mass are grams (g) and kilograms (kg). A penny has a mass of about 2 g. A kilogram is one thousand times the mass of a gram. A large cantaloupe has a mass of about 1 kg.

Other units are also used for measuring mass in the metric system. For example, the mass of a very light object could be measured in milligrams (mg). One milligram is equal to one thousandth ($\frac{1}{1000}$) of a gram.

Volume

The **volume** of an object is the amount of space it takes up. For example, an inflated balloon takes up more space—has greater volume—than an empty balloon. Volume can also be used to express *capacity*—that is, how much material something can hold. A swimming pool can hold a lot more water than a teacup can.

The basic unit of volume in the metric system is the cubic meter (m³). But because 1 m³ is such a large amount, the liter (L) is more commonly used. A liter (lēt'ər) is slightly larger than a quart. Many soft drinks are sold in 2-L containers. Units used to measure smaller volumes include the centiliter (cL), which is one hundredth of a liter, and the milliliter (mL), which is one thousandth of a liter.

A graduated cylinder, which is often called a graduate, is used to measure liquid volumes. Using a graduate is similar to using a measuring cup.

90
80 — meniscus
70
60

Using Math *For most liquids the surface of the liquid in the graduate curves upward at the sides of the glass. This curved surface is called a meniscus (mə nis'kəs). To find the volume of the liquid, read the mark that lines up with the bottom of the meniscus. What is the volume?*

Suppose you want to know how much water or some other liquid is in a container of some kind. First you pour the liquid from the container into a graduate. Then you measure the level of the liquid against the scale marked on the side of the graduate.

There are two methods for finding the volume of a solid. One method is used for finding volumes of solids that have regular geometric shapes, such as cubes, spheres, and rectangular blocks. For any solid with a regular shape, you can measure such dimensions as length, width, height, and diameter. Then you can calculate the volume of the solid by substituting the measurements in a mathematical formula. For example, the volume of a rectangular block can be found by multiplying its length times its width times its height.

The formula for this calculation is below.

$$V = l \times w \times h$$

Many solids do not have a regular shape. A rock, for example, is likely to have an irregular shape. The volume of these kinds of solids can be found by using the water displacement method.

Suppose you want to use the water displacement method to find the volume of a rock, such as the one shown in the picture. The first step is to find a graduate large enough to hold the rock. Next, you fill the graduate about one-third full with water. Then you lower the rock into the graduate, as shown. ■

Internet Field Trip
Visit **www.eduplace.com** to find out more about measurement.

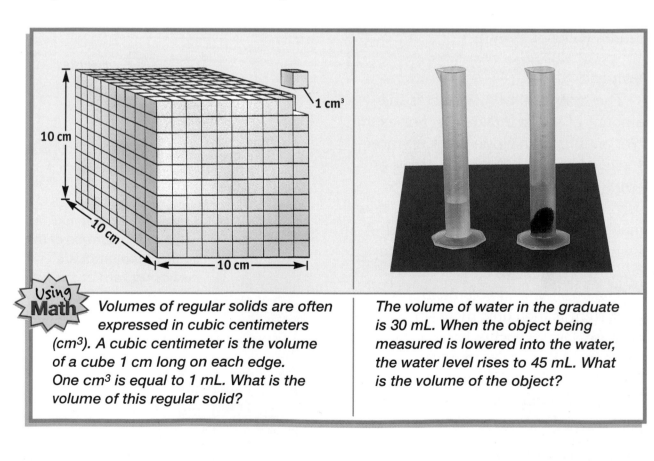

Using Math *Volumes of regular solids are often expressed in cubic centimeters (cm³). A cubic centimeter is the volume of a cube 1 cm long on each edge. One cm³ is equal to 1 mL. What is the volume of this regular solid?*

The volume of water in the graduate is 30 mL. When the object being measured is lowered into the water, the water level rises to 45 mL. What is the volume of the object?

Density

Reading Focus What is density, and how is it measured?

Imagine yourself in this situation. You have just packed and sealed two identical boxes. One box contains a down pillow, and the other box contains books. But you have forgotten which box contains which item. How can you solve this problem without opening one of the boxes? All you have to do is pick up each box. The box containing books will be much heavier than the one containing the pillow.

Density

You solved your problem by comparing the masses of two objects having equal volumes. That is, you used a property of matter—density—to solve your problem. **Density** is the amount of mass in a certain volume of matter.

Look at the photo below. What will happen if the block on the left is replaced with another block made of the same stuff, but equal in size (volume) to the block on the right? The

balance will tilt to the left. The block on the left has the greater density.

You can calculate the density of any sample of matter if you know two things—its mass and its volume. You can find the density of the sample by dividing its mass by its volume. The formula for finding density is below.

$$D = m/v$$

For example, suppose you are working with a piece of metal that has a volume of 2.0 mL and a mass of 9.0 g. By using the formula, you can determine the density of that metal. Notice that density measurements always include mass and volume units.

$$D = 9.0 \text{ g}/2.0 \text{ mL} = 4.5 \text{ g/mL}$$

Using Density to Identify Matter

Density is a characteristic property of all matter. This means that a particular kind of matter always has the same

Understanding Density
Since the two blocks balance each other, they must have the same mass. But the block on the left is obviously smaller than the one on the right—its volume is less. Thus the block on the left has a greater density than the block on the right. ▶

C13

The ball and ring are both made of brass. When they are at the same temperature (*left*), the ball fits easily through the ring. How does heating the ball affect its volume (*right*)?

density, regardless of where the matter comes from or where it is measured.

For example, the density of pure water is 1.0 g/mL. This means that a milliliter of water has a mass of 1 g. The table below gives the densities of some common materials.

Since every substance has a definite density, this property can be used to identify materials. For example, suppose you measure the mass and volume of an object and find its density is 7.9 g/mL. Could you make a reasonable guess as to what material the object is made of? You could if you had a table of densities like the one on this page. Use the table to find what the object is most likely made of.

Density and Temperature

Notice that the table lists the densities of the materials at a particular temperature—in this case, 20°C. This is done because temperature affects density. As a general rule, matter expands when it gains heat and contracts when it loses heat. In other words, the volume of a material increases as its temperature goes up and decreases as its temperature goes down.

How does a change in volume affect density? Look again at the formula for density: $D = m/v$. If the mass of a material doesn't change and the volume of the material increases, its density decreases. On the other hand, if the volume of a material decreases and its

Densities of Some Common Materials at 20°C			
Material	**Density (g/mL)**	**Material**	**Density (g/mL)**
gold	19.3	water	1.0
lead	11.3	oil	0.90
silver	10.5	wood (oak)	0.7
copper	8.9	wood (pine)	0.4
iron	7.9	oxygen	0.0014
aluminum	2.7	helium	0.0002

mass stays the same, its density increases. How does heating the ball shown on page C14 change its density?

Float or Sink?

Density can be useful in predicting whether an object will sink or float in water. The density of water is 1.0 g/mL. Any material with a density less than 1.0 g/mL will float in water. Anything with a density greater than 1.0 g/mL will sink. How might such information be useful?

Imagine you're going to boil some eggs. You want to be sure the eggs aren't spoiled. The density of a fresh egg is about 1.2 g/mL. The density of a spoiled egg is about 0.9 g/mL. If you place an egg in water and it floats, what does this tell you about the egg?

Density in Calculations

Density can also be used to answer questions about the purity of a material. Suppose you have a chunk of metal with a volume of 10 mL. You're told that the metal is pure silver. How could you find out for sure?

You could start by looking up the density of silver, which is 10.5 g/mL. This tells you that 1 mL of silver has a mass of 10.5 g. So 10 mL of pure silver will have a mass of 10 × 10.5 g, or 105 g. Now all you have to do is measure the mass of your chunk of metal. ■

Technology Link
CD-ROM

INVESTIGATE FURTHER!

Use the **Science Processor CD-ROM**, *The Nature of Matter* (Investigation 1, Good as Gold) to travel to San Francisco during the 1849 gold rush. While there, decide whether a miner is trying to sell you real gold or fool's gold.

INVESTIGATION 1 WRAP-UP

THINK IT WRITE IT

REVIEW

1. Define *mass*, *volume*, and *density*.

2. How can you find the volume of a cube and of an irregularly shaped object?

CRITICAL THINKING

3. When might you want to find the density of an object?

4. Suppose you have a 10-g cube that floats in water and a 10-g sphere that does not. What can you infer about the volume of each object? Why?

WHAT MAKES UP MATTER?

Think about what happens when water is spilled on a kitchen countertop. If you wipe the countertop with a dry sponge, where does the water go? How is the sponge different from the countertop? In this investigation you'll find out how the particles that make up matter give matter its properties.

Activity

Always Room for More

When you add sugar to a glass of iced tea, where does the sugar go? How does the sugar "fit" into the full glass?

MATERIALS
- goggles
- 2 plastic cups
- marbles
- spoon
- sand
- water
- sugar
- *Science Notebook*

SAFETY //////
Wear goggles during this activity.

Procedure

1. Fill a cup to the brim with marbles. **Infer** whether the cup is full or whether there is room for more matter. **Record** your inference in your *Science Notebook*.

2. Using a spoon, carefully add sand to the cup. Gently tap the sides of the cup as you add the sand. Continue until no more sand will fit in the cup. **Make an inference** about the space in the cup now.

3. Slowly and carefully pour water into the cup until no more water can be added.

4. Fill a second cup with water. Carefully add a spoonful of sugar and stir. **Record** your observations.

Step 1

Step 3

Step 4

Analyze and Conclude

1. Was any matter in the cup before you added the marbles? If so, what happened to it?

2. Why could the cup full of marbles still hold sand and water?

3. How would this activity have been different if you had started by filling the cup with water?

4. Use your observations of the first cup to **infer** what happened to the sugar that was added to the second cup. How does the sugar "fit" in the water?

5. Make a sketch of what you think the mixture of sugar and water would look like if you could see how the two materials fit together.

Technology Link
CD-ROM

INVESTIGATE FURTHER!

Use the **Science Processor CD-ROM**, *The Nature of Matter* (Unit Opening Investigation, What's the Matter?) to compare the characteristics of liquids, solids, and gases.

Activity

Racing Liquids

A paper towel soaks up water. Do other types of paper do the same? Paper strips can help you model how particles are packed in different materials.

MATERIALS
- goggles
- metric ruler
- scissors
- paper towel
- brown paper bag
- typing paper
- waxed paper
- filter paper
- hand lens
- tape
- wire coat hanger
- large flat pan
- water
- food coloring
- *Science Notebook*

Procedure

1. Cut a strip 2.5 cm wide and 15 cm long from each kind of paper in the Materials list. Cut one end of each strip to form a point.

See **SCIENCE** *and* **MATH TOOLBOX** page H6 if you need to review *Using a Tape Measure or Ruler.*

2. Study dry samples of each kind of paper with a hand lens. In your *Science Notebook*, **describe** how they are different. **Predict** which paper strip water will move through most quickly.

3. Tape the strips to the bottom of a coat hanger so that the points of the tips hang the same distance below the hanger.

4. Pour water into a pan and add a few drops of food coloring to the water. Hold the coat hanger above the pan so that the tips of the paper strips touch the water.

5. **Observe** as the water "races" up the strips. When the water reaches the top of one strip, remove the hanger. Then lay all five strips of paper on a flat surface.

SAFETY

Wear goggles during this activity. Handle scissors with care.

Step 4

Analyze and Conclude

1. Using the distances that water traveled through the strips, **list** the types of paper in order from fastest to slowest.

2. Imagine that you could observe the water and paper through an extremely high powered microscope. **Make a sketch** showing how you think the water moves through the paper.

3. Do samples of matter contain "empty" spaces? **Give evidence** to support your conclusion. Then reexamine your conclusion and determine what additional information, if any, is needed to support your conclusion.

Structure of Matter

Reading Focus What are some effects of the motion of particles of matter?

▲ **Even in still air, specks of dust dance and dart about.**

Picture yourself sitting in your room on a summer afternoon. There's nothing to do. You're so bored that you begin staring at the specks of dust dancing in a beam of sunlight. You notice that the specks dart about as if they were being stirred by an invisible hand. What could be moving the dust around?

Particles in Motion

The moving specks of dust offer evidence of the structure of matter. Matter is composed of very tiny particles that are constantly in motion. These particles are much smaller than the tiniest speck of dust. They are so small that they can't be seen, even with the best microscope in your school.

Air is made up of such particles, moving through space. As the particles of air move about, they collide with each other and with everything in your room, including the specks of dust. The movements of dust specks are caused by particles of air bouncing the specks of dust around!

Inflated objects, such as balloons and basketballs, provide evidence that air is made up of particles. When you put air into a container, the moving air particles continuously bang against the sides of the container. It's these collisions that keep objects inflated.

Air, of course, is a gas. Actually it's a mixture of several different gases. Because gases are invisible, it's easy to think of them as being made up of tiny moving particles. But what about other forms of matter? What evidence do we have that liquids and solids are made up

Evidence for Particle Motion

▲ A colored liquid being added to water

▲ The mixture 5 minutes later

▲ The mixture after an additional 10 minutes

of moving particles? Look at the photographs at the left on this page.

❶ Like still air in a room, the water in the jar seems calm. Yet the water and the colored liquid mix together. This mixing shows that liquids, like gases, are made up of moving particles.

❷ As the particles of water and colored liquid bump into each other, the particles spread out and mixing occurs.

❸ If left to stand, the particles of colored liquid and water continue to move until they are evenly mixed together.

So evidence indicates that gases and liquids are made up of tiny moving particles. What about solids? It's hard to visualize something as hard and unchanging as a rock or your desk being made up of moving particles. But it's true! You'll find out about evidence that supports this idea as you read on.

States of Matter

Think about some kinds of matter that you see every day, such as air, water, and cloth. They can all be classified into one of three major categories, or states. The three common **states of matter** are solid, liquid, and gas. Study the drawings and descriptions of these states on page C21.

As you have just read, solids, liquids, and gases are all made up of tiny particles in constant motion. The particles that make up a substance are attracted to each other to some degree. The state in which a substance is found depends on two things: how fast the particles are moving and how strongly the particles are attracted to each other.

The forces of attraction among particles are different for different substances. For example, particles of helium gas barely attract each other at all. These particles fly around even when moving at fairly slow speeds.

Particles of water have slightly stronger attractions to each other.

These particles have to be moving at a pretty good speed before they actually separate and fly around. The chemical forces between particles of iron are very strong. These particles have to be moving at very high speeds before they overcome the forces of attraction and fly around. ■

States of Matter

SOLIDS
In a solid, chemical forces hold the particles in place. The particles vibrate back and forth but don't leave their positions. This is why a solid keeps its shape.

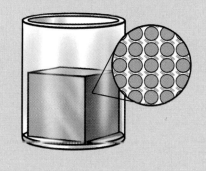

LIQUIDS
In a liquid, particles move faster and farther apart than particles in a solid. The particles in a liquid can slip and slide past each other. This is why a liquid has no definite shape.

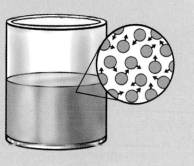

GASES
In a gas, particles move so fast that chemical forces can't hold them together. This is why particles in a gas spread out to fill their container and why gas has no definite shape or volume.

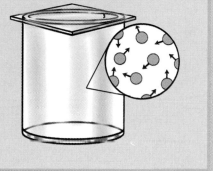

─── **INVESTIGATION 2 WRAP-UP** ───

REVIEW

1. What is matter made of?

2. Why do solids have a definite shape but liquids and gases do not?

CRITICAL THINKING

3. Iron expands when it is heated. Draw a sketch of how the particles of a piece of iron might look at 10°C and at 50°C.

4. If you add 2 mL of sugar to 100 mL of water, the volume of the water does not change. What do you think will happen if you keep adding more and more sugar? Why?

How Does Energy Affect Matter?

What happens when you put some hard kernels of corn in a pan, hold the pan over a fire, and shake it? A few minutes later you have popcorn! In this investigation you'll find out how energy changes matter in different ways.

Activity

Cooling Race

Suppose you are enjoying a glass of lemonade on a hot day. What happens to your drink when you add ice cubes? How do the ice cubes change? Can these changes be described in terms of energy?

- -

Procedure

1. **Make a chart** in your *Science Notebook* like the one below.

2. Half fill two plastic cups with water. Put a thermometer in each cup. **Record** the water temperature under *Start* in your chart.

MATERIALS
- 2 plastic cups
- 2 thermometers
- water
- 2 different colored markers
- ice cubes
- 2 small plastic bags
- balance and masses
- spoon
- crushed ice
- timer
- graph paper
- *Science Notebook*

Water Temperature						
	Start	**3 min**	**6 min**	**9 min**	**12 min**	**15 min**
Water + Ice Cubes						
Water + Crushed Ice						

3. Put two ice cubes in a plastic bag and set them on one pan of a balance. Place a second bag on the other pan. Use a spoon to add crushed ice to this bag until the pans balance.

4. Add the ice cubes to one cup and the crushed ice to the other cup.

5. At three-minute intervals, **measure** the temperature of the water in each cup. **Record** each measurement in your chart. Continue for 15 minutes.

6. **Make a line graph** that shows how the temperature of the ice-water mixtures changed over time. Use a different color for each line on your graph.

See **SCIENCE** and **MATH TOOLBOX** page H13 if you need to review **Making a Line Graph**.

Analyze and Conclude

1. **Describe** how the ice in each cup changed.

2. In which cup did the ice change faster?

3. In which cup did the water cool more quickly? What difference between the ice cubes and the crushed ice might explain why the water in one cup cooled faster?

4. Heat energy is needed to melt ice. **Suggest a hypothesis** to explain where the heat energy came from. **Give evidence** to support your hypothesis.

5. The water contained more heat energy at the start of the activity than it did at the end. **Hypothesize** what happened to this heat energy. Support your hypothesis.

INVESTIGATE FURTHER!

EXPERIMENT

Predict the changes that would occur if you added an equal number of ice cubes to both a glass of cold water and a glass of warm water. Try the experiment and check your predictions.

C23

Activity
Speeding Up Change

Wet your finger and hold it up in the air. How does it feel? Does the feeling change when you blow on the finger? What does energy have to do with these changes?

MATERIALS
- dropper
- water
- 4 small dishes
- timer
- *Science Notebook*

Procedure

1. Use a dropper to place a small drop of water in a dish. Place a drop of the same size in a second dish. Set one dish in direct sunlight and the other in a cool, shaded spot. **Predict** what will happen to the two drops of water.

2. Allow the dishes to stand undisturbed, checking on the water drops every few minutes. Each time you check, **record** your observations and the time in your *Science Notebook*.

3. Between observations, **brainstorm** with members of your group. Try to think of ways to make a drop of water evaporate faster. **Record** your suggestions.

4. Put identical drops of water in two dry dishes. Leave one drop alone. **Experiment** with the other drop to see if you can make it evaporate.

5. Repeat step 4 for each technique you try. **Record** each technique and **describe** your results.

Step 4

Analyze and Conclude

1. Which drop of water from step 1 evaporated more quickly? **Suggest a hypothesis** to explain your results.

2. What techniques were successful in causing a drop of water to evaporate faster? Explain why you think each technique was successful.

3. **Make a general statement** about what causes water to evaporate.

Particle Energy

Reading Focus How is the motion of particles involved in changes of state?

Using Math

Water is the only common substance that can be found in all three states of matter at the same time and place. Earth's atmosphere contains only 0.001 percent of all the fresh water on Earth. What fraction is equivalent to 0.001 percent?

Picture in your mind a sample of iron. You probably see a hard, grayish solid. This is the state in which iron is usually found. But under the proper conditions, iron can also exist as a liquid. It can even exist as a gas!

Most forms of matter can exist in all three states—solid, liquid, and gas. Perhaps the best example of a substance in all three states is water. You are familiar with water as a solid (ice), a liquid, and a gas (water vapor).

You have also seen water change state. You have seen ice melt, puddles "dry up," and water vapor change to a liquid and fog up a mirror. In the activities on pages C22 to C24, water

changes from the solid state to the liquid state; it also changes from the liquid state to the gas state.

Materials change state when energy is added to them or taken away from them. These changes can be understood by thinking about the motion of the particles that make up all matter.

Energy and Temperature

You know that a thrown ball or a falling rock has energy. These objects have energy because of their motion. This energy of motion is called **kinetic energy**. Even the particles that make up matter have kinetic energy. Look back at the drawings on page

C21, which show the motion of particles in the three states of matter. Would you like to know how fast the particles of a material are moving? Take its temperature! **Temperature** is a measure of the average kinetic energy of the particles in a material.

The term *average* indicates that not all particles in a material are moving at the same rate of speed. Some are traveling (or vibrating) a little bit faster or slower than most of the particles.

Temperature and Heat

Many people think that temperature and heat are exactly the same. Although temperature is related to heat, the two are quite different. To help you understand the difference, study the two wasp nests in the drawing.

Now think of a glass of water and a bathtub full of warm water at the same temperature. Just like the wasps, the particles of water in each container have the same average speed. But because there are more particles in the tub, that water has more heat energy.

Heat energy includes the total kinetic energy of the particles in a material. So a large sample of matter will have more heat energy than a smaller sample of the same matter, even though both samples have the same temperature.

What would happen if you added two ice cubes to the warm water in the glass and in the bathtub? The ice cubes in the bathtub would melt faster than those in the glass because the water in the tub has more energy to give them.

This example helps to define heat. **Heat** is energy that flows from warmer to cooler regions of matter. In both the glass and the bathtub, energy travels from warm water to cool ice.

Energy and Change of State

Energy is always involved in a change of state. When heat energy is added to a solid at its melting point or a liquid about to evaporate, the temperature does not increase. But, the energy does overcome the forces holding the molecules in solid or liquid form. In the reverse processes, energy is released, allowing a liquid or a solid to form.

Water is the best substance to study in order to learn about changes in state. Study the pictures on page C27 as you read about these changes in water.

▲ **Average Versus Total Energy**
The wasps in both of these hives have energy—they are buzzing around. The average speed of the wasps in each hive is the same. But the wasps in the larger hive have more total energy because there are more wasps.

Water Changes State

◀ Ice Changes to a Liquid

The ice absorbs energy from the Sun. This causes the particles to vibrate more. When enough energy has been added, the force holding particles together in the solid is overcome, and the ice changes state, or **melts**, to become liquid water.

◀ Water Changes to a Gas

As more energy is added, particles of liquid water escape and enter the air as a gas. The change of state from liquid to gas is called **evaporation**.

▲ Water as a Gas

Evaporation will continue until all the liquid water has changed into the gas state.

UNIT PROJECT LINK

For this Unit Project you will put on a magic show, using your knowledge of matter. Choose one of the following magic tricks to master.

1. The Disappearing Liquid What happens when you mix two different liquids and some liquid disappears?

2. The Great Tissue Bust How can a tissue be stronger than you are? Find out and then use what you learn in this unit to explain how your trick works.

TechnologyLink
For more help with your Unit Project, go to **www.eduplace.com**.

Evaporation occurs over a wide range of temperatures. And it takes place only at the surface of liquid water. If enough heat is added to liquid water, the water will eventually boil. When that happens, bubbles of water in the gas state will rise through the liquid and escape into the air.

Changes in state also take place when heat is removed from water. If enough heat is removed from a gas, it will change to a liquid. This process is called **condensation**. If enough heat is then removed from the liquid, it will change to a solid. This change from a liquid to a solid is called **freezing**. ∎

▲ Boiling is rapid evaporation that takes place throughout a liquid at high temperatures.

▲ When liquid water freezes, forces between water particles hold them in definite fixed patterns called crystals.

INVESTIGATION 3 WRAP-UP

REVIEW

1. How are temperature and heat different?

2. What happens during condensation?

CRITICAL THINKING

3. Bubbles of gas often form in tap water left at room temperature. Do you think this gas is water vapor, or is it something else? Explain.

4. If you put one hand in cold water and the other in hot water, one hand feels cold and the other feels hot. Explain these feelings in terms of the movement of heat.

REFLECT & EVALUATE

Word Power

Write the letter of the term that best matches the definition. *Not all terms will be used*.

1. The change of state from a gas to a liquid
2. The amount of mass in a given volume of matter
3. Anything that has mass and volume
4. The amount of space an object takes up
5. Energy that flows from warmer to cooler regions of matter
6. A measure of the amount of matter in an object

a. condensation
b. density
c. evaporation
d. heat
e. mass
f. matter
g. temperature
h. volume

Check What You Know

Write the word in each pair that correctly completes each sentence.

1. To calculate the density of an object, you need to know its volume and its (mass, height).
2. In a liquid the particles move faster than in a (solid, gas).
3. Energy that flows from warmer to cooler regions of matter is known as (heat, temperature).

Problem Solving

1. A 20-mL sample of grayish metal has a mass of 54 g. What is the density of the metal? After you've found its density, use the table of densities on page C14 to identify the metal.

2. Water is an unusual substance in that it expands when it freezes. Use this information to explain why ice cubes float in liquid water.

Study the drawings of the empty box and the football. Then, in your own words, describe how you would determine the volume of each object.

CHAPTER 2

KINDS OF MATTER

Solids, liquids, and gases of countless different kinds make up Earth's lands, waters, and the air. Since prehistoric times, people have used Earth's materials to make things. For example, artists use clay, a kind of matter that comes from the land, to create works of art that are both beautiful and useful.

Connecting to Science
ARTS

Pueblo Pottery Pueblo artist Nancy Youngblood Lugo creates pottery that is known for its bold, fluid designs, which are modern, yet traditional. Youngblood Lugo is a descendant of the Native American Tafoya family, whose name stands for creativity and excellence in Pueblo art.

The matter in moist clay has the property of being easily shaped. To make one of her pots, Youngblood Lugo first shapes clay into a form. As shown in the photo, she then carves a design on the clay. Another property of clay is its ability to hold its shape after drying and firing. In the traditional way of the Tafoyas, Youngblood Lugo fires her pots in an open flame. At the end of the firing, the flame is put out in a way that changes the matter of the clay to another kind that is hard, shiny, and dark. The finished pots in the lower picture have these properties.

Coming Up

◀ Nancy Youngblood Lugo carving a design on a clay pot called a melon bowl *(top);* four more clay pieces by the artist *(bottom).*

HOW CAN MATTER BE CLASSIFIED?

If you were asked to organize all the matter in the world into groups, how many groups do you think you'd need? What characteristics would you choose to identify each group? In this investigation you'll classify matter into two groups: kinds of matter that cannot be broken down and kinds that can.

Activity
Testing Your Metal

Aluminum and copper are kinds of matter. This activity will help you decide which group they belong in.

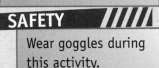
Procedure

Obtain samples of aluminum and copper. In your *Science Notebook*, **list** some properties of each of these metals. **Brainstorm** with members of your group about things you can do to change these samples. **Make a list** of your ideas and, after getting your teacher's approval, carry out your plans. **Describe** your actions and **record** all changes in the samples.

Analyze and Conclude

1. Based on your observations, what properties do copper and aluminum have in common? How are the two metals different?

2. Did any of the changes you caused produce any new materials? Explain your answer.

C32

Activity

A Change for the Wetter

Sugar is a kind of matter. Can sugar be broken down into other materials? Heat some sugar and find out.

Procedure

1. Sprinkle a small amount of sugar on a sheet of black paper. Examine the grains of sugar with a hand lens. **Make a sketch** of a sugar grain in your *Science Notebook*.

2. Obtain about a half spoonful of sugar. Place a candle in the center of a shallow dish and ask your teacher to light the candle. Your teacher will hold the spoon over the candle so that the flame just touches the bowl of the spoon.

3. As the sugar is heated, use tongs to hold a glass square 2–3 centimeters above the sugar.

4. **Observe** the sugar and the glass square carefully. Continue heating the sugar until all the white crystals have disappeared. **Record** your observations of the sugar and the glass.

Analyze and Conclude

1. What was the first sign that a change was taking place?

2. **Compare** the appearance of the material in the spoon at the end of the activity with the sugar you started with. What evidence is there that you've produced different kinds of matter from the sugar?

3. What appeared on the glass square? **Infer** where this material came from.

Step 2

Elements

Reading Focus What are elements, and how are they organized?

The materials shown below have one thing in common. They are all matter. Matter can be identified by its properties, or characteristics. **Physical properties** are characteristics that can be measured or detected by the senses. Color, size, odor, and density are examples of physical properties. **Chemical properties** describe how matter changes when it reacts with other matter. The fact that paper burns is a chemical property of paper.

Scientists classify all matter into two groups—substances and mixtures. Each group can be divided into smaller groups, as shown on page C35. A **substance** is a material that always has the same makeup and properties. The gold, aluminum, sugar, and water shown are all substances.

There are two kinds of substances— elements and compounds. An **element** is a substance that cannot be broken down by simple means into any other substance. The activity on page C32 shows that aluminum and copper cannot be changed into simpler kinds of matter. Aluminum and copper are elements.

A **compound** is a substance made up of two or more elements that are chemically combined. Sugar and water are compounds. In the activity on page C33, sugar changes into two simpler substances. One is the compound water. The black material that forms is the element carbon.

A **mixture** is a combination of two or more substances. The milk shown in the photo is a mixture. You'll learn about mixtures later in this chapter.

What properties can be used to identify these different materials? ▼

Classifying Matter

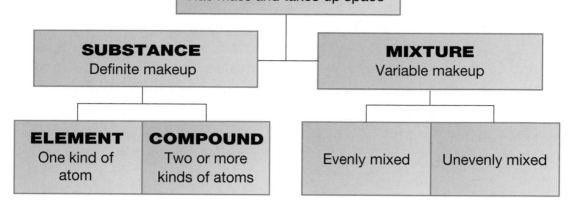

MATTER
Has mass and takes up space

SUBSTANCE
Definite makeup

MIXTURE
Variable makeup

ELEMENT
One kind of atom

COMPOUND
Two or more kinds of atoms

Evenly mixed

Unevenly mixed

Identifying Elements

Elements have been described as the building blocks of matter. All matter, regardless of its form, is made up of one or more elements. What, then, are elements made of?

Recall that all matter is made up of very tiny particles. Think about cutting a small piece of aluminum in half and then cutting one of the halves in half. Now imagine continuing to divide the aluminum into smaller and smaller pieces. Eventually you would have a particle so small that it could not be divided anymore and still be aluminum.

The tiny particle would be a building block of aluminum—an aluminum atom. An **atom** is the smallest particle of an element that has the chemical properties of the element.

All the atoms of a particular element are the same. Gold, for example, is made up only of gold atoms. Aluminum atoms make up the element aluminum. Gold atoms differ from aluminum atoms, and both differ from the atoms of all other elements.

Today, scientists know of 112 elements. Ninety elements are found in nature. Many metals, such as iron, copper, and silver, are pure elements. Some other substances, such as oxygen and carbon, are elements that are not metals. From just these 90 elements are built the many kinds of matter that make up the universe!

Twenty-two of the known elements are not found in nature. Scientists have produced these elements artificially in the laboratory.

Technology Link
CD-ROM

INVESTIGATE FURTHER!

Use the **Science Processor CD-ROM**, *Nature of Matter* (Investigation 2, Sorting Space Stuff) to explore a new planet and test the materials you discover. Decide which ones are compounds, which ones are mixtures, and which ones are elements.

Chemical Symbols

Chemists use a kind of shorthand for the names of elements. A **chemical symbol** is one or two letters that stand for the name of an element.

Many symbols consist of letters in the elements' English names, such as O for oxygen and Ca for calcium. Some symbols, such as Fe for iron and Au for gold, come from Latin names for elements. These are *ferrum* for iron and *aurum* for gold.

The Periodic Table

The idea that there are certain basic kinds of matter—elements—is an old one. Some early scientists thought there were four elements—fire, earth, air, and water. However, by the seventeenth century, scientists had identified a number of elements. By the nineteenth century, more than 50 elements were known.

In 1869 a Russian chemist, Dmitri Mendeleev, published a table of the 63

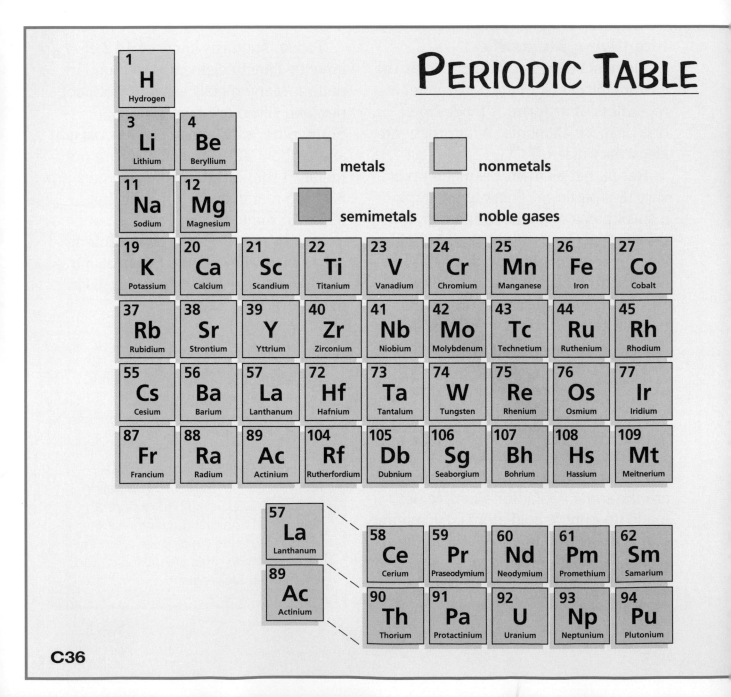

PERIODIC TABLE

elements known at that time. Mendeleev organized the elements into a table according to the weights of their atoms and their properties. The elements in each column of the table had similar properties. The table below is a modern version of Mendeleev's table. It is called the Periodic Table of Elements.

Each block of this periodic table includes information about a particular element. For example, hydrogen is the simplest element. That is, hydrogen

atoms have the simplest structure. For this reason, hydrogen is listed first and it is given the atomic number 1.

Using the Periodic Table

In addition to information about each element, the periodic table tells you something about groups of elements. Like Mendeleev's table, this table is organized so that the elements in the same column have similar properties. For example, except for hydrogen, all

OF ELEMENTS

2 He Helium					

Atomic Number

6 C Carbon

Symbol

Name

5 B Boron	6 C Carbon	7 N Nitrogen	8 O Oxygen	9 F Fluorine	10 Ne Neon
13 Al Aluminum	14 Si Silicon	15 P Phosphorus	16 S Sulfur	17 Cl Chlorine	18 Ar Argon

28 Ni Nickel	29 Cu Copper	30 Zn Zinc	31 Ga Gallium	32 Ge Germanium	33 As Arsenic	34 Se Selenium	35 Br Bromine	36 Kr Krypton
46 Pd Palladium	47 Ag Silver	48 Cd Cadmium	49 In Indium	50 Sn Tin	51 Sb Antimomy	52 Te Tellurium	53 I Iodine	54 Xe Xenon
78 Pt Platinum	79 Au Gold	80 Hg Mercury	81 Tl Thallium	82 Pb Lead	83 Bi Bismuth	84 Po Polonium	85 At Astatine	86 Rn Radon
110 *	111 *	112 *						

*No official names have been given to these elements.

63 Eu Europium	64 Gd Gadolinium	65 Tb Terbium	66 Dy Dysprosium	67 Ho Holmium	68 Er Erbium	69 Tm Thulium	70 Yb Ytterbium	71 Lu Lutetium
95 Am Americium	96 Cm Curium	97 Bk Berkelium	98 Cf Californium	99 Es Einsteinium	100 Fm Fermium	101 Md Mendelevium	102 No Nobelium	103 Lr Lawrencium

Classifying Elements

Group	Examples	Properties
Metals	iron, copper, aluminum	Usually shiny; can be formed into sheets and wire; good conductors of heat and electricity
Nonmetals	sulfur, carbon, chlorine	Dull; cannot be easily shaped; poor conductors of heat and electricity; some are gases
Semimetals	silicon, boron	Have some properties of both metals and nonmetals
Noble Gases	helium, neon, radon	Do not combine readily with other elements

the elements in the left-hand column are chemically active metals. Their symbols are Li, Na, K, Rb, Cs, and Fr. Use the periodic table on pages C36 and C37 to find their names and atomic numbers. All the elements in the right-hand column are inactive gases. What are their symbols, atomic numbers, and names?

Now look for chlorine, Cl, in the periodic table. What are the names and symbols of the other elements in the same column as chlorine?

Another way to classify elements is into four groups: metals, nonmetals, semimetals, and noble gases. These groups are shown in the table above. ■

Science in Literature

A UNIVERSE OF ELEMENTS

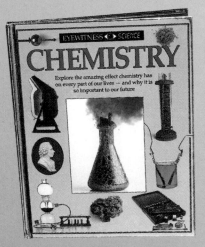

Eyewitness Science: Chemistry
by Dr. Ann Newmark
Dorling Kindersley, 1993

"Hydrogen is the simplest element. Over 90 percent of the Universe is made up of hydrogen created at the time of the Big Bang—the explosion that produced the Universe. All other heavier elements have been formed from hydrogen by nuclear reactions. . . . The elements in a meteorite, such as iron and nickel, are identical to those found on Earth. . . ."

Read *Eyewitness Science: Chemistry* by Dr. Ann Newmark to find out more about elements. For example, which do you think contains more oxygen, air or Earth's crust? The answer may surprise you.

Compounds

Reading Focus How are compounds formed?

One of the most beautiful materials found in the laboratory is a reddish-orange powder sometimes known as red precipitate (prē sip'ə tit). The photographs show what happens to this powder if you heat a small amount of it in a test tube.

In the photos you can see the contents of the test tube change from a reddish-orange solid to a dark powder and then to a shiny liquid on the sides of the test tube. What you can't see is the gas escaping from the mouth of the test tube. How can you tell that red precipitate is *not* an element?

The Composition of Compounds

Red precipitate is a compound of mercury and oxygen. Its scientific name is mercuric (mər kyoor'ik) oxide. It forms when the elements mercury and oxygen combine. When elements combine to form a compound, their atoms become chemically linked, or joined. In most compounds, such as water, the linked atoms form **molecules** (mäl'i-kyoolz). In some compounds, such as salt, or sodium chloride, the atoms are held together in hundreds or thousands of units, forming crystal-like structures.

When elements join to form compounds, the joined elements lose their original properties and take on new ones. For example, mercury is a shiny liquid metal. Oxygen is a colorless, invisible gas. But the compound made up of these elements, mercuric oxide, is a reddish-orange powdery solid.

▼ As it is heated, mercuric oxide separates into mercury and oxygen.

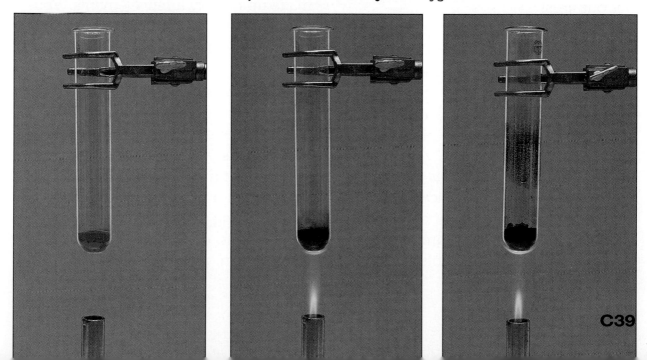

C39

▲ Sodium is a soft metal that reacts explosively with water.

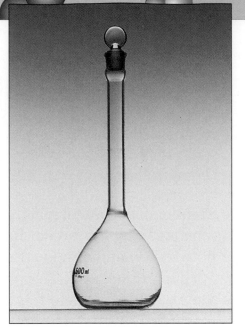

▲ Chlorine is a poisonous, greenish-yellow gas.

Water and salt are two substances that show how elements can change when they form compounds. Water is made up of the elements hydrogen and oxygen, which are both colorless gases. Hydrogen burns with a hot blue flame. Oxygen helps other substances to burn but does not burn itself.

So what are the properties of the compound that is made when these two gases combine? Water is a liquid that does not burn. In fact, it can be used to put out fires!

Sodium chloride, or table salt, is made up of sodium and chlorine. The photos above show what these elements are like. It's hard to believe that table salt is made up of such dangerous elements!

Chemical Formulas

Just as chemical symbols are used to represent elements, chemical formulas are used to represent compounds. A **chemical formula** is a group of symbols that shows the elements in a compound. For example, the chemical formula for water is H_2O. This formula shows that a molecule of water is made up of two hydrogen atoms and one oxygen atom. The formula for sodium chloride, NaCl, shows that a unit of this compound contains one atom of sodium and one atom of chlorine.

Elements in Common Materials

As you've read, there are 90 elements in nature. Yet most materials are made up of only a few elements. You know, for example, that mercuric oxide (HgO), water (H_2O), and sodium chloride (NaCl) each contain just two elements. So do many other common materials, such as sand, or silicon dioxide (SiO_2), and octane (C_8H_{18}), found in gasoline. As you shall see, many compounds that make up living things also contain just a few elements. In fact, 99% of living tissue is made up of only six elements: carbon, hydrogen, nitrogen, oxygen, phosphorus, and sulfur.

Compounds of Carbon

Carbon is an element found in all living things. The sucrose, or table sugar, you may put on your cereal has the chemical formula $C_{12}H_{22}O_{11}$. Like most common materials, this compound contains only a few elements. But like many compounds that come from living things, its molecules are complex. And even sucrose molecules are simple compared to those of cholesterol (kə les'tər ôl).

Cholesterol is a compound found in cells of many living things. Too much of this compound can cause heart disease in humans. The chemical formula of cholesterol is $C_{27}H_{45}OH$.

How many atoms are present in a single molecule of cholesterol? You would probably agree that this molecule is, indeed, complex. But carbon is a very "linkable" atom. The number of different carbon compounds seems to be endless. And many of these compounds are even more complex than cholesterol. ■

UNIT PROJECT LINK

Here are some more magic tricks. Choose one to work on with your group.
1. What Color Is Blue Ink? Is ink a mixture or a compound?
2. The Invisible Force Can an index card be used as a cap to keep a glass full of water from spilling?
3. The Leakproof Strainer How can one liquid keep another liquid from passing through the holes in a strainer?

TechnologyLink

For more help with your Unit Project, go to **www.eduplace.com**.

Eggs and fried foods are sources ▶ of cholesterol.

Using **Math**

A molecule of sugar, or sucrose, has the formula $C_{12}H_{22}O_{11}$. What is the ratio of hydrogen to oxygen in sucrose?

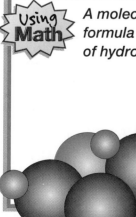

Ancient Elements

Reading Focus How has our understanding of elements changed over time?

Chemistry got its start as an experimental science in the Middle Ages with the alchemists (al′kə-mists). The goal of the alchemists was not scientific knowledge. Alchemists were mainly interested in wealth and long life. Much effort was spent trying to change iron and lead into gold and searching for a substance that could give everlasting life.

Though many of the ideas of the alchemists were wrong, much good came from their efforts. The time line shows that alchemists helped pave the way for modern chemistry. ■

The term *element* is coined by Plato, a famous Greek philosopher. The Greeks consider the four basic kinds of matter, or elements, to be fire, water, air, and earth.

400–300 B.C.

1550 B.C.
Plows made of bronze are used in what is now Vietnam.

The earliest metal objects are made. In the Middle East, small jewels and tools are carved or cut from gold, copper, and silver.

10,000 B.C.

3200 B.C.
Copper is mined on a large scale in Egypt. Copper is used in the making of bronze during the Bronze Age.

C42

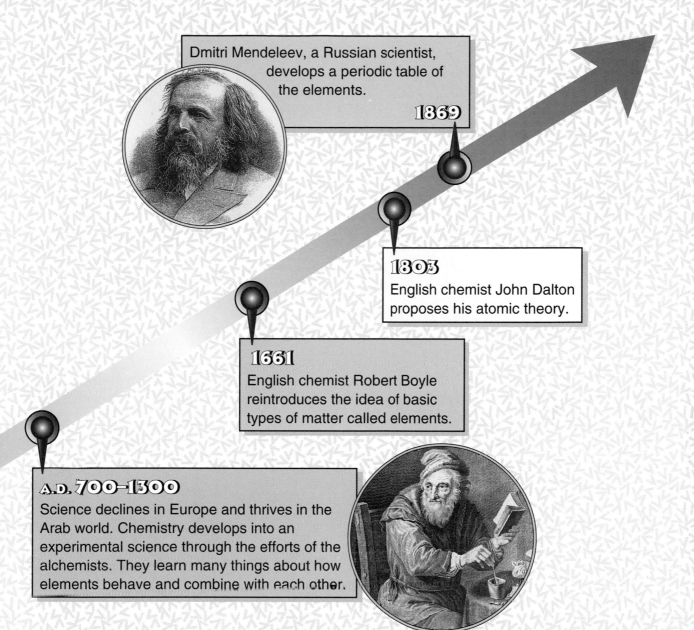

Dmitri Mendeleev, a Russian scientist, develops a periodic table of the elements.

1869

1803
English chemist John Dalton proposes his atomic theory.

1661
English chemist Robert Boyle reintroduces the idea of basic types of matter called elements.

A.D. 700–1300
Science declines in Europe and thrives in the Arab world. Chemistry develops into an experimental science through the efforts of the alchemists. They learn many things about how elements behave and combine with each other.

INVESTIGATION 1 WRAP-UP

REVIEW

1. What do elements and compounds have in common? How do they differ?

2. What is the meaning of the formula H_2O?

CRITICAL THINKING

3. The formula for carbon dioxide is CO_2. The formula for sulfur trioxide is SO_3. The formula for carbon tetrachloride is CCl_4. Infer the meanings of the prefixes *di-*, *tri-*, and *tetra-*.

4. A certain element has the atomic number of 53. What is its name and symbol? Is it more similar to oxygen or to chlorine? Explain.

INVESTIGATION 2

WHAT IS A MIXTURE?

Perhaps the two most common kinds of matter at Earth's surface are rocks and ocean water. Neither is a substance. Both kinds of matter are made up of different elements and compounds mixed together. Find out about mixtures in this investigation.

Activity
Working With Mixtures

How can you tell if something is a mixture? With some things, such as chocolate chip ice cream or vegetable soup, it's easy to tell. With others, such as vanilla ice cream or salt water, it's more difficult.

Procedure

1. Cut a piece of aluminum foil and a piece of copper foil into small pieces. Add the pieces to a clear jar.

2. Add 2 or 3 spoonfuls of sugar to the jar. **Predict** whether the properties of any of the materials in the jar will be changed by being mixed together. Place the lid on the jar and shake the jar vigorously.

Step 2

3. Use a hand lens to examine the contents of the jar carefully. In your *Science Notebook*, **describe** the contents of the jar and tell how you would separate the parts of this mixture.

4. Add 2 spoonfuls each of aquarium gravel and sand to another jar. Cover the jar and shake it vigorously.

5. Brainstorm with your partner to **plan an experiment** for separating the parts of the sand-gravel mixture. After showing the plan to your teacher, obtain the necessary materials and carry out your plan.

6. Return the sand and gravel to the jar. Add 2 spoonfuls of sugar to the jar and repeat step 5 for this mixture.

Step 3

Step 4

Analyze and Conclude

1. Were any properties of the aluminum, copper, or sugar changed by being mixed together? How do you know?

2. What can you **infer** about the differences between a mixture and an element? a mixture and a compound?

3. Describe your method for separating the mixture of sand and gravel. Were you able to use the same method to separate the mixture of sand, gravel, and sugar? Why or why not? If not, **describe** the method you used to separate this mixture.

INVESTIGATE FURTHER!

EXPERIMENT

Wearing disposable gloves and goggles, mix a spoonful of sand and a spoonful of iron filings. Think of a property of iron that you could use to help separate this mixture. Write up a plan for separating the mixture. Show the plan to your teacher. If the plan is approved, carry it out.

Activity
Racing Colors

Is black ink a substance or a mixture? Find out if you can separate it into parts.

Procedure

1. Fill a jar with water to within a few millimeters of its rim.

2. Cut a small hole in the center of a piece of filter paper. Use a water-based black ink marker to make a circle of round dots near the hole in the filter paper, as shown.

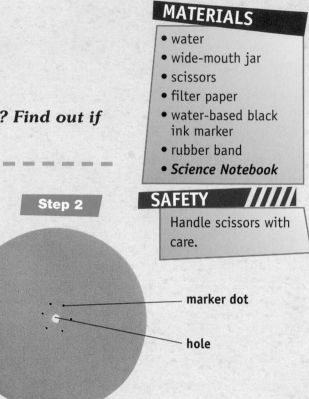

Step 2

marker dot

hole

3. Stretch the filter paper over the mouth of the jar and hold it in place with a rubber band.

4. Cut a second piece of filter paper in fourths. Roll up one of the fourths to make a cone. Insert the tip of the cone through the hole in the filter paper covering the jar until it touches the water.

5. **Predict** what will happen as water moves up the cone and past the marker spots. **Record** your prediction in your *Science Notebook*.

6. **Observe** the setup until the water has reached the edge of the jar. **Record** your observations.

Step 4

Analyze and Conclude

1. **Describe** what happens to each marker spot.

2. Is ink a substance or a mixture? What evidence can you give to support your answer? Indicate whether further information is needed to support your conclusion.

Activity

A Mixed-Up State

Some mixtures behave like a liquid. Some behave like a solid. The behavior of some mixtures, as you will discover, is not easy to describe.

- goggles
- cornstarch
- spoon
- shallow dish
- dropper
- food coloring
- water
- plastic cup
- tongue depressor
- plastic knife
- marbles
- *Science Notebook*

SAFETY

Wear goggles during this activity.

Procedure

1. Place four or five spoonfuls of cornstarch in a dish. **Predict** how the cornstarch will change if you add water to it.

2. Add several drops of food coloring to some water in a plastic cup. Add this colored water, a few drops at a time, to the cornstarch. Stir with a tongue depressor until you have a wet ball of cornstarch.

3. Describe the material you have created. Pick some up and **observe** its properties. **Record** your observations in your *Science Notebook*.

4. Try cutting the material with a plastic knife. Try rolling it into various shapes. Place marbles on the material and describe what happens.

Step 2

Analyze and Conclude

1. Why is the material produced in this activity a mixture?

2. **Describe** the ways that the material acts like a liquid and the ways it acts like a solid.

3. Do you think the mixture can easily be separated into its original parts? Explain your answer.

Mixtures

Reading Focus How is a mixture different from a compound?

The chemical formula for water is H_2O. This formula tells you that water is made up of 2 parts hydrogen and 1 part oxygen. Is water a mixture of hydrogen and oxygen? This question may confuse people who are just beginning to study chemistry. The answer to the question is no. About the only thing that compounds and mixtures have in common is that each is made up of two or more different kinds of matter.

Keeping Their Properties

In the activity on pages C44 and C45, aluminum, copper, and sugar are mixed together in a jar. Even after the jar is shaken, it's possible to recognize the different substances in the mixture.

The activity provides a clue as to how mixtures are different from compounds. All the substances in a mixture keep their original properties. When substances combine to form a compound, the properties of the substances that make up the compound are gone. Those properties are replaced by the unique properties of the compound.

Suppose you were to mix iron filings with salt. No matter how well you mixed the two substances, you would still have iron and salt. Both substances would still have their original properties. For example, one physical property of iron is that it is attracted to a magnet. Mixing the iron with salt has no effect on this property, as the photo below shows.

◀ Iron is magnetic, and it keeps this property in a salt-iron mixture.

▲ **Is this fruit punch a mixture or a compound?**

When substances combine to form a compound, the substances change. Water, for example, is nothing like the hydrogen and oxygen that combine to make up water. And water's properties are very different from those of hydrogen and oxygen.

The Makeup of a Mixture

Ice cream is a mixture. There are many flavors of ice cream, and each contains different ingredients. Mixtures, including the various flavors of ice cream, don't have chemical formulas. The reason is that two mixtures of the same materials can be quite different in makeup. This explains why the same flavor of ice cream may taste different from brand to brand.

To understand how mixtures of the same materials can differ, think about two bowls of fruit punch made with the same ingredients. One person might mix two bottles of orange juice, one bottle of club soda, some strawberries, some cherries, and a cut-up orange. Someone else might mix one bottle of orange juice, two bottles of club soda, and the same kinds of fruit but in different amounts. So a single formula could not accurately represent the makeup of such a mixture.

Unlike a mixture, a compound always has the same composition. For example, no matter where it comes from, salt always contains one part sodium and one part chlorine. Water always contains two parts hydrogen and one part oxygen. That's why you can use a chemical formula to represent a compound. The chemical makeup of a given compound never changes.

Some Common Mixtures

Most matter in the world around you exists as mixtures. You just have to look out the window to see evidence of this. In fact, the glass in your classroom windows is a mixture. Most window glass is made up of silicon dioxide (sil'i kän dī äks'īd) and other substances. The amount of each substance in glass can vary from sample to sample.

Beyond your window you may see a variety of materials, such as bricks, cement, and asphalt (as'fôlt). All these building materials are mixtures. As you observe these mixtures, you are looking through, and are surrounded by, a natural mixture—air.

Air is a mixture of gases. This mixture consists of about four-fifths nitrogen gas and one-fifth oxygen gas. But air also contains small amounts of other gases, such as carbon dioxide and water vapor. The percentages of these gases vary from place to place and from time to time.

You don't have to look outside the classroom to find mixtures. In fact, you don't have to look any further than your own body. The human body contains many different mixtures. Blood, sweat, and saliva are among the mixtures that make you what you are.

Separating Mixtures

The different materials in a mixture can almost always be separated from each other by physical means. For example, a variety of methods are used to

▲ The composition of air changes from time to time and place to place.

separate different mixtures in the activity on pages C44 and C45.

The method used to separate a mixture depends on some difference in the physical properties of the materials in the mixture. One important property used in separating a mixture is the size of the pieces making up the mixture. For example, if you had a pocketful of pennies, dimes, nickels, and quarters, you could easily separate the mixture by hand. But suppose you had a shopping bag full of coins. It would be much easier to use a sorting machine, like the one shown, to separate the mixture.

A mixture of salt and sand would be more difficult to separate than a mixture of coins. It would be almost impossible to separate the materials by hand. And a sorting machine wouldn't work, because the pieces of salt and sand are similar in size. So you have to find another method for separating the mixture.

Think about salt and sand. Do either of these materials have some property you could use to separate them? Yes, salt dissolves in water and sand does not. If you add water to a mixture of

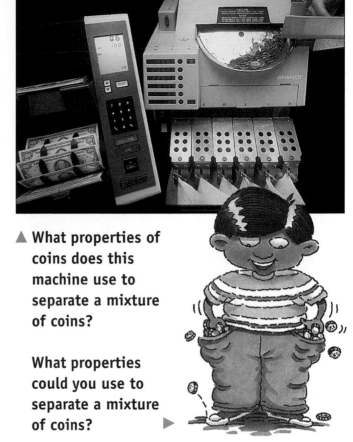

▲ What properties of coins does this machine use to separate a mixture of coins?

What properties could you use to separate a mixture of coins? ▶

salt and sand, the salt will dissolve in the water. You can then pour off the salt water and collect the sand, which remains behind. How might you get the salt back from the salt water? ■

INVESTIGATION 2 WRAP-UP

REVIEW

1. Explain why a mixture cannot be represented by a chemical formula.

2. What is the difference between a mixture and a substance?

CRITICAL THINKING

3. Suppose you had a mixture of iron pellets, pebbles, and small wood spheres, all about the same size. How would you separate this mixture?

4. How can mixtures of the same substances differ?

WHAT ARE LIQUID MIXTURES LIKE?

What do milk, soft drinks, and ocean water have in common? Your first thought may be that they are all liquids. But if you consider it more carefully, you'll realize that they are all liquid mixtures. Study the properties of these mixtures in this investigation.

Activity
Mixing Solids Into Liquids

Sugar dissolves in water and seems to disappear. What factors affect how fast the sugar disappears?

Procedure

1. In your *Science Notebook*, **make a chart** like the one shown.

Conditions	Time
Cold Water	
Water at Room Temperature	
Warm Water	
Warm Water + Stirring	
Warm Water + Crushed Sugar + Stirring	

 See **SCIENCE** and **MATH TOOLBOX** page H11 if you need to review *Making a Chart to Organize Data.*

2. Fill one cup with ice-cold water, a second cup with water at room temperature, and a third cup with warm water. Use equal amounts of water in each cup. Use a marker to label the cups as shown here.

3. **Predict** which water will most quickly dissolve a sugar cube. Then add a sugar cube to each cup. Time how long it takes for each sugar cube to dissolve. **Record** the times in your chart.

4. Pour out the water and rinse the cups. Refill one cup with warm water and add a sugar cube. This time, stir the mixture until the sugar cube dissolves. **Record** the time.

5. Use a spoon to crush a sugar cube. Repeat step 4, using the crushed sugar. **Record** the time.

Step 4

Analyze and Conclude

1. How did the temperature of the water affect the rate at which the sugar dissolved in it?

2. What effect did stirring have on the rate at which the sugar dissolved in water?

3. What effect did crushing the sugar into small particles have on the rate at which the sugar dissolved?

4. What can you **infer** about the size of the sugar particles that are dissolved in a mixture of sugar and water?

5. **Suggest a hypothesis** that relates the effects of water temperature, stirring, and smaller pieces of sugar to the rate at which sugar dissolves.

INVESTIGATE FURTHER!

EXPERIMENT

Once salt is dissolved in water, how can you get the salt back? Design an experiment to get the salt out of salt water.

Activity
To Mix or Not to Mix

Shake that bottle of salad dressing before you pour it on your salad. If you don't, you may get only part of the mixture.

Procedure

1. Add water to a jar until it is about one-fourth full.

Math Hint *To estimate the one-fourth line of a container, measure the height of the container and round the height to the nearest whole unit. Then divide by 4.*

2. Add a few drops of food coloring to the water. Swirl the water around in the jar until the water is evenly colored throughout.

3. Add the same amount of vegetable oil to the jar as you did water. Screw the lid tightly on the jar.

Step 3

4. Shake the jar several times and stand it on the table. **Observe** what happens to the liquids in the jar. **Record** your observations in your *Science Notebook*.

5. Turn the jar upside down and hold it that way. **Observe** what happens to the liquids and **record** your observations.

Analyze and Conclude

1. Does water mix with food coloring? **Give evidence** to support your answer.

2. Do water and oil mix? **Give evidence** to support your answer.

3. What happened when you turned the jar upside down?

4. Based on your observations, what can you **infer** about the ability of different liquids to mix?

Step 4

Activity
Making Water Wetter

What happens if you try to clean a greasy dish with plain water? The water runs off the dish. The water doesn't seem to wet the dish. Can you mix something with water to make it "wetter"?

Procedure

1. Spread a sheet of wax paper on the table.

2. Use a dropper to carefully place one drop of an unidentified blue liquid on the paper. Use a toothpick to probe the drop and **observe** how it behaves. In your *Science Notebook*, **record** your observations, including the color of the drop and what shape the drop takes.

3. Using a clean dropper, place a drop of an unidentified red liquid on the paper. Use the toothpick to probe the drop and **observe** how it behaves. **Record** your observations.

4. Repeat step 3 with a drop of plain water.

Step 3

Analyze and Conclude

1. Describe the shapes of the two colored drops and **compare** their behavior when you probed them with a toothpick.

2. One colored liquid is plain water mixed with food coloring; the other is water mixed with food coloring and detergent. **Infer** which is which. **Give evidence** to support your inference.

3. Which liquid seemed to "wet" the wax paper better?

4. Suggest a hypothesis to explain how detergent in water helps clean grease.

What's the Solution?

Reading Focus What factors affect the rate at which solutions form?

When viewed from space, Earth is a lovely planet. Satellite photographs of our planet show cloud patterns, oceans, and continents—in other words, air, sea, and land. These three nonliving parts of our planet are mixtures. Air is a mixture of many gases. Rocks are mixtures of minerals. And sea water is a mixture of water and different minerals.

More Mixing

Look back at the graphic organizer on page C35. Notice that mixtures are divided into two groups—unevenly mixed and evenly mixed. Most mixtures fall into the unevenly mixed group.

Suppose you added equal amounts of sand, salt, and sugar to a container. You could try everything to mix the materials evenly, but some parts of the mixture would be just a little different from the other parts.

Now think of a sugar-water mixture. The sugar and the water mix so completely that the solid sugar seems to disappear. If you could take samples from different parts of the mixture, you would find that every part is exactly the same as every other part. The drawing below of sugar water shows how the particles are evenly spread.

When sugar mixes with water, the sugar spreads evenly throughout the water and seems to disappear. ▼

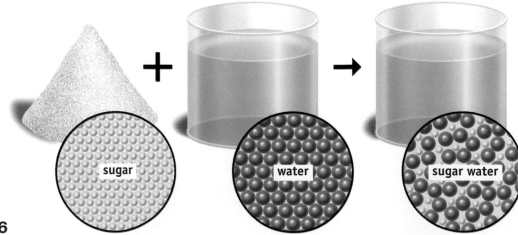

sugar

water

sugar water

Salad dressing is an example of a suspension. A suspension is a liquid mixture in which some particles are temporarily suspended in the mixture.

Even after it is shaken, the salad dressing ▶ is not a solution. If the bottle is left to stand, the dressing separates into its different parts.

A mixture in which the different particles of matter are spread evenly throughout is called a **solution**. A solution has two main parts. The **solvent** (säl′vənt) is the material that is present in the greater amount. The **solute** (säl′yo͞ot) is the material present in the smaller amount.

Rate of Solution

Which dissolves faster in water—a sugar cube or a spoonful of loose sugar grains? Dissolving takes place only on the surface of the sugar, where the water is in contact with the sugar. Small cubes, or grains, of sugar dissolve faster than a large sugar cube. The drawing below shows why.

Temperature also affects the rate at which things dissolve. For example, sugar dissolves faster in hot water than in cold water. The particles of hot water are moving faster than the particles of cold water. The fast-moving particles bump into the sugar harder and more frequently, helping to break the sugar into smaller pieces.

Stirring a mixture also helps speed up the rate at which things dissolve. Stirring causes the particles of solute to mix more quickly with the particles of solvent. ■

Internet Field Trip

Visit **www.eduplace.com** to find out more about solutions.

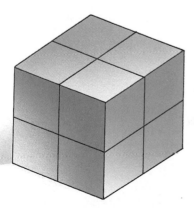

▲ This sugar cube has six sides. Each side has a surface area of 4 cm². The total surface area of this cube is 6 × 4 cm² = 24 cm².

◀ This is the same amount of sugar. The total surface area of 1 small cube is 6 × 1 cm². There are 8 small cubes. So the total surface area of 8 cubes is 8 × 6 cm² = 48 cm².

Bubbles

Reading Focus How can the force of attraction between water molecules be changed?

Have you ever seen a water strider? It's an insect that can walk on water! How does the water strider manage to stay on the water's surface? If you look closely at the surface, it seems to be covered with a thin skin. The shape of the water strider's feet allow it to glide across this skin without breaking it.

A force of attraction called cohesion exists among water particles. This force produces *surface tension*, which accounts for the "skin" on the water.

Have you ever tried to produce large bubbles like the one shown, using plain water? It's not possible. In fact, because of cohesion, you can't even get water to form a film on the bubble wand. But if you add a little soap to the water, it's a different story. Like the girl in the picture below, you can form delicate bubbles that float in the air.

When soap is added to water, surface tension is greatly reduced. If the water strider stepped onto the surface of soapy water, it would enjoy a swim rather than a stroll.

▲ Reduced cohesion makes it possible for the soap-water mixture to be stretched out into a thin film, or bubble. Some soap bubbles are no more than one or two particles in thickness.

Alloys

Reading Focus What are some common alloys and how are they used?

Question: When is a metal not an element? Answer: When it's an alloy. An **alloy** is a solution of two or more metals with properties of its own. For example, stainless steel is an alloy made of iron, chromium, carbon, and nickel, which are all elements. Stainless steel is stronger than iron, lighter than iron, and resists rusting.

An alloy is made by melting two or more metals and mixing them together. The mixture is then allowed to cool and harden to a solid. In its final form an alloy consists of a solution in which the metals are evenly mixed together.

Some Important Alloys

Alloys have been important to humans for thousands of years. One of the first alloys ever prepared was bronze, a mixture of copper and tin. Some bronzes also contain zinc.

The earliest bronze items have been dated at about 3500 B.C. The introduction of bronze was such an important event that a whole period in human history—the Bronze Age—has been named after this alloy.

▲ These bronze objects are more than 1,000 years old.

Common Alloys

Alloy	Composition	Use
Amalgam	70% Ag, 18% Sn, 10% Cu, 2% Hg	dentistry
Brass	70% Cu, 30% Zn	hardware, plumbing
Bronze	90% Cu, 10% Sn	artwork, domes of buildings
Gold alloy	70% Au, 15% Ag, 10% Cu, 1% Pt, 1% Zn, 1% Pd	dentistry, jewelry
Pewter	85% Sn, 7% Cu, 6% Bi, 2% Sb	cups, candlesticks
Solder	60% Pb, 40% Sn	connecting metal pieces together
Stainless steel	74% Fe, 18% Cr, 8% Ni	cutlery
Steel	99% Fe, 1% C	bridges, buildings
Sterling silver	93% Ag, 7% Cu	jewelry, tableware

The table above lists some common alloys and tells what metals they contain and how they are used. Refer to the periodic table on pages C36 and C37 for the names of the metals whose chemical symbols are given.

Alloys are useful because their properties are different from those of the metallic elements from which they are made. For example, alloys of gold are much harder and less expensive than pure gold. A unit called a karat (kar'ət) is used to express the purity of a sample of gold. Pure gold is 24 karats. It is too soft to use in jewelry. A piece of jewelry made with 18 karat gold contains 75% gold.

Some alloys have unusual properties. For example, Wood's metal is an alloy of bismuth (biz'məth), lead, tin, and cadmium (kad'mē əm). This alloy has a melting point of 70°C. It will melt on your stove at a relatively low temperature setting. Can you see how this alloy can be used in automatic sprinklers?

Another interesting alloy is misch (mish) metal, which is made of cerium (sir'ē əm), lanthanum (lan'thə nəm), and other metals. Misch metal has the unusual property of giving off sparks when it is rubbed. Because of this property, misch metal is used in the manufacture of flints that are used for lighting butane stoves. ■

INVESTIGATION 3 WRAP-UP

REVIEW

1. Explain why salad dressing is not a solution.

2. What do compounds and mixtures have in common?

CRITICAL THINKING

3. Why is an alloy both a mixture and a solution?

4. What methods would you use to dissolve a large crystal of salt, known as rock salt, in water? Explain all the factors that affect the rate at which the salt will dissolve.

REFLECT & EVALUATE

Word Power

Write the letter of the term that best matches the definition. *Not all terms will be used*.

1. Characteristics that can be measured or detected by the senses
2. The smallest particle of an element that has its chemical properties
3. A group of symbols that show the elements in a compound
4. Characteristics that describe how matter changes when it reacts with other matter
5. A group of atoms that are chemically linked
6. A solution of two or more metals

a. alloy
b. atom
c. chemical formula
d. chemical properties
e. element
f. molecule
g. physical properties
h. solvent

Check What You Know

Write the word in each pair that correctly completes each sentence.

1. Metals, nonmetals, semimetals, and noble gases are four different types of (elements, compounds).
2. When elements are joined in a compound, they (lose, keep) their original properties.
3. Glass is a (mixture, compound).
4. When soap is added to water, its surface tension (increases, decreases).

Problem Solving

1. Explain why all the elements that appear in the same column of the periodic table are commonly referred to as a family.
2. How could you quickly separate a mixture of brass tacks and iron tacks?
3. Explain why salt cannot be removed from a salt-water mixture by pouring the mixture through a paper filter.

Study the section of the periodic table shown. Use the section to determine which elements are more similar in chemical and physical properties—copper and zinc, or copper and silver. Explain how you know.

| 29 Cu Copper | 30 Zn Zinc |
| 47 Ag Silver | 48 Cd Cadmium |

3

HOW MATTER CHANGES

Have you ever been camping? A good campfire may have helped warm you. A campfire builder usually has to cut large pieces of wood into smaller pieces for the fire. When this wood burns, it leaves only ashes. In this chapter you'll find out about the physical and chemical changes that matter undergoes.

PEOPLE USING SCIENCE

Bioprospector Petrona Rios collects plants and insects in the rain forests of Costa Rica. As a bioprospector (bī ō-prä′spek tər), she gathers these specimens so that chemists can analyze them for use in developing new medicines.

Along with other bioprospectors, Petrona Rios continually crisscrosses the rain forest, gathering plant and insect specimens. The collected specimens are processed at INBio (Instituto Nacional de Biodiversidad) and sent to the University of Costa Rica. There, chemists make samples of the materials and send them to a major drug company. Chemists at the drug company thoroughly test the samples, looking for substances that can be used in new medicines.

As the samples are tested, they go through many chemical and physical changes. What chemical and physical changes do you see every day?

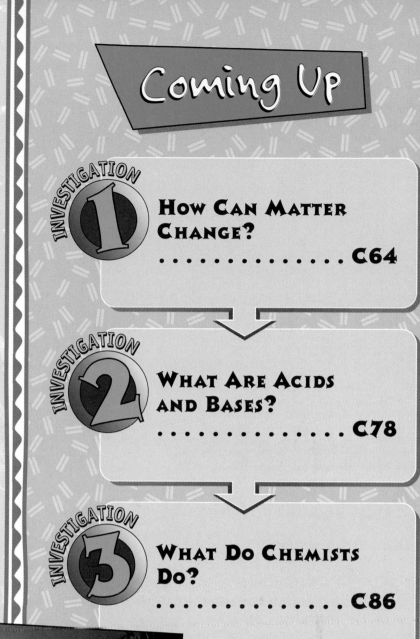

Coming Up

◄ Petrona Rios (*center*) with student assistants

HOW CAN MATTER CHANGE?

You can tear a piece of paper into hundreds of smaller pieces. Yet each piece, no matter how small, is still paper. You could recycle the small pieces and make new paper from them. But what would you have if you were to burn the paper? Find out about changes that matter can undergo in this investigation.

Activity

Balloon Blower

Blowing up a balloon can be a lot of work. How would you like to have a balloon that inflates by itself? In this activity you can combine some materials and make an automatic balloon inflater with the changes that result.

MATERIALS
- goggles
- balloon
- funnel
- measuring spoon
- baking soda
- vinegar
- narrow-necked bottle
- *Science Notebook*

SAFETY

Wear goggles during this activity.

Procedure

1. Blow up a balloon and let the air out several times. This action will stretch the rubber, making the balloon easier to inflate.

2. Place the stem of a funnel in the neck of the deflated balloon. Pour two spoonfuls of baking soda into the balloon. Gently shake the balloon to make sure the baking soda settles to the bottom of the balloon. Remove the funnel from the balloon.

3. Add several spoonfuls of vinegar to a narrow-necked bottle.

Step 2

4. Stretch the opening of the balloon over the mouth of the bottle, as shown in the picture. Make sure no baking soda escapes from the balloon.

5. Lift the balloon and hold it above the bottle so that the baking soda falls into the bottle.

Step 4

6. Observe the changes that take place when the baking soda mixes with the vinegar. **Record** your observations in your *Science Notebook*.

Analyze and Conclude

1. A **chemical change** involves the formation of new substances. What evidence is there that a chemical change took place inside the bottle after the baking soda dropped into the vinegar?

2. What happened to the balloon? From your observation, what can you **infer** about one of the substances produced when vinegar and baking soda react?

3. Hypothesize about the action of the baking soda and vinegar. Are both substances still present, or have they changed into new types of matter? **Give evidence** to support your hypothesis.

Technology
Link
CD-ROM

INVESTIGATE FURTHER!

Use the **Science Processor CD-ROM**, *The Nature of Matter* (Investigation 3, More Matter?) to travel back in time to 1789 and visit Antoine Lavoisier's laboratory. Conduct an experiment to find out what happens when you heat tin.

Activity

Making a Fire Extinguisher

In the last activity a chemical change produced a gas. In this activity you can see why this gas makes a useful fire extinguisher.

MATERIALS

- goggles
- spoon
- vinegar
- 2 jars
- baking soda
- shallow dish
- 2 long fireplace matches
- *Science Notebook*

SAFETY

Wear goggles during this activity. Be very careful when working around open flames. Secure loose clothing and tie back long hair.

Procedure

1. Add three spoonfuls of vinegar to one jar and one spoonful of baking soda to another jar.

2. Your teacher will insert a burning match first into the jar containing baking soda and then into the jar containing vinegar, as shown in the picture. The flame will not touch the contents of the jars. Look for any changes in the flame and then blow out the match. **Record** your observations in your *Science Notebook*.

3. Hold the jar containing baking soda firmly on the tabletop while you carefully pour the vinegar into this jar. **Describe** what happens.

4. Your teacher will light another fireplace match and insert the tip of the burning match into the jar containing the vinegar and baking soda. **Observe** what happens and **record** your observations.

Analyze and Conclude

1. Oxygen must be present for burning to take place. **Infer** whether oxygen was present above the baking soda and the vinegar in each jar before you mixed these materials. **Explain** what your inference is based on.

2. What **inferences** can you make about the gas released when you mixed the vinegar and the baking soda? **Give evidence** to support your inferences.

Step 2

Activity

Solids From Liquids

If you have ever made water turn into ice, you've made a solid from a liquid. In this activity you'll make a solid from two liquids by causing a chemical change.

Procedure

1. Obtain samples of unknown liquids *A* and *B*. Study the liquids and **record** your observations in your *Science Notebook*.

2. Mix the two liquids by carefully pouring the contents of one container into the other container.

Step 2

3. **Observe** the mixture for five minutes. **Record** any changes you observe.

Analyze and Conclude

1. What did you observe happening when you mixed the two liquids together?

2. What evidence indicates that the change you observed taking place was a chemical change?

3. **Hypothesize** whether liquids *A* and *B* are the same material or different materials. Support your hypothesis.

Physical and Chemical Change

Reading Focus How are chemical changes different from physical changes?

Picture yourself in this situation. You're getting ready to go to a party. You're all dressed except for your favorite wool sweater, which just came from the cleaners. You take the sweater from its protective plastic and pull it on. But it's too small—much too small!

You take the sweater off and hold it up. It's about half the size it's supposed to be! What went wrong?

Changing but Staying the Same

The case of the shrunken sweater is an example of a physical change. A **physical change** is a change in the size, shape, or state of a material. No new matter is formed during a physical change. The wool of the sweater is still the same. It just takes up less space now!

You see physical changes every day. When you sharpen a pencil or rub chalk on the board, you cause physical changes to take place. The pencil shavings and the chalk dust produced by your actions are different from the objects they came from. But the shavings are still made up of wood, and the dust is still made up of chalk.

In nature, physical changes can turn one kind of landscape into another. For example, over many millions of years, a river can carve its way down through solid rock to form a deep canyon. Pounding waves, over time, can transform rock cliffs into fine sand. In both cases, the rocks may be changed in size and appearance, but they are still made of the same substances.

Water is a good substance to use when studying physical changes. Many substances dissolve in water. The act of dissolving is a physical change. Changes in state—melting, freezing, evaporation, and condensation—are physical changes.

Why is making a baseball bat from a piece of wood an example of a physical change? ▼

Changing but *Not* Staying the Same

Have you ever smelled milk that has turned sour? Milk is a mixture. When bacteria digest part of the mixture, a new substance, called lactic acid, is produced. This change is similar to the one that occurs when two liquids are mixed together in the activity on page C67. Any change in which new substances are formed is a **chemical change**.

Water can also be changed chemically. Recall that water is a compound of the elements hydrogen and oxygen. The drawing shows how water can be changed into its component elements.

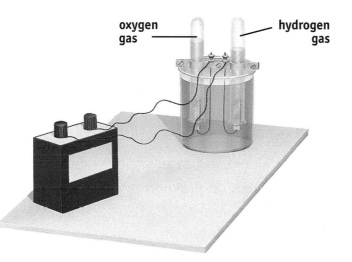

oxygen gas   hydrogen gas

▲ An electric current can be used to separate water into its elements, oxygen gas and hydrogen gas. The gases can be collected in test tubes.

Chemical changes are common in nature. The rusting of iron is one example of such a change. Rust is produced when oxygen from the air combines with iron. The product is neither iron nor oxygen, but a new substance called iron oxide, or rust.

▲ Plants use energy from sunlight to change water and carbon dioxide gas into sugar. Plants use the sugar as food.

▲ Animals use plants as food. Chemical changes occur when food is digested. These chemical changes release energy that animals need to grow and be active.

▲ Some chemical changes are not helpful. For example, rusted parts on a bicycle don't move smoothly and may crumble.

Describing Chemical Changes

Chemical changes are triggered by chemical reactions. In a chemical reaction, one or more substances interact to form new substances. To describe a chemical reaction, scientists write "chemical sentences." These sentences are written in the form of equations.

Suppose you want to describe the reaction in which water breaks down into hydrogen and oxygen. The chemical equation for the reaction is shown here.

$$2H_2O \longrightarrow 2H_2 + O_2$$

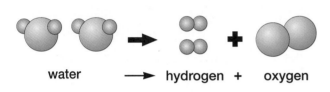

water $\longrightarrow$ hydrogen + oxygen

To express this reaction in words, you would say that two molecules of water produce two molecules of hydrogen and one molecule of oxygen. The arrow is read as *produce*, and the plus sign is read as *and*.

Look at the equation for the reaction in which iron and oxygen combine to produce iron oxide, or rust.

$$4Fe + 3O_2 \longrightarrow 2Fe_2O_3$$

How would you write this chemical sentence in words?

Many changes, such as the freezing of water to form ice, are physical. No new substances are formed. Other changes, such as those that occur when a fuel is burned or a piece of iron rusts, result in new substances being formed. Such changes are chemical changes. ■

Science in Literature

HOW METALS REACT

"Potassium and tin behave differently when put into contact with water. Potassium . . . reacts vigorously, and so much heat is generated that the hydrogen gas produced catches fire and burns with a lilac flame. Tin . . . reacts hardly at all with water. If diluted acid is used, potassium reacts even more vigorously, and tin reacts very slowly to produce hydrogen."

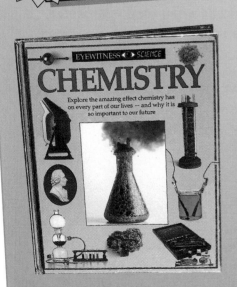

Eyewitness Science: Chemistry
by Dr. Ann Newmark
Dorling Kindersley, 1993

Look at page 25 of *Eyewitness Science: Chemistry* by Dr. Ann Newmark to see pictures of these reactions. Then read on to find out about many other chemical changes.

Atomic Structure and Chemical Change

Reading Focus What are the parts of an atom, and how are they arranged in a Bohr model?

As you have read, each of the 112 known elements is made up of atoms. All chemical changes involve atoms. So to understand these changes, you need to know more about atoms.

What Is a Model?

Atoms are much too small to see with most microscopes. But scientists use special instruments to create images of individual atoms and molecules. The picture on this page is an example of one of those images.

The structures of atoms are much too small to be shown in such images. How, then, do scientists learn about what's inside an atom? They learn from indirect evidence gathered by studying how matter behaves.

Based on this evidence, scientists have developed various models of the atom. In science, a **model** is a way to represent an object or to describe how a process takes place. Models are often used to describe things that are too big or too small to be studied directly.

What Is an Atom Like?

Modern scientific models of atoms describe them as being made up of tiny parts. Most of an atom's mass is contained in a central core called a **nucleus** (n$\overline{oo}$'klē əs). This nucleus contains protons (prō'tänz) and neutrons (n$\overline{oo}$'tränz). A **proton** is a particle that has a positive electric charge. A **neutron** is a particle that has no electric charge.

Traveling around the nucleus are one or more electrons (ē lek'tränz). An **electron** is a particle that has a negative electric charge. An electron is much smaller and lighter than a proton or a neutron.

◄This image of atoms enlarged about a billion times was made with a *scanning tunneling microscope*, known as a STM for short. It shows atoms of the element iron on a copper surface. The iron atoms appear in blue and the copper surface appears in red. The colors seen in STM images such as this one are added by artists to make the individual atoms easier to see.

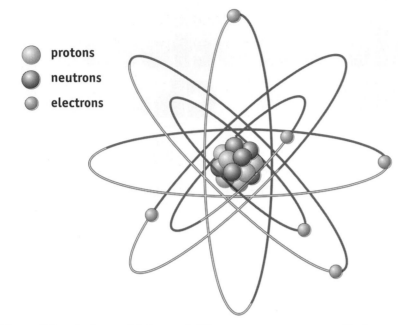

protons
neutrons
electrons

◄ The drawing shows a model of a carbon atom. This atom has six protons and six neutrons in its nucleus and six electrons outside the nucleus. This type of atomic model is known as a Bohr model, after Niels Bohr, the Danish physicist who developed it.

Two Models—Old and New

Look at the Bohr models of a helium atom and a lithium (lith'ē əm) atom below. Notice how the electrons are shown moving around the nucleus in paths called orbits. The helium atom has one orbit and the lithium atom has two orbits. A Bohr model is also called a planetary model of the atom.

Bohr suggested his model in 1913. As scientists learned more about atoms, they found that electrons do not travel in definite orbits. Rather, they "swarm" around the nucleus, much like bees swarm around a hive. Because the electrons travel so fast, they are like a "cloud" surrounding the nucleus, as shown in the drawing below.

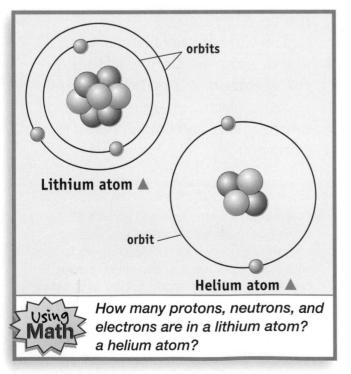

orbits

Lithium atom ▲

orbit

Helium atom ▲

Using Math *How many protons, neutrons, and electrons are in a lithium atom? a helium atom?*

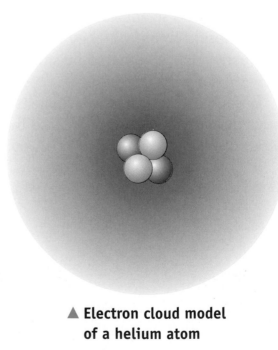

▲ **Electron cloud model of a helium atom**

Roles of Protons and Electrons

The number of protons in the nucleus of an atom gives the atom its identity. An atom of hydrogen has one proton. An atom of oxygen has eight protons. That's what makes hydrogen what it is and oxygen what it is.

Recall from the periodic table on pages C36 and C37 that every element has a different atomic number. The **atomic number** of an element is the number of protons in an atom of that element. The atomic number of hydrogen is 1. Look at the periodic table. What is the atomic number of oxygen?

Electrons are the smallest of the three types of atomic particles. Yet, because electrons move around outside the nucleus, they determine how an atom reacts with other atoms. In other words, the electrons give the atom its chemical properties.

Atoms With a Charge

Usually the number of protons in an atom equals the number of electrons. So the positive and negative charges balance each other. This balance leaves the atom electrically neutral.

Sometimes, however, an atom may capture one or more electrons from another atom. Then, both atoms become electrically charged. An electrically charged atom is called an **ion** (ī′ən). The drawing shows how positive and negative ions form.

Positive and negative ions attract each other. If the attraction is strong enough, the ions are held tightly together and form an ionic compound, such as sodium chloride. Ionic compounds are not made up of molecules. Instead, the basic unit of any ionic compound is made up of one or more positive ions and one or more negative ions.

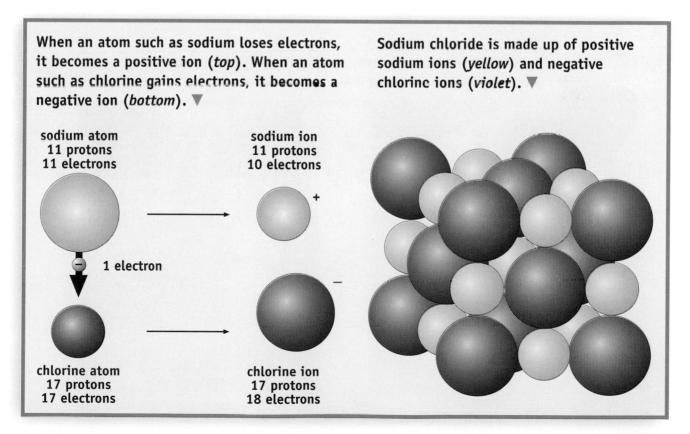

When an atom such as sodium loses electrons, it becomes a positive ion (*top*). When an atom such as chlorine gains electrons, it becomes a negative ion (*bottom*). ▼

Sodium chloride is made up of positive sodium ions (*yellow*) and negative chlorine ions (*violet*). ▼

sodium atom
11 protons
11 electrons

sodium ion
11 protons
10 electrons

+

1 electron

–

chlorine atom
17 protons
17 electrons

chlorine ion
17 protons
18 electrons

Atoms and Molecules

Many compounds, such as water, are made up of molecules. In forming molecules, atoms share electrons. For example, when hydrogen reacts with oxygen to form water, two hydrogen atoms and one oxygen atom share electrons, as shown in the drawing. Chemists call this type of compound a covalent compound.

Making and Breaking Bonds

Energy is always involved in the making or breaking of chemical bonds. Usually when bonds form between atoms, energy is given off. However, sometimes a little energy must be added to get such a reaction started. For example, a spark is needed to get hydrogen to combine with oxygen. But once the reaction starts, energy is given off rapidly, as shown in the photograph.

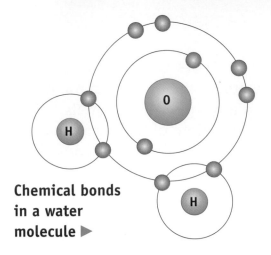

Chemical bonds in a water molecule ▶

Energy is also involved in breaking chemical bonds. Recall that water can be broken down into hydrogen and oxygen by passing electricity through it. The electricity provides the energy needed to break the bonds between the hydrogen atoms and oxygen atoms that make up water. ■

Internet Field Trip

Visit **www.eduplace.com** to find out more about chemical bonding.

In 1937, disaster struck the hydrogen-filled *Hindenburg*. A spark ignited the ship's hydrogen, and energy was released as the hydrogen combined with oxygen in the air. ▼

Conservation of Mass

Reading Focus What is the law of conservation of mass?

When a piece of wood burns, the mass of the ashes that remain is less than the mass of the original piece of wood. On the other hand, when a piece of tin is heated, it gains mass. Three hundred years ago, these and similar observations led scientists to wonder: Is matter destroyed when wood burns? Is matter created when tin is heated?

Over the years the work of many scientists provided answers to these and other questions about matter. For example, when wood burns, some of its mass goes into gases that are produced. These gases escape into the air. Today we know that matter cannot be created or destroyed by any chemical reaction. This statement of fact is known as the law of conservation of mass.

Albert Einstein publishes his theory of relativity, which includes the equation $E = mc^2$. This theory establishes the relationship between mass and energy.

1905

Working independently, two scientists—Karl Wilhelm Scheele and Joseph Priestley—discover oxygen.

A.D. 1772–1774

$E = MC^2$

1890–1910
Marie Curie's work with radium leads to a better understanding of radioactivity.

450 B.C.
Greek philosophers Leucippus (lōō sip′əs) and Democritus (di mäk′rə təs) first state the ideas set forth in the law of conservation of mass.

1789
Antoine Lavoisier, a French chemist, discovers that when matter such as tin burns, it combines with oxygen. This discovery leads to the law of conservation of mass.

Radioactive Elements

Reading Focus What is a radioactive element?

On March 1, 1896, French scientist Henri Becquerel wrapped a sheet of photographic film in paper that light couldn't penetrate. He placed the package in a desk drawer, together with a few small rocks, and closed the drawer.

A few days later, Becquerel developed the film, expecting to see an unexposed white negative. Instead he was shocked to see darkened areas on the film. Something had changed the chemicals on the film—but what?

▲ **Becquerel discovers radioactivity.**

Nuclear Radiation

Becquerel's film had been exposed to nuclear radiation (rā dē ā′shən), invisible energy that came from the rocks. The rocks contained the radioactive element uranium (yōō rā′nē əm). A **radioactive element** is made up of atoms whose nuclei (*nuclei* is the plural of *nucleus*)

break down, or decay, into nuclei of other atoms. When a radioactive element decays, it changes into a different element. This happens because some of the radiation released is in the form of protons and neutrons. And when an atom loses protons from its nucleus, its atomic number changes.

Recall that an element is identified by its atomic number. The drawing shows how a uranium nucleus decays to form a thorium (thôr′ē əm) nucleus.

When a nucleus decays, large amounts of energy are released. The particles released from the nucleus will have lots of energy. Sometimes high-energy rays called gamma rays are produced as well.

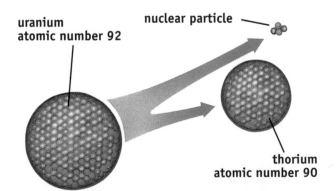

uranium
atomic number 92

nuclear particle

thorium
atomic number 90

▲ **When a uranium nucleus decays, it loses 2 protons and 2 neutrons, leaving a nucleus with 90 protons. The element with atomic number 90 is thorium.**

C76

▲ In a chain reaction, particles released when a nucleus splits go on to split even more nuclei.

Using Energy From Atoms

Radioactive elements occur naturally. Scientists have also learned how to split the nuclei of some atoms by bombarding them with neutrons. This reaction is called **nuclear fission** (no͞o′klē ər fish′ən). *Fission* means "splitting."

The drawing shows how neutrons are used to split nuclei of uranium atoms. Each time a nucleus splits, two new atoms form. Energy and more neutrons are also released. Some of the neutrons strike and split other nuclei, producing a chain reaction.

An uncontrolled nuclear chain reaction releases energy so fast that an explosion takes place. In a nuclear reactor, a nuclear chain reaction is controlled. In a controlled chain reaction, energy is released slowly.

Radiation—Helpful and Harmful

Nuclear reactors provide energy that is used to generate electricity. Reactors are also used to make radioactive forms of many elements. These elements are used in medical research and in the treatment of certain illnesses.

Nuclear energy has many uses. But nuclear radiation can also damage human tissues. Thus, radioactive materials must be handled safely. ■

INVESTIGATION 1 WRAP-UP

REVIEW

1. How does heating sugar in a spoon differ from dissolving it in a cup of hot water?

2. Write the following chemical equation in words.

$$2H_2O \rightarrow 2H_2 + O_2$$

CRITICAL THINKING

3. When might a Bohr model of an atom be more helpful than an electron cloud model?

4. If two neutrons escaped the nucleus of an atom, what would be the effect on the atom's atomic number and its total electric charge?

C77

INVESTIGATION 2

WHAT ARE ACIDS AND BASES?

Vinegar, orange juice, soap, baking soda, and antacid tablets are all things you can probably find around your home. Some of these materials are acids, and some are bases. In this investigation you'll find out what acids and bases are and how to use some simple tests to tell the difference.

Activity

Cabbage-Juice Science

Some substances, called indicators, are one color in an acid and a different color in a base. In this activity you can see for yourself how an indicator works.

- - - - - - - - - - - - - - - - - -

Procedure

1. In your *Science Notebook*, **make a chart** like the one shown.

Cup	Material	Observation
1	Vinegar	
2	Lemon juice	
3	Baking soda	
4	Powdered lime	

See **SCIENCE** and **MATH TOOLBOX** page H11 if you need to review *Making a Chart to Organize Data.*

MATERIALS

- goggles
- 6 small plastic cups
- juice of a red cabbage
- marker
- 2 droppers
- vinegar
- lemon juice
- baking soda
- powdered lime (calcium oxide)
- pineapple juice
- liquid soap
- *Science Notebook*

SAFETY ///////

Wear goggles during this activity. Do not touch or taste any chemicals.

C78

2. Half fill four small plastic cups with red cabbage juice and number the cups with a marker.

3. Use a dropper to add a few drops of vinegar to the cabbage juice in cup 1. Use a clean dropper to add a few drops of lemon juice to cup 2. **Record** in your chart any changes that you observe.

4. Add a small amount of baking soda to cup 3 and a small amount of powdered lime to cup 4. **Record** any changes that you observe.

5. **Predict** what would happen if you tested red cabbage juice with pineapple juice and with liquid soap. Carry out the tests in clean cups and check your predictions.

6. **Predict** what would happen if you added vinegar to the cup containing the baking soda and cabbage juice. Carry out the test. **Record** your results.

Step 4

Analyze and Conclude

1. In which cups did chemical changes occur? How do you know?

2. Cabbage juice is an indicator. What evidence is there that some of the materials you tested are acids or bases?

3. **Infer** which of the materials is the most similar to vinegar. **Give evidence** to support your inference. These materials are acids.

4. **Classify** all the substances you tested into two groups, based on how they react with the cabbage-juice indicator.

INVESTIGATE FURTHER!

EXPERIMENT

Use additional cabbage juice to test different liquids, including plain water and carbonated water. Group the liquids by the color changes they produce.

Activity
The Litmus Test

Litmus paper is an indicator. Blue litmus paper turns red in an acid. Red litmus paper turns blue in a base. See if you can identify the acids and bases in this activity.

MATERIALS
- goggles
- 3 pieces of red litmus paper
- 3 pieces of blue litmus paper
- 3 liquids in containers—one labeled *A*, one labeled *B*, and one labeled *C*
- *Science Notebook*

SAFETY //////
Wear goggles during this activity. Do not touch or taste any of the chemicals used in this activity.

Procedure

1. In your *Science Notebook*, **make a chart** like the one shown.

Solution	Red Litmus Paper	Blue Litmus Paper
A		
B		
C		

2. Place a piece of red litmus (lit′məs) paper and a piece of blue litmus paper beside three containers labeled *A*, *B*, and *C*. Remember, blue litmus paper turns red in an acid; red litmus paper turns blue in a base.

3. Dip the tip of a piece of blue litmus paper and the tip of a piece of red litmus paper in each liquid. Leave each piece of litmus paper beside the container in which it was dipped.

4. **Observe** each piece of litmus paper for any change in color. In your chart, **record** your observations.

Step 2

Analyze and Conclude

1. Which liquids were acids? How do you know?

2. Which liquids were bases? How do you know?

3. Write a rule for using litmus paper to identify a liquid that is neither an acid nor a base.

Step 3

Acids, Bases, and Salts

> **Reading Focus** How can you find out if a compound is an acid or a base?

It's a hot day, and you've just finished mowing the lawn. Now you're looking forward to a cool, refreshing drink of lemonade. You take the pitcher from the refrigerator, pour yourself an ice-cold glass, and take a deep gulp. Immediately your mouth puckers and your eyes begin to water. It's not lemonade—it's lemon juice! And it's sour!

You have just discovered a telltale property of some important chemical compounds—acids. And you used a test that you wouldn't be able to use in the laboratory—the taste test.

Telltale Colors

Compounds have certain properties that can be used to classify them. Acids and bases are two important groups of compounds. As the pictures below show, these compounds are found in many household products.

One property of acids and bases is their effect on indicators (in'di kāt ərz). An **indicator** is a substance that changes color when mixed with an acid or a base. Cabbage juice and litmus paper are used as indicators in the activities on pages C78 to C80.

ACIDS The substances below are acids. An **acid** is a compound that turns blue litmus paper red. ▼

BASES The substances below are bases. A **base** is a compound that turns red litmus paper blue. ▼

C81

Properties of Acids and Bases

Acids have a sour taste. Some acids, like the natural acids in vinegar and citrus fruits, are weak. Strong acids, such as sulfuric (sul fyoor′ik) acid are poisonous and can burn the skin. Many acids can eat away metals. Digestive juices in your stomach contain a strong acid. However, this acid is very dilute (di-lōōt′). This means that a small amount of the acid is mixed with a large amount of water. Diluting a strong acid can reduce some of its harmful effects.

Bases taste bitter and feel slippery. Like acids, some bases are weak and some are strong. Baking soda and antacid tablets are examples of weak bases. Like strong acids, strong bases, such as sodium hydroxide (hī dräks′īd), or lye, are poisonous.

The Strong and the Weak

Acids and bases are usually found dissolved in water. For example, lemon juice and orange juice are solutions of citric acid in water. If you add a small amount of acid to a large volume of water, the solution won't be very acidic. On the other hand, if you add a large amount of acid to a small volume of water, the solution might be very acidic.

The acidic or basic strength of a solution is measured on a scale known as the pH scale. The pH scale has units from 0 to 14. The smaller the unit, the more acidic a solution is. The larger the unit, the more basic it is. Thus, a

Using Math *What is the median number on the pH scale?*

The pH Scale

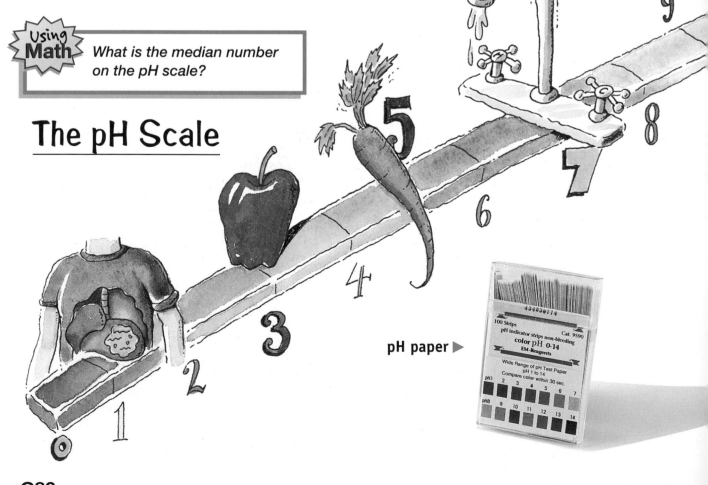

pH paper ▶

solution with a pH of 1 or less is very acidic. And a solution with a pH near 14 is very basic. Solutions with a pH near the middle of the scale are neutral. Pure water has a pH of 7.

How can you find the pH of a solution? Indicator paper made with special dyes is used for this purpose. The paper turns different colors depending upon how acidic or basic the solution that's being tested is.

Canceling Out Each Other

Antacid tablets, which are weak bases, are often used to relieve acid indigestion. This condition occurs when the stomach produces too much acid, resulting in a burning sensation. The word part *ant* in the term *antacid* comes from the prefix *anti-*, which means "against" or "opposed to." The base in the tablet reacts with the acid and cancels out, or neutralizes (nōō′trə-līz əz), its effects.

The reaction between an acid and a base is called **neutralization** (nōō trə-li zā′shən). When an acid and a base react, two substances—water and a

salt—are produced. A **salt** is a compound that can be formed when an acid reacts with a base.

Common Properties of Salts

Look again at the drawing on page C73, showing how the ions of sodium chloride, which is a salt, are arranged. All salts are ionic compounds. Recall that ions are electrically charged particles. When a salt is melted or dissolved in water, its ions move about. As a result, molten, or melted, salts and solutions of salts are good conductors of electricity.

Salts have many other properties in common. For example, salts are solid at room temperature and have high melting points. Salts also consist of crystals that have definite shapes.

Acid Rain

Reading Focus What is acid rain, and how does it damage the environment?

A gentle wind blows constantly across the land. The wind sweeps across cities, villages, factories, and power plants like an invisible broom. And like a real broom, the wind carries all sorts of dirt along with it. This dirt includes soot, dust, and smoke as well as harmful gases.

Pickup and Delivery

When the wind moves over farm areas, it picks up dust and traces of fertilizers and chemicals used to control weeds and insects. Over cities and industrial regions, the wind picks up gases produced by the burning of gasoline, coal, and oil. These gases include compounds of sulfur and of nitrogen.

Where acid rain is "born" ▼

Acids From the Sky

As sulfur and nitrogen compounds mix with water in the air, they react to produce two strong acids—sulfuric acid and nitric acid. At first these acids are dissolved in tiny droplets of water that remain in the air. They are part of the clouds that form. However, over time these droplets begin to collect into larger and larger drops. Eventually the drops fall as rain, snow, sleet, or hail.

If you were to measure the pH of this precipitation, also known as acid rain, you might discover readings as low as 2.0. Acid solutions this strong can damage both living and nonliving things. People in many parts of the world have experienced lung, skin, and eye irritations caused by acid rain.

Modern windmills use clean wind energy to generate electricity. ▶

The stone and metal of famous statues and buildings have been damaged or eaten away by acids from the sky. Forests and lakes in many regions of the world have been affected by acid rain. In Germany's Black Forest, acid rain has killed trees in an area of more than 5,000 km² (2,000 mi²). In Sweden, thousands of lakes have become so acidic that many plants and fish can no longer live in them. Similar events and conditions have been reported in the United States and Canada.

What can be done to stop the destruction caused by acid rain? The obvious answer is to reduce air pollution. The major source of air pollution is the burning of fossil fuels—coal, oil, and gas. We use these fuels to run cars, heat homes, produce electricity, and power factories.

Scientists and engineers worldwide are seeking ways to reduce dependency on fossil fuels. Some promising alternative sources of energy are being used. These sources include hydroelectric plants, which use the energy of moving water to generate electricity. Other sources of clean energy being explored are wind energy and solar energy.

In cases where fossil fuels are commonly used—such as in power plants, factories, and automobiles—methods have been developed to keep pollutants from escaping into the air. Various measures for reducing air pollution are being used in many countries. ∎

INVESTIGATION 2 WRAP-UP

THINK IT WRITE IT

REVIEW **1.** How are acids and bases alike? How are they different?

2. When would you use an indicator?

CRITICAL THINKING **3.** What effect would a solution with a pH of 11 have on litmus paper? How would you neutralize this solution?

4. What are some ways you and your family can help prevent acid rain?

WHAT DO CHEMISTS DO?

Suppose you read about a mysterious material beneath the Antarctic icecap that scientists have discovered. How would you learn about such a material? A chemist would study its chemical and physical properties. You can do the same thing.

Activity

Mystery Powders

Imagine that you find six jars, each containing a different powder. On the floor near the jars, you find six labels—sugar, salt, baking soda, cornstarch, powdered milk, and plaster of Paris. How will you identify the powders?

Procedure

1. Study the table on page C87. It contains information about the appearance and behavior of six materials.

2. In your *Science Notebook*, **make a chart** with the same headings as the table on the next page, but don't fill in your chart yet. Instead of names of substances in column 1, **record** the letters *A* through *F*.

3. Sprinkle a sample of one mystery powder on a sheet of black construction paper. **Observe** the powder with a hand lens. Under the heading *Appearance*, in the appropriate row, **record** how the powder looks. Repeat this step for each powder.

4. Place three small samples of one powder on a piece of foil. Add a few drops of water to one sample and stir the mixture with a toothpick.

Name	Appearance	Water	Vinegar	Iodine
Sugar	white; grains of different shapes	dissolves, forming clear solution	no reaction	no reaction
Salt	white; small crystal cubes	dissolves, forming clear solution	no reaction	no reaction
Baking soda	small grains of different shapes	dissolves, forming clear solution	bubbles form	no reaction
Cornstarch	white powder; tiny particles	forms gooey mixture	no reaction	turns dark blue
Powdered milk	white powder; tiny particles	forms cloudy mixture	no reaction	no reaction
Plaster of Paris	white powder; tiny particles	forms cloudy mixture that slowly hardens	no reaction	no reaction

5. **Record** your observations. Add vinegar to the second sample and iodine to the third. Mix and **observe** each sample and **record** your observations.

6. Repeat steps 4 and 5 for each powder.

Analyze and Conclude

1. Study your chart and **compare** it with the table above.

2. **Identify** each powder, based on the properties you observed. Write the names in your chart.

Step 4

INVESTIGATE FURTHER!

EXPERIMENT

Think of a powder you did not use in this activity. Check with your teacher to be sure that your choice is safe. Then have your classmates test your mystery powder. Have them tell which of the six powders studied in this activity is most like your mystery powder.

Activity

"Slime" Time

Look around you. Many objects in your classroom are made of materials that were "invented" by chemists working in laboratories. Plastics and synthetic fibers are good examples of such materials. In this activity you'll make some "slime." Is this a good name for your substance?

MATERIALS
- goggles
- water
- white glue
- food coloring
- borax
- plastic cup
- plastic spoon
- *Science Notebook*

SAFETY //////
Wear goggles during this activity. Do not put any of the materials in your mouth.

Procedure

1. Study samples of water, white glue, food coloring, and borax. **List** them in your *Science Notebook*. **Describe** the appearance of each material and **list** as many properties of each material as you can.

2. Add equal amounts of the water and white glue to a plastic cup. Add a few drops of food coloring and stir the mixture thoroughly with a plastic spoon.

3. **Observe** how the mixture looks. If you wish, you may keep adding more food coloring until the mixture is the color you want.

4. Gradually add the borax to the mixture while you stir it. **Observe** and **record** any changes in the appearance of the mixture.

5. Add borax until no more liquid is visible. Touch the mixture and **describe** how it feels. You can adjust the amount of borax to give your slime exactly the slimy feeling you want it to have.

Step 4

Analyze and Conclude

1. Pick up and handle your slime. **Describe** as many of its properties as you can.

2. **Compare** the properties of your slime to the properties of the materials you mixed together to make it.

3. Think of some possible uses for your slime. **Describe** the uses in your *Science Notebook*.

Polymers and Plastics

Reading Focus What are some organic compounds found in nature, and what are some made by scientists?

SCIENCE TECHNOLOGY & SOCIETY

Scientists once believed that compounds containing carbon were produced only by living things. Because living things are called organisms, compounds containing carbon were called organic compounds.

Carbon, the Supercombiner

Scientists have identified about 11 million different compounds. Of these, more than 10 million contain carbon.

One of carbon's unique properties is its ability to join, or form bonds, with other atoms. Because of the arrangement of its electrons, a single carbon atom is able to bond with as many as four other atoms.

This bond-forming ability makes it possible for long chains of carbon atoms to form. Each carbon atom in a

chain can also form bonds with atoms of other elements. For example, there are hundreds of ways that compounds can form from the elements carbon and hydrogen.

Not all organic compounds are complex. A molecule of methane (meth'ān), the simplest organic compound, is made up of only five atoms. Models of molecules of methane and two other organic compounds are shown below.

Vitamin C—$C_6H_8O_6$ ▼

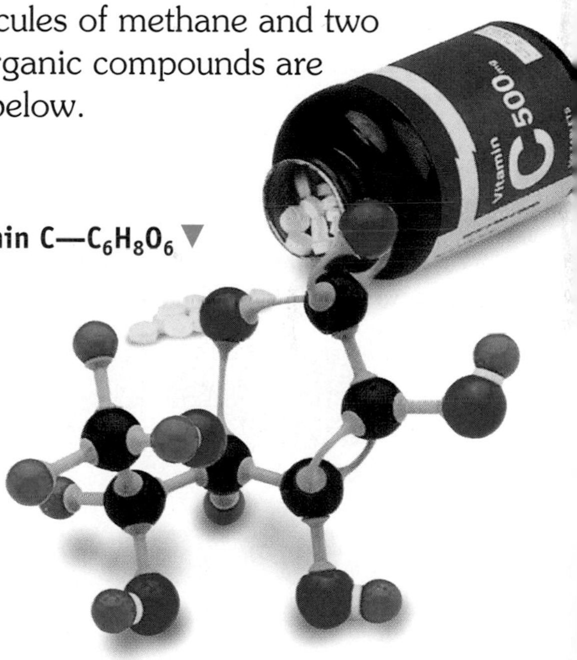

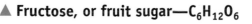

Methane—CH_4 ▼

▲ Fructose, or fruit sugar—$C_6H_{12}O_6$

C89

Polymers—Chemical Giants

The next time you use table sugar, or sucrose, think of its formula:

$$C_{12}H_{22}O_{11}$$

One molecule of this sugar contains 45 atoms! As you have read, a molecule of this sugar is pretty complex. Look again at the model of sucrose on page C41.

Now look at the model of a small part of a protein molecule on this page. Proteins are the building blocks from which your body is made. They are probably the most complex organic compounds found in nature.

Proteins are polymers (päl'ə mərz). A **polymer** is an organic compound that contains a very long chain or chains of carbon compounds. The word *polymer* means "many parts."

Part of a protein molecule ▼

Plastics are synthetic polymers. To make a polymer, chemists start with a simple organic molecule. This molecule

▲ **Some useful products made of plastic**

is one part of the polymer. Hundreds or thousands of these parts are put together to form the carbon chain. Other molecules are added to the sides of the chain.

The side chains of a polymer determine its properties. For example, side chains can make a polymer hard, flexible, or tough. Just think of all the different kinds of plastics and the wide range of properties they exhibit. ■

INVESTIGATE FURTHER!

EXPERIMENT

Work with a partner to create a paper-clip model of a polymer. Use paper clips of different sizes and colors as shown here. When you're finished, describe the polymer's properties.

What Chemists Do

Reading Focus What are the two main categories of work that chemists do?

Chemistry is the study of matter—what it's made of and how it behaves. Now think back to the title of this unit—"The Nature of Matter." The unit title could have been "An Introduction to Chemistry." So all this time you have been studying chemistry and doing some of the things chemists do!

Analysis and Synthesis

The things that chemists do can be divided into two large categories—analysis (ə nal'ə sis) and synthesis (sin'thə sis). In simple terms, *analysis* means "taking things apart" and *synthesis* means "putting things together." Many of the materials you use in everyday life are products of chemical research. Research chemists are constantly inventing and testing new drugs and medicines. The making of polymers, as described earlier in this chapter, is an example of synthesis.

Types of Chemical Reactions

In conducting research, chemists observe different types of chemical reactions. Most reactions can be classified into one of four major groups—synthesis, decomposition (dē käm pə- zish'ən), single replacement, and double replacement. Take a closer look at these reactions. It might surprise you to know that many of the changes that occur during the activities in this unit involve reactions such as these.

A chemist at work in the laboratory ▼

SYNTHESIS   *Synthesis* means "putting things together." The reaction in which hydrogen gas and oxygen gas combine to produce water is an example of a synthesis reaction in which a water molecule is "put together."

synthesis

DECOMPOSITION   Decomposition involves the breaking down of a substance into simpler substances. In the activity on page C33, sugar is heated, causing it to break down into simpler substances—carbon and water.

decomposition

SINGLE REPLACEMENT   In this type of reaction, one of the elements in a compound is replaced by another element. Such a reaction can be used to coat a piece of metal, such as copper, with a thin layer of another metal, such as silver.

single replacement

DOUBLE REPLACEMENT   In this type of reaction, elements from two different compounds change places, something like two couples changing partners at a dance. Such a reaction produces a solid from two clear liquids in the activity on page C67.

double replacement

Now you know a lot more about matter than you did at the beginning of this unit. You know what matter is made up of. You know what happens when things change. You know how to tell whether a change is chemical or physical. And you have an idea of what causes things to change. Congratulations! You are officially a beginning chemist in good standing. ■

INVESTIGATION 3 WRAP-UP

REVIEW

1. What is a polymer?

2. What are four types of chemical reactions?

CRITICAL THINKING

3. What type of reaction is involved when many small molecules combine to form a polymer?

4. Explain what happens to the atoms when a water molecule undergoes decomposition.

CHAPTER 3 REVIEW

REFLECT & EVALUATE

Word Power

Write the letter of the term that best completes each sentence. *Not all terms will be used.*

1. An organic compound made up of a very long chain of carbon compounds is a (an) ____.
2. A substance that changes color when mixed with an acid or a base is a (an) ____.
3. A change from the solid to the liquid state is a (an) ____.
4. One or more new substances are formed in a (an) ____.
5. When an acid reacts with a base, a (an) ____ forms.
6. A negatively charged particle in an atom is a (an) ____.

a. chemical change
b. electron
c. indicator
d. neutron
e. nucleus
f. physical change
g. polymer
h. salt

Check What You Know

Write the word in each pair that correctly completes each sentence.

1. On the pH scale the numbers are higher for solutions that are more (acidic, basic).
2. The number of carbon compounds is more than 10 (thousand, million).
3. A particle with a positive electric charge is a/an (proton, electron).
4. The planetary model of the atom was proposed by (Bohr, Einstein).

Problem Solving

1. Tungsten is an element with 74 protons and 109 neutrons. What is tungsten's atomic number? How many electrons does a tungsten atom have?

2. Sodium (an element) reacts with water (a compound) to produce sodium hydroxide (a compound) and hydrogen gas (an element). What kind of chemical reaction is this? Explain how you know.

Study the photographs. Then use the photographs to explain what happens during a physical change and a chemical change.

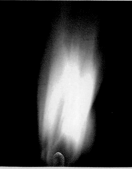

Cause and Effect

When you read, it is important to figure out what happens and why it happens. What happens is called the *effect*. Why things happen is called the *cause*.

Use these hints to determine cause and effect.

- Look for signal words: *because, and so, as a result*

- As you read, ask yourself why something is happening.

Read the paragraphs below. Then complete the exercises that follow.

Rate of Solution

Which dissolves faster in water—a sugar cube or a spoonful of loose sugar grains? Dissolving takes place only on the surface of the sugar, where the water is in contact with the sugar. Small cubes, or grains, of sugar dissolve faster than a large sugar cube. . . .

Temperature also affects the rate at which things dissolve. For example, sugar dissolves faster in hot water than in cold water. The particles of hot water are moving faster than the particles of cold water. The fast-moving particles bump into the sugar harder and more frequently, helping to break the sugar into smaller pieces.

Copy each statement. Write *C* in the blank after each cause. Write *E* in the blank after each effect.

1. Sugar will dissolve ____ where water is in contact with the surface of the grain of sugar ____.

2. Fast-moving particles of hot water ____ bump into the sugar harder and more frequently ____.

3. Hot water bumps into sugar harder and more frequently ____, helping to break the sugar into smaller pieces ____.

 **Equations and Formulas**

Density is the amount of matter in a given space. If you know the mass and the volume of an object or a substance, you can use the formula below to find the density of that object or substance.

density = mass ÷ volume

Suppose an object has a mass of 4 g and a volume of 16 cm³. Its density is 0.25 gram per cubic centimeter (0.25 g/cm³).

$$d = m \div v$$
$$d = 4 \text{ g} \div 16 \text{ cm}^3$$
$$d = \frac{4}{16} = \frac{1}{4} = 0.25 \text{ g/cm}^3$$

Use the density formula to complete the exercises that follow.

1. An object has a mass of 110 g and a volume of 20 cm³. What is the density of the object?

2. At a temperature of 4°C, the density of water is 1 g/cm³. If the density of an object is greater than that of water, the object sinks. If its density is less than that of water, the object floats. Suppose the temperature of water in a pail is 4°C. A block made of an unknown substance has a density of 0.78 g/cm³. Will the block sink or float? Explain.

3. Water at 20°C has a density of 0.998 g/cm³. A clear glass is filled with water at 20°C. A penny placed in the glass immediately falls to the bottom of the glass. What can you infer about the density of the penny?

You may wish to use a calculator for Exercise 4.

4. The density of gold is 19.3 g/cm³. The density of silver is 10.5 g/cm³. The density of nickel is 8.9 g/cm³. A block made of an unknown but pure substance has a mass of 634.125 g and a volume of 71.25 cm³. Is the material pure gold, silver, or nickel? Explain how you know.

C95

WRAP-UP!

On your own, use scientific methods to investigate a question about matter.

THINK LIKE A SCIENTIST

Ask a Question

Pose a question about matter that you would like to investigate. For example, ask, "How does the acidity of rainwater in my area compare with the acidity of distilled water?"

Make a Hypothesis

Suggest a hypothesis that is a possible answer to the question. One hypothesis is that the rainwater in my area is more acidic than distilled water.

Plan and Do a Test

Plan a controlled experiment to compare the acidity of rainwater in your area with the acidity of distilled water. You could start with rainwater, distilled water, several clean containers, and pH paper. Develop a procedure that uses these materials to test the hypothesis. With permission, carry out your experiment. Follow the safety guidelines on pages S14–S15.

Record and Analyze

Observe carefully and record your data accurately. Make repeated observations.

Draw Conclusions

Look for evidence to support the hypothesis or to show that it is false. Draw conclusions about the hypothesis. Repeat the experiment to verify the results.

WRITING IN SCIENCE
Summary

Write a one-paragraph summary of "What Chemists Do," pages C91–C92. Use these guidelines in writing your summary.

- Write one sentence stating the main idea or ideas.
- Include only important details for each main idea.
- Sum up the content in a concluding statement.

Compare your summary with that of a partner.

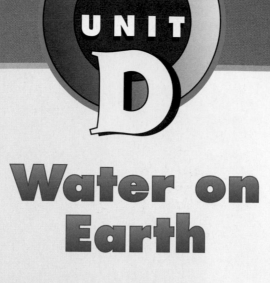

UNIT D

Water on Earth

Theme: Models

THINK
LIKE A SCIENTIST

OCEAN VIEW

The waves of the great Pacific Ocean lap endlessly along the entire length of the California coast. As seen in this view at Pigeon Point Lighthouse, the wavy ocean surface extends toward the horizon as far as one can see. Looking at a globe, you can see that oceans cover most of Earth's surface. Scientists who study water have learned where else this important resource can be found, and they continue to discover more about using water wisely and protecting water.

THINK LIKE A SCIENTIST

Questioning In this unit you'll study where water is found, how water is used, and how people can help protect water. You'll investigate questions such as these.

- How Does Nature Move Water?
- How Does Your Community Get Water?

Observing, Testing, Hypothesizing
In the Activity "Where Is the Water?" you'll model the water in different places on Earth. You'll observe where most of Earth's fresh water is found and consider whether you might be able to get drinking water from that source.

Researching In the Resource "Making Water Clean," you'll find out how water that's been used can be treated and used again. You'll also find out how water is made drinkable.

Drawing Conclusions
After you've completed your investigations, you'll draw conclusions about what you've learned—and get new ideas.

CHAPTER 1

THE WATER AROUND US

Water is all around you. But have you ever been thirsty when there seemed to be no water around? Or have you ever turned on a faucet and found that no water came out of it? If water is all around you, where is it? In this chapter you'll find out.

PEOPLE USING SCIENCE

Physical Oceanographer Since she was 15 years old, Dr. Leslie Karen Rosenfeld has known that she wanted to be an oceanographer—a scientist who studies the oceans. After two years of study, she decided that her main area of interest was physical oceanography.

Physical oceanographers study the properties of sea water. They investigate waves and currents and the winds and tides that drive them. Using ships, airplanes, satellites, and submersibles, Dr. Rosenfeld has studied the ocean "from the bottom looking up and the top looking down." Her goal, and the goal of all physical oceanographers, is to learn how the ocean behaves and why.

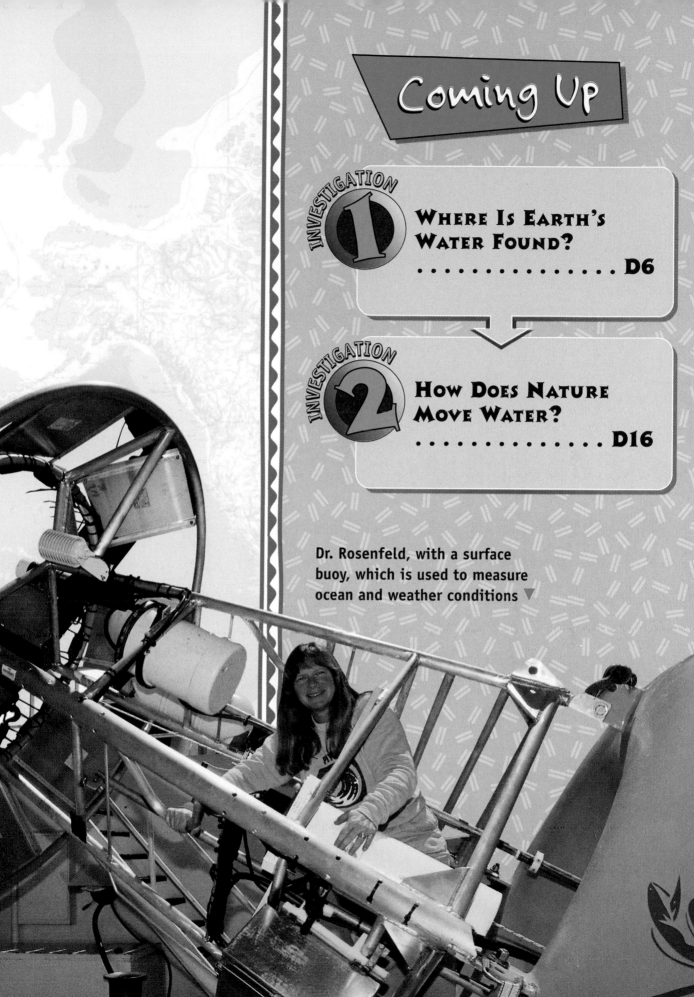

Coming Up

Dr. Rosenfeld, with a surface buoy, which is used to measure ocean and weather conditions ▽

WHERE IS EARTH'S WATER FOUND?

You might think that a place called the Water Planet exists only in a science-fiction story. But the planet on which you live is sometimes referred to as the Water Planet. That's because about three fourths of Earth's surface is covered by water. You'll learn about the distribution of Earth's waters in this investigation.

Activity

Where Is the Water?

Where's all the water on Earth? It's in different places, such as rivers and oceans. In this activity you'll use bottles to model, or represent, the amount of water in different locations on Earth.

Procedure

1. Label each of five 1-L bottles with one of the following labels: *Oceans; Underground Water; Glaciers; Rivers and Lakes; Atmosphere.*

2. Use a graduate to **measure** 1 L of water. Empty the water into a sixth 1-L bottle. Add one drop of blue food coloring to the water. This bottle of water represents all the water on Earth.

MATERIALS

- goggles
- 6 plastic bottles (1 L)
- graduate
- water
- dropper
- blue food coloring
- calculator
- *Science Notebook*

SAFETY /////

Wear goggles during this activity. Clean up spills immediately.

Step 2

WATER ON EARTH		
Location	Percent	mL That Represent Each Percent
Oceans	97.220	
Glaciers	2.150	
Underground Water	0.620	
Rivers and Lakes	0.009	
Atmosphere	0.001	

3. In your *Science Notebook*, **make a chart** like the one above. The chart shows the percent of Earth's water in different locations. Use a calculator to find how many milliliters represent one percent of 1 L. Recall that there are 1,000 mL in 1 L. **Record** your answer.

Math Hint *To find one percent of a number, multiply the number by .01.*

4. Using the information in the chart, work with your group to **calculate** the number of milliliters of water that represent the percent of water found in each location. **Record** each amount in your chart.

5. Use a graduate to **measure** each amount of water from the full 1-L bottle and pour each one into the bottle labeled for that location. To measure small amounts, use a dropper. There are about 20 drops in one milliliter

Analyze and Conclude

1. How much water did you measure for the *Oceans* bottle? the *Glaciers* bottle? the *Underground Water* bottle? the *Rivers and Lakes* bottle? the *Atmosphere* bottle?

2. How does the amount of salt water on Earth compare to the amount of fresh water? (Count all water except ocean water as fresh water.)

3. Where is most fresh water on Earth found? How easy or difficult do you think it would be to get drinking water for your community from that source? Explain your answer.

Technology Link CD-ROM

INVESTIGATE FURTHER!

Use the **Best of the Net—Science CD-ROM,** Earth Sciences, *The Great Lakes Information Network* site to learn about the five Great Lakes, which together contain one fifth of Earth's fresh surface water. You'll learn about the plants and animals living in these lakes and how the activities of humans have affected the quality of the water.

Activity

Water Races

Did you know that water can flow through some kinds of rock? Find out which kinds of rock material water flows through fastest.

MATERIALS
- goggles
- newspaper
- 5 clear plastic cups
- gravel
- sand
- clay soil
- graduate
- water
- timer
- *Science Notebook*

SAFETY

Wear goggles during this activity. Clean up spills immediately.

Procedure

1. Cover your work surface with newspaper. Fill a clear plastic cup three-fourths full of gravel. Fill another cup three-fourths full of sand. Fill a third cup three-fourths full of clay soil. Tap the bottom of the cups on the work surface to settle the materials.

2. **Observe** the material in each cup. **Predict** which material water will flow through fastest. Then **predict** which material water will flow through most slowly. **Record** your predictions in your *Science Notebook*.

3. Use a graduate to **measure** 100 mL of water. Have a partner pour this water into the cup containing gravel. As your partner pours, use a timer to **measure** how long it takes for the water to flow through the gravel. Start timing as soon as the pouring begins. Stop timing when you first see water reach the bottom of the cup. **Record** your results.

4. Repeat step 3 for the cup containing sand and then for the cup containing clay soil.

Step 3

5. Prepare a cup of gravel and a cup of sand as you did in step 1. **Observe** the gravel and the sand. Look for spaces between particles in each material. The spaces between particles in materials are called pores. **Record** which material you think has the most total space between its particles.

Step 5

6. Use the graduate to **measure** 100 mL of water. Pour enough of this water into the cup of gravel to just cover the gravel. You may need to fill the graduate again. **Measure** the amount of water remaining in the graduate. **Calculate** the amount of water poured. **Record** this number.

7. Repeat step 6 for the cup containing sand.

8. **Make a bar graph** to show how long it takes for the water to flow through each material. **Make another bar graph** to show the total volume of the pores in the gravel and of the pores in the sand.

See **SCIENCE** and **MATH TOOLBOX** page H3 if you need to review *Making a Bar Graph.*

Analyze and Conclude

1. If the pores in a material are connected, water can flow through the material. Such a material is said to be **permeable** (pʉr′mē ə bəl). Which of the materials tested are permeable?

2. Which of the materials tested is most permeable? How do you know? Which is least permeable? **Compare** your predictions in step 2 with your results.

3. The greater the volume of pores in a material, the more **porous** (pôr′əs) is the material. Which tested material is more porous, sand or gravel?

4. Layers of permeable rock, such as that made up of rock, sand, and pebbles, are often good sources of water. **Hypothesize** why this is so.

Finding the Water

Reading Focus Where is water found on Earth?

Water is everywhere on Earth—on its surface, underground, in the air, and even in living things. It exists as a liquid, a solid, and a gas. Water exists on other planets and moons in our solar system. But Earth is unique in that it has so much water compared to other planets. In addition, Earth has vast amounts of liquid water. This is not the case with any of the other planets in our solar system.

Water on the Surface

Most water found on Earth is liquid. When you look at a globe or at satellite photographs of Earth, you can see how much of the planet is covered with water. About three fourths of Earth's surface is water; only one fourth is land.

The largest part of Earth's water is contained in its oceans. The Pacific, Atlantic, Indian, and Antarctic oceans are all connected. Together these oceans form one continuous body of salt water. This continuous ocean covers about 70 percent of Earth's surface.

Water Under the Surface

Although surface water makes up the greatest portion of Earth's water, important quantities of water are also found underground. You can find water nearly anywhere in the world—even in the driest deserts—if you dig deep enough. This underground water supply is called **ground water**. Ground water is usually fresh water—salt-free.

Water, Water, Everywhere

Surface Water

Ground Water

Water in the Air

Water, as a gas, can be found in the blanket of air that surrounds Earth. Water in its gaseous state is called **water vapor**. The invisible water vapor plays an important role in the processes through which Earth's water is recycled. Water in the air also exists as groups of tiny droplets that can be seen. These groups of liquid-water droplets are called clouds.

Water in Living Things

All living things contain water. The human body, as well as the bodies of most other kinds of mammals, is about 60 percent water. Your body takes in water, uses it, and releases it as perspiration and as urine. Plants also take in water, use it, and release it into the air through their leaves.

The Total Picture

As the activity on pages D6 and D7 shows, about 97 percent of all the water found on Earth is contained in Earth's oceans. Glaciers and icecaps make up about 2 percent of the water on Earth. Fresh water in rivers and in lakes accounts for only about .009 percent, and ground water makes up about .620 percent of the total amount of water. Finally, water vapor in the air makes up only about .001 percent of Earth's water. But even that relatively small amount, if released all at once, would cover Earth with 2.5 cm (1 in.) of rainfall.

Water vapor accounts for a very small portion of Earth's total water volume. However, it plays a key role in keeping Earth supplied with fresh water. Most of the fresh water in rivers and lakes flows into the salty oceans. Water vapor in the air is Earth's natural faucet, supplying Earth with fresh water.

Internet Field Trip

Visit **www.eduplace.com** to learn more about Earth's supply of fresh water.

Water Droplets in Air

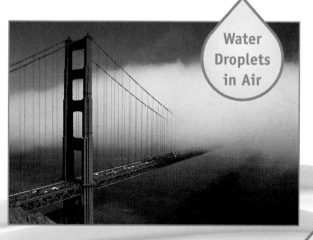

Water in Living Things

Water Under the Ground

Reading Focus How does water get underground?

As you may remember, 97 percent of all the water on Earth is salt water found in Earth's oceans. Although all of Earth's water supports life, not all of it is safe for humans to drink. Saltwater fish and a variety of other marine life forms need salt water to live. But many shipwrecked sailors have died of thirst while surrounded by ocean water.

No human can tolerate the amount of salt found in ocean water. A person's kidneys can safely filter up to a 2.2 percent salt solution. If you were to drink a few glasses of ocean water, which is 3.5 percent salt, water would move out of your body's cells. In time, you would die of dehydration (dē hī drā′shən).

◄ **Healthy human blood cells**

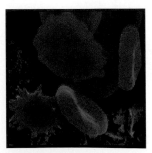

Dehydrated human blood cells ▶

The human body requires fresh water, as well as food and oxygen, to function properly. People also use fresh water for many activities. Bathing, washing clothing, and watering plants all require fresh water.

There's Enough for Everyone

About 3 percent of Earth's water is fresh water. This amount is enough for the needs of everyone in the world. Unfortunately, that water isn't distributed equally to all people on Earth. Scientists estimate that 66 percent of the fresh water on Earth is stored in icecaps and glaciers. The remainder is underground and in bodies of water such as lakes and rivers.

Fresh water that's above the ground in lakes, ponds, rivers, and streams is plentiful in some areas and scarce in others. For example, rain rarely falls in the deserts of California. When it does rain there, the puddles dry up quickly.

Soak It Up

Underground water, or ground water, is a major source of fresh water. The activity on pages D6 and D7 shows that the amount of fresh water found underground is about 70 times greater than

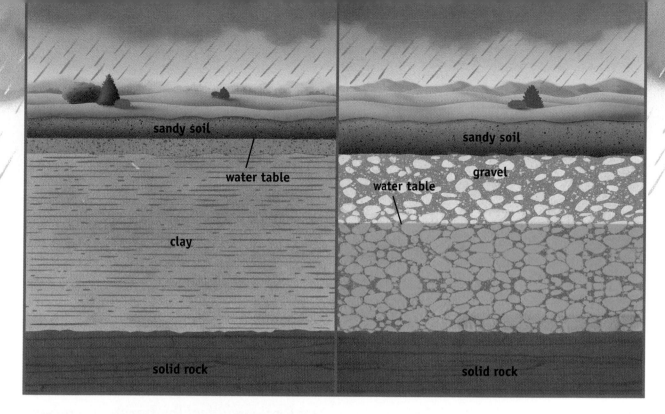

▲ The type of soil in an area can affect the location of the water table and the depth of saturated soil.

the amount found in Earth's rivers and lakes. How does water get underground? Most of the water from rain and melting snow soaks into tiny spaces, or pores, between the particles that make up the soil.

Soil that contains many pores between particles is said to be **porous** (pôr′əs). The volume of the pores in a material compared to the total volume of the material is known as the porosity (pō räs′ə tē) of the material.

It would seem that the more pores that a soil contains, the easier it would be for water to soak into that soil. In most cases this is true. However some soils, such as clay, are made up of tiny particles packed tightly together. So, even though clay is porous—has lots of spaces between particles—the spaces are not connected and are too small to allow water to enter them easily.

Move It

Soil is **permeable** (pʉr′mē ə bəl) when water can flow easily through it. In the activity on pages D8 and D9, three soil types are compared. Gravel is shown to be most permeable and clay to be least permeable.

As water seeps down through a permeable soil, it moves from pore to pore until it meets a layer of solid rock or tightly packed clay. At that point the water begins to fill the pores in the soil above that layer. When all the pores are filled with water, the soil is said to be saturated.

The surface of the water in a layer of saturated soil is called the **water table**. The level of the water table may rise or fall depending on rainfall amounts and how much water is pumped out of the ground. But most of the time the water table remains fairly stable.

Let It Flow

When water can no longer filter into deeper layers of soil, it flows horizontally from pore to pore. However, it doesn't flow like a river underground. Instead, it travels slowly through each pore in the soil, covering a broad area. An underground layer of rock or soil through which water flows easily and in which water collects is called an **aquifer** (ak′wə fər). Water obtained by drilling a well may come from an aquifer.

In the early 1900s, many California miners turned to farming following the gold rush. They drilled wells and then

Water flows underground through aquifers. ▼

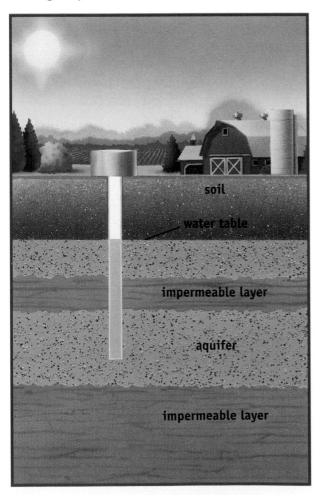

soil

water table

impermeable layer

aquifer

impermeable layer

watered their crops with water pumped from an aquifer. In some parts of Santa Clara County, the ground sank as much as 13 m (43 ft). This occurred because water was pumped out of an aquifer more quickly than it was replaced by rain. When there is adequate rainfall or snowfall and the ground remains porous and permeable, water taken from the ground is replaced.

Too Little Water

There are times when much less rain falls than usual. Periods of little or no rainfall are called droughts. Droughts that last for years affect the health and growth of all living things.

One method of adapting to a climate that is subject to droughts is dryland farming. Dryland farmers use mulch to help keep their crops moist. They keep their fields free of weeds that compete for the available water. Dryland farmers also plant crops that scientists have developed to grow quickly and that need little moisture.

People in drought areas learn to live with little water. For example, they might take fewer and shorter showers and not water their lawns. At times they might need to purchase truckloads of water from other areas where water is plentiful.

Too Much Water

Floods are the opposite of droughts. Floods occur when too much rain falls in a short period of time. During a flood period, the soil is not able to absorb all the rainfall. In such a situation, the excess rain runs off into rivers and often floods lowlands.

Engineers try to reduce the damage from floods by building dams to contain excess water. With the use of dams, flood waters can be captured and then released slowly over time and during times of drought.

Don't Drink the Water

Water can become polluted from different sources. Natural substances such as ash from a volcanic eruption can pollute water. But people are the major cause of pollution. Industries and vehicles can pollute both the air and the water.

One cause of water pollution is runoff from roadways. **Runoff** is rainfall that is not absorbed by the soil. Runoff carries particles of antifreeze, oil, rubber, brake fluid, and salt used to melt ice and snow from roads and highways. Pesticides and lawn chemicals also add to the problem of water pollution.

Some pollutants, or substances that cause pollution, are filtered out by water treatment plants before water is piped to homes, schools, and businesses. Some pollutants are filtered out naturally by the soil. But any amount of pollution lessens the amount of drinkable fresh water that is available to living things.

▲ **Dams like the one shown here provide flood control and hydroelectric energy.**

EXPERIMENT

Obtain local soil samples from two different places. Take one sample from an area in which puddles always seem to form during a rainstorm. Take the other sample from an area where puddles rarely form. Make a plan to find out which sample material is more permeable. Then carry out your plan. Share your findings with your class.

═══════════ **INVESTIGATION 1 WRAP-UP** ═══════════

REVIEW

1. Discuss the distribution of water on Earth.

2. What is an aquifer?

CRITICAL THINKING

3. How might an increase in Earth's overall temperature affect the amount of water in Earth's atmosphere?

4. How might dumping harmful chemicals on porous soil pollute ground water?

HOW DOES NATURE MOVE WATER?

It's likely that most of the water on Earth has been used at least once by a living thing. But once it's used, water is not used up—it's recycled in nature's water cycle.

Activity

Recycled Water

In this activity you'll make a model of the water cycle to see how water is recycled by nature.

- -

Procedure

1. Cover your work surface with newspaper. Use a measuring cup to **measure** 50 mL of water. Pour the water into a plastic cup. Stir one half spoonful of soil and one half spoonful of salt into the water. Then pour a small amount of the mixture into a jar lid.

MATERIALS

- goggles
- newspaper
- measuring cup
- water
- plastic cup
- plastic spoon
- moist soil
- salt
- 2 jar lids (or shallow dishes)
- large clear plastic bag
- piece of heavy cardboard
- small rock
- twist tie
- *Science Notebook*

SAFETY //////

Wear goggles during this activity. Clean up spills immediately.

Step 1

2. In a sunny location, lay a large clear plastic bag flat on a piece of heavy cardboard. Place about 400 mL of moist soil inside the bag, spreading the soil evenly.

3. Carefully place the jar lid containing the mixture of soil and salt water on the soil inside the bag. Place a second, empty jar lid in the bag near the center.

4. Gently blow into the bag to inflate it. Then, using a twist tie or tape, seal the bag securely.

5. Put a small rock on top of the bag, directly over the empty jar lid, as shown. The rock will make a dent in the bag.

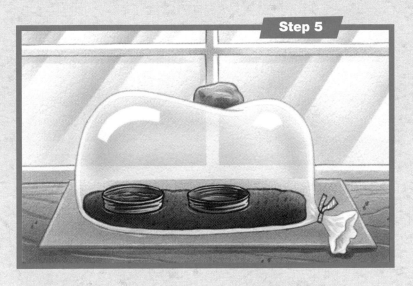

Step 5

6. Leave the bag in sunlight for at least one hour. Carefully **observe** the two jar lids and the inside surface of the bag. **Record** your observations in your *Science Notebook*.

Analyze and Conclude

1. After one hour, was there water in the second jar lid? If so, **compare** that water to the water mixture in the first jar lid.

2. Was there any water on the inside surface of the plastic bag? If so, **describe** its appearance.

3. **Talk with your group** and **hypothesize** what happened to the mixture of soil and salt water. The events observed in the plastic bag model the water cycle. **Infer** how your model water cycle is similar to the real water cycle.

UNIT PROJECT LINK

Imagine your company has been chosen to design a water system for Waterville, a planned community. What questions will you need to answer before selecting a source of water for the town? Study the brochure on Waterville and then choose a water source for the town.

Technology *Link*

For more help with your Unit Project, go to **www.eduplace.com**.

How Water Moves

Reading Focus What changes occur in the water cycle?

What do you think is the answer to this riddle: How is the amount of water on Earth like the date of your birth? The diagram below may help you figure out the answer.

The path of water is shown by a series of arrows. As you follow the arrows, notice that the path water takes is a circle. Circles have no end—they go round and round. So what happens to water occurs again and again. Such a pattern is called a cycle. In this case, it is the **water cycle**, the ongoing movement of water into the air and back to Earth's surface. When water moves through the water cycle, it changes from one state to another as heat energy is added or taken away.

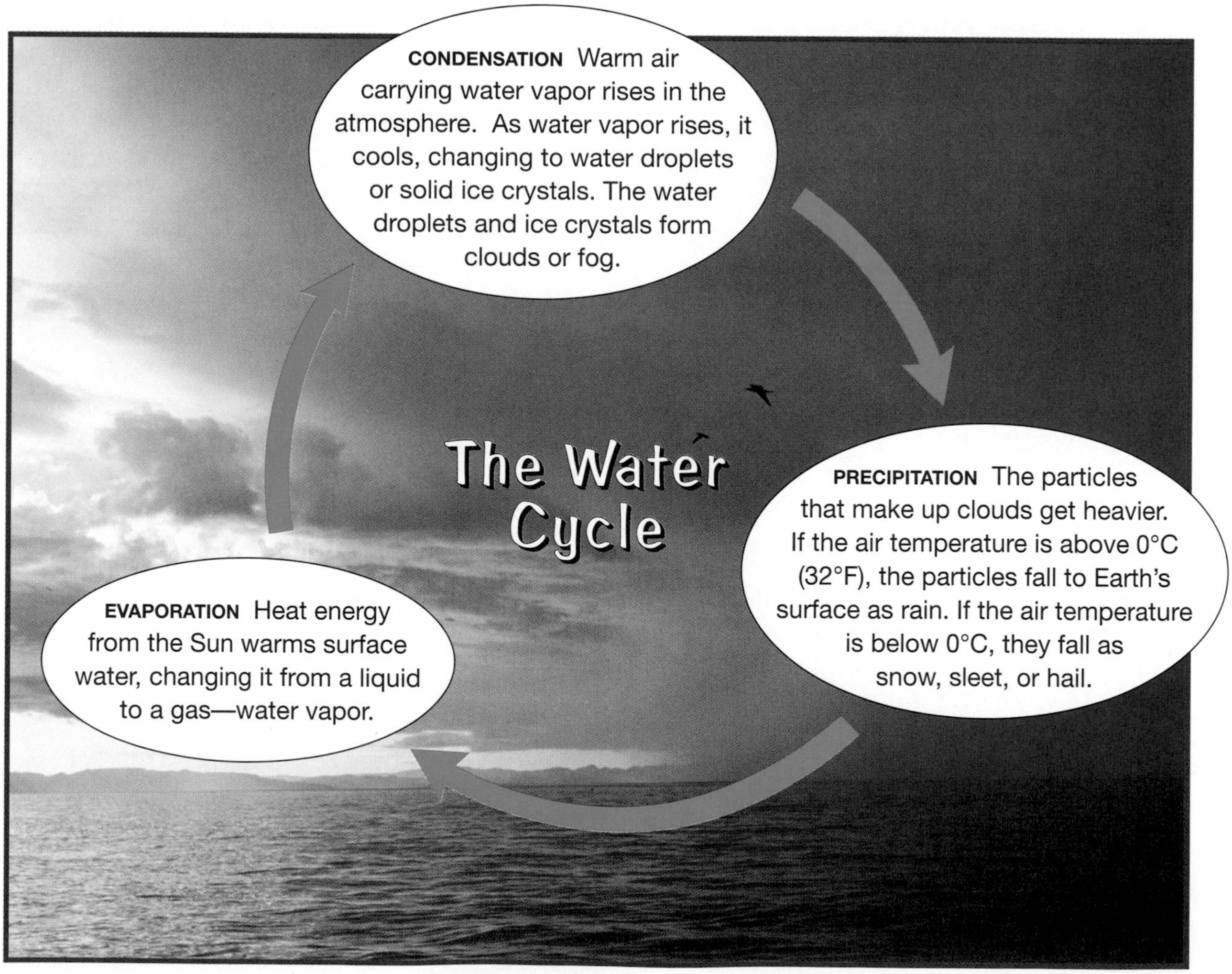

CONDENSATION Warm air carrying water vapor rises in the atmosphere. As water vapor rises, it cools, changing to water droplets or solid ice crystals. The water droplets and ice crystals form clouds or fog.

The Water Cycle

PRECIPITATION The particles that make up clouds get heavier. If the air temperature is above 0°C (32°F), the particles fall to Earth's surface as rain. If the air temperature is below 0°C, they fall as snow, sleet, or hail.

EVAPORATION Heat energy from the Sun warms surface water, changing it from a liquid to a gas—water vapor.

The Heat Is On

The water cycle is modeled in the activity on pages D16 and D17. Dirty salt water, representing the surface water on Earth, is warmed in a plastic bag by heat energy from the Sun. This warming causes the liquid water to change to water vapor, which enters the bag "atmosphere." A change like this, from a liquid to a gas, is known as **evaporation** (ē vap ə rā'shən). In the real water cycle, water vapor is also added to the atmosphere by plants.

Through the process of **transpiration** (tran spə rā'shən), a plant releases moisture through small openings in its leaves.

In the activity, the water vapor in the model water cycle cools, causing water droplets to form on the inside surface of the bag. A change like this, from a gas to a liquid, is known as **condensation** (kän dən sā'shən). The droplets that fall into the empty jar lid model **precipitation** (prē sip ə tā'shən), or any form of water that falls from the atmosphere to Earth's surface.

About 77 percent of precipitation falls into the ocean. Some precipitation sinks into soil, becoming ground water. Some water is surface water that collects in puddles, ditches, streams, lakes, and rivers. This water evaporates or empties into the oceans.

TRANSPIRATION Plants release water vapor from their leaves into the atmosphere.

FREEZING Some water becomes locked as ice in glaciers.

The main processes of the water cycle are evaporation and condensation. These processes involve heat energy. Evaporation absorbs heat and therefore has a cooling effect. Condensation releases heat and therefore has a warming effect.

Cleaning Dirty Water

In the activity on pages D16 and D17, the water that falls into the empty jar lid is cleaner than the mixture of soil and salt water because the soil and salt are left behind after evaporation. As the model water cycle in the activity shows, water is cleaned, or purified, in the real water cycle.

Around and Around It Goes

Ever since Earth formed, it has had about the same supply of water. This means that the amount of water on Earth, whether in the form of a solid, liquid, or gas, has stayed about the same for billions of years. It never changes. Now can you answer the riddle in the first paragraph on page D18?

Although the amount of water on Earth stays the same, water does not stay in one location. It moves around in an ongoing pattern that is fueled by heat energy from the Sun. In this pattern—the water cycle—water moves continuously between Earth's surface and the atmosphere.

Science in Literature

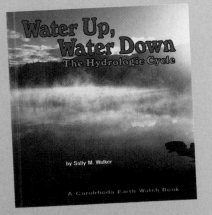

Water Up, Water Down: The Hydrologic Cycle
by Sally M. Walker
Carolrhoda Books, 1992

"SNOWFLAKE" BENTLEY

"In 1880 Wilson Alwyn Bentley, a 15-year-old boy who lived in Jericho, Vermont, began examining snowflakes through a microscope. He noticed that snowflakes were crystals. Although he was not the first person to notice this, what he did five years later had never been done before and led to a lifelong study of snowflakes."

To find out what Bentley did that had never been done before and to explore the role of snowflakes in the water cycle, read *Water Up, Water Down: The Hydrologic Cycle* by Sally M. Walker.

Plant Connection

Reading Focus What role do plants have in the water cycle?

Plants are unique in their importance as the source of food for living things. As you may know, plants make their own food. In the process of making food, plants take in carbon dioxide and give off oxygen. All living things need oxygen to survive.

On pages D18 and D19, you learned about another very important function of plants. That function is to return water to the atmosphere in the process of transpiration. Of all living things, plants are the greatest movers of water in the water cycle.

④ Water vapor released through transpiration moves into the atmosphere. Rising warm air carries the water vapor higher. What happens next in the water cycle?

③ Water vapor moves out of the plant through tiny openings called stomata (stō′mə tə), which means "little mouths." Most stomata are on the undersides of leaves. Leaves have many stomata.

② Tubes in a plant's roots and stem move water from the roots to all the living cells of the plant.

① A plant takes in water from the soil through its roots. Plants take in a great deal of water. Each plant cell needs a constant supply.

Using Math *A cucumber leaf has more than 60,000 stomata in one square centimeter of its surface! About how many stomata would a cucumber leaf with a surface area of 28 cm² have?*

D21

Using Math

Each year every tree in the rain-forest canopy, or the highest layer of trees, returns about 760 L (200 gal) of water to the atmosphere. How many gallons would 100 rain-forest trees return?

Rain, Don't Go Away!

You know that transpiration in just one plant returns water in the form of water vapor to the atmosphere. Think how much water is returned to the atmosphere by a whole forest. The amount of water vapor returned to the atmosphere by the trees of the rain forest is staggering.

Tropical rain-forest plants receive plenty of water and bright, direct sunlight. So plants there have ideal conditions for making food. In the food-making process, plants release oxygen. In fact, plants of the rain forest release about 15 billion tons of oxygen into the atmosphere each year!

Going, Going, Gone?

Rain-forest plants provide many products and materials that people want or need. These include rubber, timber for building, fiber for clothing, and compounds for making medicines.

People are cutting down the rain forests to get these products and materials. Vast tracts of rain-forest land are also being cleared to make room for farms and pastures. Each minute, more than 23 hectares (57 acres) of rain forests are destroyed. If this rate of destruction continues, Earth's tropical rain forests will be gone within about 100 years. How would this loss affect the water cycle?

INVESTIGATION 2 WRAP-UP

REVIEW

1. Make a labeled drawing to show the path of water through the water cycle.

2. What kind of energy is being added or taken away throughout the water cycle?

CRITICAL THINKING

3. Describe and compare the roles of evaporation and condensation in the water cycle.

4. Suppose you are casting a play about the water cycle. A leaf and a raindrop are the starring roles. What would you say to convince the two best players that the roles are equally important?

REFLECT & EVALUATE

Word Power

Write the letter of the term that best matches the definition.
Not all terms will be used.

1. Any form of water that falls to Earth's surface
2. Soil that contains many spaces between the particles of dirt
3. The process in which a plant releases moisture through small openings in its leaves
4. Water in its gaseous state
5. The supply of fresh water found beneath Earth's surface
6. Rainfall that is not absorbed by the soil
7. Allowing water to flow through easily

a. condensation
b. evaporation
c. ground water
d. permeable
e. porous
f. precipitation
g. runoff
h. transpiration
i. water vapor

Check What You Know

Write the term in each pair that best completes each sentence.

1. The process in which heat energy changes liquid water to a gas is (precipitation, evaporation).
2. An underground layer of rock or soil through which water flows easily is called a/an (river, aquifer).
3. The surface of the water in saturated soil is the (ground water, water table).

Problem Solving

1. The garden area in your yard has clay soil. Another area has sandy soil. How could you make sure your garden will be well-drained?

2. Your family is moving to a farm in an area that has frequent periods of drought. What measures might you take to make best use of your limited water supply?

PORTFOLIO

Study the drawing. Explain in your own words how the water cycle purifies water on Earth. Then infer why this process is important to human life.

CHAPTER 2

USING WATER RESOURCES

Fresh water is one of the most valuable resources on Earth. No living thing can survive long without it. Yet, in many parts of the world, fresh water is in short supply. Sometimes this problem can be solved by moving water from places where it is plentiful to places where there isn't enough.

Connecting to Science
ARTS

Landscape Architect From an early age, Walter Hood has been fascinated with building things and with drawing. Those interests led him to study architecture and eventually to the field of landscape architecture. In his work, Dr. Hood transforms the natural features of a place to create a space for people to enjoy. And as a professor of landscape architecture at the University of California at Berkeley, he teaches his students how to create such spaces.

Water is an important element in Dr. Hood's landscape designs, which include fountains and channels of water. "Water can calm us through its stillness and sound, and it can excite us through its movement and roar," says Dr. Hood. In this chapter you'll find out about many other uses of this valuable resource.

Coming Up

◀ Dr. Walter Hood, with
his design for a city
park, which includes
a lighted channel of
water running across
a grassy mound

HOW IS FRESH WATER USED?

Although most water on Earth is salt water, most of the water that people use is fresh water. In this investigation you'll explore some everyday uses of water and learn about different water environments.

Activity

Salty Soil

Watering crops with ocean water has been a practice for many years in some parts of California. Over time the soil in those areas has become salty. Can salty soil affect plant growth? Find out in this activity.

MATERIALS

- goggles
- newspaper
- small pots or paper cups
- metric measuring cup
- potting soil
- seeds or seedlings
- measuring spoons
- salt
- water
- *Science Notebook*

SAFETY //////

Wear goggles during this activity. Clean up spills immediately.

Procedure

1. Choose one of the following questions to investigate. Or, if you prefer, pose a question of your own about plant growth in salty soil and then investigate it.

- How does salty soil affect the growth of plants?

- Do some kinds of plants grow better in salty soil than others do?

- What is the least amount of salt in the soil that will affect the growth of plants?

2. Now change your question to a statement that will be your hypothesis. For example, you might use this hypothesis: "Some plants will not grow as well in salty soil as in soil that is not salty."

3. **Design an experiment** that will test your hypothesis. For example, if you use the hypothesis in step 2, decide how you will know if some plants will not grow as well in salty soil as in soil that is not salty. Decide how many seeds or seedlings you will plant. **Record** your ideas in your *Science Notebook*.

4. **Identify** all the variables in your experiment.

- The **independent variable** is the factor you will change in order to see what happens.

- The **dependent variable** is the factor you will observe to determine any effect of the independent variable.

- The **controlled variables** are the factors that you will keep constant, or identical, for all your setups.

5. **Record** your plan and discuss it with your teacher. Then, with your teacher's permission, **work with your group** to carry out your experiment. Each day, record your observations.

Analyze and Conclude

1. If any of your data can be shown on a line graph, construct the graph.

See **SCIENCE** and **MATH TOOLBOX** page H13 if you need to review *Making a Line Graph.*

2. Did the data from the experiment support your hypothesis? Explain.

3. **Write a report** that includes your research question, your hypothesis, your procedure, your observations, and your conclusions.

Using Water

Reading Focus What are some everyday uses of water?

Did you know that every time you take a shower about 19 L (5 gal) of water go down the drain each minute? The amount of water used for different activities may not always be as obvious.

In the Home and Community

Water is part of most food recipes. That's because so many substances dissolve in water to form solutions. A **solution** (sə lo͞o'shən) is a mixture in which the different particles of matter are spread evenly throughout. In a solution the material present in the greater amount is the **solvent** (säl'vənt). The material present in the smaller amount is the **solute** (säl'yo͞ot). If you add salt to boiling water, as shown below, you get a solution of salt water.

Cleaning and gardening are also important household uses of water. Huge amounts of water are used, for example, in washing clothes, scrubbing floors, washing cars, and watering lawns.

Cities and towns use great amounts of water. Fire engines can pump thousands of gallons of water each minute when putting out a fire. Mechanical sweepers can use thousands more gallons in cleaning streets. In rural communities, trucks sometimes spray water on dirt roads to keep dust from blowing into the air.

On the Farm

Water is extremely important to farmers because no plant can be grown without it—not even a cactus! In many

Everyday Uses of Water

Water for cooking

Water for safety

Water for cleaning

D28

parts of the world, rainfall provides the water needed to grow crops. In other parts the water must come from rivers, lakes, and deep wells.

The process of supplying crops with water, called **irrigation** (ir ə gā′shən), can be done in several ways. Farmers in California's Central Valley get water through a system of ditches and canals. Some farmers rely on pipes full of tiny holes that allow water to drip at a slow, steady rate. Other farmers use large sprinkler systems.

In Industry

Many industrial machines are cooled by water. And the manufacturing processes of industry require millions of gallons of water. Water is used to make sulfuric acid, a very important industrial compound. This acid is used in the manufacture of many products, including paints, plastics, dyes, explosives, medicines, and fertilizers. Found in almost every automobile and truck battery in the world, this acid helps produce the electrical energy needed to start cars.

Water is also important in papermaking. Wood pulp, bleaches, and dyes, all of which are used in making paper, contain water.

For Fun

People use quite a bit of water for recreation. It takes thousands of gallons of water to fill a swimming pool. Without water, there would be no grassy playing fields for football, soccer, and baseball, and there would be no ice rinks for hockey or skating. Without water, you probably couldn't even get to a recreation area—most cars, trucks, and buses are cooled by water.

For Life

Of the many ways water is used, growing food and drinking are the most important uses for people. Without food, people can survive for a few weeks. Without water, people can survive for only a few days.

As you can see, water is important to your everyday activities and even for your life. So water must be used wisely. What can you do to help use less water? To start, you can save up to 19 L (5 gal) of water a day just by turning the faucet off while you brush your teeth!

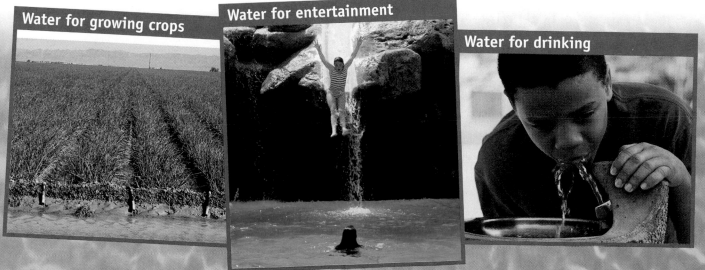

Water for growing crops

Water for entertainment

Water for drinking

They're All Wet!

Reading Focus How are areas of wetlands important, and how are they used?

As their name suggests, wetlands are lands that are always wet. **Wetlands** are environments in which the land contains significant amounts of water. The soil in wetlands is saturated by ground water most, if not all, of the time.

Wetlands are important ecosystems, or areas where living and nonliving things interact. Saltwater wetlands are found along the seacoast. Freshwater wetlands, of which there are several types, are located inland. The activity on pages D26 and D27 shows that the salt content of water can affect the growth of plants in areas such as wetlands.

Kinds of Wetlands

There are several different kinds of wetlands, such as marshes, bogs, and swamps. Marshes lack trees. Bogs have spongy ground on which moss grows. The moss in a bog can soak up more than a hundred times its weight in water. Swamps have trees as well as grasses and other plants.

Wetlands include bottom lands, which are hardwood forest lands on flood plains. Wetlands also include prairie potholes, shallow ponds, and lands that are found along the banks of rivers, lakes, or ponds.

Wetlands are among the most important natural areas left in the world today. Yet more than half of those in the United States alone have disappeared in the last 300 years, having been replaced by cities and towns.

Why Wetlands Are Important

Wetlands are important for two main reasons. First, they are home to hundreds of plants and animals that could not survive anywhere else. Second, wetlands act as natural water storage areas.

The Arcata Marsh in California, like other marshes, is home to a variety of plants and animals such as this egret. ▶

▲ Bog, with sphagnum moss

▲ Swamp, with bald cypress trees

Much of the water from rainfall and melted snow collects in underground pockets of the wetlands called tubs.

Because of the importance of wetlands, government and private agencies are active in trying to protect them. Such protection benefits endangered plants and animals. And it also helps protect people. Because wetlands hold water, they help protect against flooding. In rainy seasons, wetlands help control flooding by soaking up water. The evaporation of water from wetlands is part of the water cycle. The destruction of wetlands can contribute to drought in some areas.

Wetlands are unique environments for a variety of living things. In addition to protecting these environments, government agencies also maintain wildlife preserves in wetlands. There, both plants and animals are protected. Fisheries, places in which biologists raise fish in large tanks, are located in some wetlands. When the fingerlings, or young fish, are large enough, they are released into rivers and lakes.

Using Wetlands

Not only do wetlands help protect people, but they also provide areas for recreational activities such as boating, fishing, bird-watching, walking, and other outdoor activities. The natural beauty of wetlands is an important factor in drawing people to them.

INVESTIGATION 1 WRAP-UP

REVIEW

1. Explain the difference between a solution and a solvent.

2. Describe three uses of water. Make sure that at least one use relates to wetlands.

CRITICAL THINKING

3. You are writing to the local newspaper about a proposal to build a housing project on wetlands near your town. Explain your opinion about such a proposal.

4. As a farmer in an area that receives little rainfall, explain how you might get water to your crops.

INVESTIGATION 2

HOW DOES YOUR COMMUNITY GET WATER?

To get water, you probably simply turn on a faucet. But have you ever wondered how the water gets to your faucet and where it comes from? In this investigation you'll find out about some sources of water and some ways in which a community gets water from its source.

Activity

Taste Test

How does pure water taste? Actually, pure water has no taste. But the water you drink isn't pure. It contains air and has solid materials dissolved in it. Find out if the things dissolved in water affect its taste.

Procedure

1. Label three small paper cups *D, T,* and *B.*

2. Using a measuring cup, pour 100 mL of the following kinds of water into each cup: distilled water into cup *D*, tap water into cup *T*, and bottled water into cup *B*. Use a paper towel to dry the measuring cup after each measurement.

 See **SCIENCE** *and* **MATH TOOLBOX** page H7 if you need to review **Measuring Volume.**

3. Taste the water in cup *D*. Roll it around on your tongue before you swallow it. In your *Science Notebook*, **record** a description of how the water tastes.

MATERIALS

- goggles
- marker
- 3 small paper cups
- metric measuring cup
- distilled water
- tap water
- bottled water
- paper towels
- *Science Notebook*

SAFETY /////

Wear goggles during this activity. Clean up spills immediately.

4. Repeat step 3 for the water in cup *T* (tap water) and cup *B* (bottled water).

5. **Rank** the water samples by taste. Rank number 1 the sample that has the taste you like most. Rank number 3 the sample that has the taste you like least. **Record** your rankings.

Analyze and Conclude

1. Which water sample has the taste you like most? Which did you like least?

2. Distilled water is almost pure water. Why do you think distilled water tastes as it does? What might be dissolved in distilled water?

3. What materials might be dissolved in tap water and in bottled water that could affect their taste?

UNIT PROJECT LINK

How will water travel from its source to homes and businesses in Waterville? How will the water be cleaned so that it's safe to drink? Study the map of Waterville and the surrounding area. Then design a system to clean and transport water to the town. Construct a simple model to show the town's water system. Show how the water will get to homes and other places that use water.

TechnologyLink

For more help with your Unit Project, go to **www.eduplace.com**.

Step 3

D33

Activity

Well, Well!

Many communities and rural homes get their water from deep wells drilled into an aquifer. In Chapter 1 you learned that an aquifer is an underground layer of rock or soil through which water flows easily and in which water collects. In this activity you'll build a working model of an aquifer.

MATERIALS
- goggles
- clear plastic shoebox
- sand
- metric ruler
- wax paper
- scissors
- sharpened pencil
- modeling clay
- clear plastic straw
- plastic cup
- water
- *Science Notebook*

Procedure

1. **Make a model** of an aquifer. Place a layer of sand, about 2 cm thick, in the bottom of a plastic shoebox. To represent the slope of a mountain, build up one end with more sand, as shown. Make sure to level the top of your model mountain.

2. Cut two sheets of wax paper just large enough to cover all the sand. Lay one sheet of the paper on a flat surface and press a thin layer of modeling clay onto it. Make sure the clay extends to the edges of the wax paper, all the way around.

3. Place the clay-covered wax paper on the sand. Arrange it so that about 1 cm of the paper extends above the top of the model mountain, as shown. Then press the clay firmly against the sides of the shoebox that it touches. This layer of clay and the bottom of the shoebox represent impermeable rock—rock that water cannot pass through.

4. Use the second sheet of wax paper to cover the layer of clay. Press this sheet of wax paper into place on top of the clay.

5. Use a pencil to poke a hole through the layers of wax paper and clay into the sand. Insert a drinking straw into the hole, as shown. The bottom of the straw should be just above the bottom of the shoebox. Seal the space around the straw by pressing the clay that is between the sheets of wax paper tightly around the straw. The straw represents a well.

SAFETY //////

Wear goggles during this activity. Clean up spills immediately.

Step 1

Step 3

Step 5

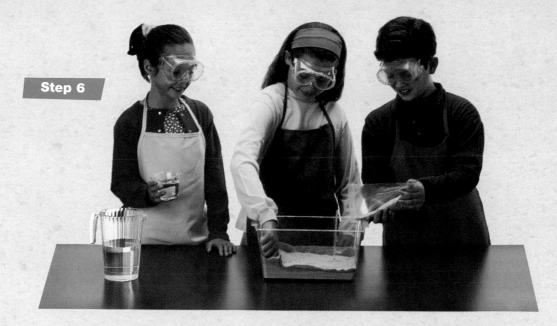

Step 6

6. Place a layer of sand over the top sheet of wax paper, as shown. By pressing on the sand in the level surface at the top of the "mountain," form the bed of a "lake."

7. Use a plastic cup to carefully add water to the "lake" bed. Continue adding water until no more water sinks into the sand and water fills the "lake."

8. Observe where the water goes and what happens in the straw. Look for any leaks. **Record** your observations in your *Science Notebook*.

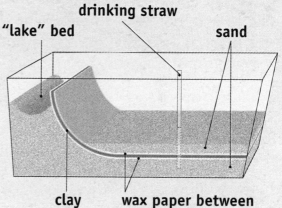

drinking straw
"lake" bed   sand

clay   wax paper between
              sand and clay

Analyze and Conclude

1. Which layer represents the aquifer? What happens in an aquifer?

2. Why is it important that an aquifer be porous? Why is it important that an aquifer be permeable?

3. What does the layer of impermeable rock do?

4. The top of the water in the "well" (the straw) shows the level of the water table. Is the water table above or below ground level in your model?

5. Suppose the straw were cut off at ground level. **Infer** whether water would flow by itself, or whether it would have to be pumped.

6. A leak in your model could be called a "spring." Did you observe any "springs" in your model aquifer? If so, tell where they occurred.

INVESTIGATE FURTHER!

RESEARCH

Different communities may obtain water from different types of sources. Research the source of water used by the community in which you live. Find out how the water is delivered to homes and businesses. If possible, make a simple drawing to show how water is supplied to your community.

Where Your Water Comes From

Reading Focus What are the main sources of fresh water, and how does fresh water reach homes and businesses?

You turn on the faucet, let the water run, fill your glass, and drink. Ahhhh, cold fresh water. But how does that water get to your home? The water that comes into your home travels there through a series of underground pipes. When these pipes arrive at your home, they branch out throughout your home. The pipes connect to showers and faucets.

At the Source

What are the water sources that supply fresh water to homes? For most homes, there are three main sources of water—ground water from wells and surface water from reservoirs and rivers. The source of water affects the way water

tastes. In the activity on pages D32 and D33, the materials dissolved in different samples of water cause those samples to vary in taste.

Freshwater Reservoirs

A **reservoir** (rez′ər vwär) is a place where water is collected and stored. Some reservoirs are natural lakes or ponds in which water collects. Other reservoirs have been created by building dams across rivers. One example is Lake Mead in Arizona. Lake Mead was created when Hoover Dam was built.

Reservoirs provide recreational areas and are sources of fresh water to nearby cities. Some reservoirs help provide

Sources of Fresh Water

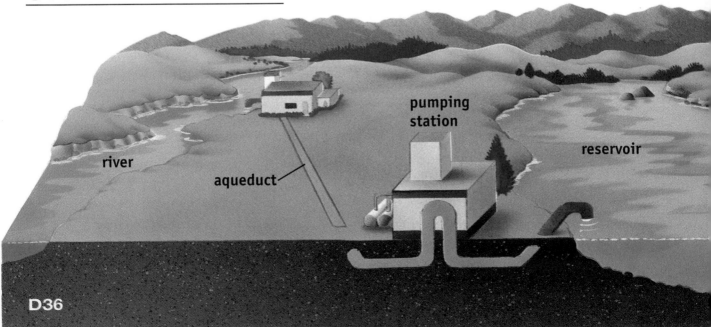

river

aqueduct

pumping station

reservoir

power to cities. Vast amounts of electricity can be produced when water from a reservoir is released through a dam and used to turn electric generators.

Rivers

Many people get fresh water from rivers. Large pumping stations situated next to rivers pump water from the rivers through pipes to homes and businesses.

Millions of California residents get their water from river systems. Cities and farms in the southern part of the state get most of their water from rivers in the northern part of the state and from the Colorado River. The Colorado flows along California's southeastern border with Arizona.

Cities and farms in the central part of the state get much of their water from the San Joaquin (san wä kēn′)–Sacramento River system. This system flows through the central part of California.

Aqueducts (ak′wə duktz) move water from river systems to reservoirs. An

▲ **California aqueduct**

aqueduct is a system of channels, pipes, tunnels, and pumps that carries water from a distant source. An aqueduct carries water from the source to a reservoir that may be hundreds of kilometers away. Pumping stations then move water from the reservoir to homes and businesses. Such a water delivery system is necessary because fresh, clean water is vital to the survival of all living things.

Internet Field Trip

Visit **www.eduplace.com** to find out more about freshwater sources and delivery systems.

well

Ground Water From Wells

A well is a deep, narrow hole in the ground that contains water. Water fills the well up to the water table. The level of the water in the well rises and falls with the level of the water table.

Many people in rural areas have their own wells. In urban areas most wells are owned by the community in which the wells are located. These wells provide water for all the people whose homes are connected to the system.

Wells tap into aquifers that lie beneath Earth's surface. The activity on pages D34 and D35 shows how water moves through an aquifer to a well. In areas where the water table is close to the surface, people dig wells by hand. However, most wells are dug by using machines. Machines drill holes into the ground and lower pipes that reach below the water table.

Pump It Up

Different kinds of pumps are used to raise water out of wells. Hand pumps and windmills were widely used during the early part of the century. They are still used today in many areas of the world. In this country many farmers still use windmills to draw water for their livestock.

Electricity is the most common power source for pumps in the United States. Electric pumps come in many sizes—from pumps that draw a few gallons a minute to pumps that can draw hundreds of gallons a minute. ■

Science in Literature

RAIN, RAIN, DON'T GO AWAY!

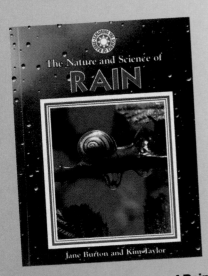

The Nature and Science of Rain
by Jane Burton and Kim Taylor
Gareth Stevens, 1998

"Rain is essential to our planet. Heavy rain can be exciting, but also dangerous. Raindrops come pelting down, the ground gets soaked, and puddles form. Swirling water fills the rivers and may burst over the banks. But after a heavy rain when the Sun shines again, leaves are fresh and green, birds sing, and flowers open."

Read *The Nature and Science of Rain* by Jane Burton and Kim Taylor to learn more about rain, which provides most of the water used by living things.

Ancient Water Systems

Reading Focus How did the ancient Romans and Aztecs move water to where it was needed?

Throughout history, civilizations have developed near bodies of water. The once-thriving ancient civilizations of Sumer, Egypt, Rome, South America, and Mexico, for example, all settled near large bodies of water.

Water's Uses

Why did civilizations make their homes near water? People and their animals needed water for drinking. People also needed water for growing crops, cleaning, cooking, and even making tools and weapons.

In addition, water provided a means of transportation. Some ancient people created simple canoes by hollowing out logs. Over time, they learned to build huge barges and riverboats. These boats carried both passengers and cargo.

Water From Afar

As populations grew, people were forced to live farther from freshwater supplies. That meant relying on rainfall and snowfall as sources of fresh water. The Egyptians and the Greeks dug wells to get fresh water. That's because these ancient people had both the knowledge and the tools to dig wells. Another way to get fresh water in areas that were far

▲ **Remains of an ancient Roman aqueduct**

from water supplies was to move the water from the source to where it was needed. So people learned to build systems for moving and storing water.

Rome's Solution

To solve their water-supply problem, the early Romans built aqueducts. Recall that aqueducts are a complicated system of ditches and tunnels through which water can flow. The Roman aqueducts moved water from the Tiber River to wherever in the city of Rome it was needed.

The Romans also built reservoirs to collect and store water. They had enough water in reservoirs to supply water for the public baths and the homes of the wealthy.

Aztec Answers

Around A.D. 1400 the Aztec Indians in Mexico built a beautiful city on an island in the middle of a lake. The city was named Tenochtitlán (te nôk tē tlän'). Aqueducts supplied fresh water from the nearby mainland to this island city.

The Aztecs also grew crops for food on islands of dirt that floated on the lake. This method of agriculture supplied the Aztecs with plenty of fresh water for their crops.

Water Is Power

Water also provided a source of power for ancient people. Water wheels were built that used the power of moving water to grind grain. The force of water falling on or pushing against the paddles of a water wheel turned the wheel. This harnessing of water's power helped civilizations grow and become more industrial. At one time, water and wind were the most widely used energy resources.

▲ Tenochtitlán *(top)* and an ancient Sumerian water wheel *(bottom)*

INVESTIGATION 2 WRAP-UP

REVIEW **1.** Why did many early civilizations choose to settle near a body of water?

2. What are the two main river systems that provide water to California residents? To which part of the state does each system supply water?

CRITICAL THINKING **3.** What system did the Romans build to move water to areas where it was needed? How might their civilization have been affected if they had not developed such a system?

4. Compare the major sources of fresh water. How does water from each source get to the community where it is used? Which source does your community use?

REFLECT & EVALUATE

Word Power

Write the letter of the term that best matches the definition.
Not all terms will be used.

1. A place where water is collected and stored
2. The process of supplying crops with water
3. A mixture in which the particles of different substances are mixed evenly throughout
4. The material in a solution that is present in the greater amount
5. A system of ditches, channels, and tunnels that carries water from a distant source

a. aqueduct
b. irrigation
c. reservoir
d. solute
e. solution
f. solvent
g. wetlands

Check What You Know

Write the term in each pair that best completes each sentence.

1. A hole in the ground that taps into an aquifer is a (spring, well).
2. A holding place for storing water is a/an (aqueduct, reservoir).
3. Marshes and bogs are ecosystems called (wetlands, bottom lands).
4. In wetlands, water collects in underground pockets called (bogs, tubs).

Problem Solving

1. Suppose your family depends on an electric pump to supply water. If you lose power for several days, how might you get enough water for drinking, cooking, and cleaning?

2. Due to a drought, your local government has to set limits on water use. In your opinion, which uses should be limited first, and which uses are too important to limit?

Study the photo shown here. Explain the importance of this kind of ecosystem to living things on Earth.

CHAPTER 3

PROTECTING WATER RESOURCES

From drinking to bathing to watering plants and cooling down machinery, the human population requires an enormous amount of water. Because some areas do not have enough water, it needs to be used wisely. It also needs to be kept clean. Find out how in this chapter.

PEOPLE USING SCIENCE

Hydrologist Hugo A. Loaiciga (lō ī'sē ga) became interested in water issues as a young man in Costa Rica. He was part of a project that was set up to deliver water to disadvantaged farmers. This experience made him aware of water's importance and the problems involved in having enough water in the right place at the right time. His interest in water led him to learn all he could about this precious resource. His studies dealt with the properties of water, its conservation, and the environmental issues involving water.

Today, Dr. Loaiciga helps to ensure a clean and plentiful water supply for our future by "educating people on ways to conserve, maintain, and protect our world water resources."

◀ Dr. Loaiciga tests lagoon waters with a special meter.

INVESTIGATION ①

HOW CAN WATER BE CONSERVED?

Although the amount of water on Earth stays the same, the demand for water and the availability of water change. Because of these changes, people must learn to conserve water, or use it wisely. You'll find out more about conserving water in this investigation.

Activity

Drop by Drop

Water that is wasted one drop at a time can really add up. In this activity you'll see how wasting water drop by drop can easily lead to a loss of many liters.

MATERIALS
• plastic containers
• timer
• *Science Notebook*

SAFETY //////
Clean up spills immediately.

- - - - - - - - - - - - - - - - - - -

Procedure

1. Choose one of the following questions to investigate. Or, if you prefer, **pose a question** of your own about water use or water waste and then investigate it.

- How much water does a dripping faucet waste in 10 minutes? in a day? in a month? in a year?

- Do you use more water to take a shower or to take a bath?

- How much water is saved by turning off the water faucet while brushing your teeth?

- How much water goes down the drain while you wait for running tap water to get cold (or hot)?

- How much water does the toilet in your home use with each flush?

2. **Design an experiment** to measure water use or water waste in order to answer the question you chose. **Record** your plan in your *Science Notebook*.

3. With your teacher's permission, carry out your plan. **Measure** how much water is used or wasted according to your plan. **Record** your results.

See **SCIENCE** *and* **MATH TOOLBOX** page H7 if you need to review *Measuring Volume.*

4. **Compare** your data with that of your classmates.

5. **Compare** your class data with the data in the table on page D46.

Analyze and Conclude

1. Think about the results of your experiment. Use what you learned to help you **infer** ways to conserve water. Then **list** suggested ways to save water.

2. If you saved water in the ways you suggest, about how much water would be saved by one person in one day? in one month? in one year?

3. Find out how many students attend your school. If each student followed your suggestions, about how much water would be saved by these students in one year?

UNIT PROJECT LINK

To protect Waterville's water supply, the town officials propose producing a special 12-month calendar. Each month will carry a message about how to protect the town's water from pollution and suggest ways to conserve water. Write 12 messages to help create this "Conserve and Care" calendar for each school and family in Waterville to use.

Technology
Link

For more help with your Unit Project, go to **www.eduplace.com**.

Activity

Down the Drain

MATERIALS
• *Science Notebook*

How much water do you and the other members of your household use each day? Could you use less? Find out!

- -

Procedure

1. Think about each activity in which you or others in your home use water during one day. Then **make a list** of these activites. **Record** your list in your *Science Notebook*.

2. The table below shows how much water is used during certain activities. **Record** the amounts for the activities on your list. **Estimate** the amount of water used to do any activity on your list that does not appear on the table.

Activity	Water Used (in gallons)
Taking a bath	25
Taking a ten-minute shower, using a regular shower head	50
Taking a ten-minute shower, using a water-saver shower head	25
Flushing the toilet	1.5 to 5
Allowing water to run while brushing teeth	2
Allowing water to run while washing dishes	30
Washing one load in a dishwasher	10
Washing one load in a washing machine	32

3. Add the number of gallons of water used doing each activity during one day. Then **calculate** the amount of water used the entire day.

Analyze and Conclude

1. What surprised you most about how your household uses water?

2. How could you use less water?

RESOURCE

Using Water Wisely

Reading Focus How do the supply of water and the demand for water affect its use?

You may have heard the terms *supply* and *demand* as they are used to describe the economy. *Supply* is the amount of a product or service that is available. *Demand* is the degree to which a product or service is wanted.

The supply of water is fairly steady—it does not change. The demand for this resource, however, has changed. As Earth's human population has increased, so has the demand for water.

In the United States, many areas use more fresh water than they receive from rain and snow. In other words, the demand in these areas is greater than the supply. To make up for this difference in supply and demand, people in such areas need to do two things. First, they have to find ways to use the fresh water they have wisely. Second, they have to find ways to get water from areas that receive more fresh water than those areas use.

Running on Empty

The supply of fresh water for a given area is determined by the amount of precipitation—rain, snow, sleet, and hail—the area receives. The demand for fresh water depends mainly on population. Generally, areas around big cities withdraw more fresh water from surface and underground sources than rural areas do. However, less-populated regions with many farms can also use large amounts of fresh water.

Water withdrawn from surface water and ground water is used in many ways—to produce electricity, to grow crops, and in factories, homes, schools, and businesses. ▼

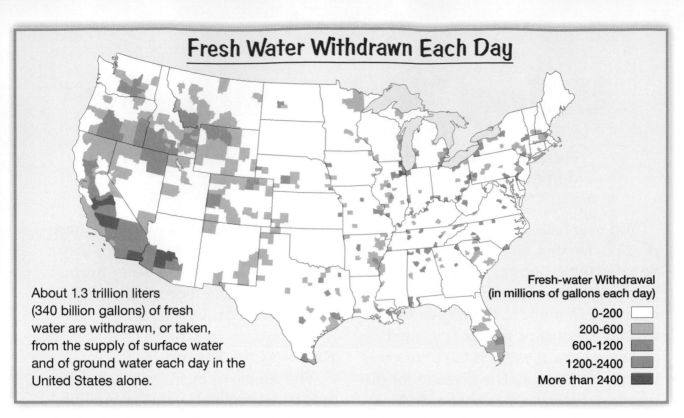

Fresh Water Withdrawn Each Day

About 1.3 trillion liters (340 billion gallons) of fresh water are withdrawn, or taken, from the supply of surface water and of ground water each day in the United States alone.

Fresh-water Withdrawal
(in millions of gallons each day)

0-200	
200-600	
600-1200	
1200-2400	
More than 2400	

Study the map on this page. It shows the amount of water withdrawn from an area each day during a single year. Which areas of the country withdraw the most fresh water? Now find your state on the map. Compare the amount of fresh water withdrawn by your state to the amount withdrawn by nearby states. Compare your area with other areas in your state.

Freshwater Needs in California

Over 33 million people live in California. About 500,000 people move to the state every year. Nearly half of these people settle in southern California. Southern California is a much drier area than the northern part of the state. To meet the great demand for fresh water in southern California, rain and melted snow are collected in reservoirs around the state. This fresh water is then piped through canals, aqueducts, and pipelines to areas where it is needed.

A number of projects have been developed in California to store and deliver fresh water to farms and homes. One of these is the State Water Project, begun in 1960. This project is responsible for bringing much of the fresh water to the people of southern California. By 1973 the first facilities were pumping much-needed fresh water into southern California. Today the project delivers fresh water to two thirds of California's population and provides water for about 1.2 million acres of farmland.

Every Little Bit Helps

Many people are beginning to recognize the importance of **conservation** (kän sər vā′shən), the wise use of Earth's natural resources. Water conservation practices include turning off the faucet while brushing teeth, taking shorter showers, and watering lawns with drip hoses. The activities on pages D44–D46 show that everyday activities can be modified to conserve water.

▲ Some landscape plans require very little water (*left*). By using such plans, water can be conserved. Other landscape plans (*right*) require a great deal of water.

People can conserve water in many creative ways. For example, many lawns in California have been replaced with grasses and other plants that are adapted to a dry climate. This practice greatly reduces the amount of water needed for watering plants. In the early 1990s, many private toilets in the Los Angeles area were replaced with newer models that use much less water. This measure saves millions of gallons of fresh water every year. ■

Science in Literature

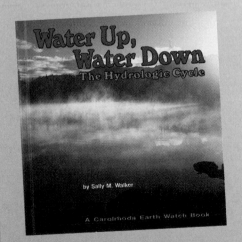

**Water Up, Water Down:
The Hydrologic Cycle**
by Sally M. Walker
Carolrhoda Books, 1992

EVERY DROP COUNTS

"Everyone, not just the people living in drought-stricken areas, should be concerned about water conservation. Simple things—like telling an adult if a faucet is dripping and in need of repair, or keeping a bottle of drinking water in the refrigerator—can save many gallons of water. You can make a difference by not wasting water."

Read *Water Up, Water Down: The Hydrologic Cycle* by Sally M. Walker to explore why it's important not to waste water and to find the answer to other questions you may have about water.

Sharing Water

Reading Focus Why must people in some parts of the world share fresh water with people in other parts of the world?

As you can see from the map on this page, some regions of the world have a great deal of precipitation. You can also see that the opposite is true in other regions. California can be thought of as a miniature example of this situation. Most of the freshwater supply is in the northern part of the state; yet most of the demand is in the central and southern parts. The state's freshwater supply, then, must be shared.

Oh, My Acre-feet!

People in California currently use about 34 million acre-feet of water per year to irrigate crops. An acre-foot (af) is the amount of water needed to flood one acre of land to a depth of one foot. One acre-foot is about 1,233,584 liters (326,000 gallons) of water.

About 193 million af of water in the form of precipitation falls over California in an average year. About three fourths of this water falls in the northern part of the state. Most of the

PRECIPITATION EXTREMES

The northern part of California receives the greatest average precipitation, and the southern part of the state receives the least. Because the greatest demand for water is in the central and southern parts, water must be shared. The freshwater supply in California is about 78 million af, but the freshwater use in the state is about 80 million af. As a result, the state must acquire water from the Colorado River.

Areas that receive the greatest average precipitation
Areas that receive the least average precipitation

freshwater demand in the state, however, is in the drier southern region. A complex maze of pipes, canals, aqueducts, and reservoirs is used to provide southern California with much of the fresh water it uses.

California has two major sources of fresh water. They are the Sacramento–San Joaquin river system and the Colorado River system. The central part of the state gets much of its water from the Sacramento–San Joaquin river system while the southern half of the state gets most of its water from river systems in the north and from the Colorado River.

The Colorado River begins high in the Rocky Mountains. The river follows its 2,350-km (1,450-mi) course through the southwestern United States before it empties into the Gulf of California. Since the early 1900s, the Colorado River and its branches have been organized to provide fresh water to seven states and parts of Mexico.

By agreement, California is allowed 4.4 million af of water from the Colorado River each year. But today, California uses about 5.3 million af from the Colorado River. California borrows the extra water from states in which the supply of water exceeds the states' demand. As the demand for fresh water in the southwestern United States increases, however, California must find other solutions to its freshwater shortage.

People in the southwestern United States have taken several steps to reduce the gap between the supply of fresh water and the demand for it. For example, federal, state, and local laws have been passed that prohibit wasting water. Recycling used water to clean floors, wash cars, and water plants is a common practice. The watering of lawns is closely monitored. Some areas such as Tucson, Arizona, even have water police. These officers enforce laws concerning water conservation.

The problems of water supply and water demand exist in many places around the world. Sharing water is one approach to help solve the problem.

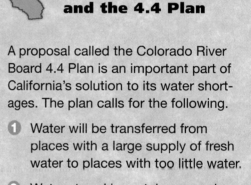

California
and the 4.4 Plan

A proposal called the Colorado River Board 4.4 Plan is an important part of California's solution to its water shortages. The plan calls for the following.

1 Water will be transferred from places with a large supply of fresh water to places with too little water.

2 Water stored in certain reservoirs across the state will be used only during periods of drought.

3 Water seeping from canals and pipes will be recovered.

4 Pipes and canals will be lined to help prevent future seepage.

Yearly, this saves millions of acre-feet of water around the state. Sharing ground water is another important part of the 4.4 Plan. Under the plan, only a certain amount of ground water from California and neighboring states can be withdrawn when it is needed.

Climate Woes

Reading Focus What are some important climate-related events in California's history?

The supply of fresh water is controlled by weather and climate. **Climate** is the average weather conditions of an area over a long period of time. Depending on where you are in California, the climate may be hot and arid or mild and humid. The southern part of the state is hotter and more arid than the milder and more humid northern part.

Floods occur when there are higher-than-normal amounts of rainfall and snowfall for an extended period of time. Floods also occur when heavy precipitation falls during short periods of time and the soil can't absorb all the water. Floods in California are often followed by droughts. As you recall, droughts are periods of time in which the amount of precipitation that falls is much lower than normal.

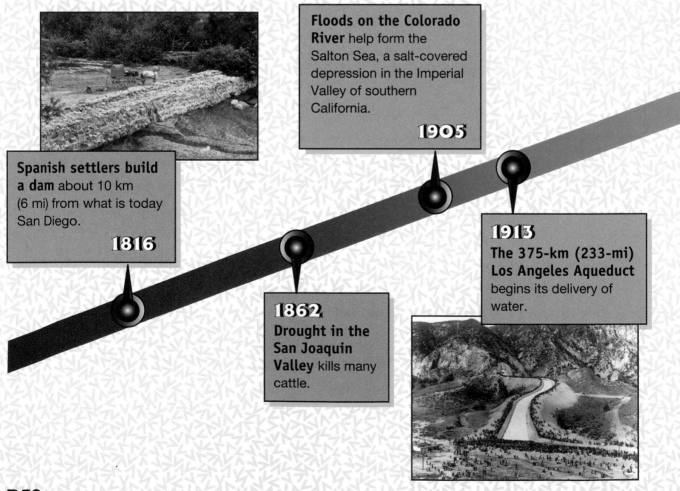

Floods on the Colorado River help form the Salton Sea, a salt-covered depression in the Imperial Valley of southern California.

1905

Spanish settlers build a dam about 10 km (6 mi) from what is today San Diego.

1816

1862
Drought in the San Joaquin Valley kills many cattle.

1913
The 375-km (233-mi) Los Angeles Aqueduct begins its delivery of water.

The Boy and the Girl

Many experts blame floods and droughts on climate events named El Niño (el nēn'yō) and La Niña (la nēn'ya), Spanish for "the boy" and "the girl." **El Niño** is a periodic warming of water in the Pacific Ocean. El Niño conditions cause air temperatures to be higher than normal. Severe storms are common during El Niño.

La Niña often follows El Niño. During La Niña, temperatures are cooler than normal. Floods are replaced by droughts. Winter weather is very harsh. Conditions typical of La Niña began to appear in June of 1998.

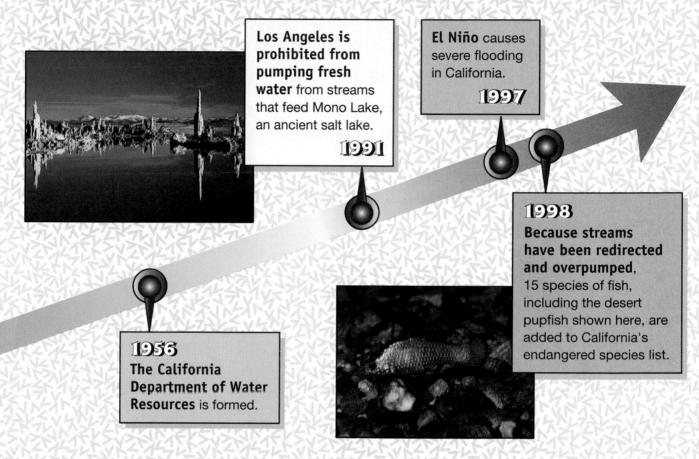

Los Angeles is prohibited from pumping fresh water from streams that feed Mono Lake, an ancient salt lake.
1991

El Niño causes severe flooding in California.
1997

1956
The California Department of Water Resources is formed.

1998
Because streams have been redirected and overpumped, 15 species of fish, including the desert pupfish shown here, are added to California's endangered species list.

INVESTIGATION 1 WRAP-UP

THINK IT
WRITE IT

REVIEW

1. Compare supply and demand in terms of the water supply in California.

2. Describe El Niño and La Niña.

CRITICAL THINKING

3. Why is it important for people to practice water conservation regardless of the freshwater supply in their area?

4. Infer why some areas of the country demand more fresh water than others.

INVESTIGATION 2

HOW CAN WATER BE KEPT CLEAN?

Water is one of Earth's most important natural resources. To insure that the water needs of all living things are met, people must not only conserve water, but they must also make sure that it is kept clean. In this investigation you'll find out some of the ways that people help keep water clean.

Activity

Pollutants Travel

Pollutants are harmful materials that end up where they shouldn't. In this activity you'll make a model of a soil profile to see how pollutants can get into ground water.

Procedure

1. **Make a model** of a soil profile. Use a piece of cotton cloth to cover the small opening of the top section of a 1-L plastic bottle that has been cut in half. Secure the cloth with a rubber band.

2. Turn the top section of the bottle upside down and set it in the bottom section of the bottle. Put sand in the top section to a depth of about 6 cm. Then add about 6 cm of soil on top of the sand. You have made a model soil profile.

soil

sand

Step 2

Step 4

3. Add five or six drops of food coloring to the soil. Then sprinkle about 5 mL of salt crystals on the soil.

4. Use a graduate to measure about 250 mL of water. Slowly pour the water over the surface of the soil. **Observe** the liquid that collects in the bottom section of the bottle. **Record** your observations in your *Science Notebook*.

Step 5

5. Use a dropper to place three drops of tap water on a microscope slide. Place three drops of liquid from the bottom section of the bottle on another slide. **Observe** the liquid on each slide. **Record** your observations.

6. Allow the liquid on each slide to evaporate. Then **compare** the slides and **record** your observations.

Analyze and Conclude

1. In step 4, what color was the liquid in the bottom section of the bottle? Did the soil and sand filter out the food coloring, or did they allow it to pass through?

2. Why was a slide with tap water used? What did you observe in step 6 after the water evaporated? Did the two slides appear the same or different? Did the soil and sand filter out the salt? How do you know?

3. What do the food coloring and salt represent? From your results, what can you **infer** about the ability of soil and sand to act as filters that prevent pollutants from getting into ground water? **Talk with your group** and **describe** how pollutants might get into ground water. Reexamine your conclusions and indicate what further information is needed to support your conclusions.

Making Water Clean

Reading Focus How can water that people have used be recycled for reuse?

Any water that living things have used is known as **waste water**. It includes the water you've used to shower, wash dishes, do laundry, flush the toilet, and so on. Most of the water used in factories becomes waste water. Even the rain that runs off roads and rooftops becomes waste water.

Round and Round It Goes!

People can recycle waste water for reuse, but it must first be treated. The drawings show some stages in the treatment of waste water.

Treated waste water has an important role in California's water cycle. During periods of drought, fresh water is scarce. **Water reclamation** (rek lə-mā'shən) projects in the state reclaim, or reuse, treated waste water. This treated waste water is not clean enough to be used for drinking and cooking, but it has other uses.

One common use for reclaimed water is to water the lawns on golf courses. Other uses include watering plants along public roads and on public property and irrigating some of California's commercial crops.

Cleaning Up Waste Water

❶ Screening A screen removes large floating materials from the water as it enters a treatment plant. The water then flows or is pumped to the next treatment stage.

❸ Removing Sludge Organic material in waste water, called **sludge**, settles to the bottom and is pumped to tanks that are called digesters.

❹ Removing Scum Light materials, such as grease, oil, and soap, float to the top, forming scum. The scum is sent to the digesters.

❷ Aerating (er'āt iŋ) Harmful gases are allowed to escape, and air is pumped through the water to replace lost oxygen. Grit settles to the bottom and is removed.

Digester Solid-waste materials are treated and returned to the environment.

Industries such as oil refineries and electrical power plants in California also use treated waste water.

Making Water Drinkable

Does the water you use in your home come from a river, a lake, or a reservoir? If so, the water goes through a water purification plant to make the water potable (pōt′ə bəl). **Potable water** is water fit for drinking.

How is water made potable? First, a screen removes objects such as twigs and insects. Then chlorine and other chemicals are added to **disinfect** (dis in fekt′) the water, or kill bacteria and other harmful microorganisms in it. Next, the water passes through filters of sand and gravel, which strain out more materials. Then the water goes into a storage tank and is treated with more chlorine. The water is then potable and ready to be piped into homes. ■

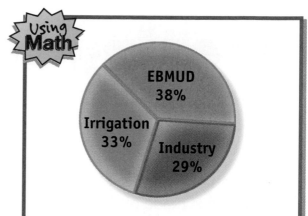

Water Reuse by 2020

Many California districts have water reuse projects. One example is the East Bay Municipal Utility District (EBMUD). EBMUD saves people in the San Francisco Bay area about 15.5 million gallons of fresh water a day! This adds up to about 5.5 billion gallons of water saved during the year 2000.

Look at the circle graph showing projected water reuse figures for California by 2020. It shows the amount of water reuse by EBMUD and for irrigation and industry.

5 Killing Bacteria Waste water is filtered and sent to a large tank where chlorine is added to kill bacteria. The treated water is tested and then discharged into a local river or the ocean, or it is stored for reuse.

▲ Water treatment plant in Oakland, California

Keeping Water Clean

Reading Focus What are some things that make water dirty, and what is being done to keep water clean?

Water is a fairly simple compound. Each molecule is made of two atoms of hydrogen and one atom of oxygen. That's why water has the chemical formula H_2O. But despite its simple formula, water is a complex substance with many unique properties. Unlike most other substances on Earth, for example, water expands when it freezes. This property makes ice less dense than liquid water. And because of this lesser density, ice cubes float in liquid water!

As you may recall, water has another unique property. Water is able to dissolve many other substances. In most ways, this ability is a useful property. But as the activity on pages D54 and D55 shows, it is because of this property that water can so easily contain and then carry pollutants.

Many laws have been passed to reduce and prevent water pollution and to ensure water quality. Some are federal, or national, laws. Others have been passed by states and by cities.

▼ **The pollutants in water can come from many sources.**

The Clean Water Act

In 1972 the United States government passed the Clean Water Act, which addresses these concerns.

- It requires that sources of fresh water be kept clean.
- In 1987, requirements were added to help reduce pollution caused by pollutants that come not from a single point, but from various sources. As shown in the picture on page D58, these sources might include streets, farms, fields, construction sites, and leaking storage tanks.
- It requires that money be provided for building water treatment plants and for control of runoff.

The Safe Drinking Water Act

In 1986 the federal government passed the Safe Drinking Water Act, which addresses these concerns.

- It requires that drinking water be made potable.
- In 1996 it was changed to make sure that drinking water is tested for organisms that can cause disease. This change is necessary because even water that looks clear can contain organisms that bring about diseases such as dysentery (dis'ən ter ē) and hepatitis (hep ə tīt'is). In 1993, *Cryptosporidium* (krip tō spō rid'ē əm) got into the water supply of the city of Milwaukee. More than 400,000 people developed severe nausea and diarrhea after drinking the contaminated water, and more than 100 people died.

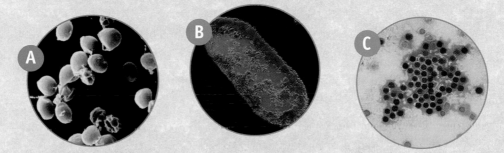

▲ Organisms that can carry digestive tract illness (*A*), dysentery (*B*), and hepatitis (*C*) in unclean drinking water

The Porter–Cologne Act

California passed its own clean water act. This act, called the Porter-Cologne Water Quality Control Act, addresses these concerns.

- It helps ensure that all waste water is properly treated before it is pumped back into the environment. In doing so, it helps ensure that California wetland areas that receive used water, such as water recreation areas, shellfish habitats, and coastal areas, will not be damaged by the water they receive.
- It requires that harmful and toxic substances be treated at their sources.
- It requires factories and power plants along the California coast to be properly designed to reduce the harmful effects of pumping waste water back into the ocean.

Other Water Quality Issues

In addition to being concerned about the pollution associated with waste water, people in California are also concerned about pollutants from other sources in their water supply. One such pollutant is a fuel additive that helps prevent air pollution. However, when the additive leaks into lakes and rivers from boats that use such fuels, the substance pollutes groundwater sources. Bills have been drafted in hopes of removing this pollutant from the gasoline used in the state.

Another substance causing concern in California is a compound used to make rocket fuel. Studies have found that the compound is present in large amounts in wells around the state. High levels of the compound have also been detected in the Colorado River. Recall that this river supplies a large amount of the state's fresh water.

About half of the fruits and vegetables produced in the United States come from California. Pesticides are used on commercial crops to control crop-destroying insects. Many of these

▲ Keeping water clean helps protect the living things in water habitats.

harmful chemicals are polluting California's water supplies. Some of this polluted water eventually reaches sensitive wetland areas.

It is important to remember that all living things need clean fresh water. Every person should do his or her part to help conserve fresh water and to keep water supplies clean. ■

Internet Field Trip

Visit **www.eduplace.com** to learn more about cleaning up water.

INVESTIGATION 2 WRAP-UP

REVIEW

1. In a wastewater treatment plant, what is the purpose of adding chlorine to the waste water?

2. Name two laws designed to help keep water clean and describe what each law requires.

CRITICAL THINKING

3. Compare the advantages and disadvantages of using fuel additives. Do you think the advantages outweigh the disadvantages? Explain your answer.

4. Explain why clear water is not necessarily safe to drink.

REFLECT & EVALUATE

CHAPTER 13 REVIEW

Word Power

Write the letter of the term that best completes each sentence. *Not all terms will be used.*

1. Water fit for drinking is referred to as ——.
2. Any water that people have used, including water used to wash dishes, brush teeth, or do laundry, is called ——.
3. The reuse of treated water is ——.
4. The wise use of Earth's natural resources is ——.
5. A periodic warming of the water in the Pacific Ocean is called ——.

a. conservation
b. disinfect
c. El Niño
d. potable water
e. waste water
f. water reclamation

Check What You Know

Write the term in each pair that best completes each sentence.

1. Waste water is treated with (sand, chlorine) to kill bacteria.
2. The amount of a product or service that is available is the (supply, demand).
3. When waste water is treated, the organic material that settles to the bottom of tanks and is removed is called (debris, sludge).

Problem Solving

1. In many areas, people may have only one bucket of water to use all day. Describe how you would use and conserve water if you only had one bucket for the entire day.
2. California uses more than its allotted amount of water from the Colorado River. Explain why this is a problem. Infer what could happen if California continues using more water than is available.

PORTFOLIO

Study the photo. Explain how this person could use water more wisely.

Summarizing

Summarizing helps you remember what you have read. A summary is a short paragraph that states the main points of a selection. Follow these guidelines to write a good summary.

Use these guidelines to write a summary.
- List topic sentences.
- Restate main ideas.
- Group similar ideas.
- Omit unimportant ideas.

Read the paragraphs. Then complete the exercises that follow.

There's Enough for Everyone

About 3 percent of Earth's water is fresh water. This amount is enough for the needs of everyone in the world. Unfortunately, that water isn't distributed equally to all people on Earth. Scientists estimate that 66 percent of the fresh water on Earth is stored in icecaps and glaciers. The remainder is underground and in bodies of water such as lakes and rivers.

Fresh water that's above the ground in lakes, ponds, rivers, and streams is plentiful in some areas and scarce in others. For example, rain rarely falls in the deserts of California. When it does rain there, the puddles dry up quickly.

1. **Write the letter of each statement that you would put in your summary.**

   a. About 3 percent of Earth's water is fresh water.

   b. Water isn't distributed equally to all people on Earth.

   c. Scientists estimate that 66 percent of the fresh water on Earth is stored in icecaps and glaciers.

   d. Rain rarely falls in the deserts of California.

2. **Write a summary of the paragraphs, using the four guidelines.**

Circle Graph

The circle graph shows the use of ground water in the United States.

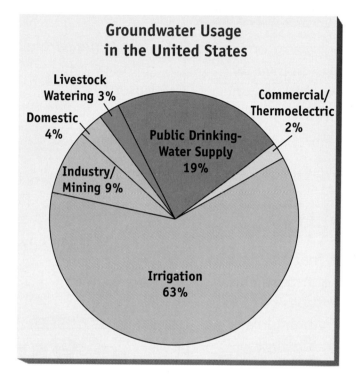

Groundwater Usage in the United States

Livestock Watering 3%

Domestic 4%

Industry/Mining 9%

Public Drinking-Water Supply 19%

Commercial/Thermoelectric 2%

Irrigation 63%

Use the graph to complete the exercises that follow.

1. What percent of the ground water is not used for irrigation?

2. For which purpose is $\frac{1}{50}$ of ground water used?

3. For which purpose is about $\frac{1}{5}$ of ground water used?

4. Represent each part of the circle graph as a decimal and as a fraction in simplest form.

Use the data in the table on page D7 to complete Exercise 5.

5. Make a circle graph showing the location of water on Earth.

WRAP-UP!

On your own, use scientific methods to investigate a question about water on Earth.

THINK LIKE A SCIENTIST

Ask a Question

Pose a question about water on Earth that you would like to investigate. For example, ask, "How might you reduce the amount of water needed to maintain a lawn?"

Make a Hypothesis

Suggest a hypothesis that is a possible answer to the question. One hypothesis is that some types of grass require less water than others do and that a lawn planted with this type of grass could be maintained with less water.

Plan and Do a Test

Plan a controlled experiment to find out if, over time, different types of grass seed grow equally well with a small amount of water. You could start with several types of grass seed, containers in which to grow the seed, and potting soil. Develop a procedure that uses these materials to test the hypothesis. With permission, carry out your experiment. Follow the safety guidelines on pages S14–S15.

Record and Analyze

Observe carefully and record your data accurately. Make repeated observations.

Draw Conclusions

Look for evidence to support the hypothesis or to show that it is false. Draw conclusions about the hypothesis. Repeat the experiment to verify the results.

WRITING IN SCIENCE
Interview

To learn about protecting local freshwater resources, interview an expert, such as a conservationist or a hydrologist. Write up your interview for your class newsletter. Follow these guidelines.

- Prepare questions before the interview.
- Take notes and, with permission, record the interview.
- Use a question-and-answer format in writing up the main points of the interview.

UNIT E

Weather and Climate

Theme: Constancy and Change

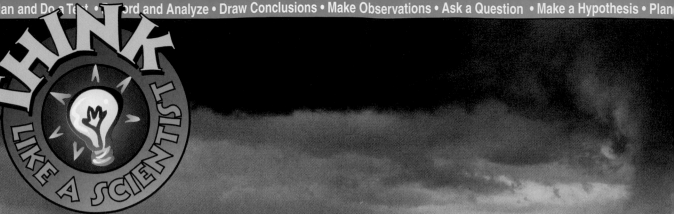

THINK LIKE A SCIENTIST

TORNADO WARNING

Tornadoes, such as this one seen over a Texas prairie, can have wind speeds up to 500 km/h (310 mph). Tornadoes are the most violent storms on Earth. Hundreds of tornadoes strike the United States each year. Scientists study actual tornadoes, measuring conditions that occur within them. Artificial tornadoes are also studied in laboratory experiments. Although scientists still don't fully understand how tornadoes develop, they try to predict where and when tornadoes will strike. Early warnings to people who may be in the path of a tornado can help prevent loss of life and damage to property.

THINK LIKE A SCIENTIST

Questioning In this unit you'll study tornadoes and other types of storms. You'll investigate questions such as these.

- What Is Air Pressure?
- What Can Clouds Tell You About the Weather?

Observing, Testing, Hypothesizing
In the Activity "Tornado Tube," you'll make observations about the motion of swirling water. You'll also hypothesize about the motion of air in a tornado.

Researching In the Resource "The Fiercest Storms on Earth," you'll gather more information about the nature of tornadoes, and hurricanes too!

Drawing Conclusions
After you've completed your investigations, you'll draw conclusions about what you've learned— and get new ideas.

CHAPTER 1

THE AIR AROUND US

What do you need air for? You need it to breathe, of course. But is air important for anything else? Learning about air is a good way to begin learning about something that affects you every day. That something is weather.

PEOPLE USING SCIENCE

Meteorologist   On Sunday, March 11, 1888, a storm stalled over New York City, dumping 53 cm (21 in.) of snow. Wind gusts of 117 km/h (73 mph) piled up 6-m (20-ft) high snowdrifts, stranding New Yorkers in trains and horse-drawn carriages. There had been no warning that a major blizzard was coming. People lost their lives.

On January 7 and January 8 of 1996, almost 70 cm (28 in.) of snow fell on New York City. Before that snowstorm arrived, meteorologists (mēt ē ər äl′ə jists) such as Al Roker were able to give people lots of warning. A meteorologist is a scientist who studies the condition of the atmosphere and forecasts the weather. Thanks to meteorologists, New Yorkers were spared tragedies like those suffered in the Blizzard of 1888.

Coming Up

◄ Meteorologist Al Roker not only forecasts the weather but has fun announcing his forecasts on television.

WHAT IS AIR?

Suppose someone asked you to describe the air. Perhaps you'd say, "Air is something that makes your hair blow on a windy day." But what is that "something"? In Investigation 1 you'll find out.

Activity

An Empty Cup

If you had a cup filled with hot chocolate, would you say that the cup is empty? Of course not. But what if you were to drink all the hot chocolate? Would the cup be empty then? Find out!

Procedure

1. Fill a clear bowl with water. Float a plastic-foam peanut in it.

2. **Talk with your group** and together **predict** what will happen to the peanut if you cover it with a clear plastic cup and then push the cup under the water to the bottom of the bowl. **Write** your prediction in your *Science Notebook*. **Draw** a picture to show your prediction.

Step 1

MATERIALS

- large clear plastic bowl
- water
- plastic-foam peanut
- clear plastic cup
- clear plastic cup with small hole
- *Science Notebook*

SAFETY

Clean up spills immediately.

E6

3. **Test** your prediction. Turn a cup upside down and push it *straight down* over the peanut until the rim of the cup touches the bottom of the bowl. **Record** what happens to the peanut.

Step 4

4. Repeat step 3, using a clear plastic cup that has a small hole in its side, near the base. **Record** your observations.

Analyze and Conclude

1. **Compare** your results in step 3 with your prediction. What happened to the peanut? Write a **hypothesis** to explain why this happened. Give reasons to support your hypothesis.

2. What happened to the peanut in step 4? **Hypothesize** why this happened. Based on this hypothesis, **predict** what would happen if you were to cover the hole with a finger or piece of tape and then repeat the experiment.

3. Was the cup empty or not? Explain your answer. What can you **infer** about air from this activity?

INVESTIGATE FURTHER!

EXPERIMENT

Use a straw to blow air into the bottom of the bowl of water you used in this activity. Blow as hard and as steadily as you can. Have a partner observe what happens to the level of the water in the bowl as you blow into the straw. Infer what's causing a change in water level.

Activity

An Ocean of Air

Have you ever gone swimming in the ocean? Can you remember the feeling of water pressing against you? In this activity you'll find out about the "ocean" that presses against you on dry land!

MATERIALS

- goggles
- thin wooden slats
- newspaper
- scissors
- *Science Notebook*

SAFETY

Wear goggles during this activity.

Procedure

1. Lay a wooden slat across your desk so that about one half of the slat hangs over the edge of the desktop.

Math Hint *To find the midpoint of the wooden slat, measure the length of the slat. Divide that measurement by 2.*

Step 2

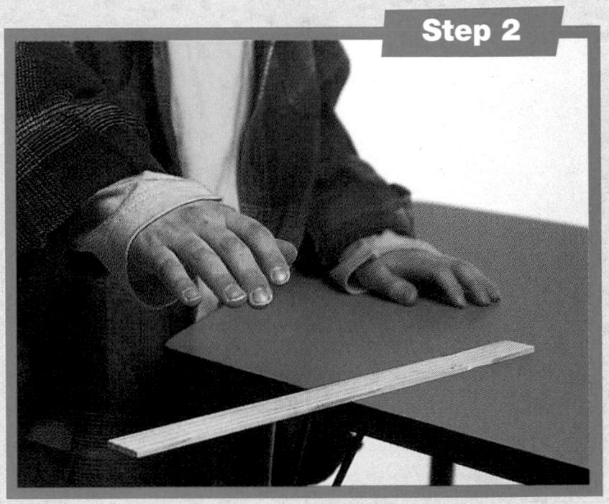

2. Use the palm of your hand to strike down on the end of the slat that is hanging over. **Record** what happens in your *Science Notebook*. Then put the slat back in the same position as before.

3. Place a sheet of newspaper over the part of the slat that is on the desk. Strike the slat as you did in step 2. **Record** your observations.

Step 3

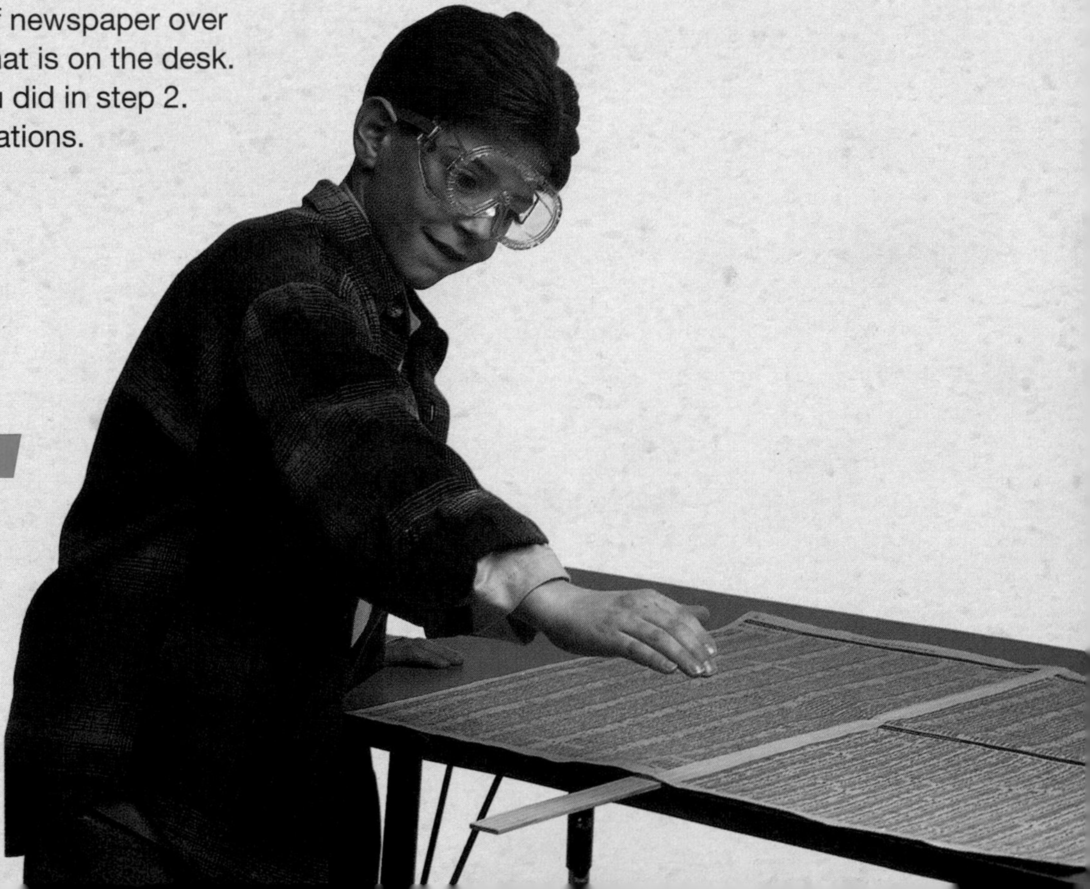

4. Place a slat on the desk in the same position you placed it in step 1. Cut the newspaper in half. Lay one half of the paper over the part of the slat that is on the desk. With other group members, **predict** what will happen when you strike the slat this time. **Record** your prediction and then test it. Be sure to strike the slat as you did in step 2. **Record** your observations.

Step 4

Analyze and Conclude

1. **Compare** what you observed in step 2 with what you observed in step 3. **Describe** the difference in your results.

2. **Describe** what happened in step 4. How does it **compare** with your prediction?

3. **Describe** what was holding down the newspaper when you struck the slat in step 3. Infer whether that same "thing" was holding down the half sheet of newspaper in step 4. What property of this "thing" caused the difference in your results? Give reasons for your answer.

Technology Link **CD-ROM**

INVESTIGATE FURTHER!

Use the **Science Processor CD-ROM**, *Weather and Climate* (Investigation 1, Up, Up, and Away) to take an imaginary ride in a weather balloon. Find out about the layers of the atmosphere. Ride the balloon higher and higher to learn which gases you'll float through at each layer.

It's Got Us Covered

Reading Focus What gases make up air, and how do these gases make life possible?

▲ **Air is matter, just as all of the objects shown are matter.**

You feel it when a gentle breeze touches your face. You hear it rustling leaves. You see its force bend tree branches. What is this thing that hints of its presence but is tasteless, odorless, and unseen? It's the air.

It's a Mix of Matter

Air is made up of matter. Like the objects that you can see, air takes up space and has weight. The activity on pages E6 and E7 shows that air takes up space. When a cup is pushed down over a plastic-foam peanut floating in a bowl filled with water, the water does not rise to fill the cup. That's because the cup is already filled with air. The activity on pages E8 and E9 demonstrates the effect

of the weight of air when a wooden slat covered with newspaper is struck. The weight of the air holds the newspaper down over the slat as it is struck.

Air is an invisible mixture of different gases. Like all matter, these gases are made up of tiny particles that are in constant motion.

The circle graph on the next page shows the mixture of gases that make up air. The largest part of air is made up of **nitrogen** (nī′trə jən). The second most plentiful gas is **oxygen** (äks′i jən). The small portion of air that's left is made up of other gases, including **carbon dioxide** (kär′bən dī äks′īd) and **water vapor**. Water vapor is water in the form of a gas.

E10

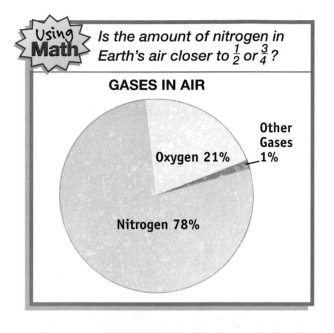

Using Math

Is the amount of nitrogen in Earth's air closer to $\frac{1}{2}$ or $\frac{3}{4}$?

GASES IN AIR

Other Gases 1%

Oxygen 21%

Nitrogen 78%

A Life-Support System

Life on Earth depends on the gases in air. For example, all animals need oxygen from the air to release the energy that is found in the food they eat. Plants need carbon dioxide in order to make food. Water vapor can form clouds. Clouds can produce rain.

Study the picture below to see how air provides a life-support system for the living things on Earth. Look for one way in which oxygen, which is used by animals, is added to the air. Find ways in which nitrogen supports life, too.

▼ **The gases in air make life possible.**

Carbon dioxide from the air is used by plants to make food.

Water vapor makes clouds, and therefore rain, possible.

Animals release carbon dioxide into the air.

Oxygen is given off to the air when plants make food.

Oxygen from the air is used by animals to release energy from food.

Nitrogen from the air is used by bacteria on plant roots. Bacteria change nitrogen into materials that plants use to grow.

Water and nitrogen-containing materials in the soil are used by plants to make food and to grow larger.

Earth's Blanket of Air

Imagine that you are riding in a space shuttle. You look out the window and see clouds in constant motion floating above Earth. These clouds are part of a blanket of air that surrounds Earth. This blanket of air, made up of gases, liquids, and some solid matter, is called the **atmosphere**. The atmosphere reaches from the ground to about 700 km (435 mi) above Earth's surface.

As you can see in the diagram on the next page, the atmosphere is made up of four main layers. The farther a layer is from Earth's surface, the farther apart are the particles of air in that layer. Likewise, the closer a layer is to Earth, the closer together are the particles.

Of the four main layers, the one farthest from Earth's surface is called the thermosphere (thur'mō sfir). The particles of air in this layer may be as far apart as 10 km (6 mi)!

Only the lowest layer of the atmosphere has enough air to support life. This layer, called the **troposphere** (trō'pō sfir), starts at Earth's surface and goes up about 8 km–16 km (5 mi–10 mi) above the surface. Most of the oxygen, nitrogen, carbon dioxide, and water vapor in the atmosphere is found in this layer.

In the lower part of the troposphere, particles that make up air are packed close together. But as you travel higher, you would find it difficult to breathe.

Science in Literature

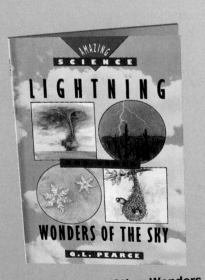

Lightning and Other Wonders of the Sky
by Q. L. Pearce
Illustrated by Mary Ann Fraser
Julian Messner, 1989

A Froggy Day

"On June 16, 1882, the people of Dubuque, Iowa, were pelted with hailstones that had tiny frogs trapped inside. These unfortunate animals were probably sucked into the clouds from nearby streams and ponds by strong updrafts, then quickly frozen and covered with layers of ice."

This story comes from *Lightning and Other Wonders of the Sky* by Q. L. Pearce. You will be amazed at what can happen in the world of weather. Read this book to learn about sundogs, sky color, rainbows, deadly fog, and all sorts of weather wonders!

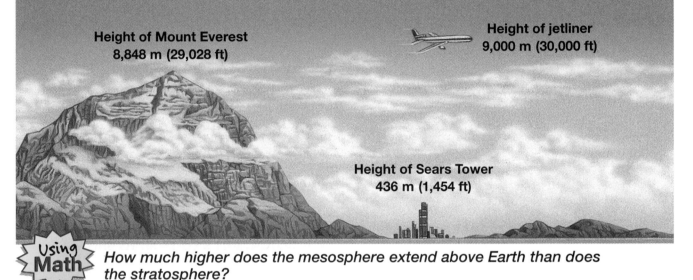

Thermosphere
extends to about 700 km (420 mi) above Earth

Mesosphere
extends to about 80 km (50 mi) above Earth

Stratosphere
extends to about 48 km (30 mi) above Earth

Troposphere
extends to about 16 km (10 mi) above Earth

Height of Mount Everest
8,848 m (29,028 ft)

Height of jetliner
9,000 m (30,000 ft)

Height of Sears Tower
436 m (1,454 ft)

Using Math *How much higher does the mesosphere extend above Earth than does the stratosphere?*

You would need a supply of oxygen to help you breathe at the top of Mount Everest. The troposphere is the layer of the atmosphere where weather occurs and where jetliners fly.

Sometimes a Wet Blanket

What's the weather like today where you live? Is it wet and chilly? Hot and dry? *Hot, wet, cold, dry, cool, warm, windy, chilly, rainy, foggy, stormy, clear, sunny*, and *cloudy* are all words used to talk about weather. Those words are actually ways of describing what's happening in the atmosphere.

Weather is the condition of the atmosphere at a certain place and time. It can change from minute to minute and from hour to hour. Air temperature and the amount of water vapor in the air greatly affect weather. Without the atmosphere, there wouldn't be any weather. What place do you know of where there is no atmosphere? What do you know about the weather there? ■

Internet Field Trip
Visit **www.eduplace.com** to explore the atmosphere.

Not Too Warm, Not Too Cold

Reading Focus How is Earth's atmosphere like the glass of a greenhouse?

SCIENCE TECHNOLOGY & SOCIETY

Have you ever visited a gardener's greenhouse? A greenhouse is usually made of glass. The glass lets in sunlight, which warms the ground and other surfaces inside the greenhouse. As these surfaces warm, they release heat into the air. The glass keeps this heat from escaping. This is similar to the way the inside of a car heats up when sunlight shines through closed windows. The air inside the greenhouse stays warm enough for plants to grow throughout the year.

Earth's Greenhouse

In some ways, Earth's atmosphere acts like the glass of a greenhouse. It allows the Sun's rays to pass through it and heat Earth's land and water. Some of the heat from the warmed Earth then goes back into the atmosphere as invisible rays. Some of these rays escape into space. But most are trapped by water vapor, carbon dioxide, and other gases that make up Earth's atmosphere. So the atmosphere warms up.

The gases send some of this heat back toward Earth's surface, as shown

Plants are grown in a greenhouse like this one. ▼

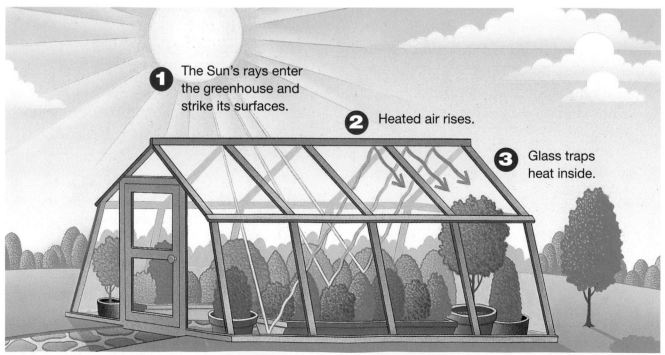

1 The Sun's rays enter the greenhouse and strike its surfaces.

2 Heated air rises.

3 Glass traps heat inside.

in the diagram below. Thus, the air in the lower atmosphere stays warm enough for life to exist. This process in which heat from Earth is trapped by the gases in the atmosphere is called the **greenhouse effect**.

Without the greenhouse effect, Earth would be a much colder place—too cold to support most forms of life. Earth would be more like the Moon, which has no atmosphere. Without an atmosphere, there is no greenhouse effect. So the Moon's surface gets much colder than any place on Earth, as low as −173°C (−279°F). The atmosphere keeps Earth's average surface temperature at about 14°C (57°F).

The amount of carbon dioxide in the air is increasing. That leads some scientists to think that the greenhouse effect may be increasing. An increase in the greenhouse effect could raise Earth's average surface temperature. Scientists are currently studying weather data to try to determine if indeed Earth's average surface temperature is increasing. ■

The greenhouse effect on Earth ▼

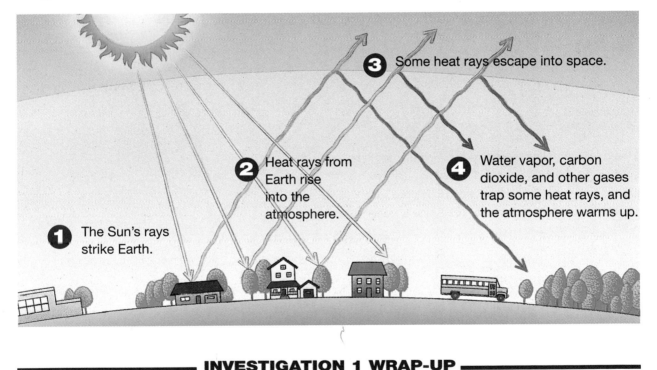

3 Some heat rays escape into space.

2 Heat rays from Earth rise into the atmosphere.

4 Water vapor, carbon dioxide, and other gases trap some heat rays, and the atmosphere warms up.

1 The Sun's rays strike Earth.

━━━━━━ INVESTIGATION 1 WRAP-UP ━━━━━━

REVIEW

1. What is air made of?

2. Which gas makes up about 78% of air?

CRITICAL THINKING

3. Give evidence to show one way in which the atmosphere is like other matter.

4. Could there be life on Earth without the greenhouse effect? What might happen if Earth lost its atmosphere?

INVESTIGATION 2

WHY DOES AIR MOVE?

Imagine that it's summertime in a big city. The air feels hot and still. What would the air feel like by the seashore or near a large lake? It's likely there would be a nice cool breeze. Why? Find out in Investigation 2 what makes the air move.

Activity

Warming the Air

What happens when the Sun's rays strike your body? Some of the light energy changes to heat and warms your body. Earth's surface is warmed by the Sun, too. Does this heating of Earth's surface change the air above it? Find out!

Procedure

1. Wrap a cardboard tube in a piece of aluminum foil. Do not cover the ends. Attach the tube to a meterstick, using a rubber band, as shown. Push the tube and rubber band along the meterstick until the bottom edge of the tube is at the 10-cm mark on the meterstick. In your *Science Notebook*, **make a chart** like the one shown.

Type of Surface	Temperature (°C)

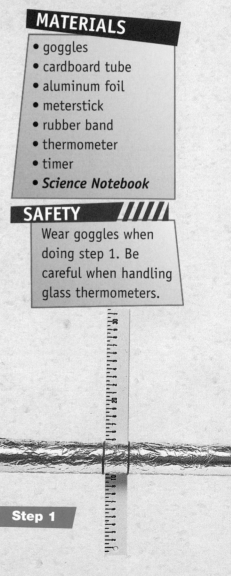

Step 1

2. Go outdoors to a grassy area. Hold the meterstick with the zero end touching the ground. Slide a thermometer into the tube. Wait at least three minutes and then **read** the thermometer. **Record** the temperature of the air.

Step 2

3. **Predict** how the temperature of the air over other types of surfaces will vary. Repeat step 2 over three very different surfaces, such as concrete, bare soil, and gravel. **Measure** the air temperature for three minutes each time. **Record** your data.

4. Repeat steps 1–3 on another day to see whether your results are the same.

Analyze and Conclude

1. Make a bar graph of the temperatures you recorded.

See **SCIENCE** *and* **MATH TOOLBOX** page H3 if you need to review *Making a Bar Graph*.

2. **Compare** your results in step 3 with your predictions. What can you **infer** about the temperature of the surfaces from the temperature of the air above them?

3. Based on the information that you gathered, **draw a conclusion** about how the Sun warms the air above different surfaces. Review your conclusion and decide whether further information is needed to support it.

UNIT PROJECT LINK

For this Unit Project you'll make a class weather station and record weather-related data. In the outside area set up for your weather station, use a rubber band to attach a thermometer to a milk carton. For two weeks, record the temperature in the morning, at noon, and in the late afternoon.

Technology *Link*

For more help with your Unit Project, go to **www.eduplace.com**.

Activity

Making an Air Scale

Does temperature affect the way air moves? In this activity you'll find out!

MATERIALS
- string
- scissors
- 2 metersticks
- 2 large brown bags
- tape
- high desk or table
- heavy books
- lamp with light bulb
- thermometer
- ***Science Notebook***

SAFETY

The light bulb used in this activity will get hot. Avoid touching the bulb.

Procedure

1. Cut one 20-cm and two 10-cm lengths of string. Tie one end of the long string to the center of a meterstick.

2. Open two large paper bags fully. Turn each bag upside down. Tape one end of a 10-cm string to the center of one bag bottom. Do the same with the other bag. Tape the free end of each string to opposite ends of the meterstick. The open end of each bag should hang toward the floor.

3. On a high table, place a second meterstick between two books in a stack of heavy books. About one third of the meterstick should hang over the edge of the table. Tape the string from the center of the first meterstick to the end of this meterstick. The bags should hang freely and be in balance with one another.

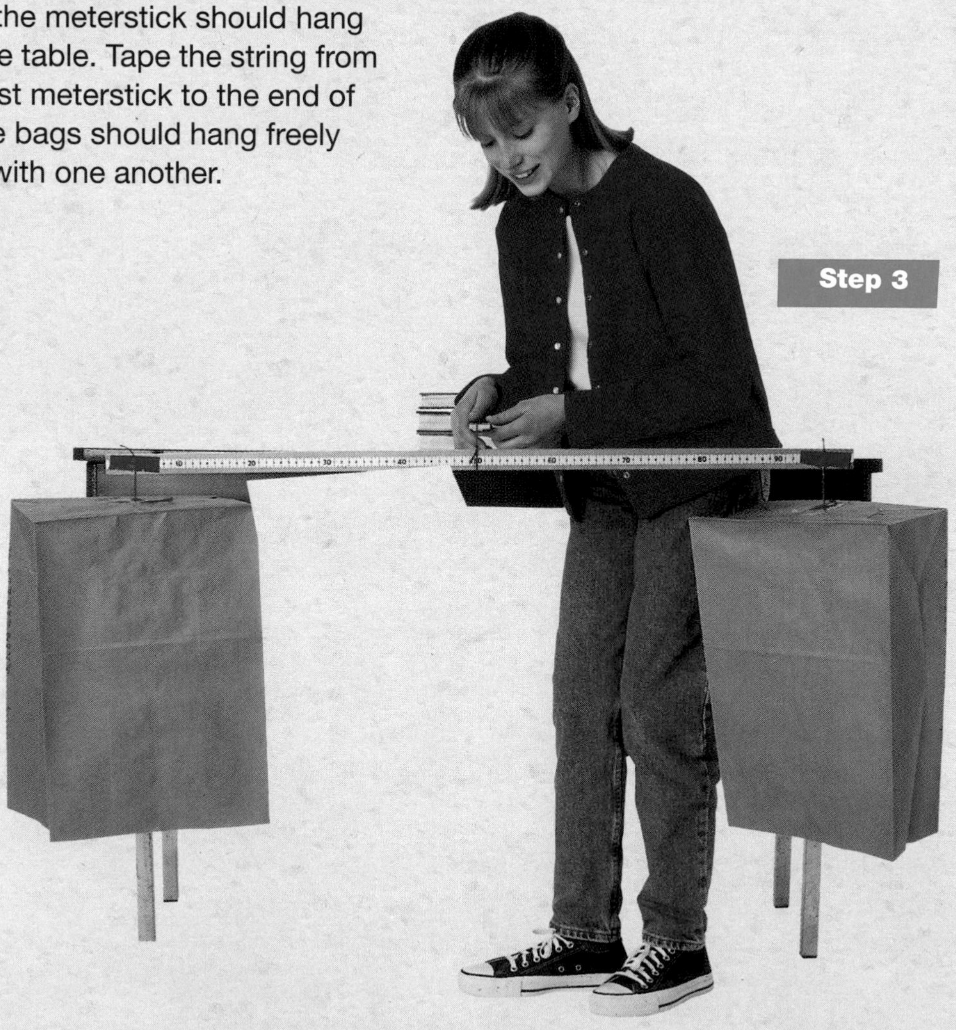

Step 3

4. Put a lamp below one of the bags, as shown. **Talk with your group** and **predict** what will happen to the bag when the lamp is turned on. **Record** your prediction in your *Science Notebook*. **Measure** and **record** the temperature inside the two bags.

See **SCIENCE** *and* **MATH TOOLBOX** page H8 if you need to review *Using a Thermometer.*

5. Turn on the lamp and **observe** what happens. Again **measure** the temperature inside the two bags. **Record** your data and observations. Let the lamp cool. Then repeat your measurements to check your results.

Analyze and Conclude

1. **Describe** what happened to the bag over the lamp. How does this result **compare** with your prediction?

2. **Compare** the temperature of the air in the two bags in steps 4 and 5. **Infer** the effect of temperature on the weight of the air in each of the bags. Give reasons for the inference you make.

Hot-Air Balloon

Reading Focus What must you do to raise and lower a hot-air balloon?

The hot-air balloon shown below doesn't look like a paper bag, does it? But it *does* work like the paper-bag scale described on pages E18 and E19. Read and find out why.

4 The pilot controls how high the balloon rises. To make the balloon rise higher, the pilot burns more fuel to heat the air more. To lower the balloon the pilot lets the air cool.

3 Heat makes the particles of air inside the balloon move farther apart, so the air gets lighter. Outside the balloon the particles of air are more closely packed together, so this air is heavier. As the warm air rises and fills the balloon, the balloon goes up.

1 The pilot and passengers stand in the basket. The fuel tanks are also inside the basket. Hot-air balloons use propane gas as fuel.

2 A fuel line feeds gas to the burner. The burner hangs above the basket and below the mouth of the balloon. Flames from the burner heat the air in the lower part of the balloon.

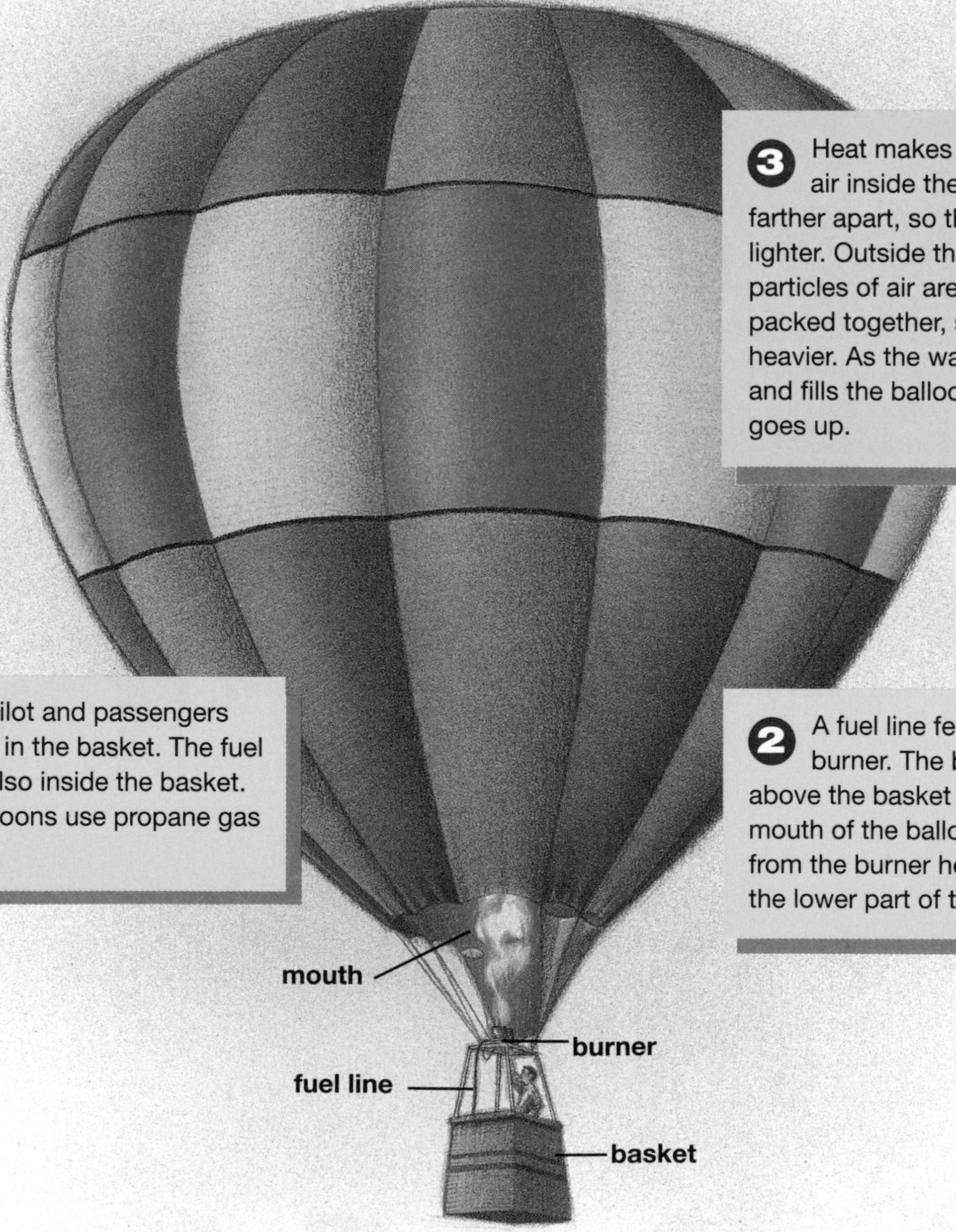

mouth

burner

fuel line

basket

Feeling the Air

Reading Focus What causes wind or moving air?

The activity on pages E16 and E17 shows that some surfaces on Earth are warmed more than others. This leads to the unequal heating of Earth's surface. How does this unequal heating of Earth's surface affect the air?

Moving Air

Look at the photos on this page. They show some of the different materials that make up Earth. In general, dark-colored materials heat up more rapidly than light-colored materials do. Therefore, the air above dark-colored surfaces, such as dark soils, is warmer than the air above light-colored surfaces, such as snow.

The activity on pages E18 and E19 shows how heating the air in a paper bag makes that bag lighter than an unheated bag. The bag with the heated air moves upward.

When an area of air is warmed, the particles of the warm air spread out. The warm air becomes lighter than the cooler air above it. The warm air rises and the cooler air sinks. The movement of air is called **wind**. Wind is caused by the uneven heating of Earth's surface.

Although you can't *see* air, you can *feel* it when the wind blows! Wind can be gentle or strong. It can cause a leaf to settle softly on the ground, or it can blow down an entire tree.

▲ **Which of these surfaces is likely to heat up most rapidly?**

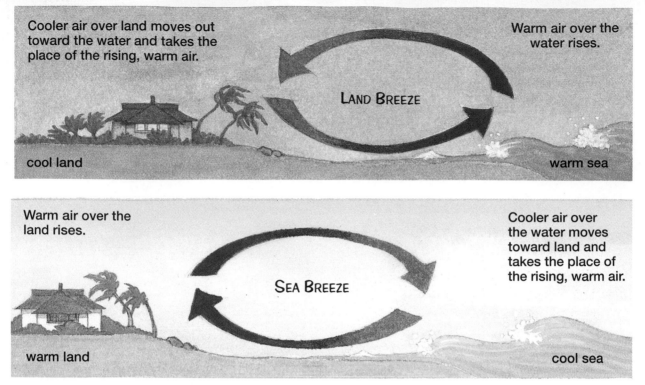

Cooler air over land moves out toward the water and takes the place of the rising, warm air.

Warm air over the water rises.

LAND BREEZE

cool land

warm sea

Warm air over the land rises.

Cooler air over the water moves toward land and takes the place of the rising, warm air.

SEA BREEZE

warm land

cool sea

▲ The uneven heating of land and water causes land and sea breezes.

Land and Sea Breezes

Let's look at the movement of air between two very different areas on Earth's surface: water and land. Land loses heat faster than water. So at night, the air over land cools off more than the air over water does. Land also heats up faster than water. So during the day, the air over land is heated more than the air over water is. Thus, land and water are heated unevenly.

How does it feel when you walk barefoot on the hot sand at a beach? Your feet may feel as if they are burning. But when you go into the cool ocean water, your feet stop burning. Your body may feel a cool breeze when you come out of the water. Such breezes can make a shoreline a very comfortable place to be in hot weather. Look at the drawings to learn more about what causes land and sea breezes. ■

INVESTIGATION 2 WRAP-UP

REVIEW

1. Which heats up more rapidly—a dark surface or a light surface?

2. Which loses heat faster—land or water?

CRITICAL THINKING

3. What is the link between the uneven heating of Earth's surface and air movement?

4. Would you expect the temperature near a ceiling to be the same as or different from the temperature near the floor? Explain.

REFLECT & EVALUATE

Word Power

Write the letter of the term that best completes each sentence. *Not all terms will be used.*

1. Water that is in the form of a gas is called ——.
2. The gas that makes up the largest part of air is ——.
3. The condition of the atmosphere at a certain place and time is known as ——.
4. The gas that makes up about 21% of air is ——.
5. The blanket of air that surrounds Earth is the ——.
6. The lowest layer of air surrounding Earth is the ——.

a. air
b. atmosphere
c. nitrogen
d. oxygen
e. troposphere
f. water vapor
g. weather
h. wind

Check What You Know

Write the word in each pair that best completes each sentence.

1. Land loses heat (faster, slower) than water does.
2. The layer of air farthest from Earth's surface is the (stratosphere, thermosphere).
3. When air is heated, it (sinks, rises).
4. Weather occurs in the (stratosphere, troposphere).

Problem Solving

1. Why is carbon dioxide important to the survival of life on Earth? Name one other gas in Earth's atmosphere and explain its importance to living things.

2. You're in a spaceship that takes you high above the troposphere. What would the weather be like there? Explain your answer.

Study the drawing of a greenhouse. In your own words, explain how a greenhouse works. Then explain what the greenhouse effect is. Use the arrows to help you explain.

CHAPTER 2

OBSERVING WEATHER

Have you ever noticed that the leaves on trees sometimes flip upside down in the wind? When the leaves turn like this, some people think it's a sign that rain is on the way. What signs do you observe in nature that make you think it's about to rain?

Connecting to Science
CULTURE

Weather Sayings   Long ago, people lived closer to nature. Their very lives depended on the weather. Here are some old-fashioned weather sayings from different countries. What weather sayings do you know?

Windy March and rainy April
Bring a flowery and beautiful May.
From Spain

If woolly worms are fat and black
*   in late fall,*
Expect bad weather.
If they are light brown,
Expect a mild winter.
From the United States

Red sky at night,
Sailor's delight.
Red sky in morning,
Sailors take warning.
From England

When spiders weave their
*   webs by noon,*
Fine weather is coming soon.
From Japan

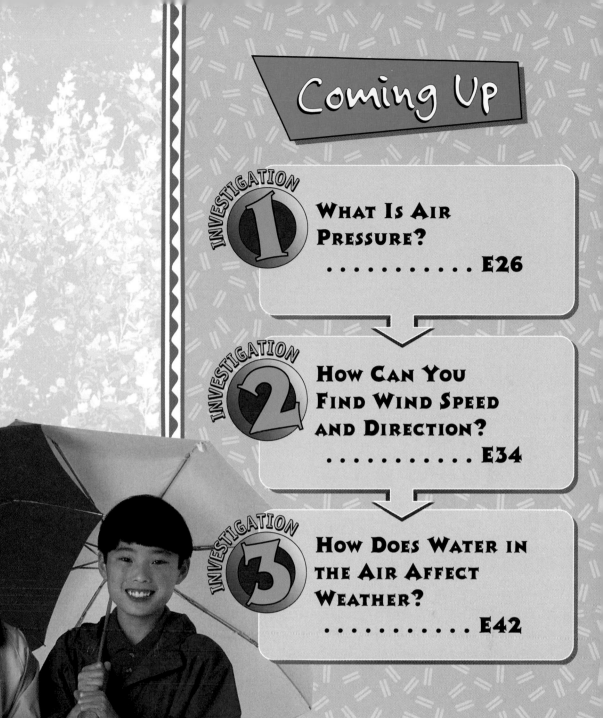

Coming Up

◄ What other weather sayings, rhymes, or songs do you know that tell about the weather?

WHAT IS AIR PRESSURE?

Air pushes down on Earth's surface. Air pushes up and sideways, too. How does the way that air pushes against things affect weather? You'll begin to find out in this investigation.

Activity

It's a Pressing Problem

Air pressure is the push of air against its surroundings. Is air pressure always the same, or can it change? This activity will help you to find out.

MATERIALS

- plastic soda bottle with cap (2 L)
- 2 small plastic dish tubs
- hot tap water
- ice water
- timer
- *Science Notebook*

SAFETY

Be careful when using hot water. Clean up spills immediately.

Procedure

1. Unscrew the cap of an empty plastic bottle. Wait a few seconds. Tightly screw the cap back on.

2. Fill a plastic dish tub with hot water from the tap. Fill a second plastic dish tub with ice water.

3. **Talk with your group** and **predict** what will happen to the capped bottle when it is put into hot water and then into cold water. **Explain** why you made the prediction you did. **Record** your prediction in your *Science Notebook*.

4. Lower the bottle into the tub of hot water. Hold as much of the bottle as you can below the water level. Keep it there for one minute. Remove the bottle and **record** your observations.

See **SCIENCE** *and* **MATH TOOLBOX** page H14 if you need to review *Measuring Elapsed Time.*

5. Repeat step 4 with the tub of ice water.

Step 5

Analyze and Conclude

1. Describe what happened to the bottle after step 4 and after step 5.

2. Compare your results with your prediction. **Talk with other groups** about their results.

3. Infer what the results have to do with **air pressure**—the push of air against its surroundings. **Explain** what led you to this inference.

INVESTIGATE FURTHER!

EXPERIMENT

Fill the plastic bottle with hot water. Let the water sit in the bottle for one minute. Hypothesize what will happen if you empty the bottle and then quickly screw the cap back on tightly. Test your hypothesis. Compare your results with those from the activity.

Activity

Measuring Air Pressure

To find out how hot or cold the air is, you use a thermometer. But how can you measure air pressure? In this activity you'll make a simple barometer to measure air pressure.

MATERIALS
- scissors
- large round balloon
- small coffee can
- rubber band
- tape
- plastic straw
- cardboard strip
- *Science Notebook*

Procedure

1. Cut a large balloon lengthwise. Stretch it over the open top of a coffee can. Secure it with a rubber band. Tape the edge of the balloon to tightly seal the air inside the can.

2. Cut one end of a plastic straw to form a point. Tape the uncut end to the center of the stretched balloon. You have now made a **barometer** (bə-räm′ət ər), a device that measures air pressure.

3. Tape a cardboard strip on a wall so that the bottom of the strip is level with the table, as shown on the next page. Place your barometer next to the strip so that the straw pointer just touches it.

4. In your *Science Notebook*, **make a chart** like the one shown below.

Step 1

Date	Time	Air Pressure Reading	Weather Conditions
Day 1			

See **SCIENCE** and **MATH TOOLBOX** page H11 if you need to review **Making a Chart to Organize Data.**

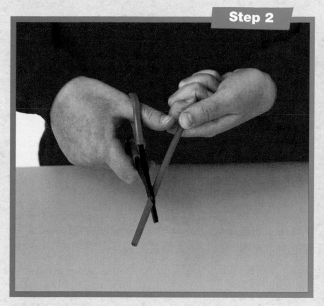

Step 2

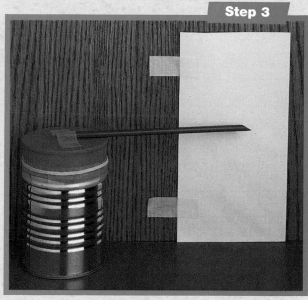

Step 3

5. Each day for one week, take a barometer reading. Draw a line on the cardboard where the straw is pointing. Label the line with the date, time, and weather conditions, such as *cloudy*, *windy*, or *rainy*.

6. Record this data in your chart. Under the heading *Air Pressure Reading*, **record** whether the pressure is higher, lower, or the same as the day before. The higher the line is on the cardboard, the higher the air pressure is.

Analyze and Conclude

1. Describe how the pointer moved from day to day. **Explain** how you could tell whether the air pressure was higher or lower than the day before.

2. Compare the readings on your barometer to your observations about the weather.

3. Look for a relationship between changes in air pressure and the weather. **Make a hypothesis** about your observations.

4. Decide if you have enough information to **draw conclusions** about the relationship between air pressure and weather conditions. If you do not have enough information, what do you need, and how can you gather it?

INVESTIGATE FURTHER!

RESEARCH

During the days that you are recording air pressure, find other sources of air pressure readings. Every day for five days, research weather reports on the radio, television, in the newspaper, or on the Internet. Weather reports always include air pressure readings. Make a chart with the date, the barometric pressure, the weather conditions, and the source (radio, newspaper, and so on). How do these readings compare with those you kept in class? If there are any differences, suggest why they occurred.

Torricelli's Barometer

Reading Focus What events led to the making of the first barometer?

A **barometer** (bə-räm′ət ər), a device that measures air pressure, is made in the activity on pages E28 and E29. More than 350 years ago, the very first barometer was made by accident.

A scientist named Evangelista Torricelli (tôr ə chel′ē) was trying to make a vacuum (vak′yōōm), a space in which there is no air or any other kind of matter. He used a large bowl and a long glass tube that was open at one end and closed at the other.

Torricelli filled the tube with a heavy liquid metal called mercury and turned the tube upside down in the bowl. Some mercury flowed out of the tube, leaving a space at the top. The empty space was the vacuum that Torricelli wanted to investigate.

Torricelli wondered why *all* of the mercury didn't flow out of the tube. He also questioned why the height of the mercury changed from day to day. He inferred that air was holding up the mercury in the tube.

As the diagram shows, air pushes down on the surface of the mercury in the bowl. This air pressure keeps some of the mercury inside the tube. The greater the air pressure, the higher the mercury rises in the tube. And because air pressure keeps changing, the mercury level keeps changing.

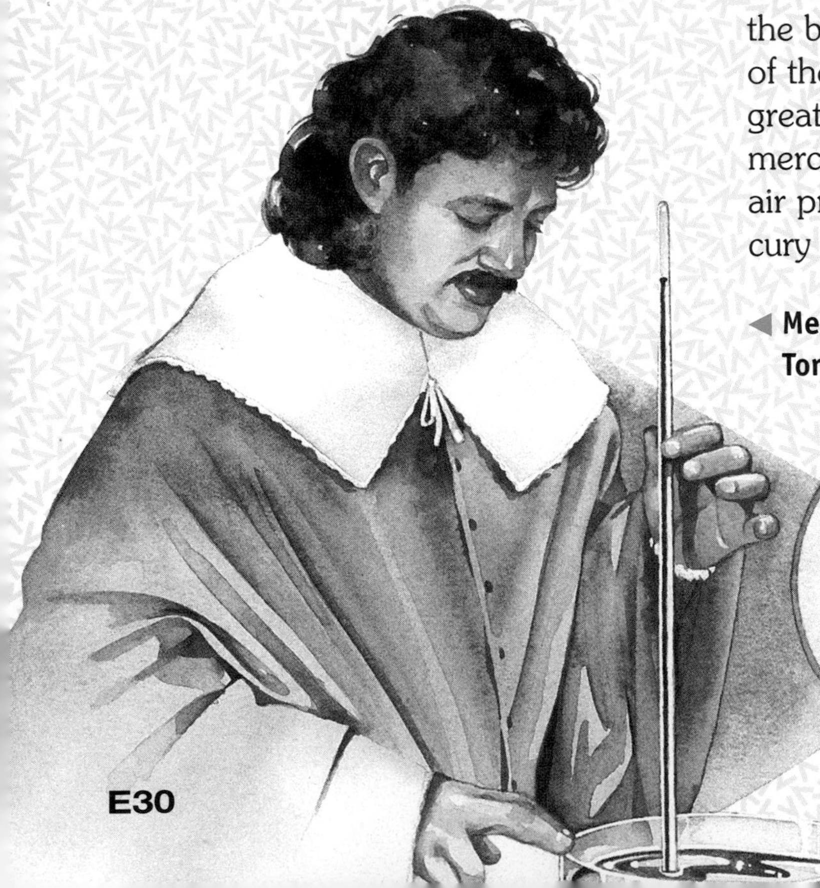

◀ **Mercury barometers very similar to Torricelli's are still used today.**

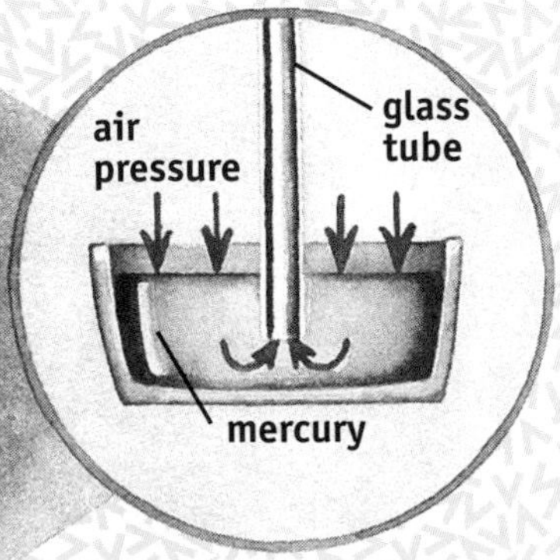

air pressure   glass tube

mercury

E30

All About Pressure

Reading Focus What causes air pressure to differ from place to place?

You live in an atmosphere in which the billions of particles that make up air are in constant motion. These particles move in all directions—up, down, and sideways. When air particles bump into things—a tree, a mountain, a dog, a pencil, a person, or other air particles—they push against them. The push of air against its surroundings is called **air pressure**.

You can see the effect of air pressure when you blow up a balloon. As you blow air into the balloon, air particles push equally in all directions at once against the inside of the balloon. The push of the particles, or air pressure, causes the balloon to inflate.

▲ **Blow up a balloon to feel the effect of air pressure.**

Gravity Rules

Look at the drawing. It shows air particles high on a mountain and at sea level. Are the particles of air closest together near sea level or at the top of the mountain? Do you know why?

Air is matter. Like all matter, the particles that make up air are pulled toward Earth's surface by a force called gravity. Therefore, the closer you are to sea level, the more particles of air there are squeezed into a given space. Suppose you climbed to the top of the highest mountain, Mount Everest. Three quarters of all the particles of air in the atmosphere would be below you.

▼ **The particles of air are closest together near sea level.**

Internet Field Trip

Visit **www.eduplace.com** to learn more about Earth's atmosphere and air pressure.

E31

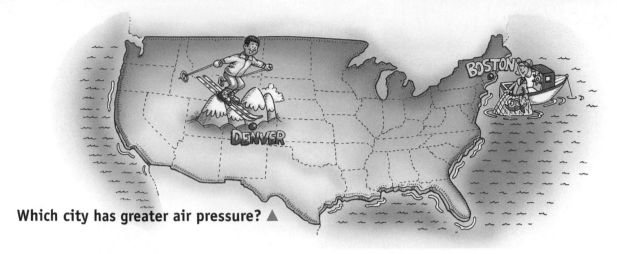

Which city has greater air pressure? ▲

Who's Under Pressure?

What difference does it make how many particles of air are squeezed into a given space? A lot! The closer the air particles are to each other, the more pressure the air has.

Denver is called the Mile High City because it is about a mile above sea level. Boston is just above sea level. In which city are people under greater air pressure? If you said "Boston," you're right! People who live at sea level are at the "bottom" of Earth's atmosphere. All the air of the atmosphere is above them.

People living in Denver are also under pressure. But the higher you go, the farther apart are the particles of air. That's because you are farther from Earth's center, so the force of gravity is less. The higher you go, then, the less air pressure there is.

Measuring Air Pressure

Air pressure is measured with a barometer. There are two main kinds of barometers—mercury barometers and aneroid (an'ər oid) barometers.

A mercury barometer works like Torricelli's barometer described on page E30. A column of mercury in a tube rises and falls as air pressure changes.

An aneroid barometer is made with a sealed metal can. The can expands or contracts when air pressure changes. This barometer is similar to the one that is made in the activity on pages E28 and E29.

Air pressure is usually measured in inches of mercury. Air pressure varies from place to place. It can also vary in the same place. At sea level when the temperature is 0°C, the height of the column of mercury is 29.92 in. (75.99 cm). This is called standard air pressure. As air pressure changes, the height of the mercury column changes.

Using Math

Suppose the air pressure, according to this aneroid barometer, is 30.06 in. How much higher is this air pressure than standard air pressure?

Air Pressure and Temperature

The activity on pages E26 and E27 shows that air pressure in a bottle increases when the air inside is heated. When the air inside the bottle is cooled, the air pressure decreases. Air pressure in the atmosphere changes with temperature as well. But air pressure in the atmosphere works in the opposite way from air pressure in a closed space, such as a bottle.

When air in the atmosphere is warmed, air pressure becomes lower because the particles of air can move away from each other. When air in the atmosphere is cooled, air pressure becomes higher because the particles move closer together.

Areas where the pressure is higher than the surrounding air are called **high-pressure areas**. Areas where the pressure is lower than the surrounding air are called **low-pressure areas**. The difference in air pressure between such areas can cause air to move. Air moves from high-pressure areas to low-pressure areas. This movement of air is called wind. ■

Which cube of air has greater pressure? ▼

INVESTIGATION 1 WRAP-UP

REVIEW

1. What is air pressure, and how is it measured?

2. Are the particles of air in a given space closer together at sea level or at the top of a mountain?

CRITICAL THINKING

3. You carry a barometer with you to the top of a very tall building. You notice that the barometer reading goes down as you ride up to the 107th floor. Explain what happened and why.

4. Explain how pressure would change as the air temperature falls.

How Can You Find Wind Speed and Direction?

Look out a window to observe a flag, a tree, or some leaves on the ground. What can these observations tell you about the wind? In Investigation 2 you'll discover even better ways to measure wind speed and find wind direction.

Activity

A Windy Day

Which way is the wind blowing? In this activity you'll build a wind vane to find out!

- -

Procedure

1. Draw a large cross with its center on a hole in the middle of a wooden board. Mark the end of each line of the cross with one of the letters *N, E, S,* and *W* to stand for *north, east, south,* and *west*.

 Math Hint *Each angle of the cross should be 90° in order to form a right angle.*

2. Remove the rubber bulb from a dropper. Carefully push the pointed end of the dropper into the hole in the wooden board.

3. Tape the middle section from a plastic bottle to a wire hanger. Then insert the straightened end of the wire hanger into the dropper.

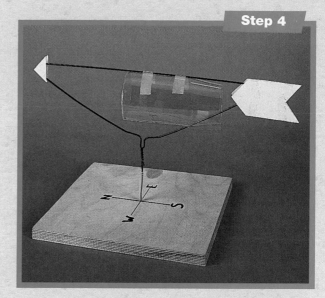

4. Cut out an arrowhead and arrow tail from cardboard. Attach these to the hanger as shown. You have made a wind vane.

5. Place the wooden board in an open area outdoors. Use a compass to find north. Then turn the wooden board so that *N* is in the direction of north.

6. **Observe** such things as flags and leaves to see how they move in the wind. **Discuss** your observations **with your group** members. **Infer** the direction from which the wind is blowing.

7. A **wind vane** is a device that shows the direction from which the wind is blowing. The arrow of your wind vane will point in the direction from which the wind is blowing. Use the wind vane to **find** the wind direction and **record** it in your *Science Notebook*.

8. **Make a chart** like the one shown. For one week, **observe** and **record** the wind direction. **Record** other weather conditions at the same time.

Date/Time	Wind Direction	Weather Conditions

See **SCIENCE** and **MATH TOOLBOX** page H11 if you need to review *Making a Chart to Organize Data.*

Analyze and Conclude

1. **Compare** your findings in step 7 with the inference you made in step 6.

2. Use the data in your chart to **infer** whether the wind comes from the same direction on warm days as it does on cool days. What connections do you see between the direction of the wind and other weather conditions over a period of time? What patterns do you see? Explain.

Activity

How Fast the Wind Blows

Have you heard a weather reporter talk about the speed of the wind? Perhaps you've wondered how wind speed is measured. In this activity you'll build an anemometer, a device to measure wind speed.

MATERIALS

- goggles
- stapler
- 4 plastic straws
- 4 small paper cups
- tape
- crayon
- straight pin
- pencil with a new eraser
- timer
- *Science Notebook*

SAFETY

Wear goggles during this activity. Be careful when handling the straight pin.

Procedure

1. Staple one end of a plastic straw to the outside of a paper cup, near the rim. Do the same thing with three other straws and paper cups. Each straw should be sticking out to the *right* of its cup.

2. Place two cups on their sides with the straws pointed toward each other. The open ends of the cups should be facing in opposite directions. Overlap the tips of the straws about 1 cm and tape them together.

3. Repeat step 2 with the other two cups. Then crisscross the two pairs of straws, as shown. Tape the two pairs of straws together at their midpoints. Mark the bottom of one cup with an *X*.

Step 3

Step 1

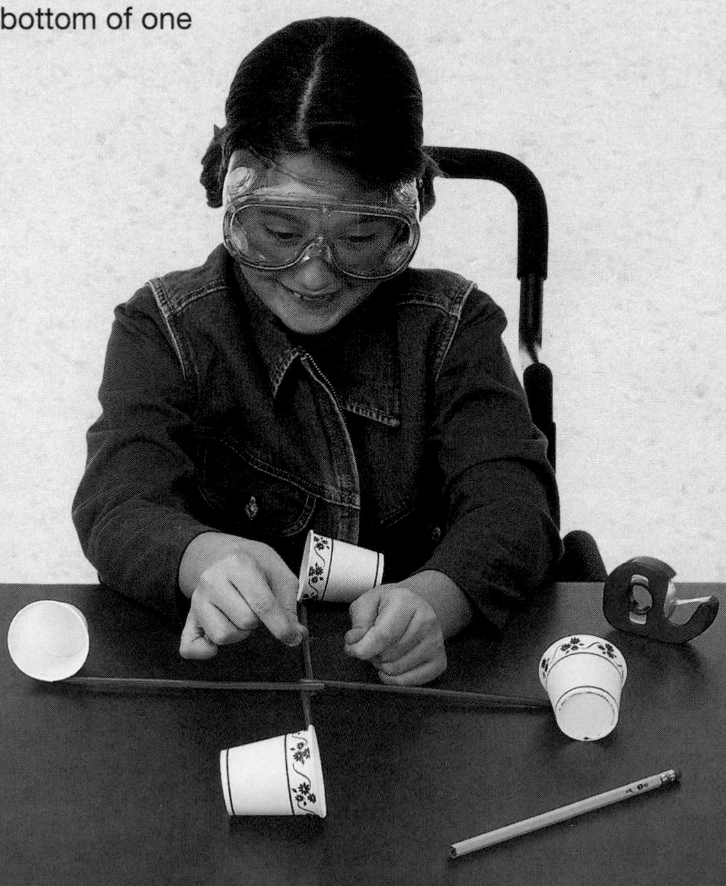

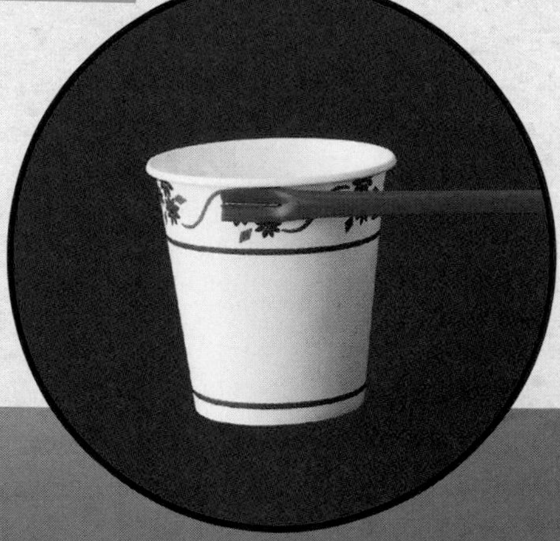

4. Your teacher will insert a straight pin through the center of the cross and into the top of a pencil eraser. Don't push the pin all the way in. Your anemometer (an'ə mäm'ət ər) is complete.

5. Test your anemometer by holding the pencil and blowing into the cups. The cups should spin freely. You can watch for the cup marked X on the bottom to tell when the anemometer has made one complete spin.

6. Talk with your group members and **hypothesize** how your anemometer can be used to measure wind speed. **Record** and **explain** your hypothesis in your *Science Notebook*.

Step 5

7. Make a chart like the one shown. Take your anemometer outside. **Count** how many times it spins in one minute. **Record** the number of spins at different times of the day or at the same hour each day for one week. **Record** other observations about weather conditions at the same time.

Date	Time	Spins in 1 min	Weather Conditions

Analyze and Conclude

1. Study the data in your chart. **Compare** differences in wind speed at different times and under different weather conditions. **Describe** any patterns you see.

2. Compare the hypothesis you made in step 6 with your results.

Technology
Link
CD-ROM

INVESTIGATE FURTHER!

Use the **Science Processor CD-ROM**, *Weather and Climate* (Investigation 2, Windswept) to find out how wind speed is related to various weather conditions.

Which Way Is the Wind Blowing?

Reading Focus How can you find wind direction and wind speed?

Wind is moving air. In Chapter 1 you learned that the uneven heating of Earth results in the uneven heating of air. Differences in air temperature affect air pressure. Differences in air pressure between two areas of air that are near each other produce wind. Recall that wind is produced when air moves from areas of high pressure to areas of low pressure.

Finding Wind Direction

The direction of the wind is the direction from which it is blowing. A wind blowing from the east to the west is called an east wind.

A **wind vane** is a device that shows wind direction. Most wind vanes are shaped like a long arrow with a tail. When the wind blows, the arrow points into the wind. It shows the direction from which the wind is blowing. If the arrow points south, the wind is blowing from the south.

Another instrument used to find wind direction is a windsock. A **windsock** is a cloth bag that is narrow at one end and open at both ends. Air enters the wide end and causes the narrow end to point away from the direction that the wind is blowing. This is opposite to what a wind vane does.

Measuring Wind Speed

What makes some winds stronger than others? The greater the difference in air pressure between two areas, the stronger are the winds produced. Also, the closer the areas are to each other, the stronger are the winds produced.

A wind vane points into the wind. On this wind vane, the head of the horse points into the wind. ▶

▲ A windsock points away from the wind.

An **anemometer** (an'ə mäm' ət ər) is a device used to measure wind speed. It often consists of cups on spokes attached to a pole. Scientists use an anemometer like the one shown below to record wind speed in kilometers per hour (km/h). The activity on pages E36 and E37 uses spins per minute to record wind speed.

If you don't have special devices to measure wind speed, you can use the Beaufort (bō'fərt) scale. In 1805 a British naval officer named Sir Francis Beaufort made a scale that divides wind strength into 12 different categories. Each category is based on observable effects of wind. Part of the Beaufort scale is shown below. ■

THE BEAUFORT SCALE			
Beaufort Number	Speed in km/h (mph)	Description	Observations on Land
2	6–11 (4–7)	light breeze	leaves rustle, wind felt on face; wind vanes move
4	20–28 (13–18)	moderate breeze	dust and paper blow; small branches sway
6	39–49 (25–31)	strong breeze	umbrellas hard to open; large branches sway
8	62–74 (39–46)	gale	walking is very difficult; twigs break off trees
10	89–102 (55–63)	whole gale	much damage to buildings; trees uprooted
12	117 and up (72 and up)	hurricane	violent, widespread destruction

◀ **An Optical Broadcasting Wind Indicator measures wind speed and direction.**

The faster the wind blows, the faster ▶ the anemometer's cups spin.

Wind Power

Reading Focus How can people use wind energy to do work?

SCIENCE
TECHNOLOGY
& SOCIETY

The activity on pages E36 and E37 shows how to make a device called an anemometer, which measures wind speed. The harder the wind blows, the faster an anemometer will spin. What if all that spinning energy could be put to work?

Early Wind Machines

Windmills are machines that put the wind to work. They were first used in the Middle East, perhaps as long ago as the seventh century. In those early windmills, a wheel made of cloth sails was attached to a tall structure. As the wind blew, the sails spun. The turning motion was used to grind grain.

In the fourteenth century, the Dutch began using windmills to pump water out of low-lying land, to grind corn, and to press oil from seeds and nuts. The traditional Dutch windmill has four arms attached to cloth sails or wooden blades. The sails or blades spin like the propeller of a plane. They can turn only when the wind blows directly at them.

▲ Many modern windmills work the same way as this traditional Dutch windmill.

The long curved blades of the modern Darrieus wind turbine can catch wind coming from any direction. ▶

Today's Windmills

Modern windmills are designed to work at much higher wind speeds than are traditional ones. They are usually made of aluminum or other light metals. Some modern windmills, called wind turbines (tur'binz), are used to produce electricity.

The largest wind turbines are over 90 m (300 ft) tall. The blade tips travel as fast as 400 km/h (250 mph). The wind turbine operates a generator that produces the electricity.

Worldwide Use of Wind Energy

Wind power may be one of the answers to today's energy needs. Unlike many other sources of energy, wind can't be used up and it doesn't pollute the air. Also, wind turbines can be built fairly quickly.

But wind power is not a perfect answer to energy needs. The direction and speed of winds change over time and from place to place. Sometimes,

▲ **Wind farm in Altamont Pass, California**

of course, the wind doesn't blow at all. Wind power works best where wind speeds are high and fairly steady. Wind turbines are placed in areas where there are few trees, houses, or other things that might block the wind.

In some areas, to harness wind as an energy source, wind farms are built. A wind farm is a system of 50 or more wind turbines working together. Each turbine turns a generator. The Altamont Pass wind farm has over 5,000 wind turbines. This wind farm produces enough electricity to supply several towns in California. Wind farms are being developed in other states as well as in Canada, Australia, Europe, India, China, and other parts of the world. ■

INVESTIGATION 2 WRAP-UP

REVIEW

1. Name one device used to find wind direction and one device that measures wind speed.

2. In which direction does an east wind blow? How do you know?

CRITICAL THINKING

3. Most people would agree that wind turbines offer benefits as an energy source for producing electricity. Identify two problems in using wind turbines as a source of energy.

4. Compare how a windsock works with how a wind vane works.

HOW DOES WATER IN THE AIR AFFECT WEATHER?

Water vapor is a very important gas in Earth's atmosphere. In Investigation 3 you'll find out how the amount of water vapor in the air affects weather.

Activity

Make a Rain Gauge

Rainfall is measured with a device called a rain gauge. Make one in this activity.

MATERIALS

- flat wooden stick
- metric ruler
- marker
- aluminum soda can, top removed
- plastic soda bottle (2 L), cut in half
- *Science Notebook*

Procedure

1. Place a flat wooden stick on your desk. Use a metric ruler and a marker to draw a line 3 cm from the lower end. Label this line *1 cm*. Draw another line on the stick 3 cm above the 1-cm line. Label this second line *2 cm*. Then draw another line 3 cm above the 2-cm line. Label this third line *3 cm*.

2. Divide the space between the lower end of the stick and the line labeled *1 cm* into ten equal parts. Repeat this for each of the other two spaces. Your stick should look like the one shown.

Math Hint *Each of the ten equal parts has a measure of $\frac{3}{10}$ cm or 3 mm.*

Step 2

3. Place an aluminum can, with the top removed, inside the bottom half of a cut plastic soda bottle.

4. Turn the top half of the bottle upside down. Insert the neck of the bottle into the can, as shown. The top half of the bottle will serve as a funnel. You've made a simple rain gauge (gāj).

5. In your *Science Notebook*, **make a chart** like the one shown.

Date	Amount of Rainfall

6. Put your rain gauge outdoors in an open area where it won't be disturbed. In your chart, **record** the amount of rainfall every day for one month. To **measure** rainfall, put the marked wooden stick along the inside wall of the can. Then empty the can. Be sure to measure rainfall the same way each time. You might want to add your readings and then find the total rainfall for the month. You can use a calculator to help you.

 See **SCIENCE** and **MATH TOOLBOX** page H4 if you need to review *Using a Calculator.*

Analyze and Conclude

1. How would you measure the rainfall if the water overflowed the can?

2. How could you use your rain gauge to measure snowfall?

3. **Talk with your group** and **predict** how the amount of rainfall where you live will vary during different seasons in the coming year. What information will you need in order to make such a prediction?

Choose one of each weather device you have made—barometer, wind vane, anemometer, rain gauge—to put in your class weather station. Explain each choice you made. Use the devices to collect more weather-related data.

 **Technology** Link

For more help with your Unit Project, go to **www.eduplace.com**.

Step 4

E43

Snow Around the World

Reading Focus How does snow affect people's lives around the world?

Over 2,000 years ago, the Chinese scholar Han Ying observed that snowflakes have six points. About 1,700 years passed before people in other places discovered this fact.

You don't have to know about the shape of a snowflake to know how much fun, or how much trouble, snow can be. Take a look at some ways that people around the world deal with "the white stuff."

▲ **UNITED STATES** In 1880, Wilson A. Bentley began photographing snow crystals through a microscope. He took thousands of pictures, but not one snowflake looked exactly like another.

◀ **JAPAN** Sapporo, a city in northern Japan, has long winters with lots of snow. Every February the city holds a week-long snow festival in which groups compete in a snow-statue contest. The sculptures made are very large. Trucks bring in 40,000 tons of extra snow in order to make them.

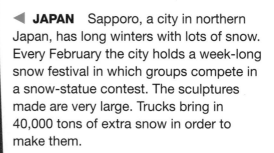

Using **Math** *Explain how you could use mental math to find how many pounds of extra snow are brought in for the festival.*

LAPLAND   Cars aren't practical in regions with heavy snowfall. The Saami (sär′mē) are a people who live in the northern parts of Norway, Sweden, Finland, and Russia. Instead of using cars, they train reindeer to pull sleds over the snow. ▶

◀ **THE ALPS**   The northern side of the Alps Mountain range receives about 305 cm (120 in.) of snow a year. People who live there must find ways to avoid avalanches (av′ə lanch əz). An avalanche is a sudden sliding of snow down a mountain. Some avalanches weigh thousands of tons and move at speeds of 160 km/h (100 mph).

THE ARCTIC   The Inuit (in′o̅o̅ wit) are a people who live in the Arctic, which is frozen under snow and ice for as long as nine months a year. To survive, the Inuit join together to fish and to hunt. Snow is so much a part of Inuit life that their language has more than two dozen words to describe different kinds of snow. ▶

The Water Cycle

> **Reading Focus** What role does water vapor play in the weather?

Water is not only found in oceans, lakes, and rivers. Water is found in air as an invisible gas—water vapor. The movement of water into the air as water vapor and back to Earth's surface as rain, snow, sleet, or hail is called the **water cycle**, shown below.

The Sun's energy heats bodies of water, causing some water to evaporate into the air. When water **evaporates**, it changes from a liquid to the gas water vapor. Water vapor rises in the air.

As the water vapor in the air cools, it **condenses**, or changes from a gas to liquid water. The water may freeze and become ice crystals depending on the temperature of the air.

Clouds are formed as water vapor in the air condenses. A **cloud** is billions of tiny drops of water that condensed from the air. Some clouds are made of ice crystals. A cloud that touches Earth's surface is called **fog**. As the drops of water in clouds grow larger, they become heavier. Finally they fall to Earth. Any form of water that falls from the air is called **precipitation** (prē sip ə tā′shən).

Rain, snow, sleet, and hail are part of the water cycle. The water that falls to Earth becomes part of the bodies of water on Earth's surface or is absorbed into the soil. As the Sun's energy causes evaporation, the water cycle continues.

THE WATER CYCLE

Drops of water in clouds become heavier and fall as precipitation.

Water vapor in air condenses and forms clouds.

The Sun warms bodies of water, causing water, through evaporation, to become water vapor.

Water from precipitation flows to bodies of water.

Measuring Precipitation

You've probably heard the amount of rainfall given in weather reports. How do weather forecasters know the amount? They use a rain gauge (gāj) much like the one made in the activity on pages E42 and E43. A **rain gauge** is a device that measures precipitation. In the United States, rainfall amounts are usually expressed in inches.

It's Relative

The amount of water vapor in the air is called **humidity** (hyōō mid′ə tē). There is a limit to the amount of water the air can hold. The amount depends on air temperature. The warmer the air, the more water it can hold.

Humidity is expressed in terms of relative humidity. **Relative humidity** is the amount of water vapor the air is holding compared to the amount it *could* hold at that temperature. If the air is holding all the water it can at a certain temperature, the relative humidity is 100 percent.

When the temperature outside is high but the humidity is low, the sweat on your skin evaporates quickly. The evaporating sweat carries heat away and you feel cooler.

At the same temperature but with high humidity, the water on your skin can't evaporate quickly. Even though the temperature is the same, you feel warm and uncomfortable.

Science in Literature

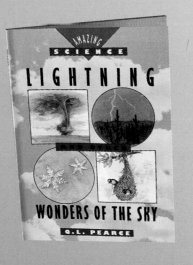

Lightning and Other Wonders of the Sky
by Q. L. Pearce
Illustrated by Mary Ann Fraser
Julian Messner, 1989

A FATAL FOG

"In some ways, fog may be the most dangerous of all clouds. If thick enough, fog can prevent you from seeing more than a few feet in front of you . . . . In 1977, thick fog contributed to the worst air disaster in history—two huge passenger jets crashed into each other on a runway in the Canary Islands."

This excerpt comes from *Lightning and Other Wonders of the Sky* by Q. L. Pearce. Fog is just one way clouds can cause disasters. Read the book to learn about a pilot who parachuted from a plane into a thundercloud.

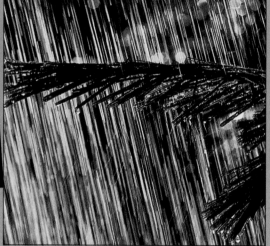

Rain is water drops that are larger and fall faster than drizzle. ▽

▲ Drizzle is very fine drops of water smaller than 0.5 mm (0.02 in.) in diameter.

Hail is particles of ice usually ranging from the size of a pea to the size of a golf ball. Some hailstones are even larger. ▽

▲ Snow is a solid form of precipitation made of ice crystals.

INVESTIGATION 3 WRAP-UP

REVIEW

1. Describe the water cycle.

2. What is used to measure precipitation?

CRITICAL THINKING

3. Imagine that it's a cold winter day. You are outside, talking with a friend. Why can you see your breath as you talk?

4. How can the relative humidity increase if the amount of water vapor in the air remains unchanged?

REFLECT & EVALUATE

Word Power

Write the letter of the term that best matches the definition. *Not all terms will be used.*

1. Device that shows wind direction
2. Movement of water into the air as water vapor and back to Earth's surface as rain, snow, sleet, or hail
3. Device used to measure air pressure
4. Amount of water vapor in the air
5. Any form of water that falls to Earth's surface

a. air pressure
b. anemometer
c. barometer
d. humidity
e. precipitation
f. water cycle
g. wind vane

Check What You Know

Write the term in each pair that best completes each sentence.

1. A device that is used to measure wind speed is called (a barometer, an anemometer).
2. When there is a great difference in air pressure between two areas, winds are (slight, strong).
3. Billions of drops of water condensed in the air form a (cloud, lake).
4. As the temperature decreases, the humidity (increases, decreases).

Problem Solving

1. Explain why an aluminum can "sweats" when you take it out of the refrigerator on a hot day.
2. How can you use a wind vane and an anemometer to help you fly a kite?
3. Suppose you want to find wind speed, wind direction, and air pressure. Which instruments would you use? Explain how each instrument works.

Study the drawing. It shows air pressure readings in inches of mercury. They were taken in different places at the same time on the same day. Explain in writing why the air pressure readings are different.

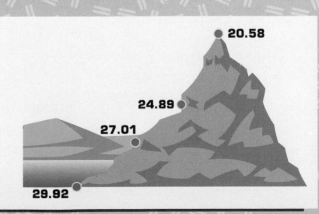

20.58

24.89

27.01

29.92

CHAPTER 3

WEATHER PATTERNS

When you listened to the radio, the weather forecaster said it was going to be sunny for your outdoor field trip. But then it rained all day. In this chapter you'll find out what goes into predicting the next day's weather.

PEOPLE USING SCIENCE

Research Meteorologist You might think that studying weather is not very exciting. But seeing how Anton Seimon learns about storms will change your mind. He flies in a plane above, around, and even into storms.

Anton Seimon is a research meteorologist. He studies storms to better understand how they form and to help other people predict storms. He uses instruments such as thermometers and radar for gathering weather data. He sometimes drops packages of instruments from the plane into a storm that is too strong to fly into. "Studying the information we collect is almost as exciting as flying into a storm," he says.

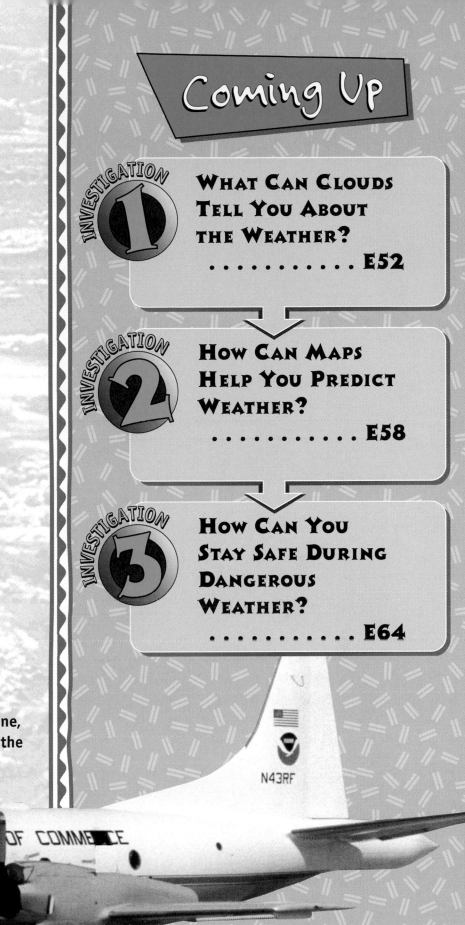

Coming Up

In a plane such as this one, Anton Seimon flies into the storms he studies. ▼

UNITED STATES DEPT OF COMMERCE

N43RF

INVESTIGATION 1

WHAT CAN CLOUDS TELL YOU ABOUT THE WEATHER?

You're about to head out the door. You notice thin, wispy white clouds high in the sky. Should you take an umbrella or your sunglasses? Find out how clouds can help you predict the weather.

Activity

Kinds of Clouds

Are there different types of clouds in the sky?
Discover the answer in this activity.

MATERIALS
• *Science Notebook*

SAFETY
Never look directly at the Sun.

Procedure

Choose three different times of day to carefully **observe** clouds. **Write a description** in your *Science Notebook* of how the clouds look and where they appear in the sky. Then **draw** pictures of the clouds. With your group, **classify** the clouds you saw. Share your results with other groups.

Analyze and Conclude

1. How many different cloud shapes did you see? Did any of the clouds change shape?

2. What colors were the clouds? How high were they in the sky?

3. **Explain** how your group classified the clouds.

Activity

Cloudy Weather

Can the types of clouds in the sky help you predict what the weather will be? In this activity you'll find out.

MATERIALS
• thermometer
• *Science Notebook*

SAFETY /////

Be careful when handling glass thermometers. Never look directly at the Sun.

Procedure

1. Think about the types of clouds you've seen in the sky. **Predict** which types of clouds may occur in certain types of weather. **Record** your predictions in your *Science Notebook*.

2. **Make a chart** like the one shown.

Date	Time	Cloud Description	Weather Conditions

3. Twice a day for one week, **observe** the types of clouds you see. **Record** a description of the clouds in your chart.

4. **Record** the weather conditions at the same time you make your cloud observations. Note whether it is sunny, cloudy, rainy, or snowy. Use a thermometer to **measure** the temperature of the air.

 See **SCIENCE** *and* **MATH TOOLBOX** *page H8 if you need to review* ***Using a Thermometer.***

Step 4

Analyze and Conclude

1. **Compare** your findings with the predictions you made. What might the weather be like tomorrow?

2. **Compare** differences in cloud types at different times and for different weather conditions. **Hypothesize** how clouds might be used to predict the weather.

The Weather From Space

Reading Focus What kinds of information do weather satellites provide?

STS
SCIENCE TECHNOLOGY & SOCIETY

Clouds are one of several factors scientists use to forecast the weather. **Weather satellites** are devices in space that are used to take pictures of clouds and to collect other weather information. One important type of weather satellite is called GOES, short for the term *Geostationary Operational Environmental Satellite.* This type of satellite travels at the same speed that Earth spins. So a GOES can keep track of weather over the same area day and night.

Weather satellites send images of the clouds over Earth to weather stations on the ground. The satellites also measure the amount of moisture in the atmosphere. They provide information about winds as well as the temperature of land and of water. Such data can help airplane pilots and sailors plan safe trips. It can also help farmers know when cold, icy weather is coming. Having this information helps farmers know when they must protect their crops.

GOES can also be used to warn people when severe weather is on the way. Weather satellites can track storms over long distances. In 1996, Hurricane Fran was tracked from space for thousands of kilometers over several days.

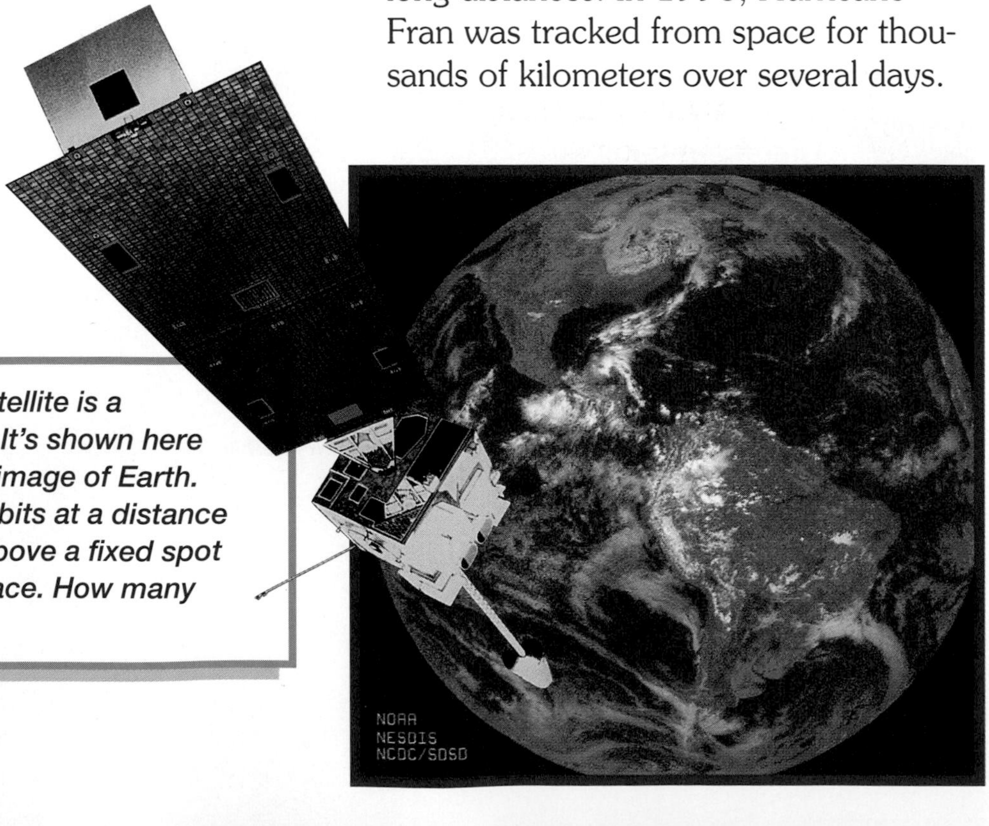

Using **Math** *This satellite is a GOES. It's shown here with a satellite image of Earth. This satellite orbits at a distance of 36,000 km above a fixed spot on Earth's surface. How many meters is this?*

NOAA
NESDIS
NCDC/SDSD

Watching the Clouds Go By

Reading Focus What are the three main types of clouds, and what type of weather is likely to occur with each?

▲ **Cumulus clouds**

Imagine that you are in a place that has no newspapers, radio, computer, or TV. How can you tell what the weather is going to be? Believe it or not, the answer is right outside your window. Just take a look at the sky. The types of clouds that you see can help you predict the coming weather.

But where do clouds come from, and what are clouds made of? You have learned that clouds form as part of the water cycle. Look at the diagram to see how a cloud forms.

Cloud Families

As you know, clouds can occur in many different shapes and sizes. The activity on page E52 suggests ways to classify, or group, clouds. In 1803 a scientist named Luke Howard found a way to classify clouds by the way they looked. He classified the clouds into three main families. These cloud families are cumulus (kyōō′myōō ləs) clouds, stratus (stra′təs) clouds, and cirrus (sir′əs) clouds.

Cumulus clouds are puffy, white clouds that look like mounds of cotton. They form when large areas of warm, moist air rise upward from Earth's surface. Cumulus clouds usually indicate fair weather.

Stratus clouds are like flat gray blankets that are low hanging and seem to cover the sky. Stratus clouds form when a flat layer of warm, moist air rises very slowly. They usually indicate rainy weather.

A cloud forms when warm, moist air rises, expands, and cools. ▼

3 Water vapor in the cooling air condenses into tiny drops of water that come together to form a **cloud.**

2 As the warm air rises, it expands and cools.

1 A large area of warm, moist air forms above the ground.

E55

TYPES OF CLOUDS

CIRRUS CLOUDS Often a sign that rainy or snowy weather is on the way

CIRROCUMULUS CLOUDS Thin, high clouds that mean changing weather

CIRROSTRATUS CLOUDS Thin milk-colored sheets that often mean rain is on the way

ALTOCUMULUS CLOUDS Fluffy gray clouds that can grow into rain clouds

ALTOSTRATUS CLOUDS Mean that stormy weather is coming soon

CUMULONIMBUS CLOUDS Thunderheads that bring thunder-storms with rain, snow, or hail

CUMULUS CLOUDS Appear in sunny skies

STRATOCUMULUS CLOUDS Mean that drier weather is on the way

STRATUS CLOUDS Low clouds that often bring drizzle

NIMBOSTRATUS CLOUDS Thick dark blankets that may bring snow or rain

▲ Stratus clouds

▲ Cirrus clouds

Cirrus clouds look like commas or wisps of hair high in the sky. Cirrus clouds form when warm, moist air rises high enough for ice crystals to form. Cirrus clouds are fair-weather clouds.

Sometimes, scientists talk about nimbostratus or cumulonimbus clouds. *Nimbus* is a Latin word that means "rain." When you see *nimbus* or *nimbo-* in a cloud name, you know the cloud is a rain cloud.

Clouds are also grouped by height above the ground. Some clouds are close to the ground, some are high in the sky, and some are in between. Clouds that form high in the sky have the prefix *cirro-* in front of their family name. Clouds that form at a medium height have the prefix *alto-* in front of their family name.

Weather Clues From Clouds

The activity on page E53 explains how to use types of clouds to help predict the weather. You may have noticed that certain types of clouds appear in the sky before a rainstorm. Or you may have seen that other types of clouds show up before fair weather.

Different types of clouds give clues about the weather to come. Some clouds can even indicate changes in temperature. Examine the different cloud types that are shown on page E56. Which cloud types might tell that rain is coming? Which might tell that the weather will be changing soon? ■

Internet Field Trip

Visit **www.eduplace.com** to learn more about cloud types.

INVESTIGATION 1 WRAP-UP

REVIEW

1. What are the three families of clouds?

2. How does a cloud form?

CRITICAL THINKING

3. You are going to a picnic when you notice that the sky is filled with a layer of gray clouds. Should you go to the picnic, or should you stay inside? Explain.

4. How can clouds seen from the ground help people predict the weather? What kinds of information do weather satellites provide?

INVESTIGATION 2

How Can Maps Help You Predict Weather?

You've probably used maps to find cities and streets. But you can also use a map to find out about weather. Investigation 2 will show you how.

Activity

Weather Maps

How can a weather map be used to predict the weather? Find out in this activity.

Procedure

1. Look on weather map 1 for a high-pressure area, marked with the letter *H*. Find the same high-pressure area on map 2. Note whether the *H* is in the same place or if it has moved. If it has moved, note in what direction it moved. Now repeat this with weather map 3. In your *Science Notebook*, **describe** what happened to the high-pressure area over the three-day period.

2. Look on the weather maps for a low-pressure area, marked with the letter *L*. Note whether the *L* is in the same place on all three maps or if it has moved. If it has moved, note in what direction it moved. **Record** what happened to the low-pressure area over the three-day period.

WEATHER MAP SYMBOLS

▨	Rain
⬚	Snow
Ⓗ	High Pressure
Ⓛ	Low Pressure
▸	Wind Direction
49/32	High and Low Daily Temperatures (°F)
○	Clear Skies
◐	Partly Cloudy
●	Cloudy
▬•▬	Warm Front
▬▲▬	Cold Front

3. Look on map 1 for the lines with the triangles and half circles. These lines show fronts. A **front** is a place where two masses, or areas, of air meet. Cold fronts are shown by the lines with triangles. Warm fronts are shown by the lines with half circles. Find the fronts on maps 2 and 3. Note whether the fronts are always in the same place or if they move. **Record** your observations.

4. **Predict** what weather map 4 will look like. **Draw** a picture of your prediction. Your teacher will give you a copy of weather map 4 so that you can check your prediction.

Analyze and Conclude

1. How do the locations of high-pressure areas, low-pressure areas, and fronts on weather map 4 compare with your prediction?

2. **Hypothesize** how weather maps can help you predict the weather.

UNIT PROJECT LINK

For five days, use the weather devices in your class weather station to collect weather-related data. Use your observations and a weather map to predict the weather each day. Keep track of how often you make the correct prediction. Do your predictions improve over time?

Technology Link

For more help with your Unit Project, go to **www.eduplace.com**.

Weather Wisdom

Reading Focus How have people from different countries used plants and animals to help predict weather?

People have been predicting the weather since long before forecasts appeared on television, radio, or in newspapers. But not everyone looks at weather devices such as barometers, anemometers, and thermometers. Instead, some people observe how plants and animals behave. Look at the map below to see some of the signs that people have used in different parts of the world to predict the weather.

UNITED STATES If a groundhog sees its shadow on February 2, winter will last for six more weeks.

ENGLAND Flowers of the scarlet pimpernel open in sunny weather and close before the weather becomes rainy.

JAPAN Strands of hanging kelp, a seaweed, swell and feel damp if rain is coming.

PERU If the leaves of this plant fold up an hour before sunset, the next day will be stormy.

CHINA "Hearing the cicadas in the rain foretells the coming of fine weather" is a saying in China.

AUSTRALIA Some believe that if mound-building termites are very active, then wet weather is on the way.

Weather in the News

> **Reading Focus** How does a weather forecaster predict the weather?

A **weather forecaster** is someone who predicts the weather. Maybe you've heard a weather forecaster predict bright, sunny skies when, in fact, it rained all day. How do people predict the weather? Why is predicting the weather such a difficult job?

The Weather Detectives

Being a weather forecaster is a bit like trying to solve a mystery. First, the forecaster must gather clues, or information, about the current weather. The forecaster gets information from all over the world. The information comes from weather balloons, weather satellites, and weather stations on land and on ships at sea. It tells about such things as wind speed and direction, cloud type, air pressure, temperature, moisture in the air, and precipitation. Much of this information comes from more than 120 local weather stations in the United States.

Once the information is gathered, the forecaster has to decide what it all means. The forecaster's job is like that of a detective who must sort through the many clues that have been uncovered. Fortunately, the forecaster gets to use computers to help solve the "mystery." All the different pieces of information are put into a computer. The computer then puts all the pieces together and produces different types of weather maps, like the ones shown below.

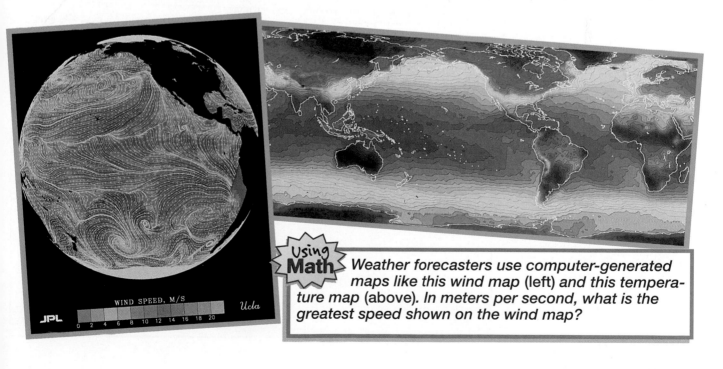

WIND SPEED, M/S

0 2 4 6 8 10 12 14 16 18 20

JPL   Ucla

Using Math *Weather forecasters use computer-generated maps like this wind map (left) and this temperature map (above). In meters per second, what is the greatest speed shown on the wind map?*

Weather Clues

Look at the weather map activity on pages E58 and E59. The activity shows the symbols used for cold fronts and warm fronts. It also shows the symbols used for high- and low-pressure areas. These fronts and areas are clues that a weather forecaster uses to make a prediction. But what do these clues mean?

You know that a blanket of air surrounds Earth. Imagine that this blanket of air is divided into large bodies, or areas. Some of these areas are warm, and other areas are cold. Each different body of air is called an air mass. An **air mass** is a body of air that has the same general temperature and air pressure throughout. Changes in the weather are caused by movements of air masses.

Often, different air masses move so that they contact each other. A **front** is a place where two different types of air masses meet. A **cold front** forms

COLD FRONT When a cold air mass meets a warm air mass, the cooler air pushes under the warm air. This forces the warm air mass to rise. Clouds form in the warm air as it is forced upward. ▶

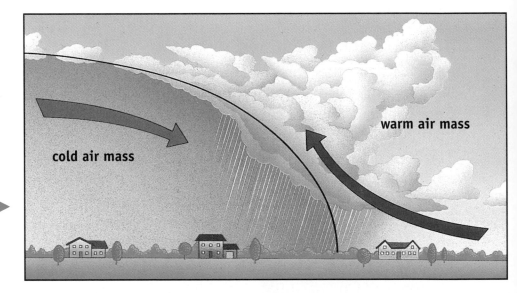

WARM FRONT When a warm air mass moves into a cold air mass, the warmer air rides up over the cooler air. Clouds form as the air rises and cools. ▶

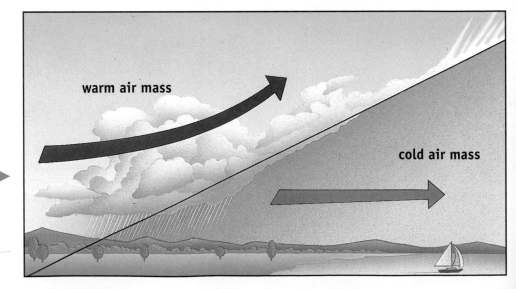

An approaching front darkens the sky and brings stormy weather. ▶

when a cold air mass moves into a warm air mass. Cold fronts often produce heavy rains and thunderstorms. A **warm front** forms when a warm air mass moves into a cold air mass. Warm fronts often produce thin, wispy clouds that spread over large areas, bringing light rain.

Weather forecasters also look at air pressure to predict weather changes. In a high-pressure area, or high, the air pressure is higher than in the air surrounding it. High-pressure areas usually bring dry, clear weather.

In a low-pressure area, or low, the air pressure is lower than in the surrounding air. Low-pressure areas usually bring wind, clouds, and rain.

Now the forecaster has enough clues to help solve the mystery. So the forecaster can make a weather prediction. Weather predictions are not always correct. Sometimes weather conditions change so quickly that the information forecasters have isn't up-to-date. And sometimes weather conditions don't follow "normal" patterns.

Scientists are developing new ways to gather weather information. These new methods will help forecasters improve their predictions. ■

Technology Link
CD-ROM

INVESTIGATE FURTHER!

Use the **Science Processor CD-ROM**, *Weather and Climate* (Investigation 3, Forecasting) to learn how to predict the weather as weather forecasters do.

INVESTIGATION 2 WRAP-UP

REVIEW

1. What kind of weather often occurs at a cold front? at a warm front?

2. What are four types of information that appear on weather maps?

CRITICAL THINKING

3. Suppose you are a weather forecaster for your town. What data would you gather to make a prediction about the next day's weather?

4. Explain why forecasting the weather can be a difficult job.

HOW CAN YOU STAY SAFE DURING DANGEROUS WEATHER?

The weather may range from calm and quiet to stormy and even dangerous. In Investigation 3 you'll find out about different kinds of dangerous weather and how you can stay safe.

Activity

Storm Safety

In this activity, find out how you can plan ahead and be prepared for severe weather.

- - - - - - - - - - - - - - - - - - -

Procedure

With your group, make a weather safety booklet. In your *Science Notebook,* list the types of severe weather that may occur in your area. These may include thunderstorms, lightning, snowstorms, hurricanes, or tornadoes. Find out which radio and TV stations to listen to in case of severe weather and what safety measures you should take. **Record** what you learn in your weather safety booklet.

Analyze and Conclude

1. Where should you go if you are warned that severe weather is about to strike your area?

2. What things should you do or not do during severe weather?

Activity

Tornado Tube

Have you ever seen a tornado? These dangerous twisting storms can cause a lot of damage. If you have never seen a tornado, don't worry. In this activity you'll be making a model of one.

MATERIALS
- 2 plastic soda bottles (2 L)
- water
- tornado tube
- *Science Notebook*

Procedure

1. Fill a plastic soda bottle about two-thirds full of water.

Math Hint *To estimate two thirds of the bottle, first measure the height of the bottle. Round the height to the nearest whole number. Divide the height by 3. Then multiply the quotient by 2.*

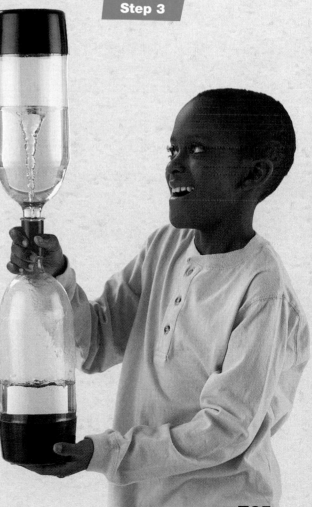

Step 3

2. Screw one end of a tornado tube onto the bottle. Make sure the end fits tightly. Then screw an empty bottle into the other end of the tube. Make sure it also is screwed in tightly.

3. Turn the bottle with the water in it upside down. Hold on to the tornado tube. Quickly move the bottles in five or six circles so that the water inside swirls. **Observe** as the water drains from one bottle into the other. **Record** your observations in your *Science Notebook*.

Analyze and Conclude

1. **Describe** the motion of the water as it moved from one bottle to the other.

2. **Hypothesize** how the movement of air in a tornado is similar to the movement of air and water in your model.

3. **Describe** how this model of a tornado is different from a real tornado.

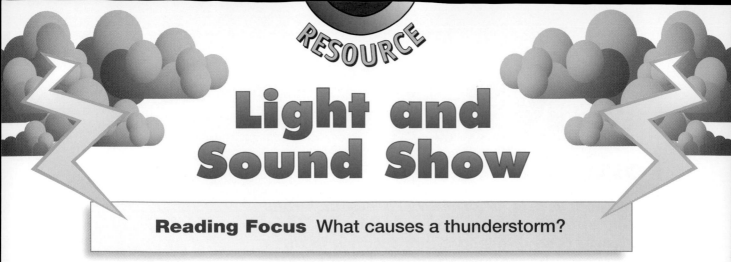

Light and Sound Show

Reading Focus What causes a thunderstorm?

KABOOM! You hear a loud, sharp crack of thunder. A **thunderstorm** is a storm that produces tall clouds, heavy rain, strong winds, lightning, and thunder. Every year there are about 16 million thunderstorms around the world. These storms occur along cold fronts and in places where the local weather is very hot and humid.

Stormy Weather

Thunderstorms begin to form when warm, moist air rises from Earth's surface. Sometimes, strong winds several kilometers above the surface make the air rise even faster and higher than usual, forming cumulonimbus clouds, or thunderheads. A single thunderhead may be several kilometers wide and up to 10 km (6 mi) high.

Strong, swirling winds within the cumulonimbus clouds carry water droplets and ice crystals up and down several times. This action causes the droplets and crystals to grow in size. When the raindrops and ice crystals become large enough and heavy enough, rain or hail begins to fall to Earth's surface.

Using Math *This time-exposure photo shows a series of lightning flashes. Lightning strikes somewhere on Earth about 100 times every second. How many times does lightning strike each minute?*

Lightning and Thunder

Water and ice particles inside a thunderhead are thrown together by strong winds. This action produces electrical charges within the storm cloud. The energy from the electricity is discharged as a flash of light and heat, called lightning. A lightning bolt can cause the air around it to become as hot as 30,000°C (54,000°F). This is more than five times as hot as the surface of the Sun!

As a lightning bolt flashes, it heats the air in its path. Because of the intense heat, the air expands very rapidly, causing the rumbling we call thunder.

Although you might not think so, lightning and thunder happen at the same time. We see lightning the instant it occurs. But we hear thunder a few seconds later, because light travels faster than sound.

Thunderstorm Problems

Although thunderstorms cool the air and ground, they can also cause problems. Sometimes there is so much rain from a sudden thunderstorm that floods occur. Sudden and violent floods are called **flash floods**. Heavy rain or hail from thunderstorms can damage crops and destroy property.

Lightning can injure and even kill people. It can cause fires. It can damage power lines and stop the flow of electricity. It can also interfere with radio and TV signals. ■

Science in Literature

MAKING RAIN TO ORDER

Professor Fergus Fahrenheit and His Wonderful Weather Machine
by Candace Groth-Fleming
Illustrated by Don Weller
Simon & Schuster, 1994

"'Good afternoon, ladies and gentlemen,' the stranger said . . . . 'My name is Professor Fergus Fahrenheit, and I represent the Wonder-Worker Weather Company. I understand you folks are in need of some rain. Well, ours is of the very best quality; and with every order we throw in a free silk umbrella.'"

This speech starts the action in *Professor Fergus Fahrenheit and His Wonderful Weather Machine* by Candace Groth-Fleming. Find out how the professor tries to help a town get rain.

Staying Safe in a Storm

Reading Focus How can you stay safe during severe weather?

In the past, people weren't able to predict when storms, hurricanes, or tornadoes would occur. But today, with the help of tools like barometers, anemometers, and weather satellites, scientists can better predict the weather.

The activity on page E64 explains how to be prepared for severe weather. What kinds of safety precautions would you include for thunderstorms, hurricanes, and tornadoes? Here are some precautions you should follow.

STAYING SAFE DURING A FLASH FLOOD

Flash floods can result from thunderstorms or hurricanes. Here are things you can do to keep yourself safe during a flood.

- Stay away from rivers, streams, creeks, and sewer drains. Water in these bodies can move very quickly.
- Don't try to walk or drive through water if you can't see the ground beneath the water.
- If a flood occurs, move to higher ground as quickly as possible.

STAYING SAFE FROM LIGHTNING

If you are outdoors,

- Go indoors. If you can't, stay away from tall buildings and trees. Lightning usually strikes the tallest objects.
- Avoid metal objects, such as metal baseball bats.
- Stay in a car, with windows up.

If you are indoors,

- Stay away from metal doors and large windows.
- Do not use the telephone.
- Unplug any TV, VCR, or computer.

E68

In the mountains outside Tucson, Arizona, a flash flood turns an arroyo (ə roi′ō), or dry gully *(left)*, into a dangerous rush of muddy water *(below)*.

STAYING SAFE DURING A HURRICANE

If you are caught in a hurricane, here are some things you should do.

- Get as far away from ocean beaches as possible. The huge waves produced by hurricanes are very dangerous.

- Stay inside in a basement, under a stairwell, or in another sheltered area.

- Stay away from windows. Hurricane winds can break glass, causing injury to people.

- Listen to local TV and radio stations.

STAYING SAFE DURING A TORNADO

If a tornado is sighted in your area, follow these precautions.

- If you are outside, try to stay in a ditch or another low area. This will help protect you from flying objects.

- If you are inside, try to stay in a basement or a storm cellar. If there is no basement or storm cellar, stay in a closet or bathroom.

- Stay away from windows and doors that lead outside. These can be blown apart by the winds of a tornado.

The Fiercest Storms on Earth

Reading Focus How are hurricanes and tornadoes alike, and how are they different?

What are hurricanes and tornadoes? What causes these storms? Where do they form? Why are they known as the fiercest storms on Earth?

Hurricanes—The Largest Storms

Hurricanes are large, violent storms that form over warm ocean water. When these storms develop over the Indian Ocean, they're called cyclones; when they form in the western Pacific Ocean, they're known as typhoons.

To be called a hurricane, the storm must have winds of at least 117 km/h (70 mph). Some hurricanes have winds of more than 240 km/h (144 mph)! They usually occur during late summer, when oceans and the air above oceans are very warm. Hurricanes are classified according to strength. The weakest hurricane is a level 1 and the strongest is a level 5. Look back at the Beaufort scale on page E39. How does the Beaufort scale describe hurricanes?

How Hurricanes Form

Hurricanes start out as small thunderstorms over an ocean. Several of these storms may join to form a larger storm. This storm grows bigger as it takes in heat and moisture from warm ocean water. As the storm grows, the wind

These satellite photos of Hurricane Andrew show the storm's location as it moved from Florida to Louisiana. The photos were taken over a three-day period in August 1992. ▼

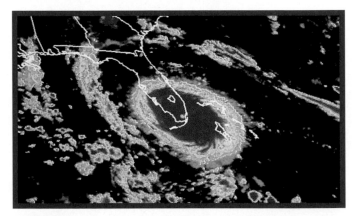

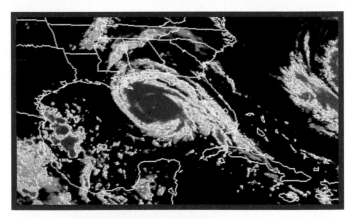

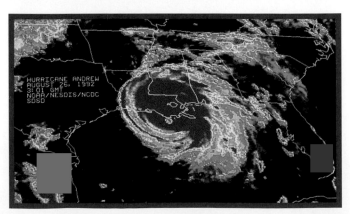

increases. This causes the clouds to spin. The diagram on this page explains how a hurricane forms.

In the middle of a hurricane is a hole, called the *eye* of the hurricane. Within the *eye* the weather is calm. There is little wind and no rain. Sometimes people are fooled into thinking that a hurricane is over when the *eye* is overhead. But it isn't over. The other half of the storm is on its way.

Hurricanes are the largest storms on Earth. A hurricane can cover a circular area as wide as 600 km (360 mi). A storm this size could cover both the states of Alabama and Mississippi at the same time.

Hurricanes on the Move

Once a hurricane forms, it begins to travel. As it moves, the winds blow harder. The winds can rip up trees and blow off roofs. Rain can cause flooding. Even more dangerous than the winds and heavy rains are the giant ocean waves. These waves can wash away beaches and sink boats. Hurricanes don't last long once they reach land. The storm loses its source of energy over land or cold ocean water.

Internet Field Trip

Visit **www.eduplace.com** to find out more about hurricanes and tornadoes.

4 A circular wall of clouds with heavy rains and strong winds develops around the eye. As the warm air moves up, it spreads out.

5 In the eye the air sinks slowly, the winds are light, and there are no clouds.

3 Warm moist air spirals up around the eye.

2 Strong surface winds at the base of the hurricane blow into an area of low pressure.

1 Warm ocean water provides the energy.

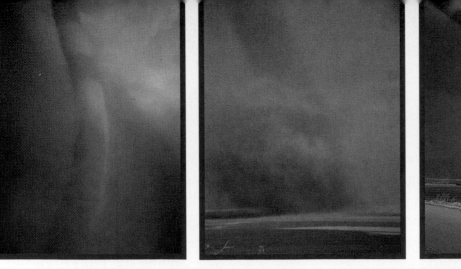

▲ A tornado may skip across the ground like someone playing leapfrog. Whatever it touches is likely to be destroyed.

Twister!

Sometimes a thunderstorm produces a tornado. A **tornado**, also known as a twister, is a funnel-shaped cloud of spinning wind. The activity that is on page E65 uses water in a bottle to model a tornado. The spinning water is shaped like a tornado. But unlike the water, air in a tornado spins upward.

Tornadoes usually occur during spring and early summer. They can develop without warning. They form when a column of warm air begins to spin. As air flows up into this swirling column, it spins very fast, forming the well-known funnel-shaped cloud.

Tornadoes are the most violent storms on Earth. Even though tornadoes don't cover as much area as hurricanes, they can be just as dangerous. The speed of the winds in the center of a tornado can be as high as 500 km/h (300 mph). That is twice the speed of the winds in the worst hurricane!

In tornadoes the air pressure is very low. The strong winds blowing into these low-pressure areas can sweep objects into the tornado, including dirt, trees, school buses, and roofs of buildings. The winds may be strong enough to move and destroy large trees, cars, trains, and houses. ■

INVESTIGATION 3 WRAP-UP

REVIEW

1. Describe the safety precautions you should take if you are outside during a thunderstorm.

2. What causes lightning? Why do you see the flash before you hear the thunder?

CRITICAL THINKING

3. Make a table to compare hurricanes, thunderstorms, and tornadoes. How are they similar? How are they different?

4. What type of dangerous weather is most likely to occur in your region? What precautions should you take if that type of weather occurs?

REFLECT & EVALUATE

Word Power

Write the letter of the term that best matches the definition. *Not all terms will be used.*

1. Where a cold air mass moves into a warm one
2. High, thin, feathery clouds made up of ice crystals
3. A large violent storm that forms over warm ocean water
4. A place where two masses of air meet
5. A low, flat cloud that often brings drizzle
6. A funnel-shaped storm of spinning wind

a. cirrus clouds
b. cold front
c. cumulus clouds
d. front
e. hurricane
f. stratus clouds
g. tornado
h. warm front

Check What You Know

Write the term in each pair that best completes each sentence.

1. When a low-pressure area moves into a region, the weather will likely be (rainy, dry).
2. Hurricanes form over (deserts, oceans).
3. The air pressure inside a tornado is very (high, low).
4. Water vapor in the air condenses into tiny drops of water that form a (front, cloud).

Problem Solving

1. Imagine that you can use only two instruments to forecast tomorrow's weather. Which two would you choose? Explain your reasoning.

2. Describe two safety precautions people can take for thunderstorms, hurricanes, and tornadoes.

3. Describe the movement of two air masses at a cold front. What kind of weather would you expect to follow once the front has passed?

Study the drawing. Then write the sequence of events that explain how a hurricane forms.

CHAPTER 4

SEASONS AND CLIMATE

Do you live in the northern part of the United States? If so, you may go sledding in winter and swimming in summer. If you live in southern California or Florida, you may not have as great a change between seasons. But every place on Earth has seasons.

Connecting to Science
CULTURE

Algonquin Moon The Algonquins, a Native American people, gave a name to each full moon to keep track of the seasons. "Crow Moon" is the name given to early spring because that is when the crows return. April is the month of Sprouting Grass Moon. At the peak of spring is Flower Moon. In June comes Strawberry Moon. The heat of summer begins Thunder Moon, and August is the time of Sturgeon Moon. Summer ends with Harvest Moon. October's moon is the Hunter, and chilly November is the month of Frost Moon. The winter brings Long Nights Moon and then the howling winds of Wolf Moon. By February, food is scarce. That month's moon is named Hunger. How would you name the moon for the seasons where you live?

Coming Up

The Algonquins might call this moon the Long Nights Moon.

INVESTIGATION ①

WHAT CAUSES THE SEASONS?

Which activities do you like to do in summer? in winter? How do the differences in weather during summer and winter affect what you do? In Investigation 1 you'll find out what causes summer and winter!

Activity

Sunshine Hours

Do the number of hours of sunlight change from season to season? Gather data to find out.

MATERIALS

- graph paper
- yellow crayon
- *Science Notebook*

Procedure

1. The table shows the times the Sun rises and sets in the middle of each month. **Interpret the data** in the table to **predict** whether the number of hours of sunlight is greater in winter or in summer. **Discuss** your prediction with your group and then **record** it in your *Science Notebook*.

2. Using graph paper, set up a graph like the one shown on page E77. Note that *Time of Day* should be on the left side and *Month of Year* should be along the bottom. Then **make a line graph**, using the data in the table.

Sunrises and Sunsets (Standard Time) for the Middle of Each Month		
Month	Sunrise (A.M.)	Sunset (P.M.)
Jan.	7:20	5:00
Feb.	6:55	5:34
Mar.	6:11	6:07
Apr.	5:23	6:38
May	4:44	7:09
June	4:31	7:30
July	4:44	7:27
Aug.	5:12	6:56
Sept.	5:41	6:09
Oct.	6:11	5:20
Nov.	6:45	4:44
Dec.	7:15	4:36

3. On your graph, mark a dot to show the time the Sun rises each month. Connect the dots.

4. Mark another dot to show the time the Sun sets each month. Connect these dots.

5. Use a yellow crayon to color the space between the two lines on your graph paper. Keep the graph in your *Science Notebook*.

Analyze and Conclude

1. What does the yellow space on your graph represent?

2. **Interpret your graph.** Are the number of hours of sunlight greater in summer or in winter? **Compare** your results with your prediction.

3. Use the data on your graph to **infer** why the temperature of the air in summer tends to be higher than the temperature of the air in winter.

INVESTIGATE FURTHER!

RESEARCH

In most parts of the United States, daylight saving time is observed from spring through fall. Find out why this practice occurs. Determine what effect it has on the time of sunrise and sunset.

E77

Changing Seasons

Reading Focus How does the tilt of Earth's axis affect surface temperatures and the seasons?

▲ **How do the changing seasons affect what you do?**

It's the first day of summer! You and your friends are planning a trip to the nearest swimming pool. At the same time, students in Australia are spending the first day of winter in school. How can it be summer in one part of the world and winter in another? And why are there different seasons at all?

The Tilting Earth

As Earth moves, or revolves, around the Sun, different places on Earth's surface receive different amounts of energy from the Sun. To understand why this happens, imagine Earth has a line running through it, from the North Pole, through Earth's center, to the South Pole. The drawing on page E79 illustrates such a line. This imaginary line is called Earth's **axis** (ak'sis).

As Earth revolves around the Sun, it also spins, or rotates, on its axis. It takes Earth about 24 hours to complete one rotation. One rotation is equal to one full day.

There is a second imaginary line which circles the middle of Earth. This imaginary line is called the **equator** (ē kwāt'ər). Find the equator in the drawing on page E79. The equator divides Earth into two equal parts. The half of Earth that is above the equator is called the **Northern Hemisphere**. The half below the equator is called the **Southern Hemisphere**.

When Earth revolves around the Sun, its axis is not straight up and down. Instead, Earth's axis is tilted slightly. The tilt of Earth's axis stays almost the same throughout the year. So as Earth revolves around the Sun, at times the Northern Hemisphere is tilted toward the Sun, and at times it is tilted away from the Sun.

AXIS Earth's axis is an imaginary line that runs from the North Pole through Earth's center to the South Pole.

EQUATOR The equator is an imaginary line that divides Earth into the Northern Hemisphere and the Southern Hemisphere.

Science in Literature

OUT OF THIS WORLD!

The Third Planet: Exploring the Earth From Space
by Sally Ride and Tam O'Shaughnessy
Crown Publishers, 1994

"The Space Shuttle streaks through space at 17,500 miles per hour. It crosses the United States in just a few minutes, and circles the whole planet in just an hour and a half . . . . I could take pictures of giant glaciers in Alaska one minute and of the shallow waters off the Florida coast 15 minutes later."

Here, astronaut Sally Ride describes what it's like to look down on Earth from a spacecraft. Her quotation is from the book *The Third Planet*, which she and Tam O'Shaughnessy wrote together. The photographs are out of this world!

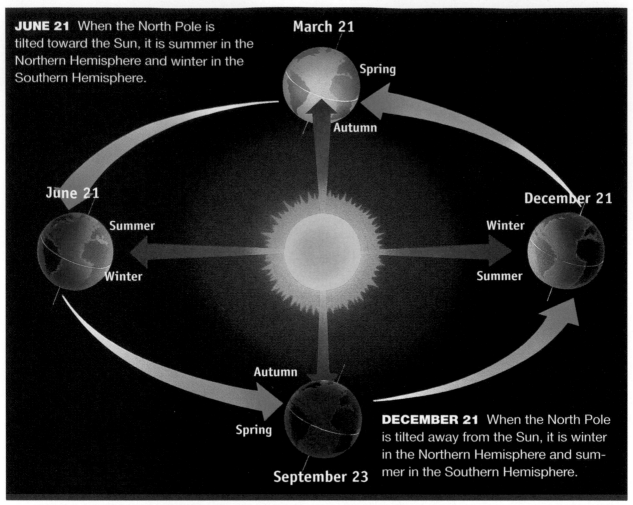

JUNE 21 When the North Pole is tilted toward the Sun, it is summer in the Northern Hemisphere and winter in the Southern Hemisphere.

March 21

Spring

Autumn

June 21

Summer

Winter

December 21

Winter

Summer

Autumn

Spring

DECEMBER 21 When the North Pole is tilted away from the Sun, it is winter in the Northern Hemisphere and summer in the Southern Hemisphere.

September 23

▲ **The seasons change as Earth revolves around the Sun.**

Seasons in the Sun

Study the picture above. As Earth revolves around the Sun, there are changes in the way the Sun's rays strike Earth's surface. These changes cause the temperature of Earth's surface and atmosphere to change, leading to the change in seasons.

The tilt of Earth's axis does not change much. What *does* change is the position of the axis in relation to the Sun's position. At times, during Earth's revolution around the Sun, the axis tilts toward the Sun. At other times, Earth's axis tilts away from the Sun.

The picture on page E81 shows that, during the winter, sunlight strikes Earth

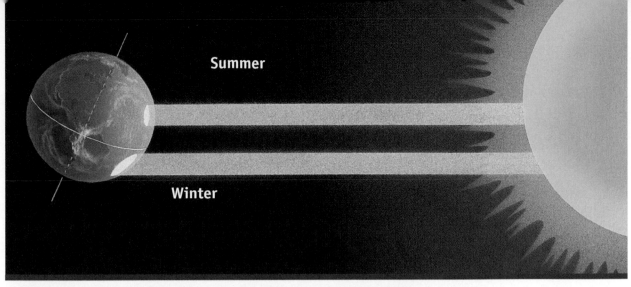

Summer

Winter

▲ **The Sun's rays strike Earth at a greater slant during winter.**

at a slant. When light strikes at a slant, it spreads out and covers more area. The greater the slant, the less energy the ground in this area receives. This is the main reason that temperatures are colder in winter than in summer.

During summer, sunlight strikes Earth more directly. The light does not spread out as much and covers less area than it does in winter. So the ground receives more energy. This is the main reason that temperatures are warmer in summer.

The number of hours of daylight also affects the temperature. When the North Pole is tilted toward the Sun, the Sun appears high in the sky. The Sun's rays strike the North Pole more directly and there are more hours of daylight. The longer the Sun shines on an area, the more energy that area can absorb, and the warmer the temperatures become.

When the North Pole is tilted away from the Sun, the rays strike at a slant, and the Sun appears low in the sky. Then there are fewer hours of daylight. Because the Sun has less time to heat an area, temperatures there are cooler. Which season, according to the table in the activity on pages E76 and E77, has the most hours of daylight? ■

INVESTIGATION 1 WRAP-UP

THINK IT WRITE IT

REVIEW

1. Give two reasons why the Sun heats an area more in summer than it does in winter.

2. Make and label a drawing to show the positions of the Northern Hemisphere in summer and in winter. Include the Sun in your picture.

CRITICAL THINKING

3. Suppose the North Pole is tilted toward the Sun. Compare daylight hours at the North Pole and South Pole. Explain your answer.

4. In what season is your birthday? What will the weather likely be on that day in your region? in Australia? Explain your answer.

INVESTIGATION 2

WHAT FACTORS AFFECT CLIMATE?

Climate is the average weather conditions of a place over a long period of time. In Investigation 2 you'll find out what factors cause Earth to have different climates.

Activity

Microclimates Everywhere!

Temperature and wind are important factors in determining climate. Why might two places close to each other have different climates? Investigate to find out.

Procedure

1. In your *Science Notebook*, **make a chart** like the one shown.

Building Side	Temperature (°C)	Wind Direction

2. Cover the outside of a cardboard tube with aluminum foil. Fasten the tube to a meterstick with a rubber band as shown. Move the tube so that the lower edge of the tube is at the 30-cm mark.

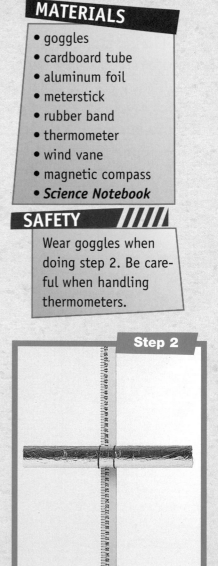
Step 2

3. **Predict** whether temperature and wind direction are the same, or different, on each of the sides of your school building.

4. Take a thermometer and a wind vane outside your school. Stay close to one side of the building and **measure** the temperature 30 cm from the ground. Use a magnetic compass to help **determine** the wind direction, too. **Record** this data in your chart.

See **SCIENCE** and **MATH TOOLBOX** *page H8 if you need to review Using a Thermometer.*

5. Repeat step 4 for the other sides of the building. **Record** all data in your chart.

Analyze and Conclude

1. **Compare** your prediction in step 3 with your results. What differences, if any, did you find on different sides of your school?

2. Different sides of a building have different microclimates. *Micro-* means "very small." From your study, how would you **define** *microclimate*?

3. Which microclimate was the warmest? Which was the coolest? **Infer** why temperature would vary on different sides of the building.

4. Was the wind direction different on different sides of the building? What factors affect the way the wind blows on one side of your school building?

Step 4

INVESTIGATE FURTHER!

EXPERIMENT

Predict what would happen if you repeated this experiment over a longer period of time. Would you get the same results? Discuss your predictions with your group. Repeat the experiment once a month for the next three months. How did your predictions compare with your results?

Florida Is Not North Dakota

Reading Focus What causes climate and what are three main types of climate?

What is the weather in your area normally like in the summer? What is the weather normally like in the winter? People in different parts of the world will have different answers to these questions. That's because different places have different climates. The **climate** of an area is the average weather conditions over a long period of time.

Hot or Cold, Wet or Dry

Two important parts of an area's climate are its average temperature and

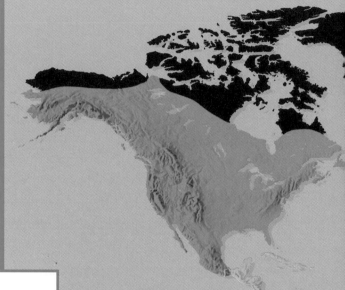

Equator

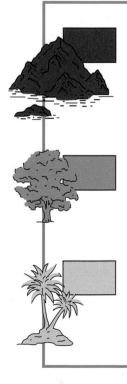

POLAR CLIMATE
In the Arctic and Antarctic, the temperature is usually below freezing all year long. These areas do not receive as much energy from the Sun as other parts of Earth.

TEMPERATE CLIMATE
Between the equator and the Poles are areas that generally have summers that are warm and dry and winters that are cold and wet.

TROPICAL CLIMATE
The places closest to the equator are usually hot and rainy for most of the year. Temperatures are high because these areas receive the most energy from the Sun.

its average yearly rainfall. The average temperature of an area depends a great deal on the distance the area is from the equator. In general, areas close to the equator are warmer than areas farther from the equator. For example, North Dakota is farther from the equator than Florida is, so North Dakota is usually colder than Florida. The map below shows the location of three main types of climates. They are polar, tropical, and temperate.

Areas with a **tropical climate** are usually hot and rainy all year round. Areas with a **temperate climate** generally have summers that are warm and dry and winters that are cold and wet. Areas with a **polar climate** are usually very cold all year round. Which climate do you think you live in?

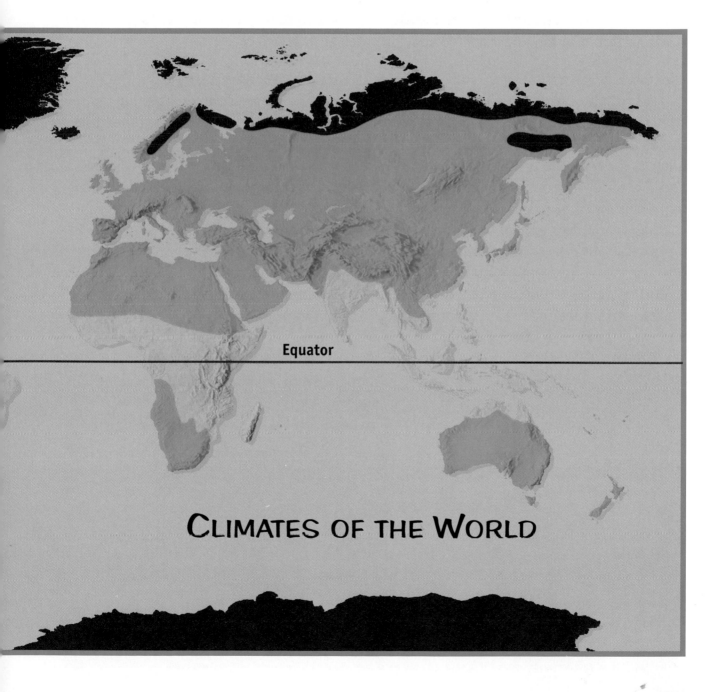

Equator

CLIMATES OF THE WORLD

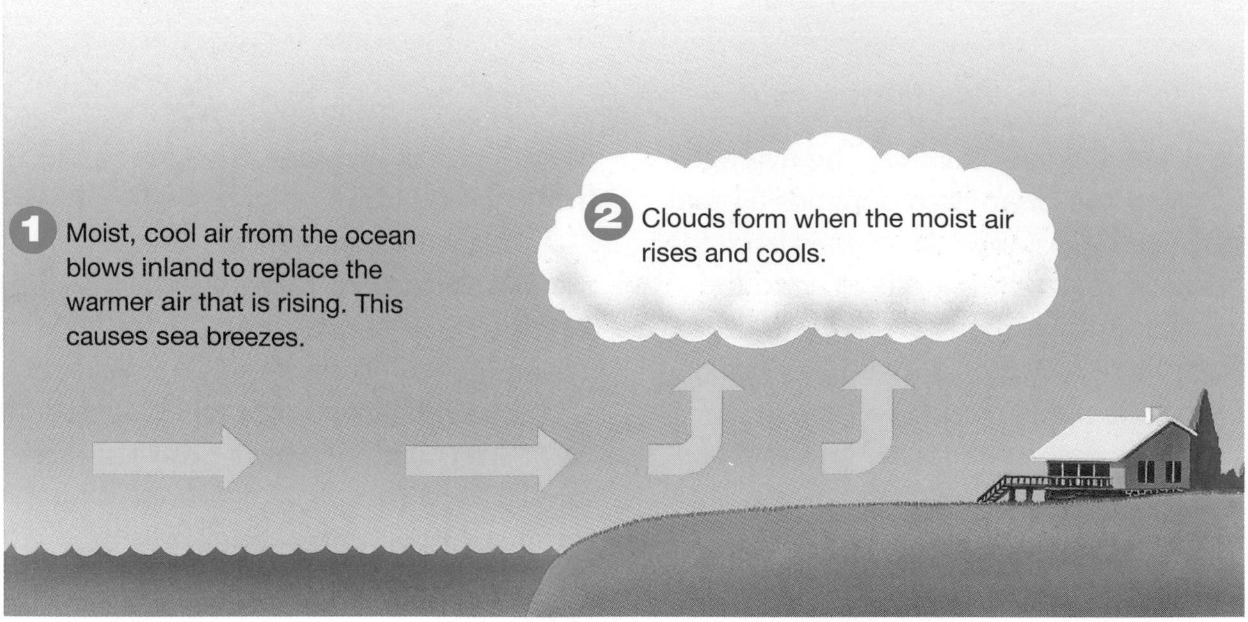

1 Moist, cool air from the ocean blows inland to replace the warmer air that is rising. This causes sea breezes.

2 Clouds form when the moist air rises and cools.

▲ **Air pattern over land near a large body of water, such as the ocean**

Climate Controls

The activity on pages E82 and E83 shows how to investigate the microclimates around your school building. Factors such as the amount of sunlight and the type of ground cover affect the temperature of an area. Other factors, such as the placement of buildings, trees, and other structures, affect the way the wind blows in an area.

Just as certain things affect microclimates, certain features, such as oceans and mountains, can affect the climate in an area. In the diagrams on this page and the next, you can see how having oceans and mountains nearby affect the climate of a region.

If you live near an ocean or a large lake, your climate may be cloudier and wetter than the climate of places farther from the water. The summers in your area may be cooler, and the winters may be warmer.

An area in the middle of the plains or far from any large body of water, such as an ocean or a lake, will likely

Air pattern over plains ▼

Plains may be cut off from the sea by mountains. Hot, dry winds blow off the mountains and across the flat land of the plains.

have a different climate. These areas will probably have little rain, hot summers, and cold winters.

If you live near a mountain on the side least protected from the wind, your area may often have strong winds and lots of rain. But if you live near a mountain on the side most protected from the wind, your climate will probably be dry and you'll have gentle winds.

El Niño

Nearness to an ocean affects climate. Changes in ocean conditions can cause a major change in climate.

The cool waters of the Pacific Ocean off the coast of South America become warmer about every four years. This causes weather patterns to change around the world! Scientists refer to this huge area of warm ocean water and the changes in weather patterns that it causes as El Niño.

Severe effects of El Niño occurred from 1997 to 1998. During the spring of 1998, rainfall was much heavier than normal in the eastern United States. California also had heavy rains and flooding. But in the southern United States and parts of Asia, drought was the effect of El Niño. El Niño also helped cause forest fires that occurred in Indonesia that year.

Scientists still don't understand all of the factors that produce El Niño, nor can they accurately predict its effects. But they continue to study El Niño and the weather changes it brings. ■

Air pattern over a mountain ▼

1 When moist air meets a mountain, the air is forced upward. As the air rises, it cools and forms clouds around the peak.

2 These clouds bring heavy rain. As the air passes over the mountaintop and flows down the other side, it becomes warmer and drier.

Clues to Earth's Climate

Reading Focus What are three ways that scientists learn about climate changes in Earth's past?

The world's climate has gone through many changes. These changes have lasted from just a few years to thousands of years. Scientists who study Earth's climate look for clues in nature to find out why these changes in climate have taken place.

Tree Rings

One way that scientists learn about climate changes is by studying trees. Most trees grow a new ring every year. These rings are called *annual rings*, meaning "a ring produced each year." You can see the tree rings in the picture. If a tree ring is wide, the weather that year was probably wetter and warmer than normal. The tree probably absorbed plenty of nutrients and grew quickly. If a tree ring is narrow, the weather was probably drier and colder than normal that year. The tree probably didn't get enough nutrients, so it grew slowly. By studying the size of annual rings, scientists can track warm and cold periods several thousand years into Earth's past.

◀ Tree rings can help scientists determine changes in Earth's climate.

▲ Finding fossils in unexpected places may indicate changes in Earth's climate.

▲ A scientist saws off a piece of an ice core for testing.

Fossil Clues

Another way that scientists learn about climate changes is by studying fossils. Fossils are the imprints or remains of animals and plants that lived in the past. Finding fossils in unusual places can be a clue that the climate in an area has changed. For example, some fossilized camel bones were found in the Arctic. Scientists hypothesize that these fossils show that the Arctic was once much warmer than it is now. Fossils can give clues to what Earth's climate was like millions of years ago.

Ice Cores

A third approach that scientists use to find out about past climate changes is to study ice samples from glaciers. Scientists drill holes in glaciers and pull out long columns of ice, or ice cores. The ice cores are analyzed for traces of certain chemicals. These chemicals can give clues about past climate changes. For example, a large amount of carbon dioxide and other gases found in an ice core sample may indicate that Earth was once warmer than it is today.

Covered in Ice

Great changes in Earth's climate usually occur very slowly. At times, Earth has been much warmer than it is now. At other times, Earth has been much colder than it is now. Then sheets of ice called glaciers covered large areas of the world. These cold periods are called **ice ages**. The last ice age ended about 10,000 years ago. During that time, glaciers covered much of Earth's surface. How do you think living things were affected by these climate changes? ■

Technology Link
CD-ROM

INVESTIGATE FURTHER!

Use the **Science Processor CD-ROM**, *Weather & Climate* (Investigation 4, Where on Earth?) to compare climate in your area with climate in other places. You'll find out which factors cause different climates throughout the world.

Weather Records

Reading Focus What are four kinds of weather records?

Have you ever thought that a certain thunderstorm was the worst one you'd ever seen and heard? Or, on a hot summer day, have you ever thought that it couldn't possibly get any hotter? Imagine what it would be like to live someplace that had no rain for 400 years. Think about what it would feel like to live someplace where the Sun shines for only half the year. Find out where these places are located as you read about some of the windiest, wettest, driest, hottest, and coldest places on Earth!

The Windiest Place
• Winds coming off Commonwealth Bay, Antarctica, can reach 320 km/h (200 mph).

The Fastest Wind Gust
• A wind speed of 415 km/h (250 mph) was recorded on April 12, 1934, on Mount Washington in New Hampshire. This area is known for unpredictable and dangerous weather.

Mount Washington, New Hampshire ▶

STOP

U.S. U.S.
FOREST SERVICE

THE AREA AHEAD HAS THE WORST WEATHER IN AMERICA. MANY HAVE DIED THERE FROM EXPOSURE, EVEN IN THE SUMMER. TURN BACK NOW IF THE WEATHER IS BAD.

WHITE MOUNTAIN NATIONAL FOREST

The Coldest Place
- Polus Nedostuphosti (Pole of Cold), Antarctica, has an average temperature of −58°C (−72°F). This area, which is near the South Pole, gets sunlight for only about half the year.

The Lowest Temperatures
- The lowest recorded temperature on Earth was −88°C (−127°F) in Vostok, Antarctica, on July 22, 1983.
- In the United States a low temperature of −62°C (−80°F) was recorded on January 23, 1971, in Prospect Creek, Alaska.

South Pole, Antarctica ▶

The Hottest Place
- Dallol, Ethiopia, has an average temperature of 34°C (93°F). Dallol is very close to the equator and is shielded from the Indian Ocean by mountains.

The Highest Temperatures
- The highest temperature recorded on Earth was in Al-Aziziyah, Libya, where the temperature reached 58°C (136°F) on September 13, 1922.
- The highest temperature recorded in the United States was 57°C (134°F) on July 10, 1913, in Death Valley, California.

◀ **Death Valley, California**

The Wettest Places

- Mawsynram, in India, has about 1,186 cm (474 in.) of rainfall per year.
- The state of Louisiana averages 142 cm (56 in.) of rainfall per year.

    In these areas the warm, wet winds blow in off the water. As the winds blow over the land, the air rises and cools. This creates thick clouds and heavy rains.

The Greatest Rainfall

- In one day, from March 15 through March 16, 1952, nearly 187 cm (74 in.) of rain fell in Cilaos, on the island of Réunion, in the Indian Ocean.

▼ **Mawsynram, India**

The Atacama Desert, Chile ▲

The Driest Places

- Arica, Chile, averages less than 0.01 cm (0.004 in.) of rainfall per year. Chile is near very cold water, so the winds blowing toward land are usually dry and don't form many clouds.
- In the state of Nevada, about 23 cm (9 in.) of rain falls per year. Much of Nevada is sheltered from ocean winds by the Sierra Nevada, a mountain range. The winds that come down from these mountains contain little water vapor.

The Longest Dry Spell

- Desierto de Atacama (the Atacama Desert) in Chile had almost no rain for 400 years! This dry spell ended in 1971.

INVESTIGATION 2 WRAP-UP

REVIEW

1. What are the two main factors that affect the climate of an area? Discuss each type of climate.

2. How are tree rings clues to climate changes?

CRITICAL THINKING

3. What would you conclude if you found the fossilized bones of an Arctic animal near the equator?

4. Suppose your business is landscaping. How can you use your knowledge of microclimates?

REFLECT & EVALUATE

Word Power

Write the letter of the term that best matches the definition. *Not all terms will be used.*

1. Climate of places in the Arctic and Antarctic
2. Climate of places closest to the equator
3. Climate with warm, dry summers and cold, wet winters
4. An imaginary line running around the middle of Earth
5. An imaginary straight line running through Earth from the North Pole to the South Pole.

a. axis
b. equator
c. ice ages
d. polar climate
e. temperate climate
f. tropical climate

Check What You Know

Write the term in each pair that best completes each sentence.

1. The greater the slant of the Sun's rays striking Earth, the (more, less) the Earth's surface is heated.
2. A very wide annual tree ring is likely to form in a year with (much, little) rainfall.
3. The average weather conditions in an area over a long period of time are its (weather, climate).
4. If you live in a tropical climate, the weather is hot and (wet, dry).

Problem Solving

1. You and a friend live in different cities. The cities are the same distance from the equator, but they have very different climates. What are some of the factors that might explain this difference?

2. Your cousin is packing shorts and bathing suits for his trip to Sydney, Australia, on July 3. During his two-week stay, he expects to spend time enjoying warm beaches. What advice would you give him about his trip? Explain.

Study the drawing. Explain in writing how the tilt of Earth's axis and the slant of the Sun's rays cause the seasons.

Compare and Contrast

Making comparisons when you read is a good way to understand new ideas. When you read, compare each new idea to an old, familiar idea.

Read the passage and complete the exercise that follows.

Look for these signal words to help you compare and contrast.

- To show similar things: *like, the same as*

- To show different things: *different from, instead*

Climate Controls

Just as certain things affect microclimates, certain features, such as oceans and mountains, can affect the climate in an area. . . . If you live near an ocean or a large lake, your climate may be cloudier and wetter than the climate of places farther from the water. The summers in your area may be cooler, and the winters may be warmer.

An area in the middle of the plains or far from any large body of water, such as an ocean or a lake, will likely have a different climate. These areas probably will have little rain, hot summers, and cold winters.

If you live near a mountain on the side least protected from the wind, your area may often have strong winds and lots of rain. But if you live near a mountain on the side most protected from the wind, your climate will probably be dry, and you'll have gentle winds.

Write the letter of each true statement about climate conditions.

   a. Areas near large bodies of water may be cloudier and wetter than are places farther from water.

   b. Areas near large bodies of water are warmer in summer and cooler in winter.

   c. Areas near mountains, on the side most protected from the wind, may have lots of rain.

   d. Areas in the middle of the plains are likely to have little rain, hot summers, and cold winters.

 **Analyze Data**

The number of seconds that elapse between a flash of lightning and the sound of thunder can be used to estimate your distance from a thunderstorm. The table below provides data that can help you make such an estimate.

Computing Distance From a Thunderstorm						
Elapsed Time Between Lightning and Thunder (s)	0	1	2	3	4	5
Distance (m)	0	346	692	1,038	?	1,730

Use the table to complete the exercises that follow.

1. How far from a thunderstorm are you if 3 seconds elapse between the time you see a flash of lightning and the time you hear the sound of thunder?

2. If exactly 4 seconds elapse between the time you see a flash of lightning and the time you hear the sound of thunder, how far are you from a thunderstorm?

3. Estimate the speed at which sound travels through air. Use a pattern from the table to explain your answer. Based on your estimate of the speed of sound, how many meters would sound travel in 6 seconds?

4. Explain how you could estimate whether it would take 2, 3, or 4 seconds for the sound of thunder to travel 1 km.

You may wish to use a calculator for Exercise 5.

5. Suppose you are 3,500 m from a thunderstorm. How many seconds will elapse between a flash of lightning and the sound of thunder from that thunderstorm? Round your answer to the nearest second.

E95

WRAP-UP!

On your own, use scientific methods to investigate a question about weather.

THINK LIKE A SCIENTIST

Ask a Question

Pose a question about weather that you would like to investigate. For example, ask, "How does wind affect air temperature in a location?"

Make a Hypothesis

Suggest a hypothesis, or possible answer to the question. One hypothesis is that wind will lower air temperature in a location.

Plan and Do a Test

Plan a controlled experiment to find the effect wind has on the air temperature in a location. You could start with two pans holding equal amounts of the same kind of soil, a desk fan, and two thermometers. Develop a procedure that uses these materials to test the hypothesis. With permission, carry out your experiment. Follow the safety guidelines on pages S14–S15.

Record and Analyze

Observe carefully and record your data accurately. Make repeated observations.

Draw Conclusions

Look for evidence to support the hypothesis or to show that it is false. Draw conclusions about the hypothesis. Repeat the experiment to verify the results.

WRITING IN SCIENCE
Persuasive Essay

Write a persuasive essay to convince scientists to research the effects of El Niño on weather patterns. Use these guidelines to write your persuasive essay.

- Discuss how being able to predict El Niño events might reduce any negative effects they cause.
- Describe the effects of droughts and floods on people's lives.
- Suggest ways in which people might prepare for drastic changes in weather patterns.

SCIENCE and MATH TOOLBOX

Using a Microscope

A microscope makes it possible to see very small things by magnifying them. Some microscopes have a set of lenses that magnify objects by different amounts.

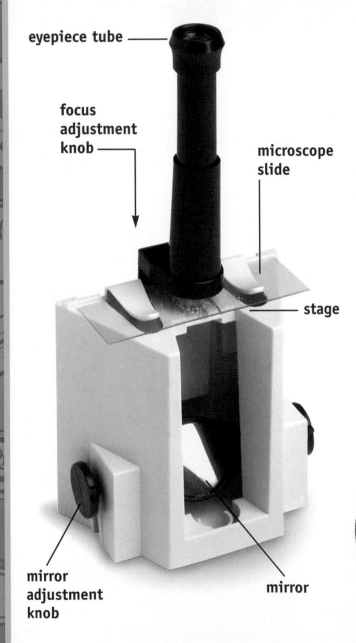

eyepiece tube

focus adjustment knob

microscope slide

stage

mirror adjustment knob

mirror

Examine Some Salt Grains

Handle a microscope carefully; it can break easily. Carry it firmly with both hands and avoid touching the lenses.

1. Turn the mirror toward a source of light. **NEVER** use the Sun as a light source.

2. Place a few grains of salt on the slide. Put the slide on the stage of the microscope.

3. Bring the salt grains into focus. Turn the adjustment knob on the back of the microscope as you look through the eyepiece.

4. Raise the eyepiece tube to increase the magnification; lower it to decrease magnification.

Salt grains magnified one hundred times (100X)

Making a Bar Graph

A bar graph helps you organize and compare data. For example, you might want to make a bar graph to compare weather data for different places.

Make a Bar Graph of Annual Snowfall

For more than 20 years, the cities listed in the table have been recording their yearly snowfall. The table shows the average number of centimeters of snow that the cities receive each year. Use the data in the table to make a bar graph showing the cities' average annual snowfall.

Snowfall	
City	Snowfall (cm)
Atlanta, GA	5
Charleston, SC	1.5
Houston, TX	1
Jackson, MS	3
New Orleans, LA	0.5
Tucson, AZ	3

1. Title your graph. The title should help a reader understand what your graph describes.

2. Choose a scale and mark equal intervals. The vertical scale should include the least value and the greatest value in the set of data.

4. Carefully graph the data. Depending on the interval you choose, some amounts may be between two numbers.

3. Label the vertical axis *Snowfall (cm)* and the horizontal axis *City*. Space the city names equally.

5. Check each step of your work.

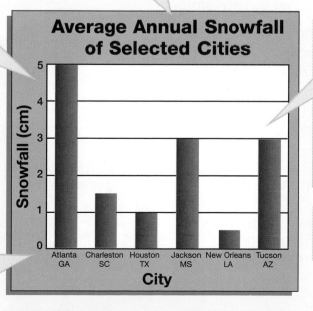

Average Annual Snowfall of Selected Cities

Using a Calculator

After you've made measurements, a calculator can help you analyze your data. Some calculators have a memory key that allows you to save the result of one calculation while you do another.

Add and Divide to Find Percent

The table shows the amount of rain that was collected using a rain gauge in each month of one year. You can use a calculator to help you find the total yearly rainfall. Then you can find the percent of rain that fell during January.

1. Add the numbers. When you add a series of numbers, you need not press the equal sign until the last number is entered. Just press the plus sign after you enter each number (except the last).

2. If you make a mistake while you are entering numbers, press the clear entry (CE/C) key to erase your mistake. Then you can continue entering the rest of the numbers you are adding. If you can't fix your mistake, you can press the (CE/C) key once or twice until the screen shows 0. Then start over.

3. Your total should be 1,131. Now clear the calculator until the screen shows 0. Then divide the rainfall amount for January by the total yearly rainfall (1,131). Press the percent (%) key. Then press the equal sign key.

214 ÷ 1131 % =

The percent of yearly rainfall that fell in January is 18.921309, which rounds to 19%.

Rainfall	
Month	**Rain (mm)**
Jan.	214
Feb.	138
Mar.	98
Apr.	157
May	84
June	41
July	5
Aug.	23
Sept.	48
Oct.	75
Nov.	140
Dec.	108

clear entry

percent

18.921309

divide

multiply

plus

equal

Finding an Average

An average is a way to describe a set of data using one number. For example, you could compare the surface temperature of several stars that are of the same type. You could find the average surface temperature of these stars.

Add and Divide to Find the Average

Suppose scientists found the surface temperature of eight blue-white stars to be those shown in the table. What is the average surface temperature of the stars listed?

Surface Temperature of Selected Blue-white Stars

Blue-white Star	Surface Temperature (°F)
1	7,200
2	6,100
3	6,000
4	6,550
5	7,350
6	6,800
7	7,500
8	6,300

1. First find the sum of the data. Add the numbers in the list.

$$
\begin{array}{r}
7,200 \\
6,100 \\
6,000 \\
6,550 \\
7,350 \\
6,800 \\
7,500 \\
+\ 6,300 \\
\hline
53,800
\end{array}
$$

2. Then divide the sum (53,800) by the number of addends (8).

$$
\begin{array}{r}
6,725 \\
8\ )\overline{\ 53,800} \\
-\ 48 \\
\hline
58 \\
-\ 56 \\
\hline
20 \\
-\ 16 \\
\hline
40 \\
-\ 40 \\
\hline
0
\end{array}
$$

3. $53,800 \div 8 = 6,725$
The average surface temperature of these eight blue-white stars is 6,725°F.

Using a
Tape Measure or Ruler

Tape measures, metersticks, and rulers are tools for measuring length. Scientists use units such as kilometers, meters, centimeters, and millimeters when making length measurements.

Use a Meterstick

1. Work with a partner to find the height of your reach. Stand facing a chalkboard. Reach up as high as you can with one hand.

2. Have your partner use chalk to mark the chalkboard at the highest point of your reach.

3. Use a meterstick to measure your reach to the nearest centimeter. Measure from the floor to the chalk mark. Record the height of your reach.

Use a Tape Measure

1. Use a tape measure to find the circumference of, or distance around, your partner's head. Wrap the tape around your partner's head.

2. Find the line where the tape begins to wrap over itself.

3. Record the distance around your partner's head to the nearest millimeter.

Measuring Volume

A graduated cylinder, a measuring cup, and a beaker are used to measure volume. Volume is the amount of space something takes up. Most of the containers that scientists use to measure volume have a scale marked in milliliters (mL).

Measure the Volume of a Liquid

1. Measure the volume of some juice. Pour the juice into a measuring container.

2. Move your head so that your eyes are level with the top of the juice. Read the scale line that is closest to the surface of the juice. If the surface of the juice is curved up on the sides, look at the lowest point of the curve.

3. Read the measurement on the scale. You can estimate the value between two lines on the scale to obtain a more accurate measurement.

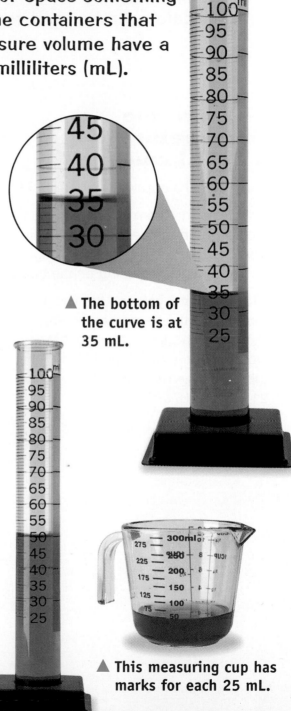

▲ The bottom of the curve is at 35 mL.

This beaker has marks for each 25 mL. ▶

This graduated cylinder has marks for every 1 mL. ▶

▲ This measuring cup has marks for each 25 mL.

Using a
Thermometer

A thermometer is used to measure temperature. When the liquid in the tube of a thermometer gets warmer, it expands and moves farther up the tube. Different scales can be used to measure temperature, but scientists usually use the Celsius scale.

Measure the Temperature of a Cold Liquid

1. Half fill a cup with chilled liquid.

2. Hold the thermometer so that the bulb is in the center of the liquid. Be sure that there are no bright lights or direct sunlight shining on the bulb.

3. Wait until you see the liquid in the tube of the thermometer stop moving. Read the scale line that is closest to the top of the liquid in the tube. The thermometer shown reads 21°C (about 70°F).

Using a

Balance

A balance is used to measure mass. Mass is the amount of matter in an object. To find the mass of an object, place the object in the left pan of the balance. Place standard masses in the right pan.

Measure the Mass of a Ball

1. Check that the empty pans are balanced, or level with each other. The pointer at the base should be on the middle mark. If it needs to be adjusted, move the slider on the back of the balance a little to the left or right.

2. Place a ball on the left pan. Notice that the pointer moves and that the pans are no longer level with each other. Then add standard masses, one

at a time, to the right pan. When the pointer is at the middle mark again, the pans are balanced. Each pan is holding the same amount of matter, and the same mass.

3. Each standard mass is marked to show its number of grams. Add the number of grams marked on the masses in the pan. The total is the mass of the ball in grams.

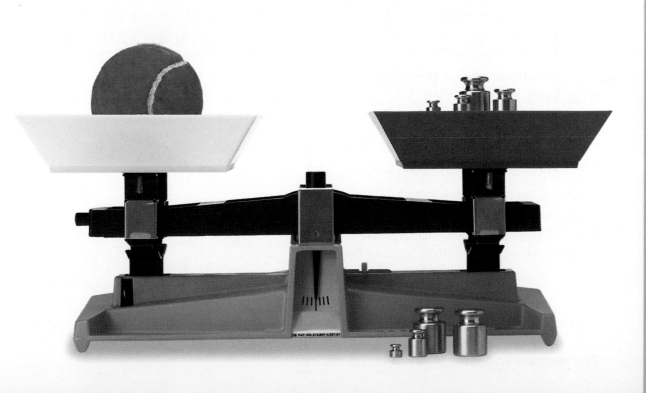

Using an Equation or Formula

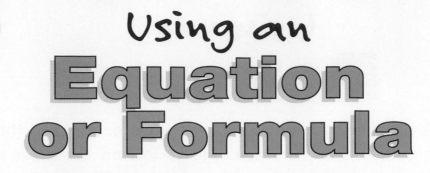

Equations and formulas can help you to determine measurements that are not easily made.

Use the Diameter of a Circle to Find Its Circumference

Find the circumference of a circle that has a diameter of 10 cm. To determine the circumference of a circle, use the formula below.

$$C = \pi d$$

$$C = 3.14 \times 10$$

$$C = 31.4 \text{ cm}$$

> π is the symbol for pi. Always use 3.14 as the value for π, unless another value for pi is given.

The circumference of this circle is 31.4 cm.

> The circumference (*C*) is a measure of the distance around a circle.

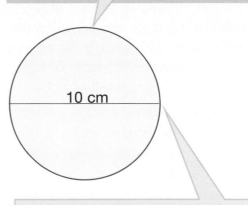

10 cm

> The diameter (*d*) of a circle is a line segment that passes through the center of the circle and connects two points on the circle.

Use Rate and Time to Determine Distance

Suppose an aircraft travels at 772 km/h for 2.5 hours. How many kilometers does the aircraft travel during that time? To determine distance traveled, use the distance formula below.

$$d = rt$$

$$d = 772 \times 2.5$$

$$d = 1{,}930 \text{ km}$$

> *d* = distance
> *r* = rate, or the speed at which the aircraft is traveling.
> *t* = the length of time traveled

The aircraft travels 1,930 km in 2.5 hours.

Making a

Chart to Organize Data

A chart can help you record, compare,
or classify information.

Organize Properties of Elements

Suppose you collected the data shown at the right. The data presents properties of silver, gold, lead, and iron.

You could organize this information in a chart by classifying the physical properties of each element.

My Data

Silver (Ag) has a density of 10.5 g/cm³. It melts at 961°C and boils at 2,212°C. It is used in dentistry and to make jewelry and electronic conductors.

Gold melts at 1,064°C and boils at 2,966°C. Its chemical symbol is Au. It has a density of 19.3 g/cm³ and is used for jewelry, in coins, and in dentistry.

The melting point of lead (Pb) is 328°C. The boiling point is 1,740°C. It has a density of 11.3 g/cm³. Some uses for lead are in storage batteries, paints, and dyes.

Iron (Fe) has a density of 7.9 g/cm³. It will melt at 1,535°C and boil at 3,000°C. It is used for building materials, in manufacturing, and as a dietary supplement.

> Create categories that describe the information you have found.

> Give the chart a title that describes what is listed in it.

Properties of Some Elements

Element	Symbol	Density g/cm³	Melting Point (°C)	Boiling Point (°C)	Some Uses
Silver	Ag	10.5	961	2,212	jewelry, dentistry, electric conductors
Gold	Au	19.3	1,064	2,966	jewelry, dentistry, coins
Lead	Pb	11.3	328	1,740	storage batteries, paints, dyes
Iron	Fe	7.9	1,535	3,000	building materials, manufacturing, dietary supplement

> Make sure the information is listed accurately in each column.

Reading a Circle Graph

A circle graph shows the whole divided into parts. You can use a circle graph to compare parts to each other or to compare parts to the whole.

Read a Circle Graph of Land Area

The whole circle represents the approximate land area of all of the continents on Earth. The number on each wedge indicates the land area of each continent. From the graph you can determine that altogether the land area of the continents is 148,000,000 square kilometers.

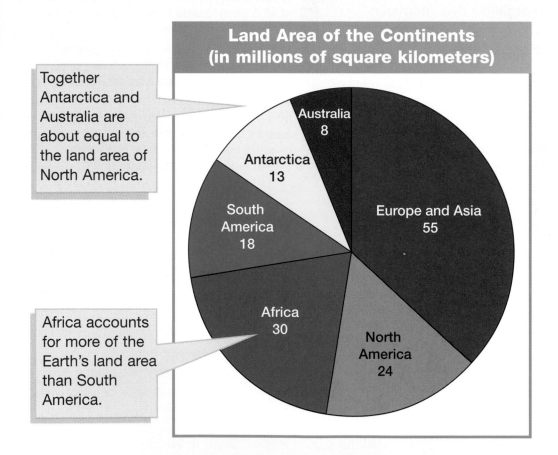

Land Area of the Continents (in millions of square kilometers)

Together Antarctica and Australia are about equal to the land area of North America.

Africa accounts for more of the Earth's land area than South America.

Australia
8

Antarctica
13

South America
18

Europe and Asia
55

Africa
30

North America
24

Making a Line Graph

A line graph is a way to show continuous change over time. You can use the information from a table to make a line graph.

Make a Line Graph of Temperatures

The table shows temperature readings over a 12-hour period at the Dallas–Fort Worth Airport in Texas. This data can also be displayed in a line graph that shows temperature change over time.

Dallas–Fort Worth Airport Temperature	
Hour	Temp. (°C)
6 A.M.	22
7 A.M.	24
8 A.M.	25
9 A.M.	26
10 A.M.	27
11 A.M.	29
12 NOON	31
1 P.M.	32
2 P.M.	33
3 P.M.	34
4 P.M.	35
5 P.M.	35
6 P.M.	34

1. Choose a title. The title should help a reader understand what your graph describes.

2. Choose a scale and mark equal intervals. The vertical scale should include the least value and the greatest value in the set of data.

3. Label the horizontal axis *Time* and the vertical axis *Temperature (°C)*.

4. Write the hours on the horizontal axis. Space the hours equally.

5. Carefully graph the data. Depending on the interval you choose, some temperatures will be between two numbers.

6. Check each step of your work.

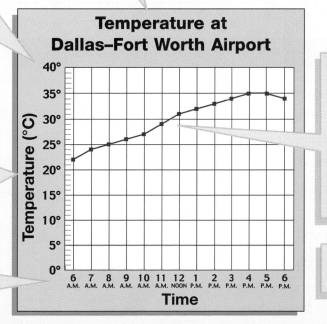

Temperature at Dallas–Fort Worth Airport

Measuring Elapsed Time

Sometimes you may need to find out how much time has passed, or elapsed. A clock is often used to find elapsed time. You can also change units and add or subtract to find out how much time has passed.

Using a Clock to Find Elapsed Minutes

You need to time an experiment for 20 minutes. It is 1:30.

Minutes

Start at 1:30. Count ahead 20 minutes, by fives to 1:50. Stop the experiment at 1:50.

20 minutes

15

10

5

Using a Clock or Stopwatch to Find Elapsed Seconds

60 seconds = 1 minute

You need to time an experiment for 15 seconds. You can use a second hand on a clock. You can also use a stopwatch to figure out elapsed seconds.

Seconds

Wait until the second hand is on a number. Then start the experiment.

Stop the experiment when 15 seconds have passed.

15 seconds

10

5

Press the reset button on the stopwatch so you see 0:00₀₀.

Press the start button to begin.

When you see 0:15₀₀, press the stop button on the watch.

Changing Units and Then Adding or Subtracting to Find Elapsed Time

If you know how to change units of time, you can use addition and subtraction to find elapsed time.

To change from a larger unit to a smaller unit, multiply.

$$2 \text{ d} = \blacksquare \text{ h}$$
$$2 \times 24 = 48$$
$$2 \text{ d} = 48 \text{ h}$$

Units of Time

60 seconds (s) = 1 minute (min)

60 minutes = 1 hour (h)

24 hours = 1 day (d)

7 days = 1 week (wk)

52 weeks = 1 year (yr)

To change from a smaller unit to a larger unit, divide.

$$78 \text{ wk} = \blacksquare \text{ yr}$$
$$78 \div 52 = 1\tfrac{1}{2}$$
$$78 \text{ wk} = 1\tfrac{1}{2} \text{ yr}$$

Another Example

Suppose it took juice in an ice-pop mold from 6:40 A.M. until 10:15 A.M. to freeze. How long did it take for the juice to freeze? To find out, subtract.

	9 h	75 min
	~~10 h~~	~~15 min~~
−	6 h	40 min
	3 h	35 min

Rename 10 h 15 min as 9 h 75 min, since 1 h = 60 min.

You can also add to find elapsed time.

	3 h	30 min	14 s
+	1 h	40 min	45 s
	4 h	70 min	59 s = 5 h 10 min 59 s

MEASUREMENTS

Volume
1 L of sports drink is a little more than 1 qt.

Area
A basketball court covers about 4,700 ft². It covers about 435 m².

Mass and Weight
A basketball has a mass of about 650 g. It weighs about 1½ lb.

Metric Measures

Temperature
Ice melts at 0 degrees Celsius (°C)
Water freezes at 0°C
Water boils at 100°C

Length and Distance
1,000 meters (m) = 1 kilometer (km)
100 centimeters (cm) = 1 m
10 millimeters (mm) = 1 cm

Force
1 newton (N) =
   1 kilogram x meter/second/second
   (kg x m/s²)

Volume
1 cubic meter (m³) = 1 m x 1 m x 1 m
1 cubic centimeter (cm³) =
   1 cm x 1 cm x 1 cm
1 liter (L) = 1,000 milliliters (mL)
1 cm³ = 1 mL

Area
1 square kilometer (km²) = 1 km x 1 km
1 hectare = 10,000 m²

Mass
1,000 grams (g) = 1 kilogram (kg)
1,000 milligrams (mg) = 1 g

Temperature
The temperature at an indoor basketball game might be 25°C, which is 77°F.

Length/ Distance
A basketball rim is about 10 ft high, or a little more than 3 m from the floor.

Customary Measures

Temperature
Ice melts at 32 degrees Fahrenheit (°F)
Water freezes at 32°F
Water boils at 212°F

Length and Distance
12 inches (in.) = 1 foot (ft)
3 ft = 1 yard (yd)
5,280 ft = 1 mile (mi)

Weight
16 ounces (oz) = 1 pound (lb)
2,000 pounds = 1 ton (T)

Volume of Fluids
8 fluid ounces (fl oz) = 1 cup (c)
2 c = 1 pint (pt)
2 pt = 1 quart (qt)
4 qt = 1 gallon (gal)

Metric and Customary Rates
km/h = kilometers per hour
m/s = meters per second
mph = miles per hour

GLOSSARY

Pronunciation Key

Symbol	Key Words
a	c**a**t
ā	**a**pe
ä	c**o**t, c**a**r
e	t**e**n, b**e**rry
ē	m**e**
i	f**i**t, h**e**re
ī	**i**ce, f**i**re
ō	g**o**
ô	f**a**ll, f**o**r
oi	**oi**l
o͞o	l**oo**k, p**u**ll
o͞o	t**oo**l, r**u**le
ou	**ou**t, cr**ow**d
u	**u**p
ʉ	f**u**r, sh**i**rt
ə	**a** in **a**go
	e in ag**e**nt
	i in penc**i**l
	o in at**o**m
	u in circ**u**s
b	**b**ed
d	**d**og
f	**f**all

Symbol	Key Words
g	**g**et
h	**h**elp
j	**j**ump
k	**k**iss, **c**all
l	**l**eg
m	**m**eat
n	**n**ose
p	**p**ut
r	**r**ed
s	**s**ee
t	**t**op
v	**v**at
w	**w**ish
y	**y**ard
z	**z**ebra
ch	**ch**in, ar**ch**
ŋ	ri**ng**, dri**n**k
sh	**sh**e, pu**sh**
th	**th**in, tru**th**
th	**th**en, fa**th**er
zh	mea**s**ure

A heavy stress mark (′) is placed after a syllable that gets a heavy, or primary, stress, as in **picture** (pik′chər).

absolute magnitude (ab'sə lo͞ot mag'nə to͞od) The measure of a star's brightness, based on the amount of light it actually gives off. (B61) The Sun's *absolute magnitude* is less than that of many other stars.

acid (as'id) A compound that turns blue litmus paper to red and forms a salt when it reacts with a base. (C81) *Acids* have a sour taste.

adult (ə dult') The final stage of an organism's life cycle. (A74) A butterfly is the *adult* form of a caterpillar.

air (er) The invisible, odorless, and tasteless mixture of gases that surrounds Earth. (E10) *Air* consists mainly of the gases nitrogen and oxygen.

air mass (er mas) A large body of air that has about the same temperature, air pressure, and moisture throughout. (E62) When warm and cold *air masses* meet, the weather changes.

air pressure (er presh'ər) The push of the air in all directions against its surroundings. (E31) You can see the effect of *air pressure* when you blow up a balloon.

air sacs (er saks) Thin-walled chambers in the lung through which oxygen moves into the blood. (A49) Each lung contains millions of *air sacs*.

alloy (al'oi) A solution of two or more metals, which has properties of its own. (C59) Pewter is an *alloy* of tin and other metals such as copper and lead.

anemometer (an ə môm'ət ər) A device used to measure the speed of the wind. (E39) The *anemometer* showed that the wind was blowing at 33 km/h.

apparent magnitude (ə per'ənt mag'nə to͞od) The measure of a star's brightness as seen from Earth. (B60) A star's *apparent magnitude* depends on the amount of light it gives off and on its distance from Earth.

aqueduct (ak'wə dukt) A system of channels, pipes, tunnels, and pumps that carries water from a distant source. (D37) Without water carried by an *aqueduct*, cities like Los Angeles could not exist.

aquifer (ak'wə fər) An underground layer of rock or soil through which water flows easily and in which water collects. (D14) Water pumped from a well may come from an *aquifer*.

arteries (art′ər ēz) Blood vessels that carry blood away from the heart. (A57) *Arteries* have thick, muscular walls.

atmosphere (at′məs fir) The blanket of air that surrounds Earth, reaching to about 700 km above the surface. (E12) Earth's *atmosphere* makes it possible for life to exist on the planet.

atom (at′əm) The smallest particle of an element that has the chemical properties of that element. (C35) Water is a combination of one *atom* of oxygen with two atoms of hydrogen.

atomic number (ə täm′ik num′bər) The number of protons in the nucleus of an atom. (C73) The *atomic number* of oxygen is 8.

axis (ak′sis) An imaginary straight line from the North Pole, through Earth's center, to the South Pole. (B13, E78) Earth makes one complete turn on its *axis* in about 24 hours.

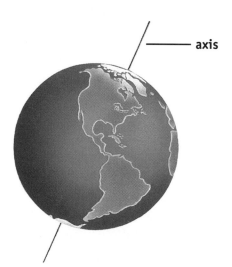

axis

barometer (bə räm′ət ər) A device used to measure air pressure. (E30) Scientists use a *barometer* to gather information about the weather.

base (bās) A compound that turns red litmus paper blue and that forms a salt when it reacts with an acid. (C81) *Bases* have a slippery feel.

big-bang theory (big′ baŋ thē′ə rē) A hypothesis, supported by data, that describes how the universe began with a huge explosion. (B39) The *big-bang theory* holds that everything in the universe was once concentrated at one tiny point.

black dwarf (blak dwarf) The cool, dark body that is the final stage in the life cycle of a low-mass star. (B65) When the Sun dies, it will become a *black dwarf*.

black hole (blak hōl) An extremely dense, invisible object in space whose gravity is so great that not even light can escape it. (B67) Scientists think that the remains of a very massive star can collapse following a supernova explosion to form a *black hole*.

blood (blud) A tissue made up of a liquid called plasma and several types of cells. (A56) *Blood* carries oxygen and nutrients to body cells.

blood vessels (blud ves'əlz) A vast network of tubes carrying blood through the body. (A56) The three main kinds of *blood vessels* are the veins, arteries, and tiny capillaries.

bronchial tubes (brän'kē əl toobz) Tubes that carry air from the trachea to the lungs. (A48) Air flows to and from the lungs through the *bronchial tubes*.

capillaries (kap'ə ler ēz) Tiny blood vessels that connect the smallest arteries with the smallest veins. (A57) Nutrients pass through the walls of the *capillaries* into the cells.

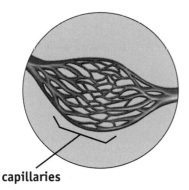

capillaries

carbon dioxide (kär'bən dī äks'īd) A colorless, odorless gas. (E10) Plants use *carbon dioxide* from the air in the process of making food.

cell (sel) The basic unit of structure of all living things. (A11) Even though plant *cells* can be of different sizes, they have many of the same structures in common.

cell membrane (sel mem'brān) A thin layer that surrounds all cells and allows water and dissolved materials to pass into and out of the cell. (A13) In plant cells, the *cell membrane* lies inside the cell wall.

cell respiration (sel res pə rā'shən) The process of using oxygen to release energy from food. (A23) Animals and plants release carbon dioxide as a waste product of *cell respiration*.

cell wall (sel wôl) The tough outer covering of a plant cell that gives the cell its rigid shape. (A13) A *cell wall* is not found in animal cells.

chemical change (kem'i kəl chānj) A change in matter that results in one or more new substances with new properties. (C69) A *chemical change* occurs when wood burns and forms gases and ash.

chemical formula (kem'i kəl fôr'myoo lə) A group of symbols and numbers that show the elements that make up a compound. (C40) The *chemical formula* for water is H_2O.

chemical property (kem'i kəl präp'ər tē) Characteristic of matter that describes how it changes when it reacts with other matter. (C34) The ability to burn is a *chemical property* of paper.

chemical symbol (kem′i kəl sim′bəl) One or two letters used to stand for the name of an element. (C36) Ca is the *chemical symbol* for calcium.

chloroplast (klôr′ə plast) A structure in plant cells that captures light energy that is used in the food-making process. (A13) *Chloroplasts* are located within cells in the leaves of a plant.

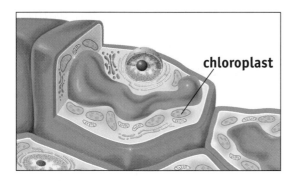

chloroplast

circulatory system (sur′kyo͞o lə tôr ē sis′təm) The transport system of the body that carries oxygen and nutrients to all cells and then removes wastes. (A56) Blood is part of the *circulatory system*.

cirrus cloud (sir′əs kloud) A thin, feathery cloud made up of ice crystals high in the sky. (E57) *Cirrus clouds* often look like wisps of hair.

climate (klī′mət) The average weather conditions of an area over a long period of time. (D52, E84) Some regions have a hot, rainy *climate*.

cloud (kloud) A mass of tiny droplets of water that condensed from the air. (E46) A dark *cloud* blocked the sunlight.

cold front (kōld frunt) The leading edge of a cold air mass that forms as the cold air mass moves into a warm air mass. (E62) Thunderstorms often occur along a *cold front*.

comet (käm′it) A small object in space, made of ice, dust, gas, and rock, that orbits a star and that can form a gaseous tail. (B24) A *comet* begins to melt and to glow as it approaches the Sun.

complete metamorphosis (kəm-plēt′ met ə môr′fə sis) The development of an organism through four stages—egg, larva, pupa, and adult. (A74) The life cycle of a butterfly is an example of *complete metamorphosis*.

compound (käm′pound) A substance made up of two or more elements that are chemically combined. (C34) Water, made of the elements hydrogen and oxygen, is an example of a *compound*.

condensation (kän dən sā'shən)
The change of state from a gas to a liquid. (C28, D19) The *condensation* of water vapor can form droplets of water on the outside of a cold glass.

condense (kən dens') To change from a gas to a liquid. (E46) Water vapor from the air *condenses* on a cold window.

conifer (kän'ə fər) A tree or shrub that bears its seeds in cones. (A91) The cones of each species of *conifer* are distinct and different from each other.

conservation (kän sər vā'shən) The wise use of Earth's natural resources. (D48) Taking shorter showers and using drip hoses to water lawns are examples of *conservation*.

constellation (kän stə lā'shən) A group of stars that form a fixed pattern in the night sky. (B10) The *constellation* known as the Little Dipper contains the North Star.

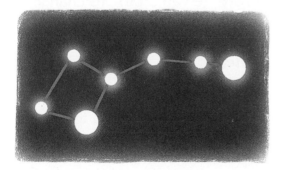

controlled experiment (kən trōld' ek sper'ə mənt) A test of a hypothesis in which the setups are identical in all ways except one. (S7) In the *controlled experiment*, only one of the four beakers of water contained salt.

controlled variable (kən trōld' ver'ē ə bəl) A factor that is kept constant, or identical, in all setups during an experiment. (D27) In an experiment that determines the effect of fertilizers on plants, the type of plant is a *controlled variable*.

cumulus cloud (kyōō'myōō ləs kloud) A large puffy cloud. (E55) White *cumulus clouds* can often be seen in an otherwise clear summer sky.

cytoplasm (sīt'ō plaz əm) The jelly-like substance that fills much of the cell. (A13) The nucleus, vacuoles, and many other structures inside a cell float in the *cytoplasm*.

density (den'sə tē) The amount of mass in a given volume of matter. (C13) Lead has a greater *density* than aluminum.

dependent variable (dē pen'dənt ver'ē ə bəl) The factor in an experiment that is observed to determine any effect of the independent variable. (D27) In an experiment to determine the effects of temperature on seed germination, the *dependent variable* is seed development time.

diaphragm (dī'ə fram) The dome-shaped muscle that separates the chest from the stomach area. (A46) When you breathe in, the *diaphragm* moves down, and air rushes into the lungs.

digestive system (di jes′tiv sis′təm) The organ system in which food is broken down into a form that body cells can use. (A38) Many medicines treat disorders of the *digestive system.*

disinfect (dis in fekt′) To kill bacteria or other harmful microorganisms. (D57) Chlorine and other chemicals are used to *disinfect* water in a water treatment plant.

donor (dō′nər) A person who gives blood for a blood transfusion. (A58) Blood banks depend on *donors* to provide blood for transfusions.

egg (eg) The first stage in an organism's life cycle. (A74) A baby bird hatches from an *egg.*

electron (ē lek′trän) A negatively charged particle in an atom. (C71) The number of *electrons* in an atom usually equals the number of protons in the nucleus of that atom.

element (el′ə mənt) A substance that cannot be broken down into any other substance by ordinary chemical means. (C34) Oxygen, hydrogen, copper, iron, and carbon are *elements.*

El Niño (el nēn′yō) A periodic warming of water in the Pacific Ocean which can cause severe storms. (D53) During the late 1990s, *El Niño* caused many unusual weather patterns in North America.

embryo (em′brē ō) An organism in its earliest stages of development; in most plants it is found inside a seed. (A85) When conditions for growth are suitable, the *embryo* inside the seed develops into a young plant.

enzymes (en′zīmz) Chemicals that help break down food. (A39) Digestive *enzymes* in the stomach break down food into smaller particles.

equator (ē kwāt′ər) An imaginary line circling the middle of Earth, halfway between the North Pole and the South Pole. (E78) On a globe, the *equator* divides Earth into the Northern Hemisphere and the Southern Hemisphere.

esophagus (i säf′ə gəs) The muscular tube that connects the mouth to the stomach. (A40) After food is swallowed, it travels through the *esophagus* to the stomach.

evaporate (ē vap′ə rāt) To change from a liquid to a gas. (E46) Some of the water boiling in the pot *evaporated.*

evaporation (ē vap ə rā′shən) The change of state from a liquid to a gas. (C27, D19) Heat from the Sun caused the *evaporation* of the water.

excretory system (eks′krə tôr ē sis′təm) The system responsible for ridding the body of harmful wastes produced by the cells. (A62) The kidneys, lungs, and skin are all organs of the *excretory system.*

extraterrestrial (eks trə tə res'trē əl) A being from outer space; any object from beyond Earth. (B88) It would be extraordinary for scientists to discover that there is *extraterrestrial* life.

fertilization (fʉrt″l ə zā'shən) The process by which a male sex cell joins with a female sex cell. (A84) In flowering plants, *fertilization* takes place in the pistil, and occurs after a pollen tube reaches the ovary.

flash flood (flash flud) A sudden, violent flood. (E67) Heavy rains caused *flash floods* as the stream overflowed.

fog (fôg) A cloud that touches Earth's surface. (E46) Traffic accidents often increase where *fog* is heavy because visibility is decreased.

free fall (frē fôl) The motion of a freely falling object, such as that of a spacecraft in orbit around Earth. (B79) Astronauts experiencing *free fall* in space feel weightless.

freezing (frēz'iŋ) The change of state from a liquid to a solid. (C28) The *freezing* of water occurs at a temperature of 0°C.

front (frunt) The place where two air masses meet. (E62) Forecasters watch the movement of *fronts* to help predict the weather.

fruit (fro͞ot) The enlarged ovary of a flower that protects the developing seeds. (A85) Some *fruits*, such as peaches, plums, and mangoes, contain only one large seed.

galaxy (gal'ək sē) A vast group of billions of stars that are held together by gravity. (B70) The Milky Way is a typical spiral *galaxy*.

gas giant (gas jī'ənt) A large planet that is made up mostly of gaseous and liquid substances, with little or no solid surface. (B47) Jupiter is a *gas giant*.

geocentric model (jē ō sen'trik mäd″l) A representation of the universe in which stars and planets revolve around Earth. (B37) Ptolemy proposed a *geocentric model* of the universe.

germination (jʉr mə nā'shən) The sprouting of a seed. (A86) After *germination*, an acorn begins to form a seedling, or tiny young plant.

greenhouse effect (grēn'hous e fekt') The process by which heat from the Sun builds up near Earth's surface and is trapped by the atmosphere. (E15) Some scientists fear that air pollution may increase the *greenhouse effect* and raise temperatures on Earth.

ground water (ground wô t'ər) Earth's underground water supply. (D10) If you dig deep enough into the ground, you will probably reach *ground water*.

H

heart (härt) The pump that pushes blood throughout the entire circulatory system. (A56) The human *heart* normally beats about 70 to 80 times per minute.

heat (hēt) Energy that flows from warmer to cooler regions of matter. (C26) *Heat* can cause matter to change from one state to another.

heliocentric model (hē lē ō sen′trik mäd″l) A representation of the relationship between the Sun and planets of the solar system in which the planets revolve around the Sun. (B37) Copernicus hypothesized a *heliocentric model* of the solar system.

high-pressure area (hī presh′ər er′ē ə) An area of higher air pressure than that of the surrounding air. (E33) Winds move from *high-pressure areas* to low-pressure areas.

humidity (hyōō mid′ə tē) The amount of water vapor in the air. (E47) Tropical climates have warm temperatures and high *humidity*.

hurricane (hʉr′i kān) A large, violent storm accompanied by strong winds and, usually, heavy rain. (E70) The winds of the *hurricane* blew at over 125 km/h.

hypothesis (hī päth′ə sis) An idea about or explanation of how or why something happens. (S6) The *hypothesis* about the expanding universe has been supported by evidence.

I

ice age (īs āj) A period of time when glaciers covered much of Earth's land. (E89) During the last *ice age*, glaciers covered parts of North America.

independent variable (in′dē-pen′dənt ver′ē ə bəl) The factor that is changed, or varied, during an experiment. (D27) In an experiment to determine the effects of light on oxygen produced by plants, the *independent variable* is the amount of light.

indicator (in′di kāt ər) A substance that changes color when mixed with an acid or a base. (C81) Paper treated with an *indicator* is used to test whether a compound is an acid or a base.

ion (ī′ən) An electrically charged atom. (C73) *Ions* form when atoms lose or gain electrons. Sodium chloride is made up of sodium ions and chlorine ions.

irrigation (ir ə gā′shən) The process of supplying crops with water. (D29) *Irrigation* allows farmers to grow crops in even the driest of places.

kidneys (kid′nēz) A pair of organs that clean and filter the blood. (A63) The *kidneys* help remove excess water and salts from the blood.

kinetic energy (ki net′ik en′ər jē) Energy of motion. (C25) A ball rolling down a hill has *kinetic energy*.

large intestine (lärj in tes′tən) The organ that absorbs water and salts from undigested material. (A43) The major job of the *large intestine* is to absorb water from wastes and return it to the bloodstream.

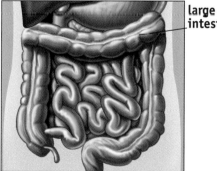

large intestine

larva (lär′və) The wormlike stage that follows the egg stage of an insect's life cycle. (A74) A caterpillar is the *larva* stage in the life cycle of a butterfly.

larynx (lar′iŋks) The part of the throat that is used in speaking. (A48) The *larynx* is another name for the voice box.

leaf (lēf) A plant part in which photosynthesis takes place. (A19) In a plant such as cabbage, it is the *leaf* that people eat.

life processes (līf prä′ses ēz) The functions that a living thing must carry out to stay alive and produce more of its own kind. (A11) Digestion is one of the essential *life processes*.

light-year (līt yir) A unit of measurement representing the distance that light travels in one year. (B61) The distance to stars is measured in *light-years*.

low-pressure area (lō presh′ər er′ē ə) An area of lower air pressure than that of the surrounding air. (E33) Storms are more likely to occur in *low-pressure areas*.

lungs (luŋz) Two spongy organs that expand when they fill with air. (A46) The *lungs* are the main organs of the respiratory system.

mass (mas) A measure of how much matter there is in an object. (C10) A large rock has more *mass* than a pebble.

matter (mat′ər) Anything that has mass and takes up space. (C10) Coal, water, and air are three kinds of *matter*.

melt (melt) To change state from a solid to a liquid. (C27) The icicles began to *melt*.

meteor (mēt′ē ər) A piece of rock or metal from space that enters Earth's atmosphere. (B25) A *meteor* is also called a shooting star.

meteorite (mēt′ē ər īt) The remaining material of a meteor that has landed on the ground. (B25) In 1902, scientists were able to examine the largest *meteorite* ever known to land in the United States.

microgravity (mī krō grav′i tē) The condition of very low gravity. (B84) Astronauts experience *microgravity* aboard the space shuttle.

Milky Way Galaxy (milk′ē wā gal′ək sē) A gigantic cluster of billions of stars that is home to our solar system. (B70) The Sun is located in one of the arms of the *Milky Way Galaxy*.

mitochondrion (mī tə kän′drē ən) The cell structure in which energy from food is released. (A13) Cell respiration occurs in the *mitochondrion*.

mixture (miks′chər) A combination of two or more substances that can be separated by physical means. (C34) This jar contains a *mixture* of colored beads.

model (mäd′′l) Something used or made to represent an object or to describe how a process takes place. (C71) The plastic *model* showed the structure of the heart.

molecule (mäl′i kyo̅o̅l) A particle made up of a group of atoms that are chemically bonded. (C39) A *molecule* of water contains two hydrogen atoms and one oxygen atom.

moon (mo̅o̅n) A natural object that revolves around a planet. (B44) The planet Mars has two known *moons*.

nebula (neb′yə lə) A huge cloud of gas and dust found in space. (B64) A *nebula* can form from a supernova.

neutralization (no̅o̅ trə lī zā′shən) The reaction between an acid and a base. (C83) *Neutralization* produces water and a salt.

neutron (no̅o̅′trän) A particle in the nucleus of an atom that has no electric charge. (C71) The mass of a *neutron* is about equal to the mass of a proton.

neutron star (nōō′trän stär) The remains of a massive star that has exploded in a supernova. (B67) A typical *neutron star* is less than 20 km in diameter.

nitrogen (nī′trə jən) A colorless, odorless, tasteless gas that makes up about four fifths of the air. (E10) *Nitrogen* is used by plants for growth.

Northern Hemisphere (nôr′thərn hem′i sfir) The half of Earth north of the equator. (E79) Canada is in the *Northern Hemisphere*.

nuclear fission (nōō′klē ər fish′ən) The splitting of the nucleus of an atom. (C77) Bombarding a nucleus with neutrons can cause *nuclear fission*.

nucleus (nōō′klē əs) 1. The cell structure that controls all of a cell's activities. (A13) The *nucleus* was clearly visible after the cell was stained. 2. The central part of an atom, made up of protons and neutrons. (C71) The *nucleus* of a helium atom contains two protons and two neutrons.

nutrients (nōō′trē ənts) Substances that are needed for an organism to live and grow. (A11) Proteins, carbohydrates, and fats are *nutrients* found in food.

organ (ôr′gən) Different types of tissue working together to perform a certain function. (A12) The lungs are *organs* of the human body.

organ system (ôr′gən sis′təm) Groups of organs working together. (A12) The digestive system is an *organ system* that includes the stomach, small intestine, and large intestine.

oxygen (äks′i jən) A colorless, odorless, tasteless gas that makes up about one fifth of the air. (E10) *Oxygen* is essential to life.

peristalsis (per ə stal′sis) A wavelike motion that moves food through the digestive system. (A41) Swallowed food is moved through the esophagus to the stomach by means of *peristalsis*.

permeable (pur′mē ə bəl) A description of soil through which water can flow easily. (D13) Gravel is the most *permeable* type of soil.

photosynthesis (fōt ō sin′thə sis) The process by which producers, such as plants, make their own food by using energy from the Sun. (A19) *Photosynthesis* takes place primarily in the leaves of plants.

physical change (fiz′i kəl chānj) A change in which the size, shape, or state of matter changes but no new substances are formed. (C68) Cutting an apple in half and freezing water into ice are examples of *physical change*.

physical property (fiz′i kəl präp′ər tē) A characteristic of matter that can be detected or measured with the senses. (C34) A *physical property* of a ball is its round shape.

pistil (pis′til) The female part of the flower. (A84) Pollen grains stick to the stigma, which is at the tip of the *pistil*.

planet (plan′it) A large body in space that orbits a star and does not produce light on its own. (B17) Saturn is one of nine known *planets* that revolve around the Sun.

polar climate (pō′lər klī′mət) A very cold climate that does not receive much energy from the Sun. (E85) The Arctic has a *polar climate*.

pollen grain (pal′ən grān) A structure produced in the male part of a flower and which contains the male sex cell. (A85) The *pollen grains* of a flower must be carried from the stamen to the pistil in order for seeds to be formed.

pollination (päl ə nā′shən) The transfer of pollen grains to the pistil of a flower. (A85) Bees often help in the process of *pollination*.

polymer (päl′ə mər) An organic compound consisting of large molecules formed from many smaller, linked molecules. (C90) Proteins are *polymers*.

porous (pôr′əs) A description of soil in which there are many pores between particles. (D13) Water soaks easily into most *porous* soils.

potable water (pōt′ə bəl) Water fit for drinking. (D57) Water purification plants make water from a reservoir *potable*.

precipitation (prē sip ə tā′shən) Any form of water that falls from clouds to Earth's surface. (D19, E46) Rain, snow, and hail are forms of *precipitation*.

proton (prō′tän) A positively charged particle found in the nucleus of an atom. (C71) The atomic number of an atom equals the number of *protons* in the atom's nucleus.

protostar (prōt′ō stär) A concentration of matter found in space that is the beginning of a star. (B64) When the temperature inside a *protostar* becomes high enough, nuclear reactions begin and the protostar turns into a star.

pulse (puls) The throbbing caused by blood rushing into the arteries when the lower chambers of the heart contract. (A57) A doctor takes the *pulse* of a patient by feeling an artery in the patient's wrist.

pupa (pyo͞o′pə) The stage in a life cycle between the larva and the adult. (A74) The cocoon is the *pupa* stage in the life cycle of a moth.

radioactive element (rā dē ō ak'tiv el'ə mənt) An element made up of atoms whose nuclei break down, or decay, into nuclei of other atoms. (C76) As the nucleus of a *radioactive element* decays, energy and particles are released.

radio telescope (rā' dē ō tel'ə skōp) A gigantic antenna on Earth designed to receive radio signals from space. (B90) *Radio telescopes* are important tools for studying distant stars and galaxies.

rain gauge (rān gāj) A device for measuring precipitation. (E47) The *rain gauge* at the weather station showed that 2 cm of rain had fallen in a 24-hour period.

recipient (ri sip'ē ənt) A person who receives blood in a blood transfusion. (A58) An accident victim is often the *recipient* of transfused blood.

red giant (red jī'ənt) A very large old reddish star that has greatly expanded and cooled as its fuel has begun to run out. (B65) As the Sun reaches old age, it will turn into a *red giant*.

reflecting telescope (ri flekt'iŋ tel'ə skōp) An instrument for viewing distant objects that uses a curved mirror at the back of its tube to gather light and produce an image. (B22) This observatory uses a *reflecting telescope* to observe faraway galaxies.

refracting telescope (ri frakt'iŋ tel'ə skōp) An instrument for viewing distant objects that uses two lenses to gather light and produce an image. (B21) The *refracting telescope* allowed the astronomer a closer look at the Moon and the planets.

relative humidity (rel'ə tiv hyōō mid'ə tē) The amount of water vapor present in the air at a given temperature compared to the maximum amount that the air could hold at that temperature. (E47) A *relative humidity* of 95 percent on a warm day can make you feel sticky and uncomfortable.

reservoir (rez'ər vwär) A place where water is collected and stored. (D36) It is very important for *reservoirs* to be protected from pollution.

respiratory system (res'pər ə tôr ē sis'təm) The body parts that work together to take air into the body and push it back out. (A46) The lungs are the central organs in the *respiratory system*.

revolution (rev ə lōō'shən) The movement of an object around another object or point. (B13) It takes about 365 days for Earth to make one *revolution* around the Sun.

root (rōōt) The underground part of a plant that anchors the plant and absorbs water and nutrients. (A16) Carrots and turnips have one large *root*.

rotation (rō tā'shən) The spinning motion of an object on its axis. (B13) It takes about 24 hours for Earth to make one complete *rotation*.

runoff (run'ôf) Rainfall that is not absorbed by soil. (D15) *Runoff* from roadways can carry pollutants into the ground water.

saliva (sə lī'və) The watery liquid in the mouth that begins the chemical breakdown of food. (A38) For most people, just the thought of food, as well as its odor and taste, will cause *saliva* to flow into the mouth.

salt (sôlt) A compound that can be formed when an acid reacts with a base. (C83) When vinegar and baking soda interact, they produce a *salt* and water.

satellite (sat''l īt) A natural or human-built object that revolves around another object in space. (B44) The Moon is a natural *satellite* of Earth.

sexual reproduction (sek'sho͞o əl rē'prə duk'shən) The production of offspring that occurs when a male sex cell joins a female sex cell. (A84) The *sexual reproduction* of flowers is greatly aided by insects.

small intestine (smôl in tes'tən) The long coiled organ where most digestion takes place. (A42) The *small intestine* is about 6 m (20 ft) long.

solar system (sō'lər sis'təm) The Sun and the planets and other objects that orbit the Sun. Also, any star and the objects that revolve around it. (B34) Our *solar system* consists of the Sun, nine known planets, and many smaller objects.

solute (säl'yo͞ot) The material present in the smaller amount in a solution; the substance dissolved in a solution. (C57, D28) If you dissolve sugar in water, sugar is the *solute*.

solution (se lo͞o'shən) A mixture in which the different particles are spread evenly throughout the mixture. (C57, D28) Dissolving salt in water makes a saltwater *solution*.

solvent (säl'vənt) The material present in the greater amount in a solution; the substance in a solution, usually a liquid, that dissolves another substance. (C57, D28) If you mix sugar and water, water is the *solvent* because it dissolves the sugar.

Southern Hemisphere (suth'ərn hem'i sfir) The half of Earth south of the equator. (E79) The island continent Australia is in the *Southern Hemisphere*.

stamen (stā'mən) The male reproductive structure of a flower. (A84) Pollen grains are produced in the *stamen* of a flower.

star (stär) A huge globe of hot gases that shines by its own light. (B17) Many *stars* may have systems of planets around them.

state of matter (stāt uv mat'ər) Any of the three forms that matter may take: solid, liquid, or gas. (C20) Water's *state of matter* depends on its temperature.

stem (stem) The part of a plant that supports the leaves and flowers and carries water to those parts. (A18) The trunk of a fully grown maple tree is a large woody *stem*.

stomach (stum'ək) The muscular organ that stores food and helps digest it. (A41) The *stomach* squeezes and churns food into a souplike mixture called chyme.

stratus cloud (strāt'əs kloud) A low, flat cloud that often brings drizzle. (E55) Large sheets of very dark *stratus clouds* covered the sky on the rainy morning.

substance (sub'stəns) Matter that always has the same makeup and properties, wherever it may be found. (C34) Elements—such as gold, silver, and uranium—and compounds—such as water, sugar, and salt are *substances*.

supernova (soo'pər nō və) An exploding star. (B66) When a massive red giant star uses up all its fuel, it collapses and explodes in a *supernova*.

sweat glands (swet glandz) Small coiled tubes that end at pores on the skin's surface. (A64) By producing sweat, *sweat glands* help to adjust the temperature of the body.

temperate climate (tem'pər it klī'mət) A climate that generally has warm, dry summers and cold, wet winters. (E85) Most regions of the United States have a *temperate climate*.

temperature (tem'pər ə chər) A measure of the average kinetic energy of the particles in matter. (C26) Water *temperature* rises as the motion of water molecules increases.

terrestrial planet (tə res'trē əl plan'it) An object in space that resembles Earth in size, in density, and in its mainly rocky composition. (B44) Mars is a *terrestrial planet*.

theory (thē'ə rē) A hypothesis that is supported by a lot of evidence and is widely accepted by scientists. (S9) The big-bang *theory* offers an explanation for the origin of the universe.

thunderstorm (thun'dər stôrm) A storm that produces lightning and thunder and often heavy rain and strong winds. (E66) When the weather is ʰ hot, and humid, *thunderstormᵚ* likely to develop.

tissue (tish′o͞o) Similar cells working together. (A12) Muscle *tissue* contains cells that contract.

tornado (tôr nā′dō) A violent, funnel-shaped storm of spinning wind. (E72) The wind speed at the center of a *tornado* can be twice that of hurricane winds.

trachea (trā′kē ə) The air tube that joins the throat to the lungs. (A46) Choking occurs when an object becomes stuck in the *trachea*.

transpiration (tran spə ra′shən) The process in which a plant releases moisture through small openings in its leaves. (D19) During *transpiration*, plants release water vapor into the atmosphere.

tropical climate (träp′i kəl klī′mət) A hot, rainy climate. (E85) Areas that are near the equator have a *tropical climate* because they receive the greatest amount of energy from the Sun.

tropism (trō′piz əm) A growth response of a plant to conditions in the environment, such as light or water. (A24) Growing toward a light source is an example of a plant *tropism*.

troposphere (trō′pō sfir) The layer of the atmosphere closest to the surface of Earth. (E12) The *troposphere* reaches about 11 km above the surface of Earth and is the layer of the atmosphere in which weather occurs.

universe (yo͞on′ə vʉrs) The sum of everything that exists. (B38) Our solar system is part of the *universe*.

urine (yor′in) The yellowish liquid containing wastes and water from the filtering units of the kidneys. (A63) A doctor may test a sample of *urine* to check a patient's health.

vacuole (vak′yo͞o ōl) A cell part that stores water and nutrients. (A13) Some plant cells have large *vacuoles*.

variable (ver′ē ə bəl) The one difference in the setups of a controlled experiment; provides a comparison for testing a hypothesis. (S7) The *variable* in an experiment with plants was the amount of water given each plant.

veins (vānz) Blood vessels that carry blood from the capillaries to the heart. (A57) The walls of *veins* are thinner than those of arteries.

vertebrate (vʉr′tə brit) An animal with a backbone. (A76) *Vertebrates* are the large group of living things that includes mammals, fish, birds, reptiles, and amphibians.

villi (vil′ī) Looplike structures in the wall of the small intestine in which nutrients are passed from the small intestine into the blood. (A43) The *villi* release mucus as well as absorb nutrients in the small intestine.

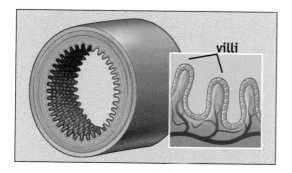

volume (väl′yōōm) The amount of space that matter takes up. (C11) A large fuel tank holds a greater *volume* of gasoline than a small tank.

warm front (wôrm frunt) The leading edge of a warm air mass that forms as the warm air mass moves forward into a cold air mass. (E63) Light rain often falls along a *warm front*.

waste water (wāst wôt′ ər) Water that living things have used. (D56) *Waste water* can be reused if it is treated.

water cycle (wôt′ər sī′kəl) The movement of water into the air as water vapor and back to Earth's surface as rain, snow, or hail. (D18, E46) The *water cycle* is powered by energy from the Sun.

water reclamation (wôt′ər rek lə-mā′shən) Projects that reclaim, or reuse, treated waste water. (D56) As a result of *water reclamation* projects, polluted water is treated so that it can be used again.

water table (wôt′ər tā′bəl) The surface of the water in a layer of saturated soil. (D13) During a drought, the *water table* drops below its normal level.

water vapor (wôt′ər vā′pər) Water that is in the form of a gas. (D11, E10) *Water vapor* from the air forms drops of water on cold glass surfaces.

weather (weth′ər) The condition of the atmosphere at a certain place and time. (E13) The *weather* today in Chicago is snowy.

weather forecaster (weth′ər fôr′kast ər) A person who makes weather predictions or reports weather conditions. (E61) The *weather forecaster* predicted rain for the next three days.

weather satellite (weth′ər sat″l īt) A human-made device in space that takes pictures of Earth and collects information about the weather. (E54) The *weather satellite* sent back pictures of clouds to weather stations in different locations on the ground.

wetlands (wet′lands) Environments in which the land contains significant amounts of water. (D30) Protecting the remaining *wetlands* in the U.S. is an important concern of environmentalists.

white dwarf (wīt dwarf) A very
small dying star that gives off very little
light. (B65) When the Sun's fuel runs
out, it will collapse into a *white dwarf*.

wind (wind) The movement of
air over Earth's surface. (E21) The
strong *wind* lifted the kite high above
the houses.

windsock (wind′säk) A device used
to show wind direction, consisting of a
cloth bag that is open at both ends and
hung on a pole. (E38) The *windsock*
showed that the wind was blowing
from the north.

wind vane (wind vān) A device,
often shaped like an arrow, used to
show the direction of the wind. (E38)
The *wind vane* on the roof of the
weather station showed that the wind
was blowing from the southwest.

INDEX

* Activity

* Activity

CREDITS

ILLUSTRATORS

Cover Olivia McElroy.

Think Like a Scientist 3–4: Garry Colby. 14: Laurie Hamilton. *border* Olivia McElroy.

Unit A 3: Olivia McElroy. 10–11: Paul Mirocha. 13: Carlyn Iverson. 16–17: Walter Stewart. 18, 20: Steve Buchanan. 22: Carlyn Iverson. 24–25: Patrick Gnan. 28: Carlyn Iverson. 30: Richard LaRocco. 34: Leonard Morgan. 39–43, 46–50, 56–57: Richard LaRocco. 58–59: Albert Lorenz. 62–63: Richard LaRocco. 64, 66: Carlyn Iverson. 72–73: Ilene Robinette. 75: Patrick Gnan. 76: Rob Schuster. 79: Michael Maydak. 84–85: Glory Bechtold. 86–87: Catherine Deeter. 88–89: Eldon Doty. 91–92: Michael Maydak.

Unit B 3: Olivia McElroy. 9: Delores Bego. 10–11: *border* Dale Glasgow. 11: Tom Powers. 13: Jeff Hitch. 14: Michael Carroll. 15: Tony Novak 17: Robert Schuster. 21: Lane Yerkes. 22: Fred Holz. 24–25: Jim Starr. 27: Tom Powers. 30: Dale Glasgow. 34–35: Dennis Davidson. 36: *b.m.* Dale Glasgow, *m.m.* Verlin Miller, *m.r.* Susan Melrath. 37: *t.l.* Dale Glasgow, Susan Melrath. 38–39: Michael Carroll. 42–43: Dennis Davidson. 44–49: Robert Schuster. 50: *t.r.* Dale Glasgow, *m.l.* Michael Carroll, *m.t.* Robert Schuster. 57: Tom Powers. 60–61: Lu Matthews. 64–65: Joe Spencer. 67: Tom Powers. 70: Michael Carroll. 71: Tom Powers. 72: Joe LeMonnier. 73: Tom Powers. 79: Terry Boles. 80: Stephen Wagner. 82–83: Nina Laden. 91: Andy Myer. 92: Dale Glasgow. 93: Terry Boles.

Unit C 3: Olivia McElroy. 10–11: Andrew Shiff. 12: *t.* Andrew Shiff, *b.* Scott Ross. 15: Terry Boles. 19–21: Scott Ross. 26–27: Robert Pasternack. 29: Patrick Gnan. 34: Bill Fox. 36–37: Paul Woods. 39–41: Nadine Sokol. 51: Bob Brugger. 56: Patrick Gnan. 57: Bob Radigan. 58: Adam Mathews. 61: Paul Woods. 69: Patrick Gnan. 70, 72–74: Nadine Sokol. 75: Eldon Doty. 76: *m.l.* George Hardebeck, *b.r.* Ken Rosenborg. 77: Ken Rosenborg. 82–83: Steven Mach. 88: Patrick Gnan. 90, 92: Robert Schuster.

Unit D 3: Olivia McElroy. 10–11: Bob Radigan.

Unit E 3: Olivia McElroy. 11, 13: Randy Hamblin. 14–15: Robert Roper. 20: Andy Lendway. 22: Flora Jew. 23: Robert Roper. 30: Susan Melrath. 31: Rob Burger. 32: Tom Pansini. 33: Rob Burger. 38–39: Pamela Becker. 46: Michael Kline. 49: Rob Burger. 55: Gary Torrisi. 56: Patrick Gnan. 60: Kristin Kest, *map*: Thomas Cranmer. 61–63: Nancy Tobin. 62: Robert Roper. 66, 68–70: Tom Lochray. 71: Gary Torrisi. 72: Tom Lochray. 73: Gary Torrisi. 77: Josie Yee. 78: Mike Quon. 79: Josie Yee. 80-81: John Youssi. 84–85: Thomas Cranmer. 86-87: Uldis Klavins. 90–92: Julie Peterson. 93: John Youssi.

Science and Math Toolbox *logos* Nancy Tobin. 14–15: Andrew Shiff. *borders* Olivia McElroy.

Glossary 19: Ellen Going Jacobs. 20: Robert Margulies. 21: Fran Milner. 23: Tom Powers. 26: Carlyn Iverson. 28: Richard Larocca. 29, 31: Robert Pasternack. 33: Gary Torrisi. 37: Robert Margulies.

PHOTOGRAPHS
All photographs by Houghton Mifflin Company (HMCo.) unless otherwise noted.

Cover *t.* G.K. & Vikki Hart/The Image Bank; *m.l.* Superstock; *m.r.* Runk/Schoenberger/Grant Heilman Photography, Inc.; *b.l.* NASA/Media Services; *b.r.* Superstock.

Think Like A Scientist 2: *b.* Chip Porter/Tony Stone Images. 3: *t.* Paul Seheult, Eye Ubiquitous/Corbis. 10: *b. bkgd.* PhotoDisc, Inc.

Unit A 1–3: Prof. P. Motta/Dept. of Anatomy/University "La Sapienza", Rome/Science Photo Library/Custom Medical Stock Photo, Inc. 4–5: *bkgd* Ron Garrison/The Zoological Society of San Diego; *inset* Ken Kelley for HMCo. 7: *t.m.* Clive Druett Papilio/Corbis; *b.m.* Kim Sayer/Corbis; *b.r.* Mitchell Gerber/Corbis; *b.l.* E.R. Degginger/Color-Pic, Inc. 9: Ken Karp for HMCo. 10: *l.* E.R. Degginger/Color-Pic, Inc.; *inset* Don & Pat Valenti/DRK Photo. 12: *t.* © P. Dayanandan/Photo Researchers, Inc.; *b.* © Dr. Brian Eyden/Science Photo Library/Photo Researchers,

Inc. 19: *l.* N. H. Cheatham/DRK Photo; *r.* Phil Degginger/Color-Pic, Inc. 20: *l.* Milton Rand/Tom Stack & Associates; *r.* © Scott Camamzine/Photo Researchers, Inc. 21: *bkgd.* Phil Degginger/Color-Pic, Inc.; *t.* © Science Source/Photo Researchers, Inc.; *inset* Tom Stack/Tom Stack & Associates. 23: *m.* Ken Karp for HMCo.; *b.* Ken Karp for HMCo. 25: *t.l.* Runk/Schoenberger/Grant Heilman Photography, Inc.; *t.r.* Runk/Schoenberger/Grant Heilman Photography, Inc.; *b.* © Franz Krenn/Photo Researchers, Inc. 32–33: *inset* Richard T. Bryant for HMCo. 45: Richard Hutchings for HMCo. 52–53: Courtesy, Rich LaRocca. 55: *r.* Richard Hutchings for HMCo. 58: David G. Houser/Corbis. 59: *l.* © A. Glauberman/Photo Researchers, Inc.; *r.* Runk/Schoenberger/Grant Heilman Photography, Inc. 68: Courtesy, Diane Hirakawa/IAMS company. 68–69: *t.* Iams Company; *b.* Cheryl A. Ertelt/ Photos & Phrases. 69: Iams Company. 74: *t.* © Alvin E. Staffan/Photo Researchers, Inc.; *b.* Anthony Bannister/ Animals Animals/Earth Scenes. 77: *bkgd.* PhotoDisc, Inc; *t.m.* Jeff Foott/Alaska Stock Images; *t.l.* Rick Rosenthal/ Masterfile Corporation; *t.r.* Jeff Foott/Alaska Stock Images; *b.l.* Michael DeYoung/Alaska Stock Images; *b.r.* Chris Arend/Alaska Stock Images; *b.* Jeff Foott/Alaska Stock Images. 79: Dwight R. Kuhn. 80: Grant Huntington for HMCo. 81: Grant Huntington for HMCo. 85: *b.l.* Dwight R. Kuhn; *b.m.* Dwight R. Kuhn; *b.r.* Dwight R. Kuhn. 87: Runk/Schoenberger/Grant Heilman Photography, Inc. 89: Bruce Coleman Incorporated. 90: *r.* Rosenfeld Images LTD/Rainbow. 91: *b.l.* Bruce Iverson; *b.m.* Doug Wechsler/Animals Animals/Earth Scenes; *b.r.* Bruce Iverson.

Unit B 1–3: © Pekka Parviainen/Science Photo Library/Photo Researchers, Inc. 4–5: *inset* Roger Russmeyer/Corbis. 5: Alan Levenson/Time Magazine. 6–8: Grant Huntington for HMCo. 10: © John Sanford & David Parker/Photo Researchers, Inc. 12: Roger Russmeyer/Corbis. 16: © Gordon Garradd/Science Photo Library/Photo Researchers, Inc. 20: Grant Huntington for HMCo. 21: Dennis Di Cicco/Sky & Telescope. 22: Roger Russmeyer/Corbis. 23: The Stock Market. 24: Frank P. Rossotto/Stocktrek. 25: *t.* Stocktrek. 26: Andrea Pistolesi/The Image Bank. 28–29: *bkgd.* Gunnar Kullenberg/Superstock; *inset* NASA Goddard Space Flight Center. 37: C. Telesco/University of Florida, Gainesville FL. 40–41: Media Services, NASA Headquarters Audio-Visual Branch, Code PM. 41: *l.* Media Services, NASA Headquarters Audio-Visual Branch, Code PM; *r.* NASA. 44: *l.* NASA; *r.* NASA/Peter Arnold, Inc. 45: *t.l.* NASA/Tom Stack & Associates; *t.r.* Stocktrek; *m.l.* NASA/MGA/Photri, Inc.; *m.r.* USGS, Flagstaff, Arizona/Corbis; *b.* Sovfoto/Eastfoto. 46: *t.l.* JPL/NASA; *t.r.* D. Simonelli/Cornell University; *m.* Media Services, NASA Headquarters Audio-Visual Branch, Code PM. 47: *l.* NASA/Tom Stack & Associates; *r.* USGS/TSADO/Tom Stack & Associates; *b.* Frank P. Rossotto/Tom Stack & Associates. 48: *t.* NASA/The Image Bank; *m.* JPL/NASA; *b.l.* NASA/JPL/TSADO/Tom Stack & Associates; *b.r.* NASA/Bruce Coleman Inc. 49: *t.l.* NASA; *t.r.* © NASA/Science Source/Photo Researchers, Inc.; *b.l.* NASA; *b.r.* NASA. 50: *t.* NASA/Tom Stack & Associates. 52–53: *bkgd.* Harold Sund/The Image Bank; *inset* Bob Sacha/Sacha Photographer. 54: Ken Karp for HMCo. 62: *l.* © Royal Observatory, Edinburgh/AATB/Science Photo Library/Photo Researchers, Inc.; *m.* MGA/Photri, Inc.; *r.* © Royal Observatory, Edinburgh/AATB/Science Photo Library/Photo Researchers, Inc. 63: *l.* Anglo-Australian Observatory; *m.* National Optical Astronomy Observatories/Phil Degginger/Color-Pic, Inc.; *r.* © Royal Observatory, Edinburgh/AATB/Science Photo Library/Photo Researchers, Inc. 67: E.R. Degginger/Color-Pic, Inc. 68: *l.* © Royal Observatory, Edinburgh/AATB/Science Photo Library/Photo Researchers, Inc.; *m.* MGA/Photri, Inc.; *r.* NASA/Peter Arnold, Inc. 69: *l.* Anglo-Australian Observatory; *m.* Frank P. Rossotto/Stocktrek; *r.* Anglo-Australian Observatory. 74: NASA/Media Services. 74–75: *bkgd.* Photri-Micro Stock; *inset* NASA/Media Services. 81: NASA. 84: NASA. 85: NASA/Media Services. 87: Donna McLaughlin/The Stock Market. 88: The Arecibo Observatory/National Astronomy and Ionosphere Center, Cornell University. 89: MGA/Photri, Inc.

Unit C 1–3: J. Jamsen/Natural Selection Stock Photography, Inc. 4: © 1993 James Zheng/Icefield Instruments, Inc. 4–5: *bkgd.* Tom Bean/The Stock Market; *inset* David S. Hik/Nunatak International. 6: Richard Hutchings for HMCo. 7: *t.* Richard Hutchings for HMCo. 9: Richard Hutchings for HMCo. 11–13: Richard Hutchings for HMCo. 18: Richard Hutchings for HMCo. 20: Richard Hutchings for HMCo. 24: Richard Hutchings for HMCo. 25: E.R. Degginger/Color-Pic, Inc. 28: *r.* © Scott Camazine/Photo Researchers, Inc. 30–31: Murrae Haynes/Indian Artist Magazine. 32: Grant Huntington for HMCo. 34: *m.* Grant Huntington for HMCo.; *r.* Grant Huntington for HMCo. 39–40: Yoav Levy/Phototake/The Creative Link. 42: *l.* © George Holton/National Archaeological Museum/Photo Researchers, Inc.; *r.* Culver Pictures Inc. 43: Culver Pictures Inc. 44–46: Grant Huntington for HMCo. 49: Grant Huntington for HMCo. 50: *l.* Robert Yager/Tony Stone Images; *r.* Bill Ross/Tony Stone Images. 51: Steve Weinrebe/ Stock Boston. 54: Grant Huntington for HMCo. 56: NASA/Tom Stack & Associates. 57: Grant Huntington for HMCo. 58: David Young Wolff/PhotoEdit. 59: *t.* Ken Lax for HMCo.; *b.l.* Boltin Picture Library; *b.m.* Boltin Picture Library; *b.r.* Boltin Picture Library. 62–63: *bkgd.* Michael Fogden/DRK Photo; *inset* Steve Winter/Black Star . 65: Ken Karp for HMCo. 67: Ken Karp for HMCo. 68: *l.* Dutch Craftsman Baseball Bat Co. 69: *t.* D. Cavagnaro/DRK Photo; *m.* John Gerlach/DRK Photo. 71: IBM Corporation. 74–75: Corbis. 80–82: Ken Karp for HMCo. 84–85: Tom Stack & Associates. 85: © Jim Corwin/Photo Researchers, Inc. 87: Ken Karp for HMCo. 90: *b.* Ken Karp for HMCo. 91: Keith Wood/Tony Stone Images. 93: Phil Degginger/Color-Pic, Inc.

Unit D 1–3: Tom Algire/Tom Stack & Associates. 4–5: *bkgd.* PhotoDisc, Inc.; *inset* Batista Moon Studio for HMCo. 10: *l.* L.D. Gordon/The Image Bank; *r.* Willard Luce/Animals Animals/Earth Scenes. 11: *t.* J.A. Kraulis/Masterfile;

Extra Practice

On the following pages are questions about each of the Investigations in your book. Use these questions to help you review some of the terms and ideas that you studied. Each review section gives you the page numbers in the book where you can check your answers. Write your answers on a separate sheet of paper.

Contents

Investigation 1 pages A6–A13

Write the term that best completes each sentence.

cell	organ	nutrient

1. A substance that is needed for an organism to live and grow is a/an ___.
2. The basic unit of living things is the ___.
3. Similar types of tissues working together form a/an ___.

Complete the following exercises.

4. How does a living thing differ from a nonliving thing?
5. How are plant and animal cells similar, and how are they different?
6. Compare and contrast how plants and animals carry out the following life processes: take in nutrients and gases; give off wastes; react to surroundings.

Investigation 2 pages A14–A25

Write the term that best completes each sentence.

leaf	root	stem

7. The plant part that anchors the plant and absorbs water and minerals is the ___.
8. The food-making factory of a plant is the ___.
9. The aboveground parts of the plant are supported by the ___.

Complete the following exercises.

10. Identify three things that a plant needs in order to make food.
11. Describe the process of photosynthesis and name the materials produced.
12. What is cell respiration?

Unit A Extra Practice

Investigation 3 pages A26–A30

Write the term in each pair that correctly completes each sentence.

13. Oxygen is brought into the body by the (respiratory system, excretory system).

14. The group of organs that works together to break down food makes up the (respiratory system, digestive system).

15. Blood is transported to all parts of the body by the (circulatory system, respiratory system).

Complete the following exercises.

16. How do both plants and animals use the nutrients in food?

17. How are nutrients carried to the body's cells?

18. How does a "waste" product of photosynthesis help humans and other animals survive?

Investigation 1 pages A34–A43

Write the term in each pair that correctly completes each sentence.

1. Dissolved nutrients pass from the small intestine through the (large intestine, villi) into the body.

2. The salivary glands and stomach produce (fats, enzymes), which help break down food.

3. The main function of the (small intestine, stomach) is to store food.

Complete the following exercises.

4. Describe the role of saliva in digestion.

5. How is food moved from the esophagus to the stomach?

6. Would it be easier to survive without a stomach, a small intestine, or a large intestine? Explain your answer.

Investigation 2 pages A44–A50

Write the term that best completes each sentence.

air sacs	bronchial tubes	larynx

7. Air is carried from the trachea to the lungs by the ___.
8. The part of the throat used in speaking is the ___.
9. The spongy tissue of the lungs contains millions of ___.

Complete the following exercises.

10. Why is "windpipe" a good name for the trachea?
11. Describe the function of the respiratory system.
12. How are sounds produced during speech?

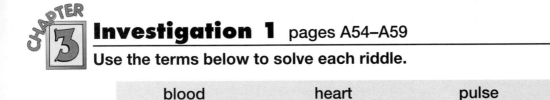

Investigation 1 pages A54–A59

Use the terms below to solve each riddle.

blood	heart	pulse

1. I am the pump that pushes blood throughout the body.
2. I am the throbbing that can be felt in arteries and is caused by the rush of blood into them after the heart contracts.
3. I am a tissue made up of several types of cells in a liquid called plasma.

Complete the following exercises.

4. What are the sections, or chambers, of the heart called?
5. How do veins and arteries differ?
6. Describe blood circulation in the heart.

Investigation 2 pages A60–A66

Write the term in each pair that correctly completes each sentence.

7. The body system responsible for removing waste products produced by body cells is the (circulatory system, excretory system).

8. The yellowish liquid produced by the kidneys and which contains excess water, salt, and minerals filtered from the body is called (sweat, urine).

9. Small coiled tubes that end at pores on the surface of the skin are called (nephrons, sweat glands).

Complete the following exercises.

10. How does the skin remove wastes from the body?

11. What organs of the respiratory system also remove wastes? Explain your answer.

12. Distinguish between the ureters, urethra, kidneys, and bladder in terms of the function of each.

CHAPTER 4 Investigation 1 pages A70–A79

Use the terms below to solve each riddle.

| egg | pupa | larva |

1. I am the first stage in a moth's life cycle.

2. I am the caterpillar stage in the life cycle of a moth.

3. I am the stage when the moth is called a cocoon.

Complete the following exercises.

4. What are the stages in the human life cycle?

5. Describe the life cycle of a salmon.

6. How does a woodpecker's instinctive behavior help it survive?

Investigation 2 pages A80–A92

Write the term in each pair that correctly completes each sentence.

7. The male part of the flower is the (stigma, stamen).

8. The female sex cell is found in the (ovary, pollen grain).

9. A male cell joins with a female cell to produce a fertilized egg during the process of (pollination, sexual reproduction).

Complete the following exercises.

10. Describe the formation of a fruit.

11. How are offspring produced in asexual reproduction?

12. Some plants reproduce from cuttings, or cut parts of plants. Do you think this is an advantage or a disadvantage? Explain your answer.

Unit B Extra Practice

CHAPTER 1

Investigation 1 pages B6–B17

Write the term that best completes each sentence.

constellation	planet	star

1. The Sun is the closest ___ to Earth.

2. A large object that circles a star and does not produce its own light is a ___.

3. A star pattern in the night sky is a ___.

Complete the following exercises.

4. What causes seasonal changes on Earth?

5. Why is Polaris known as the North Star?

6. Why do the stars appear to move from east to west across the night sky?

Investigation 2 pages B18–B26

Write the term in each pair that correctly completes each sentence.

7. Dirt particles that burn up as shooting stars are called (planets, meteors).

8. An instrument for viewing distant objects that gathers light in a curved mirror at the back of its tube is called a (reflecting telescope, refracting telescope).

9. An icy ball that contains dust and rock and travels in an elliptical orbit around the Sun is called a (meteor, comet).

Complete the following exercises.

10. What effect does the Sun have on the tail of a comet?

11. What advantages does the Hubble Space Telescope have over telescopes on Earth?

12. How are meteors related to comets?

Unit B Extra Practice

Investigation 1 pages B30–B41

Write the term that best completes each sentence.

| big-bang theory | geocentric model | solar system |

1. One explanation for the formation of the universe is the ___.

2. The Sun, nine known planets and their moons, and many comets and asteroids form a ___.

3. The astronomer Ptolemy believed in an Earth-centered model, or ___, of the solar system.

Complete the following exercises.

4. Describe the big-bang theory.

5. Identify and explain the model of the solar system described by Copernicus.

6. What do scientists believe about Mars based on Martian rocks and meteorites thought to be from Mars?

Investigation 2 pages B42–B50

Write the term in each pair that correctly completes each sentence.

7. Earth, Mercury, Venus, and Mars are known as the (gas giants, terrestrial planets).

8. The two planets that switch positions as the eighth and ninth planets are (Neptune and Uranus, Neptune and Pluto).

9. Jupiter, Saturn, Uranus, and Neptune are known as the (gas giants, terrestrial planets).

Complete the following exercises.

10. Which planet is most like Earth? In what ways are the planets similar? How are they different?

11. What are Saturn's rings made of?

12. Based only on its characteristics, is Pluto more like the inner planets or the outer planets? Explain your answer.

Investigation 1 pages B54–B57

Use the terms below to solve each riddle.

color	spectroscope	Sun

1. I am the largest body in the solar system.
2. I am a device used by astronomers to study the light given off by the stars.
3. I am closely linked with the temperature of a star.

Complete the following exercises.

4. How big is the Sun?
5. What color would the hottest stars be? the coolest stars?
6. Where does a star's energy come from?

Investigation 2 pages B58–B61

Write the term in each pair that correctly completes each sentence.

absolute magnitude	magnitude	light-year

7. The measure of a star's brightness is called its ___.
8. The distance that light travels in one year is called a/an ___.
9. The amount of light a star actually gives off is its ___.

Complete the following exercises.

10. How do astronomers use parallax to figure out distances to nearby stars?
11. What device do astronomers use to measure how bright a star appears to be?
12. On what two factors does the apparent magnitude of a star depend?

Unit B Extra Practice

Investigation 3 pages B62–B67

Write the term that best completes each sentence.

neutron star	nebula	black dwarf

13. The Sun's final stage will be as a ___.

14. A huge cloud of dust and gas that provides raw material from which stars form is called a ___.

15. The collapse of the core of a massive star can become a ___.

Complete the following exercises.

16. When does a star begin to shine?

17. What causes a star to shine?

18. Can the Sun ever become a supernova? Why or why not?

Investigation 4 pages B68–B72

Write the term in each pair that correctly completes each sentence.

19. The Milky Way Galaxy is (an elliptical galaxy, a spiral galaxy).

20. Most galaxies are moving rapidly (toward, away from) one another.

21. A galaxy shaped like a slightly flattened sphere is (a spiral galaxy, an elliptical galaxy).

Complete the following exercises.

22. Why are galaxies called the "building blocks" of the universe?

23. Describe Earth's location in the Milky Way Galaxy.

24. Is there more than one galaxy in the universe? How do you know?

Investigation 1 pages B76–B81

Write the term that best completes each sentence.

free fall	gravity	weightless

1. The motion of a freely falling object is called ___.
2. The force that pulls things toward the center of Earth is called ___.
3. In a spacecraft orbiting Earth, astronauts feel as though they are ___.

Complete the following exercises.

4. Why does someone not feel the effects of gravity in free fall?
5. Why must food and drink be kept in sealed packages during a trip into space?
6. Why do an astronaut's muscles have less work to do during a space flight?

Investigation 2 pages B82–B85

Use the terms below to solve each riddle.

carbon dioxide	International Space Station	microgravity

7. I'm a condition of very low gravity.
8. I'm a space project being built by scientists and engineers from 16 countries.
9. I'm a resource that will be recycled by astronauts living in space for long periods of time.

Complete the following exercises.

10. What is the purpose of the International Space Station?
11. What are two reasons for the astronauts on the ISS to grow their own food?
12. What are some advantages of using robots in space?

Investigation 3 pages B86–B92

Write the term that best completes each sentence.

extraterrestrial	radio telescope	SETI

13. The search for extraterrestrial intelligence is referred to as ___.

14. A being that comes from beyond Earth is called a/an ___.

15. A giant antenna that receives radio signals is a/an ___.

Complete the following exercises.

16. What was on *The Sounds of Earth,* which was carried by the Voyager probes?

17. What did the first radio telescope discover?

18. Why do many scientists think it is unlikely that we will ever be able to communicate with intelligent life from other planets?

Unit C Extra Practice

Investigation 1 pages C6–C15

Write the term that best completes each sentence.

mass	density	volume

1. A measure of the amount of matter an object contains is its ___.
2. The amount of space an object takes up is its ___.
3. The amount of matter in a given space is ___.

Complete the following exercises.

4. How can you measure the amount of matter in an apple?
5. How can you decide which of two toy dinosaurs has the greatest volume?
6. How can you calculate a rock's density?

Investigation 2 pages C16–C21

Write the term that best completes each sentence.

solid	liquid	gas

7. A ___ has no definite shape or volume.
8. A ___ keeps its shape and has a definite volume.
9. A ___ keeps its volume, but has no definite shape.

Complete the following exercises.

10. What two factors affect the state of matter in which a substance is found?
11. Compare the forces of attraction among water particles to the forces of attraction among iron particles.
12. What evidence is there to indicate that air is made up of moving particles?

Unit C Extra Practice

Investigation 3 pages C22–C28

Write the term that best completes each sentence.

temperature	condensation	heat

13. The energy that flows from warmer to cooler regions of matter is ___.

14. A measure of the average kinetic energy of the particles in a material is ___.

15. The change from a gas to a liquid is ___.

Complete the following exercises.

16. What causes water to evaporate?

17. A swimming pool full of water and a bucket full of water are the same temperature. Compare the heat energy of the water in the two containers.

18. Describe what happens when water freezes.

Investigation 1 pages C32–C43

Write the term that best completes each sentence.

compound	mixture	element

1. A substance that cannot be broken down into any other substance by simple means is a/an ___.

2. A substance made up of two or more elements that are chemically combined is a/an ___.

3. A combination of two or more substances is a/an ___.

Complete the following exercises.

4. What is the difference between the chemical properties and physical properties of matter?

5. See pages C36–C37. What are the name and symbol for the element with atomic number 50? Name three other elements that have similar chemical properties.

6. Compare the four-element classification used by early scientists to the four groups elements are classified into today.

Investigation 2 pages C44–C51

Write the term that correctly completes each sentence.

7. Water is a (compound, mixture) of two parts hydrogen and one part oxygen.

8. Air is a (compound, mixture) of gases.

9. If you add water to a mixture of salt and sand, the (salt, sand) will dissolve.

Complete the following exercises.

10. How are compounds and mixtures alike? How are they different?

11. Name some properties that can be used to separate a mixture into its component parts.

12. Why can you use a formula to represent a compound but not to represent a mixture?

Investigation 3 pages C52–C60

Write the term that best completes each sentence.

alloy	solvent	solute

13. A solution of two or more metals is a/an ___.

14. The material that is present in the greater amount in a solution is the ___.

15. The material that is present in the smaller amount in a solution is the ___.

Complete the following exercises.

16. What factors affect the rate at which a solution forms?

17. How is the attraction among water molecules changed when soap is added to the water?

18. How is an alloy formed?

Unit C Extra Practice

CHAPTER 3

Investigation 1 pages C64–C77

Use the terms below to solve the riddles.

electron	nucleus	proton

1. I am the central core of an atom.
2. I am an atomic particle that has a positive electrical charge.
3. I am an atomic particle that has a negative electrical charge.

Complete the following exercises.

4. What is a radioactive element?
5. What is the difference between a chemical change and a physical change?
6. How is rust produced?

Investigation 2 pages C78–C85

Write the term that best completes each sentence.

indicator	salt	neutralization

7. A compound that can be formed when an acid reacts with a base is a/an ___.
8. The reaction between an acid and a base is called ___.
9. A substance that changes color when mixed with an acid or a base is a/an ___.

Complete the following exercises.

10. What is acid rain?
11. Describe the pH scale.
12. What properties do salts have in common?

Unit C Extra Practice

Investigation 3 pages C83–C92

Write the term that correctly completes each sentence.

13. Compounds containing (helium, carbon) are called organic compounds.

14. The simplest organic compound is (methane, fructose).

15. The word (synthesis, polymer) means *many parts.*

Complete the following exercises.

16. What are proteins?

17. Why is carbon called the supercombiner?

18. What is the difference between single replacement reactions and double replacement reactions?

Unit D Extra Practice

Investigation 1 pages D6–D15

Write the term that best completes each sentence.

| runoff | water vapor | ground water |

1. Water in its gaseous state is called ___.
2. The underground water supply is called ___.
3. Rainfall that is not absorbed by the soil is called ___.

Complete the following exercises.

4. Why is Earth sometimes called the water planet?
5. Where is Earth's fresh water supply stored?
6. Where does the water in an aquifer come from?

Investigation 2 pages D16–D22

Write the term that best completes each sentence.

| water cycle | precipitation | transpiration |

7. The ongoing movement of water into the air and back to Earth's surface is the ___.
8. The process by which a plant releases moisture through small openings in its leaves is called ___.
9. Any form of water that falls to Earth's surface is called ___.

Complete the following exercises.

10. Name at least three services plants provide.
11. Name and describe the processes that occur in the water cycle.
12. What happens to the water that falls as precipitation?

Unit D Extra Practice

Investigation 1 pages D26–D31

Write the term that correctly completes each sentence.

1. The process of supplying crops with water is called (irrigation, dilution).
2. Without water, people can survive for a few (weeks, days).
3. A marsh is a wetland the lacks (trees, plants).

Complete the following exercises.

4. What are wetlands?
5. Give two reasons why wetlands are important.
6. Name some ways you use water in your everyday life.

Investigation 2 pages D32–D40

Write the term that correctly completes each sentence.

7. A place where water is collected or stored is a/an (reservoir, aqueduct).
8. Lake Mead in Arizona was created when (Tenochtitlán, Hoover Dam) was built.
9. The Aztecs grew food crops on (canoes, islands of dirt) that floated on a lake.

Complete the following exercises.

10. What are the major sources from which communities get fresh water?
11. How can groundwater be pumped from wells?
12. What is an aqueduct and what does it do?

Investigation 1 pages D44–D53

Write the term that best completes each sentence.

climate	El Niño	La Niña

1. The average weather conditions of an area over a long period of time determine its ___.
2. During ___, the temperatures are cooler than normal and there may be droughts.
3. The periodic warming of water in the Pacific Ocean is called ___.

Complete the following exercises.

4. How are supply and demand for water in a given area determined?
5. What can you and your family do to conserve water?
6. How much is an acre-foot of water?

Investigation 2 pages D54–D60

Use the terms below to solve each riddle.

potable	sludge	chlorine

7. I describe water that is fit for drinking.
8. I am used to kill bacteria in water.
9. I am the organic matter in waste water.

Complete the following exercises.

10. Name some sources of water pollution.
11. Describe the process used in a water purification plant.
12. What is the difference between reclaimed waste water and purified water?

CHAPTER 1 Investigation 1 pages E6–E15

Write the term in each pair that correctly completes each sentence.

1. The lowest layer of the atmosphere is the (stratosphere, troposphere).
2. The condition of the atmosphere at a certain time and place is called (temperature, weather).
3. The blanket of air that surrounds Earth is the (mesosphere, atmosphere).

Complete the following exercises.

4. What is the greenhouse effect?
5. Identify the gases that make up air.
6. What two factors greatly affect weather?

Investigation 2 pages E16–E22

Write the term in each pair that correctly completes each sentence.

7. Wind is caused by the (even, uneven) heating of Earth's surface.
8. Materials tend to heat up faster if they are (dark, light) in color.
9. When air is warmed it (rises, sinks).

Complete the following exercises.

10. How does the pilot of a hot-air balloon make the balloon rise?
11. Why is a shoreline often a comfortable place to be in hot weather?
12. Would you wear dark-colored clothing or light-colored clothing in hot weather? Explain your answer.

Investigation 1 pages E26–E33

Write the term in each pair that correctly completes each sentence.

1. A device that measures air pressure is called a (barometer, thermometer).

2. The push of air against its surroundings is called air (pressure, temperature).

3. The first barometer, made by Toricelli, was (an aneroid, a mercury) barometer.

Complete the following exercises.

4. What are high-pressure areas and low-pressure areas?

5. Why does air pressure increase the closer you are to sea level and decrease the farther you are from sea level?

6. How does heating the air in a closed bottle and the air in an open bottle affect the air pressure in each? Explain.

Investigation 2 pages E34–E41

Use the terms below to solve each riddle.

anemometer	windsock	wind vane

7. I am a device that shows wind direction. Often I am shaped like a long arrow with a tail.

8. I show wind direction. I am a cloth bag that is narrow at one end and open at both ends.

9. I am a device that measures wind speed. I am made up of cups on spokes attached to a pole.

Complete the following exercises.

10. What is the Beaufort Scale?

11. How are windsocks and wind vanes alike? How do they differ?

12. Identify three benefits and one drawback of using wind power.

Investigation 3 pages E42–E48

Write the term in each pair that correctly completes each sentence.

13. Very fine drops of water are called (hail, drizzle).

14. Any form of water that falls from the air is called (humidity, precipitation).

15. The amount of water vapor in the air is called (humidity, relative humidity).

Complete the following exercises.

16. How do clouds form?

17. What causes rain?

18. At the same air temperature, would you feel cooler if the relative humidity was 10 percent or 100 percent? Explain your answer.

CHAPTER 3 Investigation 1 pages E52–E57

Use the terms below to solve each riddle.

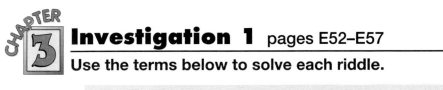

| cirrus cloud | cumulus cloud | stratus cloud |

1. I am a puffy cloud that forms when large areas of warm, moist air rise upward from Earth's surface.

2. I am a flat, gray cloud that forms when a flat layer of warm, moist air rises very slowly.

3. I am a cloud that looks like wisps of hair and I appear when air rises high enough for ice crystals to form.

Complete the following exercises.

4. What does the word part *nimbo-* mean in a cloud name?

5. How can clouds be used to predict weather?

6. How are weather satellites used in weather prediction?

Unit E Extra Practice

Investigation 2 pages E58–E63

Write the term that best completes each sentence.

air mass	front	weather forecaster

7. Someone who makes predictions about the weather is a/an ___.

8. A body of air that has the same general temperature and air pressure throughout is called a/an ___.

9. A place where two types of air masses meet is called a/an ___.

Complete the following exercises.

10. What conditions do forecasters use to make predictions?

11. Describe how a cold front forms and how a warm front forms.

12. You hear that a low pressure area will move into your region by evening. What type of weather can you expect for that night?

Investigation 3 pages E64–E72

Write the term in each pair that correctly completes each sentence.

13. A storm that produces heavy rain, strong winds, lightning, and thunder is a (flash flood, thunderstorm).

14. A funnel-shaped storm of spinning wind is a (tornado, thunderstorm).

15. A large, violent storm that forms over warm ocean water is a (hurricane, thunderstorm).

Complete the following exercises.

16. What causes a thunderstorm?

17. Name one type of severe weather and identify some ways to stay safe during it.

18. Under what conditions is a storm called a hurricane?

R24

Investigation 1 pages E76–E81

Write the term in each pair that correctly completes each sentence.

1. The imaginary line that circles the middle of Earth is called the (axis, equator).

2. The imaginary line that runs from the North Pole through Earth's center to the South Pole is the (hemisphere, axis).

3. The half of Earth below the equator is the (Northern Hemisphere, Southern Hemisphere).

Complete the following exercises.

4. How does the slant at which the Sun strikes Earth affect seasonal temperatures?

5. When the hemisphere in which you live is tilted away from the Sun, what season do you experience?

6. What season are people in the Southern Hemisphere having right now? How do you know?

Investigation 2 pages E82–E92

Use the terms below to solve each riddle.

| polar climate | temperate climate | tropical climate |

7. I am usually hot and rainy all year round.

8. I have warm, dry summers and cold, wet winters.

9. I am usually very cold.

Complete the following exercises.

10. Compare the climate of a place that is near a large body of water to that of a place that is far from a large body of water.

11. What are three methods scientists use to study climates of the past?

12. How does distance from the equator affect a region's climate?

PERIODIC TABLE

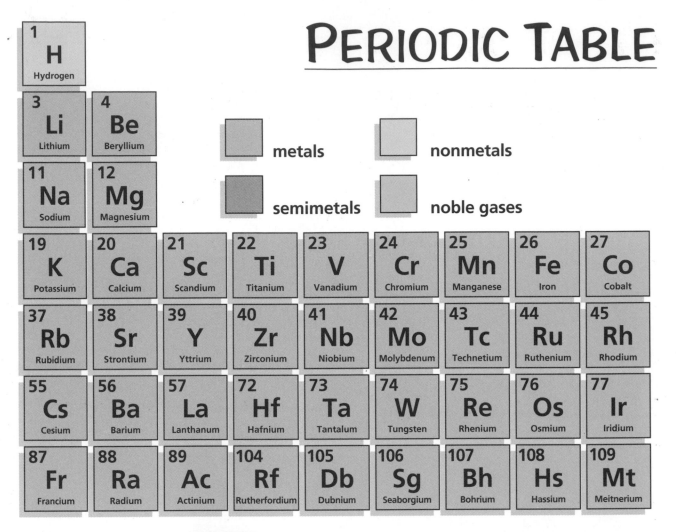

	metals
	semimetals
	nonmetals
	noble gases

1 H Hydrogen								
3 Li Lithium	4 Be Beryllium							
11 Na Sodium	12 Mg Magnesium							
19 K Potassium	20 Ca Calcium	21 Sc Scandium	22 Ti Titanium	23 V Vanadium	24 Cr Chromium	25 Mn Manganese	26 Fe Iron	27 Co Cobalt
37 Rb Rubidium	38 Sr Strontium	39 Y Yttrium	40 Zr Zirconium	41 Nb Niobium	42 Mo Molybdenum	43 Tc Technetium	44 Ru Ruthenium	45 Rh Rhodium
55 Cs Cesium	56 Ba Barium	57 La Lanthanum	72 Hf Hafnium	73 Ta Tantalum	74 W Tungsten	75 Re Rhenium	76 Os Osmium	77 Ir Iridium
87 Fr Francium	88 Ra Radium	89 Ac Actinium	104 Rf Rutherfordium	105 Db Dubnium	106 Sg Seaborgium	107 Bh Bohrium	108 Hs Hassium	109 Mt Meitnerium

57 La Lanthanum						
		58 Ce Cerium	59 Pr Praseodymium	60 Nd Neodymium	61 Pm Promethium	62 Sm Samarium
89 Ac Actinium		90 Th Thorium	91 Pa Protactinium	92 U Uranium	93 Np Neptunium	94 Pu Plutonium